# THE NEW AGE VISION

**Other works by Ron Lampi**

*Bay of Monterey, Poems of Monterey Bay*  2010
*Toward The Mythos, philosophical essays*  2010

Also published by River Sanctuary Publishing:

*From the Corridors (of the Labyrinth)*  2011
*The New Story, Two Poems*  2011
*The Poet Reflects*  2012
*On The Cruz, Poems of Santa Cruz*  2012
*Through the Labyrinth*  2013
*Poetry / Is*  2013
*A Divine Psyche Manifesto & other poems*  2016
*The Edge Manifesto*  2018
*Photons*  2018
*Technos & Psyche, A Prelude & other poems*  2019
*Lamp Light, A selection of short poems*  3rd Ed.  2020
*The Vision of Psyche & other poems*  3rd Ed.  2020

# The New Age Vision

## 2020

### Ron Lampi

*The New Age Vision*
Copyright © 2021 by Ron Lampi
www.ronlampi.com

All rights reserved. No part of this book may be reproduced in any form or by any electronic or mechanical means including information storage and retrieval systems, without permission in writing from the author.

Book design by River Sanctuary Graphic Arts
Cover by Melanie Gendron

ISBN 978-1-952194-13-9

Printed in the United States of America

Additional copies available from:
www.riversanctuarypublishing.com

River Sanctuary Publishing
P.O. Box 1561
Felton, California 95018
www.riversanctuarypublishing.com
*Dedicated to the awakening of the New Earth*

## Contents

Foreword ............................................................................. 1
Addendum 2016 ................................................................ 2
Addendum 2020 ................................................................ 3
Preface ................................................................................ 5
    *The New Age I Sing* (poem) ........................................ 9
Basic Themes for the New Age ...................................... 10
Orientation: Welcome to the New Age ......................... 13
    *I Celebrate the Lightworker* (poem) ........................ 15
1 – A Preliminary Discussion: Objections to the New Age ......... 17
2 – An Age of Crisis—*and Transition*: Postmodernity ................ 39
    Comparing Modernism/Postmodernism and the New Age ......... 64
3 – World Ages: The Astronomical/Astrological Background .... 66
    *A note on language* .................................................... 78
4 – The Water Bearer: Spirit and Soul ........................... 81
5 – Higher Self: The Aquarian Dispensation ............. 111
6 – Our Psychospiritual Evolution ............................... 138
    Comparing the Piscean and Aquarian Ages ............. 162
    *The Transformer* (poem) ......................................... 164
7 – Psyche: Mythos for the New Age ........................... 166
8 – Technos: The New Global Superpower ................. 187
9 – Gaia: Our Earth Web ............................................... 214
10 – UFOs and ET Contact: Harbingers of the Next Level ....... 240
11 – The Next Level: The Astral-Psychic ..................... 263
    *The New Human* (poem) ......................................... 296

12– Mythos-Making: Art of the New Age ........................ 298
13– The Emerging New Story of Us ............................... 320
    *We, The Aquarians* (poem) ........................................ 343
14– We Pour Forth ......................................................... 348
    *A New Age Prayer* ..................................................... 355
Addendum 1: New Age Music ...................................... 356
Addendum 2: The MYTHOS Project ........................... 357
Notes ............................................................................... 358
Bibliography .................................................................. 367
About the Author .......................................................... 370

Note: The poems above are all taken from the collection *Advent*

*This is not a Story I tell via traditional Logos,
but one I tell co-creative with Mythos.*

*There are many Threads that would go into this Story,
of which I have attempted to weave here but a few,
and only preliminary at that.*

# Foreword

I must say something here at the start about the title of this book. It was not uncommon for me to hear the suggestion, while working on the manuscript, that if I would only consider changing the title, it would probably find a better reception. When others recommended, *Why don't you consider changing the title?* they were of course always referring to the phrase 'New Age.' It surprised me how "New Age" triggered so much disfavor in others. Little did those who made these suggestions without having read any of the manuscript itself realize that the title is an integral phrase that happens to be woven throughout the work's entirety. Read any bit of it to be convinced. I was not about to coin one more clever word or phrase to replace 'New Age'; that had been done so many times already by other authors that we realize it was so often but a marketing ploy for selling yet another book about this transition time we live in. It was almost as if others were asking me, disconcertingly, not to write a book about the New Age at all. Why waste your time? (The various objections that have been made over the years to the New Age *as a movement* I have addressed in Chapter 1.) At issue then was really the question, what relevance could such a book about the New Age have today? But that is exactly what the book in its entirety addresses—is the New Age Vision not the Vision that we need today?

The challenge for me, as I worked on the manuscript on and off for 20 years, was to keep it as up-to-date as possible amidst the changes that are happening so fast all around us. Inevitably new developments and trends threatened to outstrip some of the more topical discussions in it. Hopefully, though, its philosophical drift—as I see this above all as a "soft" philosophical work—will survive as a true Vision of what this new World Age of Aquarius we are entering is all about.

## Addendum 2016

I have recently realized how auspicious it has been that I held off publishing this work for a number of years. Potentially catastrophic global developments are currently unfolding for us all; at the time I first finished a draft of the manuscript, already some years ago, this had not yet been on my radar. Now that it has come to my full attention, it would be negligent on my part not to incorporate something of these developments here, in a work, after all, that attempts to envision our evolutionary future. I refer, in particular, to both abrupt climate change and the ongoing nuclear disaster at Fukushima, Japan. Both have the potential to become game changers, not only for civilization, but for the entire biosphere of the planet. The name 'Fukushima' itself will probably sooner rather than later—outstripping the meme of a similar disaster 'Chernobyl'—become an ominous cultural meme for all future nuclear power. The threat of what is now being called "abrupt climate change" (an alternate name for global warming), some claim, has the admittedly difficult to accept potential of collapsing our entire civilization in the near future; they say, by 2030, if not sooner. (I set aside here, for now, the controversy that climate change / global warming has been labeled a hoax, as there are those who claim that it is all a front for a geoengineering and New World Order agenda. We will pick this up later.) To me, this is not simply then what has been referred to in current discourse as an unfolding ELE—an extinction level event—but, as I prefer to name it, more accurately, I feel—an *MELE*, meaning, far more globally, a *mass extinction level event*. Fukushima has the same potential, most likely in a longer-term scenario. We are undoubtedly, then, living today in the early days of a two-pronged MELE. In this transition period to a New Age that we are currently living in, we will all be witnessing this MELE firsthand that will fatefully characterize our entry into the new Aquarian Age. This development, I realize, will always be looming darkly over the New Age Vision I am presenting. Yes, it will seem at times that I am talking out of two sides of my mouth. But there is no way to get around it, unless one prefers living in denial. On one front or another, civilization is nearing The Edge. A few, who are especially hardcore "doomers," might say that presenting any such Vision of a so-called "New Age" is by now pointless. To them, there will be no "Aquarian New Age" civilization…at least, not a global civilization such as we know it today. Because of this and other contemporary developments that we will explore, it is unavoidable then that the Story I tell will seem at times to suddenly get schizoid, as I juggle scenarios with such radical, opposing implications. But then it dawns on us that this is exactly the schizoid character of our Postmodern world. Be that as it may, there is still a Story that must be told…

## Addendum 2020

Yes, this is the year of COVID-19. A pandemic is one of the possibilities I mention when I discuss the transition between Ages that we are currently living in. The social confusion and chaos we are experiencing is of the very nature of such a transition. We are right in the midst of it, and it may very well get worse as civilization approaches The Edge. But does this in any way negate the New Age Vision and the dispensation that it entails? Not at all. A New Age will unfold in one way or another no matter what we must go through.

# Preface

There are those who might contend that this book comes too late, that the New Age movement it would be assumed to be culturally based on had already come and gone in the latter years of the 20th Century. I argue otherwise. I would suggest that such a view—that the New Age movement has already played itself out—comes too early, and that, though the subject of the New Age might not be considered as topical in recent years as it previously had been, the movement is still alive and well, *and* growing. One purpose of this book is to correct the impression that the New Age is merely a fad in demise.

It is curious that the question *What really is the New Age?* has never been adequately addressed, at least not to my satisfaction. (This statement is as true today as when I first wrote it, in the year 2000.) Given all the New Age leaders and teachers who have been active over the years, we would have thought that this question would have been clearly answered by now. It remains a stumbling block, in fact, to many in the New Age movement itself. We find in the movement that there is still confusion as to what the "New Age" should actually mean. What we too often get is guessing, misconceptions, partial answers, general statements that hang in mid-air, a certain hedging, and a constant beating-around-the-bush: What we don't get is a clear exposition of what, indeed, this New Age we are entering is all about. We might well have wondered, Where are the New Age *philosophers?* Or would *this* question have been premature—until now? (Is Ken Wilber, for example, a New Age philosopher? Some might think so; he is often labelled as such. But even Wilber's Integral Vision falls far short of being comprehensive of New Age issues, as he largely ignores, to the point of belittling, whole aspects of the paranormal that are front and center of the New Age picture. For all his intellectual, historical acumen, his offering any visionary gnosis for the contemporary world also seems absent. However, despite all that, I have often drawn upon his work here.)

I hope to address this question about the meaning of the New Age in as complete and satisfactory a manner as is possible today. Keep in mind, though, this is *my* interpretation of the New Age, so is not meant to be a scholarly overview, for example, of the New Age *movement*. I am not so much interested in the movement per se as I am in the visionary meaning of the new Aquarian Age. And not that this work is a full explication of a New Age philosophy—which is still to come—or an in-depth exploration of all its many aspects—which would imply a work more rigorous and much lengthier than this—but it is, I hope, in essential outline, an attempt to at least satisfy my own observation of a lack. The New Age Vision is complex in its themes and requires a gradual unfolding. The following work proceeds in a sort of spiral fashion as these themes are developed in stages, where what was hidden in a seed is slowly revealed as a tree. New concepts and transformations of traditional concepts are branches of the tree. Some of this may come as a surprise to those who might have thought that the New Age, as a movement, had already wrapped itself up, and had essentially come to naught. Whereas those expecting to read here what so many see as simply wild, airy-fairy New Age claims may perhaps find themselves disappointed. I do believe, though, that some extraordinary directions of visionary thought will be developed. Extraordinary enough, perhaps, to even convince those who see in the New Age nothing more than the pipedream of spiritual escapism that there may actually be something significant afoot in it after all.

This is not at all then a pep talk book about how the New Age is conveying some wonderful, new, sugar-coated, utopian Vision filled with peace and love. I do not wear rose-colored glasses about the New Age or the state of the world today. The world today appears to be heading into one game changing disastrous scenario or another, and so I will call it as I see it. It *would be* a mere, wishful, pipedream to think that the New Age we are entering makes any sort of promise that everyone will somehow slip through the changes that are coming unscathed; in fact, would anyone even want to live through the more disastrous scenarios of change that are possibly coming?

This, I hope, is a work that will help bridge the meaning of the New Age, and the movement by that name, to traditional thought and ground it in its historical context. Again, what I offer is not meant to be a scholarly history of the New Age movement, nor a stand back and observe academic exercise: What I attempt here is to literally present and define the New Age Vision by having lived squarely within it, by *seeing firsthand*.

## The New Age I Sing

The New Age I sing, Advent of the Aquarian—
I sing of today's Mythos emerging, the new Word
of a new Divinity, Revelation of Psyche Divine.

For Ear & Eye, a Melody & Vision were granted me—
Now the words I weave, articulation & fulfillment
of one Voice, one Tongue, a life that gave birth
      to Song.

Will I give witness to one Power alone?
I sing to give witness to all Powers—
All Gods & Goddesses of all times & places,
whatever, whomever they might be,
all entities nonhuman & cosmic Intelligences
      of all orders of Being,
all revealing themselves through the Opening

                    I sing

And not one people alone do I sing of,
but all peoples & nations—
I sing of this Earth, and of all creatures
& persons travelling with us upon this Earth.

I sing the next chapter in the adventure of soul,
an illumination gifted to me by Spirit,
its Web connected of all orders of Being,
now presenting its Revelation—
the coming among us of Psyche Divine.

I sing the correspondences
of Above & Below.

1985

## Basic Themes for the New Age

The Aquarian dispensation: Spirit dispenses a new evolutionary lesson (a new World Age).

Enough of Postmodernism: The overcoming and transformation of Postmodernism.

Reality is more than what it appears to be: We are beginning to enter the worlds of the Invisible.

To know firsthand: To know for oneself: A return to gnosis: "I know for myself."

Openness as the Aquarian existential attunement that involves a new relationship to Being.

All that is hidden is to be revealed: *No more secrets.*

We pour forth: We pour forth into the open Air for all: The Water Bearer / The Fountain.

Reconnecting with soul via Spirit coming-to-us anew in the guise *of* soul: *Psyche.*

Connecting with the Higher Self: Key to the Aquarian dispensation.

Psyche: Spirit *of* soul as the Living Image of the Higher Self: The liberation of soul.

Psyche as The Mythos, the new Word, of the New Age: Psyche as The Water Bearer.

Developing a relationship with the Higher Self that is firsthand, ongoing, co-creative.

The integration of heart and mind / soul and Spirit.

Being a Transformer: Transforming all that has been: Transforming the Traditions.

Our psychospiritual evolution: A bi-transformational process: A dynamic, interactive inner and outer process.

Conscious evolution: We are now collectively in the position of consciously evolving ourselves.

Our encounter with *The Other*: Recognition of Other Intelligence: ETs are real: The return of the Gods.

Aquarius: Opening up to the higher mind of intuition (Higher Self) beyond the rational.

Aquarian communication as long-distance, invisible, instantaneous, collective: this defines both the Internet & the psychic realm.

The integration of Technos & Psyche: The needful integration of technology and spirituality.

A new understanding of energy involving recognition of new and alternative energies (e.g. free energy).

Gaia: The Web of all life on Earth: Our stewardship of Earth.

The Aquarius/Leo dynamic: Endless Revealing/Unlimited Creativity.

The Living Fountain: The new super-creativity.

Aquarius as the sign of androgyny: Psyche the Divine Androgyne.

The Self as our supreme creative project.

Mythos-making as the supreme New Age art: A return to Mythos.

Uranus, planetary ruler of Aquarius, as the Awakener, the Liberator.

The Next Level coming through: The astral-psychic.

Networking as an Aquarian social form.

Realizing and fulfilling our individuality within community.

We are all members of the universal human family.

# Orientation:
# Welcome to the New Age

We find many today talking about receiving Visions and strange visitations. We find many sharing extraordinary, paranormal experiences and encounters; many who claim they are being addressed by otherworldly sources; and in one way or another, many more are finding themselves awakening to a new spiritual life. Indeed, there are many today realizing that they do have a higher purpose in life. The Call of a New Age is coming through louder and clearer in a multitude of ways.

Over 40 years ago now, upon arriving in Santa Cruz, California, I knew nothing about what the New Age was even supposed to be. When I did begin to hear, soon after my arrival, what was then the current talk about it, as I met the early New Agers of that late 1970s time, my response was to intellectually criticize it. With an academic background in the sciences and in traditional Western philosophy, I was impatient with what I pushed aside as so much nebulous fluff, pretension, and delusion. But, in my own way, like the Apostle Paul, who had, before his Vision and subsequent conversion to the Christ message, persecuted the first Christians of his time, I was soon to receive a Vision.[1] As I began the long process of assimilating this Vision, I was slowly, year by year, won over to the New Age message. Eventually I came to embrace it completely. An openness to the Call of the New Age, often after having had some firsthand experience, makes it contagious. By that I mean, a new dispensation of Spirit is happening today, in our midst, and it is finding in every individual who is open to it an opportunity to awaken that individual to that dispensation more and more. It is no coincidence that this parallels exactly what happened in the ancient world at the time of the birth of Christianity.

In our early youth, there were those of us who were assured by our teachers and the society around us that science would soon provide us the Truth, most importantly, the Truth about our existence, since no religion, according to Modern and then, later, Postmodern critique, could any longer pretend to do so. That promise, of course, failed to materialize. To those, however, who still might suggest that we have not waited long enough, that science will eventually—*someday*—reveal to us all that we wish to know about ourselves, I can only reply, *I am not going to wait around for that "someday."* I am not going to wait for something that undoubtedly will never arrive, when what I need to do is to live *here and now*. Science, as so many others have said, cannot provide us the existential meaning we are in so great a need of today. Science alone—that is, the science we know of today—cannot provide the Big Picture of who we are, what our relation to the cosmos is, and where we are going. So where does that leave us? Where did that leave *me*? *In a state of existential disorientation.* For there was no returning for me into the arms of traditional religion—there was no turning in repose to *any* traditional religion. I underwent the Postmodern experience, but it became time to move beyond it—*a Vision of a New Age was opening before me…*

# I Celebrate the Lightworker

Is there a new profession under the Sun?

From ancient callings through long history converging this day,
I celebrate a new calling today, a calling evolutionary & noble,
    of the highest Ideal—
A calling going out to all who taste the taste of Light divine,
who now in your hearts dedicate yourselves lifelong
    to be Workers of Light divine.

The Lightworker I celebrate, you I envision before me—
For your selfless efforts, going about in your own individual way,
cupping your hand to taste the taste of Light divine,
you are honored as you face the challenge of this day,
you no longer guess & hedge & slink back to conventional modes
    of safety & security.
What courage this compact you make with Self to bring the gift of Light
to this planet, in this decadent, declining, material-shackled, Postmodern
    chapter of our history—
You, the Lightworker, with passionate aspiration, you bring the Vision
    of a New Age before the disillusioned & disoriented, media-drunken
    masses fed daily on confusion.
You, the Lightworker, willing to step out with your Vision into the cruel
    & callous & cynical, sharp-toothed-&-clawed social arena.
You, the Lightworker, engaged in your inner labor without guarantee
    of any material reward, you dedicate yourself to the soul work
    of self-transformation.
You, the Lightworker, guiding energy into the body with hands of etheric
    healing, clearing & opening auras & chakras, healing nerves & muscles
    & bones, you draw energy down into tissue & even cell.
You, the Lightworker, listening with Light & talking with Light,
    casting Light into shadowy & tenebrous corridors & recesses of self,
    you counsel & support & encourage others on the Path.

You, the Lightworker, focusing Light through cards, numbers, colors
& crystals, planets & signs, you skilled yourself at seeing into Time.
You, the Lightworker, medium of Light, channeling Light in hushed
rooms, clairvoyant with Light outside the limitations of our
4-dimensional space & time, you help others to peer into the multi-
dimensions of Higher Self.
You, the Lightworker, schooled in the Light of wisdom traditions taken
to heart, now the itinerant teacher sharing the honey of Light.
You, the Lightworker, embodying Light in works of visionary art,
you revitalize our profane milieu with living Spirit, you are herald
of the Mythos of the New Age dispensation.
You, the Lightworker, wanderer of worlds, incarnate from elsewhere,
you realize after such struggle & acceptance of your struggle why
you are here, what Mission on this planet among planets in all
the far-flung star systems & galaxies & parallel universes.
You, the Lightworker, in contact with Other Intelligence, you face
unjust ridicule yet prepare our people for the inevitable encounter,
you grope for new concepts to wrench us from their time-is-up
of established paradigms, shifting us into a new level
of consciousness, inviting the agents of our evolution
to draw nearer.

The New Age calls you, Worker of Light—
Herald, harbinger, guide, beacon, healer, transformer, teacher
& visionary—
You see the veils of separation & ignorance, of mental perception,
falling away,
you share Light to help make Earth whole, to help birth New Being—
I celebrate you, Lightworker, at this threshold of a New Millennium!

I celebrate all of you, Lightworkers, who open doors
into the New Millennium!

1998

# ( 1 )

## A Preliminary Discussion:
## Objections to the New Age

I thought it best that we begin our exploration of the meaning of the New Age by first addressing the objections to it that we are most apt to hear. Why the objections (and so many of them!)? What is it that people say about the New Age movement, in particular, that has given it such a poor image in the general public, that is, if they still hear about it at all? Is it still, in fact, even an active, a viable, countercultural movement? Already years ago, I remember occasionally being warned about associating myself with anything New Age. The usual implication was that the movement was just too airy-fairy, composed primarily of mushy-headed individuals who didn't appear to have any capacity for critical thinking whatsoever, and so it had hardly established for itself anything resembling credibility. By the 1980s, it had become too much of a metaphysical carnival of angels and crystals, psychic healers, channels, and smooth-talking, flashy gurus. As I have already said, I, too, at first, had been one of these critics. Why, then, would I want to identify myself with anything New Age now? But we need to look beyond all the glitter and strobing lights of the carnival.

And then there was something more—occasionally someone would imply something more troubling; there was, in fact, a danger involved in such an association, coming especially from Fundamentalists. Waving the New Age flag around was likened to making oneself a possible target of hatred. I couldn't help but note that if the persecution of New Agers had any basis at all—and as far as I knew, I hadn't heard of any specific incidents of it, but for the dismissive slights—, that it would curiously echo, however faintly, the blatant, murderous persecution of early Christians during the New Age phase of the ancient dawn of the Age of Pisces.

Today, despite all the impressions to the contrary, there is, yes, still talk about a New Age: *The Age of Aquarius.* The phrases "New Age" and "Age of Aquarius" have certainly been around for quite a number of years now. Carl Jung had already been using the phrases earlier in the 20th Century. And, after all, the Woodstock Music Festival of 1969 was subtitled "An Aquarian Exposition: 3 days of Peace & Music." For many, though, all this New Age talk is already long passé, or is merely another example of the kind of, say, "California hype" that the rest of America likes to poke fun at, which is to ignore, of course, the fact that the New Age movement has established itself worldwide. A case in point, we find that communities like Findhorn, Scotland had already been notable New Age centers, in their own right, back in the 1970s and 80s. For the religious Fundamentalists, the New Age always seemed to pose a threat. Then, we might all know New Age-oriented individuals who take up meditation, yoga, astrology, tarot, channeling, shamanism; they're into angels, crystals, past life readings, psychic healing, or any one of a number of psychotherapies; we see the growth in wholistic or alternative health care practices, the burgeoning of health food markets; and we have often heard all of these referred to as "New Age." And there is the common rebuke, *But nearly all of this has been around for centuries, if not millennia, it's all traditional wisdom really, even ancient wisdom. What's so new about it?* Or, *what's so new about any of this anymore?* But the real significance here is missed—of course, none of this taken separately is new, or especially new at this point, but what must be kept in mind is that all of this is happening in a whole new context, at the dawn of a new *Age*, meaning, in a whole new cultural, global, context. The essence of "New Age" really implies something much more significant than simply getting into meditation and yoga, or angels and crystals.

First of all, whatever one might have assumed about it, the New Age was not and is not a cultural fad. (I am slowly going to make more explicit as we proceed that the New Age movement is not the New Age per se, but is an early cultural expression of it, of a dawning new *World* Age.) We have all heard references to the New Age of Aquarius as having been some Sixties "thing." *Didn't the Age of Aquarius go out with the Sixties?* we are sure to have heard. There are many, apparently, who have gotten the impression that it did; more accurately, however, it might reasonably be suggested that it had gone out with the 1980s, when it appeared to have peaked as a fad, or, at least by the 1990s. Yet, if the phrase is indeed still currently in use, then obviously it hadn't ended with the Sixties, or the Eighties or the Nineties. I have heard it said that years ago the general notion in the media was that the New Age was simply some offbeat fad having primarily to do with angels and crystals. Now there is no doubt about it, we live in a society of fads—we find all sorts of youth fads, music fads, commercial fads, clothing fads (fashion), techno and artistic fads, and now, fads via the Internet. Fads can last anywhere from under a year—long enough for a commercial season—to two or three years, maybe even five years. Even if we might stretch the timeframe of a cultural fad to ten years—for example, the so-called Me Decade of the Seventies (as if narcissism had only peaked then!)—the New Age movement has been around much longer than that, and only continues to grow. The first references to a New Age actually started appearing as early as the 19th Century—poet William Blake called out for a New Age in the early part of that century—, with seed influences from Transcendentalism and Spiritualism, and then with Theosophy, via Helen Blavatsky, in the later 19th Century firmly anchoring it in the metaphysical community going on into the early 20th Century. Other influences were the early studies in parapsychology; and then individuals such as Guy Ballard and the "I AM" Movement, Rudolf Steiner establishing Anthroposophy, in addition to the work of Alice Bailey. All of these background influences have already been discussed by others.[1] Carl Jung in the mid-20th Century clearly saw a New Age dawning with his psychological interpretation of the Christian Piscean Age and his claim that the Piscean dispensation had exhausted its archetypal force and was coming to an end. He, in fact, even made references to astrology to back up his own observations, so the coming Age of Aquarius made perfect sense to him. We should therefore make no mistake about it: The New Age is not a passing cultural fad.

For somewhat similar reasons, the New Age is not a cult. To begin with, a cult, by definition, is not something that can be slapped onto a whole 2,000-year period we call an "Age." The more accurate question would be, What, then, about the New Age as a cultural *movement*, or the so-called New Age religions that have popped up in recent years, aren't there cults here? First, even as a movement—a movement, again, that is worldwide—, we do not find any central cult figure, no one cult center, no cult doctrines or beliefs, no cultists found under one common banner called "New Age." Certainly, there may be any number of little cults within the New Age movement—as Christianity itself certainly has—, but such cults are really an anachronism that do not genuinely represent the global reach of the new Aquarian Age. It is questionable, as a matter of fact, whether the New Age *as a movement*, at this time, can be considered any kind of *unified* movement at all. It is a loose-knit association comprising diverse groups, yes, but groups still lacking, up to now, at least, any unifying Vision.

The same can be said for any references regarding a New Age religion. Though claims might have been made by various groups that they indeed represent the New Age religion—there are many varieties of weird religion under the umbrella of New Age—, there is as of yet, though, no one generally accepted New Age religion that everyone can point to; however, that is not to say that there is not increasingly a need for such a religion. To start with, it should be made abundantly clear that none of the world's traditional religions can be considered *the* religion for the New Age. But the New Age religion that is coming will definitely be a transformation of them all. The genuine New Age religion that is coming will (potentially) have the fundamental characteristic of being a *universal* Earth-based religion because it will emerge in a new "global village" context, but with this caveat: If civilization does collapse in the near future (as the abrupt climate change doomers claim), we can imagine that any surviving remnants of humanity will find themselves in isolated pockets that would inevitably begin to create new culture in diverse ways, including new religious influences. Keeping in mind, though, that our thinking today must be global and comprehensive of all that has gone before us, the New Age religion that is coming would subsume all other major religions as earlier cultural forms of the Piscean and other previous World Ages.

We should fully realize that the New Age universal religion to come is not one that we can somehow intellectually design and then will into existence. It is not as if we can take the so-called best of all current religions and somehow blend them together in a syncretic sort of stew and expect that it will speak to us existentially. That might be an interesting scholar's exercise, but it is certainly not how a genuine religion is born. We can be sure then that the New Age universal religion to come is not going to be established by a committee of scholars based on a comparative study of the world's great religions. This would be, for one thing, to utterly misunderstand the meaning of transformation: Transformation in the New Age sense involves an originary Vision, a Revelation, an emergent spiritual Form, that is born of novelty that over time makes new previous cultural forms by assimilating them into itself and thereby giving them a new, but radically transformed, life. Any new religion, we might claim, would still require the equivalent of a *Revelation*—an equivalent perhaps, as Jonathan Zap writes[2], such as a coming *event horizon*. And this implies the reality of someone's or some group's existential situation, not some academic conference on comparative religion, giving birth to it.

Those who are active in the New Age movement are all, in one way or another, preparing for this new, universal religion, whether they fully realize it or not. I, myself, prefer to be conscious about it, and openly honest about what I see as my own life's work. Indeed, a New Age Aquarian stance is that of being more genuinely honest about how we see ourselves.

It must already be apparent that I am not afraid of the word 'religion.' There are many today, and within the New Age movement itself, who strongly dislike this word 'religion.' They will be quick to emphasize a sharp distinction between religion and spirituality. *No, I am not religious, but I am spiritual*, we have certainly all heard someone say. The usual implication is that religion is an outdated, divisive, even dangerous, restrictive, exclusionary, institutionalized system for control, whereas spirituality is considered to be directly experiential and liberating, totally open to all that Spirit might reveal. It is a new spirituality that these individuals might advocate, but not another new "religion." *The last thing we need is another religion*, I'm sure we have also heard it said. Certainly I understand the distinction they are making here, but I do not see "religion" and one's "spirituality" as mutually exclusive, or necessarily in permanent conflict. I prefer to think of religion in its original, fundamental sense, and that is, of a tying back to the Source, to Spirit, but, meaning that that tying back is taking some tangible cultural form. In other words, religion becomes the cultural embodiment of—the symbolic or Mythos form, the Great Story, for holding—the spiritual life. How often when I do hear those who insist on this distinction, after they dispose of religion and proclaim how spiritual they are, that it turns out that by "spiritual" is meant something utterly vague, abstract, nebulous, it is perhaps some mystical "feeling," that scarcely has any embodiment in form. Spirituality, in other words, is left floating in the clouds as a feeling of a great "Something," or perhaps of how we are all interconnected as one—*We are all one*, you know—, but, then, that's as far as it goes—nothing tangible is really made of it, and nothing in current culture is changed. The status quo still remains. Now, of course, *there are* concrete spiritual practices—as many who turn to the East readily find them there—that are very clearly defined, laid out in specific, definite forms, that one becomes practiced at, such as the scores of meditation techniques, yoga paths, mantra practices, tantra, tai chi, martial arts, etc. (A common flaw here is that one's "spirituality" then gets caught up in techniques, meaning then that one's connection with Spirit is all a technique.) What I am suggesting is that the new, universal religion I speak of will unfold as an organic, cultural development—ultimately as the new Great Story to be told, *The Mythos*—of the experience of New Age spirituality.

Let us consider now the claim that might be made by someone who is loyal to one of the traditional religions. We meet someone who appears to be savvy about spiritual matters who will say, for example, that Buddhism has all the answers we need, and that it is spiritually superior to the other traditions. He or she finds it completely satisfactory and fulfilling. Now that may well be the case for any given individual. I honestly do not see, however, our society turning en masse to Buddhism as the one religion we all need. Christians, of course, are quick to jump in with *their* claim. But taking Buddhism as our example, it cannot be the religion of the New Age because it comes with its own cultural baggage. To be a Buddhist seriously involves borrowing its mythology, its culture, its voluminous texts, its doctrines, and usually implies spending at least some period of time in a monastery. To be a Buddhist means accepting its age-old doctrines as though the world has not changed since ancient times. It must be stressed that the New Age is not about simply borrowing other people's culture, or religion, no matter how enlightened it might appear to be; it is about opening to Spirit anew on our own soil. Certainly we are challenged to absorb and assimilate all the religious traditions that have been passed down to us to the extent that we are able, but the New Age Vision foresees a transformation of them all. There are important realities today that any New Age religion must confront. Where in the Buddhist texts is there mention of the new physics and new biology, of all the new technologies—the cyberworld, for example—, of ecological issues in a technological world, or of how a contemporary world should handle the impact of ET contact? For that matter, where in Buddhism is there mention of Christ's mission, but then, vice versa—where in Christianity is there serious acceptance of Buddha? Though any of the world's current religions can satisfy multitudes in their respective societies—and billions today are, of course, still loyal to their religious traditions—, I do not find Buddhism, or Christianity, Hinduism, or Islam, satisfying the New Age requirement of contemporary universality.

Fundamentalist Christianity presents another issue for us. We often find Fundamentalist leaders expressing their fear of the New Age. In many of their books they will issue warnings to their Christian flock of the New Age threat to their Truth, and they often consider it a far more dangerous threat to Christianity, in fact, than any of the other traditions. What they must fundamentally fear about the New Age then is *change*. The main lesson for them is that, as with all tradition and culture, religions, too, must change with the changing of the times—"the times" symbolically meant here is exactly the changing of the Ages, which are not measured by anything like a few years, decades, or even centuries. Whereas the arts have gone through quite rapid changes in the Modern, and now Postmodern, world, and science, though traditionally conservative, has its revolutions and paradigm shifts, religions have adamantly resisted change. The reason is, as Fundamentalists of any Tradition claim, is that their religion has already embodied the Truth. (All of what is said here applies equally as well then to Fundamentalist Judaism and Islam.) *Why change what is Truth?* they say. Or, as they say more strongly, we have no right to change what has already been revealed as Truth. The misunderstanding is to think that we, the ego-self collective—collective consciousness—, can change the "Truth"; rather, it is the "Truth" that changes itself through us. To claim that Truth is some rock-solid Absolute that we can "capture" in language—that it can never change because it has been "captured" in a book—is a particular, historical, metaphysical orientation, in short, a particular, preconceived mindset that has not yet gone through the contemporary Postmodern experience. But we have come to a new orientation today: religions, too, must change as Revelation is given to us anew. This does not imply, then, in any simplistic sense, that the Traditions are rejected out of hand; no, not at all—they are to be absorbed, assimilated, and *transformed*. Fundamentalist Christians of today may yet live to see the New Age Vision transforming their Truth. It is the intention, I believe, at the very heart of our psychospiritual evolution.

We are well aware that there are some, even within the loose-knit New Age movement itself, who are simply tired of hearing the phrase 'New Age,' and often feel adamantly that the phrase ought to be dropped. I am sorry they feel that way, but to suggest that the phrase 'New Age' has somehow been used up like some commodity of contemporary consumerism is rather premature. True, someday it will undoubtedly have exhausted its relevance, but that someday is still many years away—30, perhaps 50, perhaps even a hundred years away. (As long as scholars continue to tell us that we live in a Postmodern world, we know that we have not yet even collectively entered the New Age.) Isn't it interesting that the words 'Christianity' and 'Buddhism' have not been worn out yet. We don't hear people too often complaining about the overuse of the word 'Christian,' for example. I never really hear anyone saying they are tired of hearing the word 'Christian,' or 'Buddhist,' or 'Muslim,' and yet, 'New Age,' strangely enough, provokes such strong, negative reactions in quite a number of people.

Again, among those tired of hearing 'New Age' are surprisingly some who are firmly planted within the "New Age movement" itself, however awkwardly they attempt to squirm out from being identified with it. They will say, for example, *It is time to come up with a different label now, it's time to coin a different phrase.* And so we look on as they ingeniously try to coin the new phrase, some neologism perhaps, that can somehow stamp the essence of what is happening today. So we hear of "the new consciousness," "the new spirituality," "new thought," "wholistic thought," "the new paradigm," (all phrases that are, of course, rather vague and general), or others, such as "the Awakening," "the Quickening," "the Shift." They all do sound simply like evasive variants of "New Age," but without the profound implication already packed into the growing momentum of the whole notion of a "New Age." For 'New Age,' having an astrological basis going back thousands of years, is the perfectly appropriate phrase that expresses what this transition period, this Shift, we have entered is all about, and we should be courageous in our continued use of it. I challenge anyone to suggest a better term than 'New Age' at this juncture in our human Story; it, in fact, easily absorbs the meanings of the various other terms that are currently being offered. (One movement, though, that will undoubtedly be gaining more attention in the coming years is Transhumanism. Whether it has the potential to supplant 'New Age' as better characterizing our transition period is open to debate. In fact, we will be addressing the whole issue in a later chapter.) Those who feel that they must come up with a new catch phrase every few years have only fallen prey to our society's mania for using up and throwing away faddish things. To believe that a new phrase must be coined to replace 'New Age' only muddies the water. Of course, there will always be those—for whatever reason—who want to muddy the water. (Again, lest I be misunderstood at this point—I will explain further on—I am not saying our current historical time, globally, can yet be called *the* New Age. No, not yet, not yet by a long shot. Our current historical time is still characterized by almost all scholars as Postmodern (and I include in this the merely clever Post-Postmodern phrase that is currently making the rounds). I am implying by this then that when it comes to spirituality, for example, Postmodern and New Age are utterly distinct notions. The Postmodern sensibility, in fact, is the spiritual antithesis of New Age. Obviously, though, the New Age *movement* is unfolding in a Postmodern world.)

In my twenties, I myself went through a phase where I felt disgusted every time I heard the word 'new.' We were being deluged by new this, new that, everything was being marketed as new, new, new; it was almost a disease, it seemed, started by Modernism that was still spreading into and infecting every aspect of life. My first resistance to the notion of a New Age was clearly then because of the use of the word 'new.' *What, now there's a new Age coming on too?* But this was before I understood its astrological foundation. After some time, I came to realize the profound implication of what a new World Age really meant, and to embrace the further realization that the New Age movement was what I was indeed moving in the direction of, that here was where my thinking *and my experience* were leading me.

We should mention that there are those who are uncomfortable with any label whatsoever—they want to carry on in their life independently of any label that might characterize them, and so, apparently, pinning them down. *Why does it need a label?* they ask. And they can get quite bullheaded about it too; they don't want to belong to anything that they feel limits them in any way. They would prefer not to be identified in a cultural context, or to be historically situated, by the use of any label. But the reality is is that we are all historically situated, there is really no escape from it. They are also neglecting the fact that all past historical figures participated in some cultural movement, period, era, though they may not have always seen themselves in such a context in their lifetime. (One of the positive contributions of Postmodernist thought is to alert us to such a context, that we are always already living within a context.) Or, perhaps, we can look at it this way: It is as if a Christian, or a Buddhist, or a Muslim, were to say, *Don't label me a Christian! Don't label me a Buddhist! Don't label me a Muslim!* You don't find shame associated with being a Christian or a Buddhist or a Muslim, yet, curiously, admitting that you are a New Ager is almost something you are expected to be ashamed of. Why is that? Again, we must have the courage for acknowledging who we are in the greater cultural context. And in today's hyper-self-conscious world, it is hardly possible to be unreflective about our historical self-image. It is actually disingenuous.

Another point about labeling (what can also be referred to as cultural memes), which also comes down to simply *naming* things, is that telling a story is impossible without giving names to things, places, events, and people. How can you tell a story without characters that have names? And names for places too? It should be made clear then, if I haven't made it clear already, that we are beginning in this work to tell a Story of these times, these very times that we live in. In our current Postmodern world—or, let us say, according to Postmodernist theory—such a grand Story as I am attempting to tell here is no longer considered possible; it is actually preferred to be avoided. We will see in the next chapter on Postmodernism why such a claim has been made. In a fundamental sense, then, to deny the right to label or to name things is to deny our right to storytelling, and that applies also to Big Storytelling.

Then we are hit with the retort, *There's really nothing new about the New Age at all. It's all old stuff rehashed. It has all been said before.* True, there is nothing new about mysticism or occult practices, meditation, yoga, astrology, crystals, psychics and psychic healing, Earth spirits, shamanism, even channeling. We can find all of it already in mystical Christianity, Sufism, Hinduism, Buddhism, Taoism, the occult tradition, paganism, and in Native American traditions. True, there is nothing really new about any of this; there is plenty of old Tradition under the umbrella "New Age." But the mistake is to think that the New Age is reducible to any of the above, or to all of them somehow blended together. We can safely say that the current resurgence of interest in spiritual metaphysics, in the occult, in ancient wisdom, or the turning of Westerners to the East for existential, spiritual answers, is not, in essence, what the New Age is about. One is not New Age, in the profound sense of the phrase, simply because one meditates, eats health foods, practices yoga, astrology or new alchemy, or works with crystals or herbs, or is into channeling. All of these occult and spiritual practices and areas of study—and we must include all the psychotherapies that are available today—are only a preparation, a mulch, for the cultural soil from which the tree called "New Age" will rise. In essence, the New Age is a new spiritual dispensation, and the tree of this dispensation will transform the very soil in which it grows. Those who claim not to see anything new yet are only indirectly pointing to the fact that the New Age has barely begun, that the new *collective* spiritual inspiration of Aquarius has yet to be dispensed. *But the New Age Vision is definitely here.* And there are some few of us who *are* already receiving that dispensation.

Even among "New Agers" we sometimes find this needless arguing about the newness of the New Age. We will hear, *Haven't we gone through this cycle before? Didn't the ancient or legendary so-and-so civilization know all this already?* Instead of arguing about how "new" the New Age really is, the essential point is to understand that we are entering a new *World Age*—we are moving into another astrological Age which will bring to the fore a different set of grand themes, a whole different global context, resulting in a profound shift in consciousness, unlike anything we have known in recent centuries of civilization. (To those who might pounce here and say, *Aha! So the New Age is really only an astrological claim, therefore is baseless on that alone,* we will address their criticism in another chapter.)

As for Eastern religious traditions going back thousands of years, true enough, but that was obviously *in the East.* The Eastern spiritual influence has only in recent decades burgeoned in the West, helping, yes, to create a "new" spiritual context for us. But this is still not the *new* in New Age. The same can be said for the occult arts. They had largely been practiced by an underground minority throughout the long history of Christianity. The Church had suppressed occultism—including all of paganism, for that matter—for its own dogmatic and political reasons. Under this suppression, occult "secrets" were accessible only for the few, those who sought them out for their own spiritual growth, and who knew the importance of keeping the ancient occult tradition alive. In recent centuries, modern science, too, has helped to suppress these arts, by criticizing them as so much archaic superstition. But here, too, the situation is changing as the growth of interest in spiritual/occult matters continues, openly, in the general public. Today, there is no longer, by and large, a political necessity for such secrecy. Greater numbers are taking active interest in alternative approaches to the spiritual life; the old Sunday religion, for many, is simply no longer good enough. There are those who want *more*. Specifically, they want actual, firsthand, spiritual experience, not mere beliefs, and not mere lip service. Occult "secrets" to the spiritual life are now being shared with all who have interest in them, through many venues. Consider the hundreds, no, *thousands* of books that have come out in recent years on every conceivable aspect of spirituality and occultism. The New Age, we would hope, does sound the note of an eventual spiritual awakening in more of the population. Yet, this alone still does not encapsulate the New Age. Again, the New Age is not simply a borrowing from the past or other cultures. All that we might assimilate from the past or from other cultures is but, again, preparing the mulch for the soil in which the New Age dispensation, like a tree, can take root and grow.

Another criticism we often hear regarding the New Age movement is its often blatant, notorious, commercial aspect. Look at the consumer marketing that exploits the label "New Age" (this was especially true some years ago). It was cynically contended that the "New Age" label was but a clever marketing ploy for the new therapeutic and spiritual supermarket—the "consciousness industry"—that had emerged since the Sixties, and was often affordable only for the well-to-do. Through "New Age" churches, temples, study centers, workshops, conferences, expos, lectures, bookstores, with all their books, tapes, CDs and DVDs, and magazines, every sort of religious, spiritual, and occult fare has now been laid out on the table for our consumption. And it's all simply hyped up, we hear, so that it sells. We all know people—especially in the younger generation (even if they have an ear for it)—who are turned off to anything New Age because of this commercial aspect to it. (As if no one has ever heard of a Christian bookstore!) I was cynical about anything New Age myself at one time because of this too. Why is it that everything costs money—and so much money? We should not confuse, however, the essence of the New Age with the commercial packaging so often done in its name. At the same time, we must be honest enough to put the label "New Age" in its current cultural context. We clearly live in a totally commercialized society; it would be a bit too much to assume that those in the New Age community would not want to sell their wares in the marketplace, as any craftsperson or professional would expect to be able to do. Do New Age practitioners and artists not have a right to make a living, each according to their calling? Exploiting New Age trends, however, simply to make loads of money is not exactly commendable; it can be crass. (Some have even gotten the impression that the New Age is only about manifesting prosperity, since that seems to be the major motivation in a certain percentage of those in the movement. It makes it all sound rather like another new, catchy, spiritually sneaky way of advocating a hip kind of capitalism.) But none of the above observations takes away from the New Age dispensation. Make no mistake about it: The New Age is far larger than any commercial packaging. The New Age, in its essence, is not a smorgasbord where we get to pick and choose different dishes of spirituality. (I call those who indulge exclusively in that way the "Eclectics.") Eventually, I see that those who identify with the New Age—it probably *will* have taken on a different name by then—will be in much the same position as the Christian churches are today when it comes to them providing free religious services, spiritual counseling, and being active in community and global charity work.

Then we hear the criticism that the New Age movement, for all its presumption of new spirituality, is actually quite superficial, being merely all fluff and phony sweetness and light with no substance, promoted by airy-fairy, wishful-thinking people who hanker for an empty transcendence, which is nothing other than another vain attempt at escaping from the real world. We hear it said that New Agers will simply believe anything, no matter how outrageous, as they seem to have an inability to think critically. True, that may indeed be how so many New Agers do come across. But there is no argument here. You find that this is no different than with anything else; people have always jumped on the circus bandwagon of fads and trends without having any inner gyroscope of their own. Are Christians or Muslims, for example, by and large critical thinkers? Are they not true believers in any number of outrageous doctrines? This criticism, then, in no way diminishes the profound meaning of the New Age Vision that is still to unfold and still to be shared.

For those who might still protest, *But I don't want to be lumped in with New Age, it's passé and outdated,* the fact is, as I have stated at the beginning, despite what the media or certain critics may want us to believe, the New Age has not yet even been adequately defined. That is what I find most disturbing: There are those who want to simply dismiss it before the New Age Vision has even been fully laid out. So it is incumbent upon us, *the New Age thinkers,* to do just that, to explain what this New Age Vision is all about. That is the one thing I do hope to accomplish here. The further challenge then would be to take this Vision into our own hands and co-creatively mold it into new forms of living, spiritual culture—*a new Mythos.*

Sometimes we hear talk that the New Age of Aquarius will mean a time of universal enlightenment for all humanity. What exactly is meant by "enlightenment" here is usually, though, left unclear. (Especially when we consider that cybertechnology is now part of the equation in our further evolution.) If the assumption is that everyone will be Buddha enlightened, then it is easy to brush aside any New Age aspirations as so many pipedreams. *C'mon,* we can hear the critic say, *you must be dreaming.* But if we are more modest and suggest that we will become more enlightened about our origins, about our place in the universe, about the Next Level of consciousness opening up to us, about our Higher Self, then that may very well be a better answer to what the dawning New Age is about. Any so-called universal "enlightenment"—whatever that might mean—will come in its own time.

Likewise, many have had the impression that the New Age is supposed to inaugurate a utopian Peace and Love and Light on Earth; everything, it is assumed, is supposed to be getting so much better in the world. Now looking at the world today, this is, of course, nowhere evident. On the contrary, current events highlight global tensions, conflicts, unrest, terrorism, quagmires of wars—for years in Iraq, and still in Syria and Afghanistan—, the still looming threat of nuclear war, possible economic collapse, environmental degradation, natural disasters, the out-of-control disaster at Fukushima, in addition, of course, to climate change catastrophe, and our current "pandemic." (In the following, too, we will have opportunities for referring to these dire trends in the world. And we will in no way deny that all of this is happening.) So the response we get to all this is, *There's your New Age for you—a complete bust.* But the whole notion of a New Age had guaranteed nothing regarding those early, rather naïve, impressions about the "Age of Aquarius." The New Age by no means promises any overnight utopia or mass collective enlightenment. Was it some popular song or another out of the Sixties that misled people about this that still echoes today? It is rather of the very nature of an emerging "New Age" that the current culture is in decay, that the times appear to be in chaos, that we may appear indeed to be coming upon End Times. After all, the previous World Age *is* ending. We should realize that the dispensation of a New Age is more likened to a seed that will germinate out of the mulch of cultural decay. And even in the midst of chaotic, dark, and decadent times, there can be found pockets of genius and brilliant new ideas and Visions. We should always keep in mind here that we are currently living through this chaotic time of transition between Ages, which today is called Postmodernity (aka Postmodernism). The New Age, therefore, promises nothing regarding particular world events; it announces, rather, grand new themes unfolding of the human adventure, an adventure both exhilarating to participate in and filled with its own dangers. The "New Age" is really the name of a psychospiritual, cultural frontier.

Similar to the simplistic assumptions regarding Peace and Love, there are the simplistically expressed, so-called New Age tenets. For example, we find: *We create our own reality. We are all one. We are responsible for everything that happens to us, or, for that matter, for everything that happens anywhere on the planet.* And then there's the big Secret: *You can attract anything you want to you.* (Which always seems to imply material things, including above all wealth, love, and power—all so boringly and mass media typical of our Postmodern, narcissistic, you-can-have-it-all culture. The book *The Secret* did something of a disservice to serious New Age thought in this regard.) Now this is not the moment to address these particular beliefs; but that the New Age was thought to be conceptually limited to such simplistic, generalized, platitudinous notions was unfortunate. We must make an attempt to undo the damage and correct the misconceptions, and present a more comprehensive and substantial view of what this New Age we are entering is all about.

Before we go any further, though, I should make more of an effort now to bring out a distinction so as not to create too much confusion, as I am aware that some misunderstanding here is probably unavoidable. The New Age, as we will see, does refer to the new World Age of Aquarius that we are entering, a roughly 2,000-year period. Obviously, considering the pace of change today, we cannot know what unimaginable transformations will occur for humanity in that extensive timeframe. For that matter, we can scarcely know what the world will look like 20 years from now. Yet, those who talk about a coming, but still far far off, universal enlightenment for all humanity may turn out to be right about the Age of Aquarius after all when we take into consideration such a lengthy period of time as 2,000 years. But when I refer to 'New Age,' I am speaking primarily about a much more limited timeframe, which is only that of our entry into the Aquarian Age, after which time the newness of the Age will slowly have passed. By 'New Age,' then, I am referring primarily to these next few decades, perhaps even the next hundred years, however long the "newness" of the Age of Aquarius might apply. In the midst of this timeframe will undoubtedly take place tremendously devastating events, and perhaps, because of abrupt climate change, even the extinction of most of the biosphere and humanity. At the same time, however, a growing New Age *movement* oriented in an Aquarian way (perhaps even in a surviving remnant) will be occurring. We will see in our discussion of Postmodernity, however, that, despite all the signs of a New Age movement, we are still not even close to a New Age-defined world. The New Age, in a collectively spiritual, global sense, is still barely on the mainstream radar screen. (There are some who believed, for reasons regarding Mayan prophecy, that the year 2012 was supposed to be the tipping point year for a New Age beginning. And we may well look back on 2012 as a tipping point year in which dire prophecies were just starting to unfold.)

Another attempt at undermining any allegiance to the Vision of a New Age (however dim the future might appear) is perhaps the strongest objection yet: It is the claim, usually made by right-wing Fundamentalists or conspiracy theorists with their own political agenda, that the New Age movement has been infiltrated, or is even being orchestrated, by Secret Controllers, the Illuminati, a secret global elite; in other words, that some secret elite conspiracy is manipulating it behind the scenes and using it and funding it as a front movement. Well, if that were the case, I am certainly out of the loop! They almost always reference Alice and Foster Bailey and their founding of the Lucis Trust in 1922, which was largely a trust fund for publishing Alice Bailey's books. Lucis Trust morphed into an organization (under different names) that came to have a close association with the UN, and in their literature, they apparently promoted the idea of a One World Government.[3] As if the past activities of the Lucis Trust of close to a hundred years ago and the allegation of some secret New Age conspiracy should somehow frighten us and stop us from fulfilling our life work as New Age Lightworkers. We should remain wary of giving away our power, as they say, to those who talk conspiracy in order to sidetrack us and make us doubt our own life Path. As if there were no Secret Controllers—secret societies, secret governments, puppet masters that are a global elite—behind the Church, behind elected governments, the Federal Reserve, the world banking system, The Trilateral Commission, Council on Foreign Relations, international alliances, multinational corporations, behind all our intelligence agencies, behind NASA, and all aspects of the corporate-military-industrial complex. We could just as easily talk about the apparent conspiracy of the right-wing neoconservative agenda to take over our American government in the wake of 9/11. The thing is, claims of secret conspiracies to control and manipulate can be made concerning just about anything. And don't get me wrong here, I am not denying the importance and validity of conspiracy research. But we have to be on our toes here at all times, for a conspiracy certainly is in place to keep the general public confused and in the dark about quite a number of things; the lack of truth and honesty in "official" government announcements anymore is a given. Or, we find the utter silence of officialdom on certain issues, such as global geoengineering. Yes, the reality of Secret Controllers scheming behind the scenes of our world *is* quite apparent; not to see this is to be naïve. But to think to single out the New Age movement, which is, first of all, a *spiritual* frontier, as somehow posing as the front movement for a geopolitical New World Order is not exactly offering an accurate Big Picture; it is almost beside the point. Be assured, those behind the New World Order are not interested in advancing some of the most important intentions of the Aquarian New Age, such as, *All that is hidden is to be revealed: No more secrets.* And, *We pour forth into the open Air for all.* And also, the spiritual realization of unlimited creativity. Agents of the New World Order may push simplistic New Age ideas in popular culture to muddle people's minds, but they certainly are not intending to *pour forth into the open Air* so that all can see the Big Lies of the corporate-military-industrial complex for themselves. What we usually discover is that those who most loudly make this claim about the New Age movement as a front are in fact Christians of a certain political bent. Obviously, they are out to promote their brand of religion *and* politics. Fundamentalists who go so far as to see the New Age movement as the work of "Satan" or "Lucifer" are asking us to accept an outmoded, simplistic, mythic interpretation that does extreme injustice to a complex Postmodern world. They have to wind up lumping everyone who is not enlisted in their narrowly defined Fundamentalist camp as part of the "Conspiracy."

That there is a shadow side, a dark side, to the New Age movement, and even to the dawning Aquarian Age itself, is not to be ignored. (The Piscean Age we are leaving certainly had a dark side.) Some of the things we've already discussed here could be extrapolated as the dark side of the movement. Take, for example, the "New Age" messianic UFO cult that started in the Seventies, first going by the names Human Individual Metamorphosis, then Total Overcomers Anonymous, and finally Heaven's Gate, led by The Two, also calling themselves Bo and Peep. The cult had early on been preparing for what they called the Level Above Human. The Two brainwashed their followers into believing that someday an apocalyptic sign would appear announcing that a UFO would be taking them away…to the Level Above Human. And sure enough, in 1997 that sign appeared—Comet Hale-Bopp. In the broader New Age community of that time there was a lot of chatter about Hale-Bopp being more than just a comet; it was a messenger—Hale-Bopp's companion was coming, the ETs were coming! And we know what happened next—the mass suicide of 39 people—the Heaven's Gate cult—outside of San Diego. Marshall Applewhite (who was Bo) claimed that the Mother Ship Companion had come for them, that Earth was about to be recycled, that their only chance to survive was to transcend to the next evolutionary level, requiring that they had to leave their "earthly containers," their bodies, behind.

We can also consider the possible dark side of the Aquarian future to be the unchecked rise of Technos—that what some are warning as the coming AI "God" may take complete control of Earth and may determine that merely biological Homo sapiens is obsolete, that only techno Transhumanists would be viable on the future Earth. Indeed, we have seen many sci fi dystopian scenarios of what the future Earth might be. We might even consider that the possibility of a MELE (mass extinction level event) implying the extinction, or near extinction, of humanity itself as another dark, doom and gloom, scenario of the new Aquarian Age.

So the New Age, a critic might say, is apparently then about a new, so-called World Age. An immediate question might then be: *According to whom? Astrologers? But I don't believe in astrology,* the critic will say. *And does anything like a so-called World Age even mean anything?* (Again, we will pick this theme up more extensively in a forthcoming chapter.) Indeed, it could all be, according to our hardcore Postmodern critic, a grand fabrication created by certain delusional types of individual. The fact that the world is rapidly changing today with a New Age subculture in its midst is only coincidence, the critic might say. Yet, we might just as easily ask, *Only* a coincidence? Or is the fact that the world is rapidly changing not exactly what the transition into a New Age entails? Actually, the more pointed and helpful question would initially be, *Who is in a position to adequately interpret this rapidly changing world?* Now the purpose of this book is to show that there is something more going on with the notion of a New Age than what our critic might think.

Hopefully apparent by now is the sense that despite the decades that the New Age movement has been around, despite all the already published New Age books, and despite those who think that they can easily debunk it or write it off, a comprehensive Vision of what the New Age entails has never fully been laid out. It was as if the opportunity to do so was lying fallow, only waiting for someone to plant that seed of Vision that would begin the Story. Indeed, mention should be made that there are whole aspects to the New Age that are neglected or not even thought of as belonging to it. Let us be clear about it: The New Age is not limited to being some newfangled, but narrowly-defined, spiritual movement or offbeat religion; no, it is unfolding in a multitude of ways, on various fronts. We could say to our critic, Do you mean to say there is nothing new about the high-tech world, the cyberworld, about artificial intelligence, robotics, nanotechnology? There is nothing new about Internet global communications and today's instantaneous media? They definitely all play a role in the New Age, as we will see. And why is science increasingly moving into realms of the Invisible? Is science finally catching up to what the occult traditions have always known (but could only hint at culturally through symbols)? There is a clue to the New Age here, too. And is there nothing new about UFOs and ET contact? Though they have always been with us behind the scenes since the dawn of history and before, they are certainly something profoundly new for our civilization today, a civilization in which "officialdom" still denies that there is any evidence for Other Intelligence at all. In fact, the UFO phenomenon and the ET presence is something so radical, so disturbing, so reality shattering, that a heavy-handed cover-up has been in place since the late 1940s to keep the public completely blind-sighted about it. And will someone say that we have not through the centuries developed—I would say evolved—a whole new civilization that is changing the face of Earth, and that this process in recent years—it may soon be academically called the Anthropocene—has somehow stopped? This process has not stopped, we continue to evolve, even now, today, more rapidly than ever before, more rapidly than we can even fully realize, even with our eyes wide open. As we will see, in the futuristic, high-tech arena, there are those calling themselves Transhumanists who speak about the coming evolutionary event they dub the "Singularity." There are certainly plenty of surprises coming for those who might think the human species has gone stagnant, or that there is nothing catastrophically new waiting for us upon the horizon.

# ( 2 )

# AN AGE OF CRISIS—AND TRANSITION: POSTMODERNITY

Nietzsche: *God is dead. End of Story.*
Postmodernists: *We agree. There is no Story.*

Ours is an age in crisis. This has been hammered into our ears since our youth; and still, to this day, as we have entered a new century—in fact, it's even a new millennium—we hear the same theme over and over. First, we suffered the carnage, atrocities, and Holocaust of a World War; we saw dictators slaughter millions of their own people; we entered the Nuclear Age with the horror of two atomic bombs dropped on wartime cities and have lived ever since under the threatening shadow of nuclear annihilation; the traditional social fabric of the Western world has been coming undone; scholars have written of the 20th Century's alienation, fragmentation, existential disorientation, dehumanization, the meaninglessness, emptiness, neurotic anxiety and stress of everyday life, its spiritual bankruptcy, its decadence, its nihilism; at the same time, we see the explosion of population—we are now at over 7 billion globally—; we hear the doom and gloom prophets of global ecological disaster—Earth is now heating up with a fever with dire scenarios of anthropogenic climate change…the Arctic icecap now quickly melting, how many gigatons of methane to be released that will rapidly raise the temperature of the planet—there will be no agriculture at that point, but an ongoing MELE—, a sea level rise that will wipe out major coastal cities; always predictions of new killer plagues; there is the exponential increase in information that no one individual can even come close to getting a handle on; the insertion of technology into every aspect of life, which, in the hands of secret governments, potentially threatens to bring about a New World Order that will attempt to control all life on Earth. And now we must live with the ongoing, radioactive, death-making MELE of Fukushima that is projected to go on not only for decades, but quite likely for centuries. We see an overwhelming picture of crisis from every angle. Welcome to our Postmodern Era. It does appear to be leading us into a possible coming Dark Age of civilization's collapse. Or perhaps it is not as simplistic as that.

*To move beyond the Postmodern, we should make an attempt to understand what we are moving away from.*

Let us note, first of all, that most people today will still make the assumption that we live in the Modern world. The word 'modern,' of course, is still used extensively, for example, in all manner of marketing pitches. It is an everyday word, meaning whatever happens to be current in a world continuously improved by science and technology and material production. But the collective understanding that these are now no longer Modern but Postmodern[1] times has still not sufficiently sunk in. (Scholars will usually prefer the word 'Postmodernity' to define these times, so as to make a distinction from Postmodernism as a trend defining artistic style and intellectual thought. It is not my intention here to go into all the scholarly debate in defining and distinguishing 'Postmodern,' 'Postmodernist,' 'Postmodernism,' 'Postmodernity.' It does seem obvious to me that they are all connected by common themes.) Almost every day I find individuals who are somewhat surprised to suddenly hear it put this way, that we today do live in a *Postmodern* world. This is a little discouraging, perhaps, to those of us who are now more than ready to move beyond the Postmodern to realize that mainstream society has yet perhaps many more years before the influence of Postmodernism has fully played itself out. (There are some intellectuals today making references to the Postmodern, usually in the context of the art world, as somehow having already come and gone, circa late 1990s. I believe this to be premature; it belies a Postmodernist orientation in thinking to state opinions like this to begin with. In the same vein, we might hear it put that we now live in a Post-Postmodern period, which, to me, is nothing more than the same Postmodern cleverness talking. However many Posts- you might put in front of modern, the phrase still shows the same face of the Postmodern. Or, a new phrase that's current is pseudo-Modern. As will be made apparent, I see the New Age orientation as the only "new trend" possible beyond the Postmodern. Even Transhumanism per se, at least still now, is Postmodern, since it has no strong spiritual orientation.)

The Modern period of Western civilization saw the slow undermining of the religions and metaphysical systems of Tradition. The successes of modern science; the 18th Century European Enlightenment, especially the Kantian revolution in philosophy putting a strict limit on what metaphysics was capable of; the separation of Church and State; the rise of middle class culture; the relentless critique pursued by various "schools of suspicion" (Paul Ricoeur's phrase) inspired by the famous trio of Marx, Nietzsche, and Freud; the 20th Century philosophical trends of positivism, phenomenology, existentialism, negative dialectics, linguistic analysis and language games, semiotics, structuralism and then post-structuralism, and deconstruction, and all the announcements about the death of Western metaphysics; radical theology and the numerous movements of the artistic avant-garde; to the ubiquity of mass popular culture as an industry and the dominance of mainstream media and rampant capitalist, consumer materialism—all of these contributed, in one way or another, in different arenas of life, to our progressive disorientation before the cosmos.

Even our entering the Space Age, with the celebrated feat of going to the Moon, was actually more disorienting than being a possible new orientation for humanity at the time, because the new perspective it offered of Earth was never fully integrated into culture. It had no impact really on changing the dominant mainstream and mass-conditioned perceptions of everyday life. Globally, did landing on the Moon in 1969 change the existential condition for any billions of people? It was indeed a significant milestone in our technological capability, but it failed to birth any new orienting Mythos for us. Instead of orienting us anew in the cosmos, it became but another disconnected spectacle in the Postmodern landscape.

The Grand Premise[2] of the recently completed 20th Century could be phrased in many ways, but perhaps it can be most succinctly stated as this: *We have been passing through a transition, but without a Vision.* This long transition when we are without a center, without clearly marked bearings, without a Vision, is so often experienced by us individually as an existential crisis. Let us call it our fundamental *existential disorientation*.

This nearly universal agreement that our age is one in transition coincides exactly with the astrological notion that we are living in the cusp period between two World Ages: We are passing from the Piscean Age into the new Age of Aquarius.

> *But where danger is*
> *grows the saving power also*[3]

These lines from the 19th Century German poet Hölderlin are a classic statement for our day, as Heidegger clearly saw. *Where danger is.* The danger, as we see, is all around us, it permeates this time. From the perpetual threat posed by weapons of mass destruction, to unforeseeable disasters caused by climate change; from Earth's great masses living with no clear Vision of where they are going, to Technos threatening the takeover of society under a New World Order; from potential resource shortages to food shortages to ecological collapse—and today, let us never lose sight of the beginning extinction-level scenario of Fukushima—this is a time of danger, of *crisis*. But what does 'crisis' mean, in its profound sense? It means a time when the established way of life is not only unsatisfactory, but is no longer sustainable; in a fundamental sense, it has had a deep breakdown, though those living on the surface of the culture are not aware of it yet. And this breakdown and falling away of the old can be stressful, painful, fearful, for so many, once they do realize it. So many will want to hold on, and will try to hold on, to the past, to the familiar, to the way things were, even when what is so familiar and comfortable to us is slowly destroying us. (In psychology, this has come to be called "normalcy bias.") But this breakdown essentially implies that something else has also happened—simultaneously an opportunity has opened up, an opportunity for change, for moving in some new direction, for finding our bearings again from a new orientation. It is therefore a time of turning—a turning in that new direction, a direction that promises to bring new meaning into life, a new kind of fulfillment, a direction that will hopefully give us a renewed sense of existential wholeness. From a condition of disorientation, we open ourselves to a new orientation—*the saving power*.

The word 'crisis,' coming directly from the Greek, means, in fact, a time to choose, a time for that moment of decision—in crisis, we are called upon to choose a new orientation, to head in a new direction. Our crossing the threshold of a new millennium crisis, for those of us who have experienced it, is an existential opening up to something greater than us so that we can be spoken to anew, as we first make that decision to listen.

If we are in a transition, then we must be moving in some direction, however difficult it might be to see clearly where we are headed. But, then, that is the purpose of Vision, is it not—Vision is the ability to see ahead, however far that Vision enables us to see. This transition we currently live in could be long drawn out, with apparently no end in sight, as Heidegger also saw. Scholars have labelled this period of our transition Postmodernity, or simply, the Postmodern. Personally, I have never felt comfortable with the Postmodern label. More bluntly put, I have always found it somewhat distressing to witness so many of our contemporaries wallowing in the mire of Postmodern spiritual bankruptcy.

Again, "Postmodernism," "Postmodernist thought," the "Postmodern," "Postmodernity" is a complex subject that we will not pretend to thoroughly discuss here. But there are obvious, basic questions like, What, essentially, is meant by Postmodern? Who is Postmodern? When did the Postmodern period begin? Were there already Postmodern indicators back in late Modernism? The opinions about all of this are so varied that the label 'Postmodern' can tend to get quite slippery. But we are going to make an effort here to not slip around in confusion; we should come to realize that that slipping around is itself an inherent Postmodernist sensibility. To note then: we who identify with "New Age" are no longer in the Postmodern camp, even though we do live in a Postmodern context. As we proceed with our Story, we will come to see that the New Age orientation signals a rebirth of Mythos, and Mythos, as we know, always implies in some way, on some level, a story. The thing is, it is impossible to tell a story if we are always slipping around in confusion.

'Postmodern' was originally and primarily a term used in association with the arts (in particular, with architecture first). We know that the arts, from the late 19th Century on, began to go through phases—movements (known as the cutting-edge of the avant-garde)—quite rapidly, and so it happened that the first indicators of a Postmodern sensibility breaking into collective consciousness were readily to be found in the arts. Scholars naturally argue about when Modernism as a defining cultural period came to an end; generally, though, it is thought to have occurred by at least the mid-20th Century, with Postmodern themes unfolding from that point on. I would agree and would make the case that it was World War II and the sudden new reality of nuclear weapons that was the death blow to the ideals of Modernism, especially that of enlightened Progress. The Postmodern, to me, really begins with the Mushroom Cloud and all its progeny of spiritual abandonment. So I am clear then, in the Story I am telling here, our transition between Ages coincides with the Postmodern Era, implying that, as of 2020, we are approximately 70 years into it.

Postmodernism, in its cultural expression, has been lavish, however, in art movements, from abstract expressionism, pop art, op art, minimalism, to conceptual art, "happenings," installation art, body art, performance art, electronic art, to name but the more significant among them. But what has been missing among them all is Story, any Big Story. As Postmodern, art severed its symbolic connection to any "Greater Reality," to any grand narrative of the human Story (and even to Nature), and so became increasingly self-referential; that is to say, art no longer presumed to convey meanings from any Larger Reality beyond Human Reality. This is especially meant in the metaphysical, "divine" sense, implying thereby that symbolic language was dead and mythic depth but an illusion. (That a sort of abstract spirituality could still be conveyed, say, in abstract expressionism—as in Jackson Pollack's work, for example—is a valid opinion, but it does ignore the fact that a grand narrative of the human Story is still missing. The only story we do hear about (which could be said about any Postmodern artist, really) is that of Pollack's own life and genius…and that is exactly what is Postmodern here—the ego-self as the center of all things. So an equally valid opinion could say that his work was the expression of mere subjectivity—again, another way of referencing Postmodern sensibility.) Increasingly with Postmodern art, there was no longer an "inner" depth to things, so the *surface* of things came to be glorified. (Isn't that what Andy Warhol's work and sensibility epitomized? He was the surface artist par excellence. His own personality thrived on being blatantly deadpan ordinary, merely surface.) The artwork, therefore, was said to be sufficient onto itself; one experienced it for itself alone, not because it embodied any larger Story or had any greater message to convey than that immediate aesthetic experience. This conveniently placed art into the logic of a consumer commodity. It is the mere look of something, with a recognizable name attached to it, that appeals in a strictly materialistic marketplace. And whether it is paintings, novels, or even poetry, artworks were now to be "consumed" simply as part of a cultured life-style.

Postmodernism and metaphysics, including such old-fashioned metaphysical notions as Spirit and soul, are considered quite antithetical. Postmodern culture means, in fact, the utter lack of the metaphysical (nihilism); better yet, Postmodern culture doesn't know what "metaphysical" is even supposed to mean. Symbols that at one time opened us to some Greater Reality were emptied out and became linguistic shells by the earlier Modernist project of Critique, and now the shells are further ground up by Postmodern deconstructive philosophy. The continuing outcome of this is that all fads, trends, styles, movements, experimentation, icons, become passé, because there are no genuine symbols in them to ground us existentially in the long term. It is the jaded, world-weary, We've-seen-it-all-before syndrome. The ultimate emptiness takes place when Language itself is essentially reduced to simply mouthing blah-blah-blah.

Over time, the Postmodern label was then applied by scholars to Western culture as a whole: its mass media, entertainment and pop culture, the rage of deconstruction in philosophy, the life-style of suburbanites, the culture of narcissism, divorce, breakdown of the family, gender bending, social fragmentation, cultural pluralism. Postmodernism, not only as an academic study of culture and society, but as an academic style of thought itself, fully emerged by the mid-1980s. There was scarcely an academic discipline that had not been deeply influenced by Postmodernist theory. Academics at all our universities have certainly heard the siren song of the Postmodernist thinkers.

Modernism—both in the sense of modern living improved by science and technology *and* infused by modern art—had rejected the traditional past in the name of Progress or the New (as in the arts). Modernism, as a trend of intellectual thought with beginnings in the 17th Century, set out to eventually undermine all the "superstitious nonsense" of previous Tradition (which is exactly the story of modern science). But it was especially in the arts, though, that Modernism would go even further: It continuously undermined even its own efforts (which is not to say that brilliant work was not done). It was in the arts, in particular, that a new kind of tradition had set itself against itself, as Octavio Paz[4] described it. Modernism, in other words, was a self-undermining contradiction, when it came to the arts, meaning this: it could build no foundation, lay no bricks, for a new Spirit-inspired home for our dwelling on Earth—after dispensing with Tradition—, but was set on leveling and scrapping every attempt made in its constant obsession with novelty, originality, the new new new, with the focus, the spotlight, always drawn to the genius-ego of the individual artist. If the artistic work, whatever its brilliance and originality, cannot be experienced in a spiritual way that brings soul to feel at home in its world, then its dazzling performance is but another isolated feature of a fragmented cultural landscape. (Consider the title alone of T.S. Eliot's classic modernist poem *The Waste Land* or James Joyce's literary monument *Finnegan's Wake*, written out of the cultural ruins of Tradition.) It was no surprise that Late Modernism imploded and left in its wake a spiritual emptiness. Modern life itself was characterized by a growing existential disorientation. Following upon the demise of Modernism then, Postmodernism no longer had any past to reject but became instead a decadent pirating of the ruins of the past in which all previous artistic forms, styles, movements, icons, are simply exploited for their surface value. Everything can be shuffled around and juxtaposed in a revelry of incoherence. And to this day artists have worked under strong peer pressure to deny in themselves the possibility of true Vision, that is, the possibility of any new, redeeming, spiritual orientation.

That this surface-oriented art can be visually exciting, aesthetically satisfying, is not to be denied, but, in its Postmodern context, it still leaves us spiritually hungry. Now to insist that art has nothing to do with spirituality, that it is simply the subjective expression of the creative individual, is but a reaffirmation of the conditioning brought about by our Postmodern fragmentation and disconnectedness from any Greater Reality. This view, that art is something separate from spirituality, we realize we do not philosophically have to accept. Even Modernists who broke with Tradition did not go this far, but could still have a strong spiritual orientation, as in the work of poet Rainer Maria Rilke, or the painter Wassily Kandinsky. Secular humanism is often another name given to this view that we can dispense with anything smacking of the spiritual, let alone, religion. (This is not to confuse secular humanism per se with postmodernist style and thought, though both do have in common an atheistic orientation. Secular humanism, after all, still attempts to uphold the 18th Century Enlightenment promise of Reason, objectivity, and social order, and a belief in the responsible, integrated, moral person, involving the grand narrative of Progress in which rationally enlightened individuals will eventually create a better world for all. Postmodernist theory, in contrast, has come to reject all this.) The promise of the New Age Vision is that it will someday unfold a many-branching Mythos that will allow our life to be an integrated whole again, *spiritually* whole.

So, whereas the Modern period held before it a scientifically-inspired beacon called human Progress and assumed that the wrongs of the world can be righted through enlightened practice, Postmodernist theory is a critique of any notion of Progress or rational, enlightened thought as a self-serving cultural construct of a dominating Western worldview. Yet, I would argue that the psychological undercurrent behind the real abandonment by Postmodernist thinkers of the notion that humanity was still on the road of Progress began as a result of the development of nuclear weapons and their pivotal role in the Cold War. Note that this whole Nuclear Age development was occurring by the mid-20th Century, at the same time that Postmodernist cultural trends began to emerge. That humanity had reached a point where it could annihilate itself overnight through weapons of mass destruction did not look anything like Progress whatsoever. The Modernist ideal of Progress was obliterated by the Bomb. The fate of Civilization was now set to the last minutes of a Doomsday Clock. The madness of nuclear weapons even translated into the international policy of mutual assured destruction: MAD. The fate of Civilization had become a dystopian, nihilistic nightmare. Amidst all its abundance and surface glitter, this was the unconscious face of the Postmodern world. And how many sci fi movies drudged up this dark face just beneath the surface of our daily life?

The Postmodern, become now a term defining our whole contemporary period, most notably in the West, is the epitome of nihilism: Its theoretical position takes as gospel (beginning with epistemological reasons concerning the limitations of what we can know, which started with the philosophy of Kant) that such notions as Spirit, or the spiritual realm, or call it the supernatural, transcendent, or "higher" divine realm, no longer make sense, because it is not possible to speak as Logos about them, except as subjective entertainment (again, because we cannot "know" them, in the sense of the old traditional ideal of Logos); and, yes, God is dead, therefore there are no "higher" values, including the old bogeyman "Truth"; therefore, there is nothing beyond the decadence of a totally human ego-centered, ego-obsessed, ego-incestuous, world; therefore, any attempt to tell a Big Story of who we are, like in the old days of Tradition, is futile. According to Derrida, however, it is more than merely futile; any Big Story from the past has been used to oppress and dominate and marginalize those left out of the hierarchies of power. Foucault's work also extensively explored all this. Reason itself—the traditional Logos—was an oppressor, legitimizing the agendas of the elite. (Modernism, after all, still told, and was inspired by, the Big Story of continuing human Progress. But Progress for whom, and at whose expense? The Postmodernists therefore became antagonistic to any Big Story.) This, in fact, results in what decadence means today: the human world is now carrying on a completely incestuous relationship with itself, devoid of any relationship to an *Other*. Traditionally, that was what religions fostered, a relationship to an Other, an Other in the context of some Larger Reality, i.e. a Big Story. In the Postmodern world, there is no Other that speaks to us; it had become apparent for some time that "God" had fallen silent. Postmodernism is fundamentally the position of atheism, but with intellectual implications that most atheists do not fully carry out, or even understand. Your everyday atheist simply does not believe in a God, and leaves it at that. That the New Age Vision can accommodate the everyday atheist may come as a surprise. But we will see that in our discussion of the Higher Self (chapter 5) the old, traditional notion of "God" has been transformed.

Today's mass media, as an example here, is a perfect expression of our Postmodern world. It is a world utterly and absolutely ego-intoxicated—narcissistic—, having no connection to any Larger Reality beyond the human, not even Nature. An immediate dose of our Postmodern world is available in nearly every living room—just turn on the TV and surf some 200 channels by remote control. (Again, to say that mass media has nothing, and should have nothing, to do with spirituality is but to make our point, and to reiterate our contemporary condition of cultural fragmentation.) In this context, it is the ego-self personality—thoroughly conditioned by corporate, mass consumer culture, let us add—that becomes the ultimate arbiter, the measure, of all things. That is to say, whatever is presented to the contemporary ego-self—*Here, turn the channel—try on this religion, conspiracy theory, therapy, diet, or movie—*, the ego-self is now in the almighty position of accepting or rejecting it on an almost whimsical, what next, short-term memory basis. Facebook is also a perfect example of this surface play fragmentation: anything and everything can be posted on the news feed; one can scroll and scan a grab bag of the most disjointed of juxtaposed items on a second by second basis. We see that everything is susceptible to becoming ever shifting, consumer-driven entertainments for the ego. The metaphysical, the spiritual—instead of, as formerly, confronting the ego with something larger than itself and thereby challenging it—are now considered just a more refined, though still delusional, kind of entertainment for the ego. Mass media itself is a continuous feeding frenzy of sound bites and bright, popping imagery, as everything becomes mere surface.

We often find poets in this Postmodern era given to wallowing in a sort of collective self-pity, while apathy becomes the accepted social dis-ease; and seemingly the best that could be done by the young to express any real passion was the punk rage of already some decades ago. It was the punk rock theme of the later 1970s to scream of the decline of Western Civilization. And in the 1980s the fear was that the Bomb was going to annihilate us all in a global nuclear Armageddon anyway.

Artists had increasingly gone to desperate lengths to be original in the continuing mania started by Modernism for the New. For some time now there has circulated the assumption that all styles and all possibilities for art have been exhausted, and that the artist is but left with rehashing the art movements of the past. Art itself has been critiqued and questioned in the very process of the artwork itself, which has been the main thrust behind conceptual art. It is apparent that Postmodern artists have been going round and round in the revolving door of a self-conscious nihilism. Our Western Postmodern world with its notoriously shallow pop culture continues its hysteria of narcissism in high gear without any Vision, without any hope of redemption from its ego-intoxicated mania, driven on by capitalist consumerism. To be clear and to be fair, it is not as if we can point the finger solely at artists and intellectuals for our Postmodern malaise—we certainly cannot ignore the whole military-industrial-corporate complex, aka Late Capitalism, that dominates our Postmodern way of life either. That itself is a whole focus of intellectual critique.

One discouraging, frustrating, even depressing, characteristic of our Postmodern way of life had become quite apparent in the last few decades. This applies especially to those who would be visionaries, radicals, or revolutionaries, in whatever sense. The Postmodern pluralistic arena is such that it can appropriate and accommodate just about anything. Any new idea, new Vision, new movement, or form of activism (e.g. the Occupy movement), can be absorbed, compromised, undermined, and disempowered; and the Status Quo goes on. New voices, after their 15 minutes of viral fame, simply get lost in the shuffle of the cultural supermarket. Take books—anymore, no matter how important, how revolutionary, a book's message might be, it no longer makes any real impact in the general culture, not like books had back in the 1950s and 60s. For one thing, the young are no longer seriously influenced by books. We've all sensed how authors who believe they've written the book that the culture has been waiting for, a book that lays out a proscription for real social change, wind up disappointed that it's had no noticeable traction. The book finds its place as just one more book in a marketplace of books. The same can be said for film documentary exposés; no matter how much fanfare a film may get, no matter how many film festival awards it may receive, its impact causes few ripples in the Establishment mainstream. Postmodern culture accommodates anything and everything, so one might as well be haranguing on the proverbial soapbox on a street corner.

Your hardcore, Postmodern, secular individual recognizes no consciousness, no intelligence, no voice, beyond the human ego. Literally nothing outside the human can speak to such an individual. And we all know such individuals. To them, the human ego is the only player there is, and they will even seem to insist on wanting it that way, exalting as they do in the narcissistic ego's will to power. There is a dubious sense of unfettered freedom and unlimited power when the human ego recognizes no greater or larger Intelligence than itself. Let us be honest about it: a strictly human-centered world is an insatiably ego-intoxicated, narcissistic world.

We might ask, though, a tough, philosophical question, Is humanity itself to blame for nihilism? Was it somehow our decision to turn from Spirit? Rather, what we are going through is of the very nature of living in a transition period, the cusp between Ages. The original inspiration of the waning Age has long withdrawn from consciousness, which is not to imply, however, that its collective lesson is no longer valid. The Piscean teachings of Jesus, for example, are obviously as important now as ever. But Spirit, because of its timetable with humanity, works through cycles of inspiration, coming in the highest form as Revelation, involving an active phase of "downloading" a new dispensation into the collective consciousness of humanity. On the microcosmic, individual, scale this is something quite well known: any artist knows of cycles of inspiration and waiting for inspiration (to the point of depression). The macrocosmic, collective, scale is no different: Spirit is a coming-to-us or a withdrawing-from-us on a periodic basis. We have fatefully been living in a sort of cuspal limbo, caught as we are between the passing Piscean Age and the emerging, new Aquarian Age. Nihilism itself could be considered a form of collective spiritual depression.

But we are not altogether passive either. Not only are we called to actively engage inspiration when it does come through, but we can always be preparing ourselves for it. We can actively be opening and attuning ourselves to Spirit, by inviting Spirit to speak. This is not a passive waiting around for something to happen, but is an ongoing preparation of soul. It has been said that we had witnessed a collective failure of nerve to act courageously in the 20th Century, that what we saw too often was a pathetic wallowing in an ego-self decadence.

Existentialism was the major philosophical response to spiritual abandonment in the wake of Modernism. When the metaphysical "pretensions" of the past were brought down, as it were, the existential thinkers made the call for us to find a new foundation in ourselves. If Tradition could no longer provide us a pre-established definition of who we were—what our essence is—then it was left up to us in our own individual existence to somehow take it upon ourselves to newly define ourselves, to lift ourselves up by our own bootstraps, as it were. But existentialism, for all the insights it did offer into fundamental structures of Human Reality[5], resulted, out on the street, in an anything goes, debilitating relativism where the ego got to level everything down to its own size. Fortunately, existentialism was not the final word on Human Reality; it was an understandable outcome of the Second World War shocked 20th Century. It revealed quite clearly our existential disorientation in that century, but Spirit coming-to-us anew signals that we are coming to a new understanding, a new orientation, regarding who we are.

The collective human response to the Piscean dispensation of 2,000 years ago established itself not only in the obvious institution of the Church, but, primarily since the Renaissance, installed itself in science and technology, and in the 18th Century European Enlightenment period that was pivotal in the development of critical and analytical thought. (Consider that at the peak of this period, Immanuel Kant (who we've already mentioned a couple of times) published his *Critique of Pure Reason*.) This human response to the original Piscean dispensation has had the character of astrological Virgo (which we will explore why in the next chapter). Virgo can be characterized as practical intelligence working on the material plane (science becoming, then, the handmaiden of technology). Virgo, an Earth sign emphasizing the practical and the developing of all skills and techniques, and being of service, is a definite clue then to our contemporary, collective, technological materialism and pragmatism. Yet, Virgo has a self-conscious, critical/analytical focus too; it most fully symbolizes the self—the collective self of our civilization in this case—in crisis. Which indeed brings us to where we are now. Why it had this Virgo character will become apparent soon.

Those who can plumb the collective psyche on a deep level will undoubtedly come to realize that society is destined to become weary of Postmodernism itself. (That is, short of the complete dominance of society by new technologies that threaten to turn persons into functional zombies, as we will see.) The incestuous, self-indulgent ego of contemporary culture can only go round and round its cage so many times before it exhausts itself, to the point of even becoming sick of itself, and yearns for something more, something *other*. This will be the great opportunity that the New Age dispensation will be waiting for. Of course, Traditionalists of the world's various religions will see it as *their* opportunity to draw others back into the arms of Tradition. But it would be a mistake to think that we can return to the past. There is no going back to the past and the Traditions of the past.

Let us ask this question, Where does Postmodernism, if left to its own emptiness, lead us? First, I am well aware that many Postmodernist thinkers took themselves to be liberators: As they deconstructed, dismantled, all the thought constructs of the past, all the prisons of language and systems of power, all the codifications of repression, the total social construct of subjectivity, they claimed that they were freeing us.[6] Yes, we do have to admit, to a certain extent, that is true, that is definitely true (for those capable of really understanding Postmodern thought), but, then, we can only follow them out into the wasteland of deconstruction so far. Postmodernist thought is a powerful tool against oppression and repression, and clearly reveals how we have been thoroughly conditioned from birth by the System, but as it turns out, the Postmodernist stance cannot be an end in itself. The question again is, The Postmodernist thinkers are freeing us for what? or toward what? I do not find any of them offering us a Vision of where a totally human-solipsistic world is taking us. Or, better yet, a Vision that would take us *beyond* a human-solipsistic world. (Of course, a hardcore Postmodernist might ask, *Why would you want to do that?*) Postmodernists, with their sole emphasis on critique and their inability to consider any Intelligence outside the human, had painted themselves into a corner. We saw them expending tremendous intellectual effort on textual trivialities while Rome was burning. They have effectively made themselves impotent to initiate meaningful change in response to our crisis. The more honest among them did admit this. Let *us* not be shortsighted then: We must come to see that Postmodernism itself, because its practitioners can offer no alternative but critique, which is harmlessly absorbed into our Postmodern corporate controlled context, ironically only takes us down the path towards an increasing techno-materialism that threatens to dominate all life. Corporate culture is ipso facto materialistic culture. I call this techno-materialism the new Superpower in the world today—*Technos*. The fledgling New Age that offers a Vision of an alternate future is therefore destined to have a profound confrontation with Postmodernist thought.

It is interesting to note that despite all the onslaught of Postmodernist critique, we find multitudes of individuals still practicing in the symbolic systems of the occult arts, still pursuing their spiritual Paths, still doing their etheric energy work, and still claiming contact with Visitors from elsewhere. Apparently the windows that open us to the invisible worlds have not all been darkened. Postmodern theorists, however, would probably dismiss all of this as nothing more than culturally codified delusion, mere myth forms of subjectivism. Needless to say, they never seriously look into these subjects firsthand so that they might see for themselves that something significant, a Greater Reality, beyond the utterly self-revolving culture of human ego, is still "out there." The New Age grand narrative to come—the New Story—would engage this Greater Reality, though here, too, Postmodernists find any suggestion of a grand narrative suspect. In the meantime, the spiritual smorgasbord such as we find today is undeniably still able to feed and nourish, to some degree or another, all who are spiritually hungry.

On a final note, the word 'Postmodern' itself is not exactly inspiring; we are left with the sense that we live in a time that is merely a postscript to a supposedly more determining period—the feverish high of Modernism. One way that I have personally, in a sense, tolerated living in a Postmodern world is to see it as essentially a transition period in the cycle of spiritual inspiration. Even if in our youth some of us admitted to a spiritual poverty—which was an expression of our intellectual honesty living in this Postmodern world—, we still heard the Call of something far off—the distant Call of Spirit out of the decadence of the times. It is apparent that the great majority of our artists and poets, however, have not yet realized that the new, Renaissance-level inspiration source for art that brings significant meaning back into life will be the Aquarian New Age dispensation.

One more final note: I could simply define the Postmodern as the inability to tell a Story...a Big Story.

\*

Perhaps we should make a few comments here about the 1960s. The Sixties was a most remarkable, high-level, collectively creative decade. And we have all heard the questions, Wasn't the Aquarian New Age first a Sixties phenomenon? But why did the countercultural movement of the Sixties fail to make greater impact in mainstream culture? And then, what brought it to an end? How could it have largely degenerated into a drug culture of Postmodern decadence? Why was a cultural disorientation the outcome? The Seventies following was the decade of noticeable cultural disorientation. Everyone has opinions about this, of course, including those who will swiftly and angrily protest that the Sixties counterculture never failed at all, but was put down and prevented from having any greater influence by the Establishment, which I do agree did happen. My summary view on all this is the following:

The idealistic intentions of the Sixties failed because it had no substantial spiritual foundation of its own, let alone an articulated Mythos. That the Sixties has had lasting cultural impact is without question; that important social changes, such as civil rights, resulted from those years is without question; but the revolutionary spirit it attempted to manifest *throughout* society failed miserably. That spirit couldn't have survived because there was no spiritual gyroscope to guide it, no clearly definitive spiritual inspiration to feed the new, alternative culture. Certainly there were multitudes of sincere hippies/flower children/psychedelic youth who were "into" spirituality, exploring other Traditions, and experimenting with alternative life-styles. There were plenty of youth expanding their minds with psychedelics, music, and alternative—usually Eastern—religion. There were psychedelic gurus like Timothy Leary, popular interpreters of Eastern religion like Alan Watts, Beat spokespersons like Allen Ginsberg, and of course all the music idols and political activists. There was no lack of highly intelligent and creative cultural leaders, but a new, definitive, spiritual foundation was not there. (Some thought they had found it in Buddhism.)

The 1960s were still premature for the Aquarian dispensation, despite all the popular talk about the Sixties representing the "Age of Aquarius." The spiritual foundation I speak of would have had to have been the New Age Vision. That is to say, it would have to have been a significant, globally transformative Revelation or Vision that was grounded, announcing a new World Age. The Sixties saw a few first glimmers of how the New Age might inspire a generation, but the Aquarian dispensation had not yet occurred collectively. In my earlier years, I often found fault with the Sixties leaders, complaining how they had failed us. True, many of the rock stars of the music world appeared to have sold out to the glamour of stardom—or simply couldn't help but do so by the very nature of their enormous success. The important point is, though, by and large, they fell far short in providing any spiritual leadership. The Beatles, as perhaps the best example here of a music group, during a brief window opening of opportunity, appeared to have the potential for some sort of leadership in the palm of their hand, but they obviously couldn't follow through. Admittedly, in hindsight, it was simply far too much to expect of them, or of anyone in the music world limelight. Seriously, what were we thinking—after all, The Beatles were only in their 20s, and they were only musicians, however extraordinary at that. Hardly had any of us at that time had a track record of following a spiritual Path, but for the instant mind-opener of psychedelics. What were we thinking, how naïve we all were—it was far too much to expect of any popular culture figures of that time to have grounded a spiritual Mythos for us, given the complete context of a thoroughly Postmodern, materialistically-driven society with a fiercely entrenched corporate-military-industrial complex. (None of this is meant as a criticism of the music of the Sixties, however, which, to this day, is classic and still utterly amazing.) With time, I saw that the Sixties cultural leaders could really not have done much in profoundly changing an already preset Postmodern world anyway. The truth was, so often they were reveling and enjoying themselves as the "beautiful people" in the hedonistic culture of Postmodernism, to begin with. Most of the New Age themes we will be exploring hadn't fully been on the beautiful peoples' radar yet. At the time, for example, AI was only science fiction, the Internet unheard-of; the possibility of biosphere collapse was still far off in the future; UFOs were just a cool thing to talk about. The most profound of spiritual inspiration, which is a new dispensation, a new Revelation, a new Vision, as we have suggested, has its own astrological timetable. It is either coming through or it isn't, and there is nothing much we can do to force it, to make it happen, before its time. Anyone who has experience with inspiration, whether spiritual or artistic, or of whatever kind, understands this. Always, the best we can do is to know where we stand in the moment, and to passionately work with *that*—to live in the Now of *that*.

Other reasons we might mention that influenced the demise of the Sixties' spirit probably were: One, that it was too tied in to the Vietnam War, often making it a reaction to a negativity (war). We cannot base a true cultural renaissance solely on resistance to negativity; it requires in addition a more powerful positivity (spiritual inspiration) coming through. Another reason was undoubtedly the government's, the Establishment's, own involvement in bringing the youthful countercultural movement down. Government-backed provocateurs undoubtedly infiltrated the movement, creating discord, and, as witnesses who remember will claim, brought in hard drugs, dissipating the psychedelic and natural high momentum. Most importantly, though, the pressures of living in an already firmly-established, money-obsessed, materialistic society made it impossible to uphold the free-living, countercultural life-style: It literally degenerated and was largely absorbed back into the Establishment. Which is to say, the counterculture was all along but a subculture in the enormously larger, dominant, aggressive, mainstream, military-industrial complex Establishment. So we found that the money-and-success-driven, competitive Yuppies of the Eighties were so often yesterday's love everyone flower children. But then, not all. Here and there, little pockets of hippiedom did manage to survive, and we do find to this day holdouts of Sixties individuals who have managed to keep, despite so many pressures, the flame of the old idealism still burning. I, myself, despite my criticisms, still cherish the Sixties spirit I came of age in.

\*

The previous discussion should make it clear that today's world is still far from being characterized as New Age. As of yet, the New Age movement has not managed to gain much credible recognition. Our universities are filled with Postmodern scholars who teach courses on our Postmodern world—Postmodern art, culture, life-style, sex and gender, our pluralistic society, politics, etc.; they are not offering classes on any New Age world. What we have seen thus far of genuine New Age spirituality has barely even registered in mainstream society. Whether we like it or not, we all still live in a Postmodern world.

Yet, the outer infrastructure of the New Age is being built at a furious pace. And that is the cyberworld, especially represented by the global network called the Internet, in its early days the World Wide Web; it is the virtual new worlds of cyberspace. What is yet lacking to genuinely transform it into an Aquarian New Age infrastructure is Spirit.[7]

In terms of spiritual loyalties today, I see three main camps that define nearly everyone, with a sort of fourth camp that is ambiguous where exactly its loyalties lie. The camps are: the Traditionalists, the Postmodernist, and New Age. They are by no means exclusive; most people have a foot in one of these camps, with the other foot in another. By "Traditionalists," I refer primarily to those who remain identified with one of the world's major religions—the Traditions, whether Hinduism, Buddhism, Judaism, Christianity, Islam, even Taoism; and then, there are any number of traditional "native" religions worldwide too. Altogether, the Traditions still claim the loyalties of billions. The "Postmodernist" camp largely defines the West (with a country like Japan clearly joining in), despite everywhere the continued schizoid presence of Tradition, at least on the surface. Postmodern culture, in contrast to Traditionalism, is nonreligious, nonspiritual, nihilistic, intellect-and-sensation-oriented, materialistic; it is clearly not loyal to any of the Traditions. It is, above all, the world of mainstream mass media, popular culture, television and movies—all forms of entertainment—, commerce and banking and the corporate-military-industrial complex, the educational system, the sports world, the Internet, and of course, as we saw, starting with Postmodern art, the art world. But here is my point: Even those who practice their traditional faith will almost without exception have one foot in Postmodern culture; here, in America, in the Western world in general, it is a given. You can't escape it; you simply turn on the TV or radio, buy a magazine, go to a shopping mall or movie, or get on the Internet. In our country, perhaps the Amish or certain remote Native American tribes are the only nearly pure Traditionalists left. We can readily see the reason why the highly Traditionalist Middle East countries of Islam steadfastly resist Western influence (read Americanization), and that is because of the implication it carries of Postmodern culture.

Before finishing with the New Age camp, we should mention another, fourth camp I have come to call the Eclectics. At first glance, they would appear to be in the New Age camp—and probably are—but usually they refuse to be identified with it. What they prefer is the eclectic taste, that is, periodically trying this or that spiritual practice or religious service, working with occultism as a cool thing to get into, or taking up any one of your various therapeutic techniques. They can move restlessly from one guru, one teacher, to another. They enjoy the freedom of tasting all the morsels from the consciousness smorgasbord without committing themselves to any "movement," which is as much a Postmodern life-style as it might appear to be New Age. Being eclectic, not necessarily loyal to any Tradition or movement, they often tend to flow with whatever is currently in vogue.

But, then, one might ask, What about those who identity with esotericism? occultism? the Perennial Philosophy? Where are they in this scheme? I look at it this way: If they rely solely on past teachings, whether ancient esoteric-mystery school of some kind, Hermetic, Gnostic, Neoplatonic, or even more recent Theosophical teachings, are they not still Traditionalists? But if they are pursuing their esoteric Path in the light of new Vision, a new gnosis…if they stand at The Edge of a new encounter with Being, they, to me, are clearly New Age, whether they like that label or not.

In comparison to the Traditionalists and Postmodernist camps, the New Age camp hardly registers yet on the global scene. There are tiny pockets of New Agers and New Age communities scattered here and there, but they surely represent far less than a fraction of a percent of the world's population. For now, this Postmodern transition period that we live in, which is still going strong some years now into the 21st Century, appears to have no end in sight.

I have often heard the question come up: And where are the young people in the New Age movement? Why do we find so very few? Again, though the New Age movement emerged out of the Sixties, the Sixties counterculture largely degenerated into the sex, drugs, and rock-n-roll scene of the Seventies; and then, so many who managed to survive that as New Agers rediscovered our capitalist system and found that they could promote New Age as a new marketing label for all kinds of fringe spiritual and therapeutic practices and woo-woo, resulting in the New Age movement acquiring its poor reputation for all the reasons we explored earlier. The young, as we know, are so conditioned by mainstream, pop culture that anything fringe is hardly on their radar, to begin with. Brought up on ubiquitous television, movies, big music concerts, music videos, video games, now smart phones, the Internet, and social media, besides having to deal with the real-world pressure of launching a career, why would the young even be interested in fringe woo-woo stuff anyway? As it is well known that spiritual matters usually do not become of interest until later in life, a cultural bridge representing the New Age that could span generations has scarcely been built. Even to suggest that the Internet is actually an Aquarian New Age development simply goes over their heads.

The New Age camp does have its own relation to both the Traditionalist and Postmodernist camps. It certainly has roots in all the Traditions, not only in the teachings of the Traditions, which it will eventually come to transform, but most importantly in that it recognizes as do all the Traditions that there is a Greater Reality beyond our human bubble that does have meaning for us, tremendous meaning, once we experience it and engage it. The New Age camp recognizes that fringe boundary of the paranormal where Spirit announces itself, where that Greater Reality presents itself. But the New Age camp is in another sense closer to the Postmodernist in that it accepts the evolutionary need to critique all Traditions, to deconstruct their mind prisons of outmoded myth and doctrines, so that a liberating, new, co-creative encounter with Spirit can happen. The New Age Vision accepts Postmodern pluralism as a liberation from Traditional "religionism" (in which one religion claims exclusively to possess the Truth), and from all inherited sexism, racism, and insular ethnic tribalism.

The question is, Can we as a civilization continue down the road we are going? With population growth outpacing what Earth can provide, while Earth's ecosystems are continuously dumped on with pollution and radiation; with global warming and climate patterns changing with already foreseeable devastating outcomes; with technology outstripping an appropriate spiritual response; with cities of multi-millions like human jungles, apathy a social sickness, we wonder how long this can go on without that moment of decision for changing course. The mainstream status quo gives all the appearance of being utterly oblivious to the full extent of the crisis; despite all the lip service we hear, we rarely see any desire for change in the corridors of power. (Again, we must constantly overcome our naiveté about this—the power elite have their own agenda, beginning with, staying in power.) There are those who now believe it is too late to reverse the downward spiral of civilization's collapse. It is apparent that something has got to give.

So we hear about different scenarios of what is coming: Some major Earth change or solar flare disaster that brings down the System, global pandemics or the speeding up of the climate change undermining of civilization, or Fukushima's radiation continuously spreading out to slowly kill off the greater proportion of life, or the nuclear winter of a nuclear war, or then, there is worldwide ET contact that promises to burst our human-centered bubble. Small scale disasters or conventional wars won't do to change the status quo. In fact, wars only ingrain the status quo more. *Wars are status quo.* What might change the direction in which our civilization is going, a direction, as we have seen, that is headed toward some disaster or another, and/or a Big Brother New World Order? There are those of us who say *The New Age Vision has arrived.* This is the time of its *Advent.*

## Comparing Modernism/Postmodernism and the New Age

| Modernism/Postmodernism | New Age |
| --- | --- |
| Breakdown of monocentric systems | Breakdown as transition into polycentric modes of being |
| An "Age of Chaos"—existential disorientation | A new Higher Self existential orientation |
| The drive to fragmentation, disintegration | A pluralistic world determined by Spirit |
| Schizoid / Schizophrenic | Polyphrenic |
| Emphasis on revolt, against the past, a pirating of the ruins of the past | Bankruptcy of mere revolt, rediscovery of the past, the transformation of Tradition |
| Permanent revolution—a tradition set against itself, constantly undermining itself, providing no foundation | Co-creative with Spirit building upon itself, in process |
| Progress the ideal for Modernism, but comes to be strictly scientific/technological<br>Postmodernism then abandons the notion of "Progress" | Shift in consciousness, integrating Technos (technology) and Psyche (spirituality) |
| The ascendancy of materialism | Materialism opening out into the Invisible |
| Emphasis on linear time—historicism | A recognition of multidimensional timelines—the cycles & multidimensions of Being |
| Secular humanism | A return to Spirit, a Higher Self humanism |

| | |
|---|---|
| Soul breaking through in pathological ways as the "return of the repressed" | Soul is openly accepted and liberated<br>A return to all that is Other, beyond the ego |
| Preoccupation with the ego-self in crisis, extreme subjectivity | A new collective "subjectivity"—the Higher Self |
| Nihilism, cynicism, anxiety, despair, defeat, disillusionment, the Void—tragic humanism | Existence no longer anthropocentric, but a recognition of the Other & a multiplicity of reality interpretations—all modes of Being accepted<br>A radical relativism that is yet spiritual<br>No longer despair before the Void but participation in the multiple modes of Being |
| Under the shadow of critical reason—Critique—the "schools of suspicion" (Paul Ricoeur) | Cultivation of a post-critical "second naivete" (Ricoeur)<br>Critical reaon as one mode among others |
| Self-sufficiency of the art work—analytical, language centered, the isolated image, non-referential, alienated from Nature, emphasis on technique, style, experimentation | Reconnecting to the world and Nature |
| Will to irony, obscurity, indirectness | Emphasis on spiritual attunement<br>Return to passion, Vision, full-bodied speech, narrative, ritual, symbol |
| Against rhetoric, narrative, ritual, symbol, myth | Centrality of living myth—a return to mythos-making and the vital coherency of an interconnecting Mythos—*The MYTHOS* |

# ( 3 )

## WORLD AGES:

## THE ASTRONOMICAL/ASTROLOGICAL BACKGROUND

I began writing this book in the first year of the new 21st Century. But the year 2000 was also the beginning of the much-celebrated New Millennium. But, then, even more than that, on a scale that can encompass the coming and going of whole civilizations, we were entering the time of a *New Age*. What we need to do first is to gain some understanding of what is meant, then, by "World Ages," and thereby clear up a possible confusion (which we've already touched upon) regarding the New Age. There is the New Age as a new cultural *movement*, but also, more importantly, the New Age refers to the next World Age (an older term is Aeon, the Greek Aion[1]) we are entering called *Aquarius*. Obviously, they are connected by an interpretation of history and civilization that we can now broadly characterize as New Age thinking. Thinking, then, from a new World Age perspective will go on to explain why there is a New Age movement.

*So the New Age is based on astrology. And why is that?*

The metaphysical basis of the New Age begins with astrology. In fact, astrologers should have the firmest grasp of anyone as to what the New Age means. As I am an astrologer myself, it is appropriate then that I begin here. That the New Age is thereby said to be merely a claim made by astrologers I will address shortly.

By World Ages astrologers refer to approximately 2,160-year periods (which we will often round off for convenience sake to 2,000 years). There are twelve of them, corresponding to the twelve signs of the zodiac, so that there is a complete cycle of World Ages called the Great Year, or Platonic Year, as in older texts. That is roughly a grand cycle of close to 26,000 years. In chronological time, the Ages march backwards through what astrologers know as the normal, "forward" zodiacal round (which goes from Aries to Taurus to Gemini, etc.); we are coming out of the roughly 2,000-year Age of Pisces, the two Western Christian (and Islamic) millennia; prior to that (chronologically looking backwards now) were the Ages of Aries, Taurus, Gemini, etc. When we refer to the New Age as that of the Age of Aquarius, we are talking then about these next roughly 2,000 years, however presumptuous that may sound. When this New Age begins as an even approximate date on the calendar is still a point of controversy among astrologers themselves. (A question is, Can the beginning of an Age even be pinpointed to a specific date?) Some have claimed it has already begun—perhaps years ago—, and others that we might still be 50–100 years from definitively saying we are squarely within Aquarius. A case has been made that we had actually entered it in the year 2000,[2] but then others will say more insistently that it was 2012. Personally, I am not interested in getting caught up in the arcane details of the controversy. Suffice to say, we are definitely in the transition period between the waning Piscean Age and the dawning Aquarian Age. The Ages as distinctly characterized dispensations of Spirit do not just abruptly end and begin overnight, to start with, but over time transition into one another. The transition period itself may be rather lengthy, as we have suggested in our discussion about Postmodernity.

An appropriate question is why the notion of World Ages is based on astrology. The most straightforward answer is that it is precisely astrology, which studies cosmic cycles from the perspective of Earth, that posits the notion of World Ages—World Ages *are* astrological. To ask then what astrology bases this notion on, on what particular cycle, we must briefly discuss then the astronomical phenomenon of *the precession of the equinoxes*, hopefully without getting too involved in technicalities. For the following to make sense, keep in mind that astrologers consider there to be two zodiacs: the zodiac of signs (a band of symbolic signs, so not actual stars, that encircles the

Earth) that most Western astrologers use for interpretation (called "tropical astrology"), and the zodiac of "fixed" stars, or, better yet, the zodiac of constellations (actual star patterns in the heavens) that Eastern astrology (called "sidereal astrology") is based on. These two zodiacs did at one time coincide, but have shifted in relation to each other since the ancient world, which is exactly the phenomenon of the precession of the equinoxes to be explained below. (It is probably best that a model or visual diagram be used, as the following verbal description is undoubtedly difficult to follow, if one is hearing it for the first time.)

Critics of astrology are quick to point out this discrepancy, that the zodiac that most astrologers in the West use no longer even corresponds to the actual stars in the sky because of this phenomenon of precession; they conclude, therefore, that today's astrology is invalid (if astrology, to them, ever was valid), and consider astrologers to be dunces, or shysters. What these critics don't seem to realize is that any professional astrologer knows about precession and is conscious of using the zodiac of signs—tropical astrology—if that indeed is his or her preferred system, for it has its own symbolic rationale and has proven itself over time.

Let us consider the relationship between Earth, Sun, and the "fixed" stars. Imagine that two great planes intersect through the Earth's center, one being the plane of the equator extended into space (the Celestial Equator), the other, the plane of the ecliptic, representing the apparent yearly path of the Sun (which determines the band around Earth of both zodiacs). The ecliptic is tilted from, forms an acute angle to, the equatorial plane because we know that Earth is tilted on its axis in relation to the Sun, at 23.5°. We know that the Sun does not simply revolve around the equator (from Earth perspective), otherwise these two planes would be one and the same, and the Northern and Southern Hemispheres would undoubtedly have a consistently homogeneous climate; in other words, there would be no seasons, at least not as we know them. These two great circles, which do not therefore coincide, are posited to intersect at opposite points on the globe in the zodiac of signs: at 0° Aries (always the Spring Equinox) and at 0° Libra (always the Fall Equinox). When the Sun in its annual movement reaches 0° Aries—usually March 21—, it is the first day of spring in the Northern Hemisphere, and the first day of autumn in the Southern Hemisphere. At this moment, day and night are of equal duration, which is the origin of the word 'equinox'.

Earth, as science tells us, has a slight wobble to it as it spins on its axis, no different than what we find with a spinning gyroscope. The wobble goes backwards to the spinning. This is called *precession*. This causes the Earth's polar axis (the imaginary line drawn through both poles out into space) to trace out a great circle in the sky taking approximately 26,000 years. Since this motion is slowly shifting the equatorial and ecliptical planes in relation to each other, that imaginary point of their intersection happens to be continuously shifting backwards, which is what precession means, through the zodiac of fixed stars at the rate of 1° per 72½ years. (Each zodiacal constellation is considered to be 30°, though the difficulty, when using the sidereal system based on the actual constellations, has always been to be able to demarcate exactly where one constellation ends and another begins. The Western zodiac of signs does not have this problem, since its precisely demarcated 30° for each sign defines rather a symbolic band around Earth.) The Spring Equinox point, March 21, (always 0° Aries in the zodiac of signs) has therefore been shifting backwards through the constellation Pisces (zodiac of fixed stars) for the last 2,000 years; it is in the boundary zone now with the constellation Aquarius. (Again, depending on how one draws the precise boundaries between the constellations in the zodiac of fixed stars, one can argue when that imaginary point into Aquarius has actually occurred. The stars themselves, of course, do not define for us how the outline, the perimeter, of what is in fact our imagined pictures of constellations should be drawn.) Here, simply, then, is the astronomical/astrological, cosmic cycle foundation for our entry into the next World Age—*Aquarius*.

We should mention briefly another technical point about World Ages. A World Age is astrologically defined in full by a zodiacal polarity. The Age is named by the sign that is its major dispensational theme (whatever constellation 0° Aries (zodiac of signs) is passing through, as we saw above), but, in addition, there is an undercurrent theme that is named by the sign that is its opposite on the wheel of the zodiac. Therefore, the coming Age of Aquarius is more accurately called the Age of Aquarius/Leo. The Spring Equinox point (zodiac of signs) is about to move into Aquarius (constellation of signs), at the same time that the Fall Equinox point is about to move into Leo. The passing Age of Pisces is likewise more accurately called the Age of Pisces/Virgo, and so forth, going back into previous Ages. This undercurrent theme is evident as our collective human response to, how we have embodied, that original dispensation of the Age. This will have significance as we proceed. The Leo undercurrent to Aquarius will be explored primarily in the chapter "Mythos-making: Art of the New Age."

After all this, one might ask, *So what? What does all this mean?* A fundamental astrological principle is that every cyclical motion in the heavens—cyclical motions that are *astronomical fact*—has metaphysical significance. This astrological principle is itself based on the fundamental metaphysical principle that *all things are interconnected* on the invisible planes. Therefore, the great cycles of the planets and stars in the heavens are metaphysically connected with, correspond to, events happening here on Earth. The heavens above us are a giant, symbolic, cosmic clock, and if we know how to read the time on this clock, that is, how to *interpret it*, then we can gain insight into the events and people around us. The precession of the equinoxes into different constellations, therefore, has astrological/metaphysical significance as distinct World Ages. Still, why this is so—which is really the question as to why astrology has meaning and has proven itself to those who have looked into it—would take us into a more in-depth study of the theory of astrology, which is the study of its cycles and their connection with Time.

The actual character of World Ages, and other major cycles,[3] is initiated then by a particular-timed dispensation—Spirit comes-to-us anew, dispensing the new Word that will guide the human Story forward. This dispensation can be embodied in an avatar or other spiritual visionaries and prophets who speak that new Word; that is, someone, or some few highly inspired individuals, along with some series of numinous events—such as visitation by a God (Other Intelligence)—, combine as the trigger that sets into motion a change in consciousness for humanity as a whole. Over time, collective consciousness has then shifted into a new world. This process is the manifestation of a Divine Word (we could say here "archetype") from a higher level of consciousness—superconsciousness—making its descent into the world. (I will be referring to this Divine Word, for us today, as *The Mythos*.) The dispensation is a collective lesson, a rite of passage, and a stage, for humanity in its psychospiritual evolution. At least up to now, many centuries were required for humanity to assimilate its lesson, for human consciousness, unfortunately in so many tragic ways, could not, and perhaps still cannot, undergo transformation in any short order (undoubtedly based in the material conditioning of the biochemical brain), as the evolutionary road is also filled with the conflicting agendas of many individuals, groups, and entrenched institutions, not to mention Others who have had a hand in the affairs of Earth. A World Age, accordingly, has a particular character, a grand theme, which unfolds through the numerous Threads of its Story.

Admitting that the New Age has an astrological basis naturally allows critics to retort, *But I don't believe in astrology, so why should I believe in World Ages?* First of all, there is no issue here about blind belief; belief per se is not especially a New Age—that is, an Aquarian—kind of attunement to Reality, to begin with (as we will see). Still, the contemporary scientific mind that does not accept the validity of astrology obviously sees no reason why there should be any World Ages at all. (History, as a scholarly study, does historicize in its own way, of course; it demarcates its own ages, worlds, eras: the Ancient World, the Medieval World—the Age of Belief, the Renaissance, the Modern World, and now the Postmodern, and numerous other subperiods.) But culturally, the astrological backdrop to our civilization cannot be denied. Astrology does permeate all of our religious/spiritual Traditions. But though astrology provides the symbolic, metaphysical framework that answers the question as to why there are World Ages, whether one accepts that or not changes nothing—the point is, can we deny that today we are entering a profound, new development in our civilization, one which is now completely global?

Briefly, let us initiate here some of the major themes that will bring out the distinction between the Piscean Age we are leaving and the Aquarian Age we are entering. (Keep in mind that this interpretation is not meant to apply to any given individuals. A person's natal chart is a whole other matter: a complex symbolic picture that requires an individual interpretation.) Pisces, a Water sign, defined an emotionally-based Age whose major theme is summarized in the phrase "I believe." It was a self-contradictory Age (as Pisces has a self-contradictory character), as the human ego was directed to focus on God, the Supernatural, the Universal, Higher Things (for Christians, all via the Christ Image), which meant then a divorce of Spirit from the world, which further meant that the ego was conditioned to repress its own self-expression of *soul*. Belief did provide the illusion of certainty (a psychological certainty), for the newly emerging ego in an ancient world adrift in spiritual chaos (the transition between Aries and Pisces); and when modern science was born in the 17th Century, then it was science (experimental method/analytical intellect) which was next to claim a narrowly defined certainty regarding Truth. First it was the Church, and then Science, which represented Authority regarding certainty and Truth. (We will see later that modern science has the stamp of Virgo, which refers to the Pisces/Virgo polarity of this passing Age.)

In astrology, the zodiacal signs are ruled by planets. Pisces is ruled by the planet Neptune, with an older, traditional, what we now call co-rulership, by Jupiter. Neptune, the astrological power of illusion and illusion-making in all its various forms,[4] also signifying the collective emotional tenor of the times, suggests then that these last 2,000 years were characterized by a sort of collective illusion regarding Reality—a mass Grand Delusion, we could even say. (I am not implying here that illusion and illusion-making are merely a negative and are to be, or even can be, avoided. Much of art is illusion-making, especially filmmaking. See note for the full range of Neptune's rulership.) Neptune is a higher mind planetary principle that accesses the higher, transcendental realms through their vast, oceanic nature, their interconnectedness, so that all things are ultimately experienced as One. This is why Neptune rules mysticism. Neptune is also the fount of universal, unconditional Love, the higher octave of Venus. The Neptunian mode, however, can existentially feel like swimming around in a vast, ethereal ocean (Pisces a Water sign), but without a direction. Neptunian influences are indeed notorious for spreading confusion, which is often the partner of illusion. Belief, the "I believe" of religion, is thus a powerful psychological drug (Neptune, in fact, rules drugs and alcohol) that, though promising the Truth, certainty about the Truth, tends rather to promote a Grand Delusion. The implication then is that our Piscean religions (Christianity and Islam) have deluded us in a fundamental way about Reality and what this life is about. What we were taught about God, for example, has been a masquerade for the sake of an evolutionary agenda. It is time, though, for the mask to come off—which is the Aquarian intent—, if the evolutionary agenda is to be kept on track.

The Jupiter co-rulership of Pisces refers primarily, in the context of our discussion, to the position of Authority in the Piscean Age. Jupiter originally referred to kings and kingship (Jupiter being the king, the largest, of the planets; it is Roman for the Greek Zeus, king of the Gods). Note, however, that in the earlier Age of Aries a king per se did not set out to conquer other lands and then believe that he could impose upon his new subjects what they were to think and believe; rather, his rule was primarily effective over earthly matters of territorial organization, which usually meant respecting the regional Gods and Goddesses of the conquered lands. Alexander the Great, for example, (in the waning Age of Aries) conquered lands all across the Middle East, all the way to India, but his campaign was absolutely not a crusade of trying to spread correct theological beliefs to all of its peoples. With the Age of Pisces this completely changed. The ascendancy of the Church in the Piscean Age implied Authority was not only hierarchically defined (the Pope at the head) but now held sway over what people were to believe (dogma), that is to say, what people were even allowed to think. The period of the Inquisition was undoubtedly the high point of this unforgiving theological domination. The expansive astrological principle of Jupiter (and Jupiter does rule religion and philosophy) meant that all subjects of the vast lands of the Holy Roman Empire were to be indoctrinated into the same, that is, the correct, theological dogmas. (Even in today's Islamic nations (Islam, a definitely Piscean religion) we see this authoritarian power over what Muslims must think and believe, and even how they must act in everyday affairs.) This power of Authority carried over then into modern science itself and today's scientific establishment. (We do know that maverick scientists are commonly ostracized from the scientific community and cannot get their work published.) Authority and the imposition of its interpretation of certainty regarding Reality defined then a mass, collective, Neptunian Delusion that has held sway over these last two thousand years of the Piscean Age. Our Postmodern period is, in a sense, that bubble of Delusion burst, so often leaving the individual ego-self facing an existential emptiness.

The dawning Aquarian Age is mentally-based—Aquarius is an Air sign—but not in the sense of the intellectual ego we are so accustomed to (which is better defined in terms of the later Virgo phase of the Piscean Age—Virgo, ruled by Mercury, planet of the thinking intellect); Aquarius signals rather our entry into the higher mind beyond the rational intellect; it is mind at a collective, intuitive, psychic level (different from Pisces/Neptune, which was epitomized by mysticism). Its key phrase "I know" means, *I know for myself.* This, in particular, refers to spiritual matters. It implies that I am no longer dependent upon secondhand dogma issued from Authority to inform me about Divinity, as I have come to know for myself firsthand about Divinity, because *I have seen for myself.* In other words, we are shifting away from belief with regards to spiritual/religious matters, to knowing for ourselves through direct experience. This opening up of the higher mind potentially accessible to everyone in a new democracy of Vision is already being heralded in the global, externalized world by cybertechnology, namely, the Internet, which, we should keep in mind, is still in its early childhood. And we will see that our reference to the Internet is no mere coincidence.

The sign Aquarius is ruled by the planet Uranus.[5] The Uranian principle is precisely that of accessing the higher mind beyond the rational, intellectualized, and everyday mind of Virgo. The everyday mental functioning of thinking, reasoning, evaluating, using language to speak and write and communicate, is astrologically ruled by the planet Mercury. Now Mercury happens to be the planetary ruler of Virgo, the sign that is the undercurrent theme of the latter half of the Piscean Age. It reaches its peak in cerebral, scientific, conceptual thought and analysis, the Virgo development of the ancient ideal of Logos. So the Modern Age, dominated by scientific thought, has been the perfect expression of the latter half of the Piscean Age. Uranus is often described as the higher octave of Mercury—in other words, it is a distinctively mental function, but is not limited to the ego-intellect (though a favorable birth chart Uranus can confer intellectual brilliance); it implies more the higher mental function of intuition, the so-called Third Eye, with its sudden flashes of insight, of immediate higher knowing, that then kicks into play the mental functioning of Mercury, ideally allowing that higher brilliance to be communicated. We will be exploring much more of this Uranian principle as we proceed.

Consistent with the Uranian principle of suddenness, of breaking through (as the higher mind breaks through into the everyday mind), is the revolutionary impulse of Uranus that breaks through, that shatters, old forms and structures that no longer serve us. It is that lightning bolt of intuitive genius that sees into the essence of things, that says *I know firsthand*, and by that immediacy can then behold the genuinely New. Those who are highly Uranian are often quirky, eccentric, individualistic to the extreme; they are the rebel, the revolutionary, the maverick, the individual who doesn't fit in. We could say then, in a sense, that Postmodernism is the Uranian advancing shock wave of the burst bubble of the previous Age's collective Delusion. The puffed-up importance of Authority is itself deflated. We will see here too that Aquarius implies a coming, new, collective dream (let us say this time a lucid dream) that is no longer hierarchical, no longer ruled by old men representing a stagnant patriarchy, but is based on an interactive community of equals, that is, of friendship and partnership.

Aquarius also had an older, traditional ruler (now co-rulership) in the planet Saturn. Saturn is the planet of form and structure per se. (In astrological dynamics, Uranus usually refers to the shattering of ossified Saturnine form with its implication of limitation and restriction, in order to bring in the New.) What the Saturn influence on the New Age might be will only be hinted at here (since all of these astrological themes will play out in our Story). In terms of world civilization, it might imply a developing New World Order governed not so much by traditional Authority but by a centralized Administrator we might with justification call Technos (this, one might consider the potential dark side of the Aquarian New Age). In terms of spiritual life, the Saturn influence (its preferred influence) would imply that spirituality will come to be experienced in a more concrete way, in particular forms (perhaps still in practices), but especially in a particular universal Form, with immediate clarity, linguistically and psychically, not in the vague, nebulous, Neptunian confusing manner of Pisces where metaphysical and spiritual language is stalled at big abstractions that over time come up empty, so that no one really knows what is anyone is talking about.

The Western obsession with materialism, again, as a result of the later Virgo phase of the Piscean Age (Virgo, an Earth sign), is astrologically destined to be overcome, in the sense that it will essentially be grown out of. (Consider a recent book by Charles T. Tart titled *The End of Materialism*.) Materialism, in the common, everyday meaning of the word, takes the apparent world as Reality. It will increasingly become firsthand experience that Reality is far more than that, and that also means far more than reducing everything down to molecules and atoms and sub-atomic particles; for we are beginning to enter the worlds of the Invisible. Not only will individuals come to a greater realization of the invisible worlds, but science will no longer be fixated on a narrow materialistic paradigm; it, too, is exploring further into the Invisible, and must eventually come to an expanded understanding of energy and the concept of hyperdimensions. Science will undoubtedly come to learn what the spiritual and occult traditions had already known and symbolically represented millennia ago. The new Aquarian cybertechnologies are all moving in this direction, which is away from the merely nuts and bolts, big clunky machinery of Virgo.

Though the New Age refers to this new 2,000-year World Age of Aquarius, 'New Age,' as a label, will actually become a historical term referring to the early phase of our entry into Aquarius. Within this early phase we can speak, as we see it happening now, of a New Age *movement* that will over time permeate all of society, a movement which I foresee transforming and replacing Postmodernity. At some point, however, when we are firmly planted in the Aquarian Age, the phrase 'New Age' will have lost its timeliness. But that has not yet occurred, despite what the debunkers and cynics might have us believe. We must therefore keep this distinction in mind—yes, the *new* Age is this coming 2,000-plus year period, but 'New Age' is also a historical term, implying a broad spectrum of change, spiritual, cultural, social, scientific/technological *and* political, that will come to define a relatively much much shorter period of time. At some point, simply, the "New" Age will not be new anymore.

We might ask, Was Christianity, the major spiritual force that came to define the Age of Pisces, merely a fad? We should keep in mind that the dawning Age of Pisces at the time of Jesus Christ was then the New Age of the Mediterranean world. Imagine the Romans in the years following the death of Jesus asking, *What newfangled cult is this Fish God? Who are these stubborn, self-styled Christian rabble? What is this New Age they keep talking about?* Little could the Romans then realize that their own mighty Empire would someday be converted en masse to Christianity. The early Christians were, in fact, the New Agers of their time.

The New Age has an astrological basis, a *Western* astrological basis.[6] Why it should have a Western determination is a valid point of discussion, but one which would take us too far afield. However, we who are defining the New Age live here, in the West, and this whole concept of the New Age is emerging out of *our* Tradition. Can we overlook the fact that this Tradition has become global, and continues to dominate in various ways? The grand Western—or might we say, Middle Eastern—evolutionary experiment still has a global destiny. Again, why this is so would entail an in-depth metaphysical/philosophical dissertation. Some clues, however, will hopefully be found in this work.

Last, we might wonder why there is a timetable for the evolution—and here, primarily, we are discussing psychospiritual evolution—of Human Reality at all. Why are there World Age, and other cycle, stepping stones that we—humankind—must learn to walk across? Why do the collective spiritual lessons that move us forward come in stages? This is a deep mystery regarding consciousness embodied in the material plane, regarding, in fact, Being and Time. Perhaps some clues to this will also be found along our way.

## *A note on language*

I thought it would be helpful to say something about how I am approaching language here, to be up front about it, as it were. It will become apparent that I prefer to orient myself first with an existential, phenomenological approach to words and abstractions, even as I move into some degree of speculation. It is more of an introspective method, which is much despised, I know, by the Postmodernists. But this is in keeping with the New Age Aquarian directive to know for oneself, directly. Instead of immediately launching into wild, ungrounded speculation, or accepting straight out what the Traditions have claimed, as we find in so much esoteric metaphysical literature, I want to present first what, in my own direct seeing, I have seen and can account for myself. I want to know how abstract notions relate to my concrete existence, to my soul, in the here and now. What I see is that the long-term Aquarian intent is to bring greater clarity and concrete understanding to metaphysical/spiritual Reality, implying a focus on the language by which we speak about it, especially as we come to directly experience the Greater Reality beyond the Veil for ourselves. The flip side to this is that I will practice then a certain philosophical restraint in my language when it comes to metaphysical discussion.

I hope that this in no way constricts what I really want to get across, but actually brings more substance, an existential deepening, to it.

An example of what I am referring to is readily at hand: It is quite common among New Agers to hear talk about "energies" and "frequencies." We all know the view that says that everything is really only energy, that "God" is energy, and the different planes of Reality are all but different frequencies of energy. Everything in the universe and everything beyond, we are assured, simply comes down to that. It is not that I object to this notion per se, but to be left with only this abstract idea, as if by simply mouthing it we understand all there is to know about Reality, can only result in a great poverty of thought. (Hegel, I know, would most certainly agree here.) I discovered that people, by and large, really don't have much of an idea of what they actually mean by saying "energy." We must be careful, for one thing, about borrowing words directly from physics in order to speak about superconscious realities, even though there might be parallels to be made, as explored, for example, in the popular book of years past *The Tao of Physics*, by Frijof Capra. To say, however, that everything is only energy at different frequencies is actually quite insidiously reductionistic, if one is still viewing energy, no matter how quantum savvy one is, through the lens of physics. It is also awkward, to say the least, to develop a heart-felt soul relationship to "energy." It might be helpful here to mention Jung's insight that we do not emotionally relate to abstract "archetypes" themselves, but to a living God (whoever that God might be).

There is no doubt that "energy" is a most fascinating concept[1] that we are still only coming to understand. I certainly haven't been satisfied by the vague notions about it that have been floating around for years. My main point, again, is that it too easily becomes just another abstract word that we get to hang everything on.

In addition to direct experience, my own knowing, I do rely on the abundant evidence and literature provided by other experiencers, scholars, and researchers, and by the Traditions, for the subjects we will be discussing. We cannot ignore the honored scholarship, research, and the honest experience of others, in helping us to see.

At the same time that I am advocating this greater clarity, I am quite aware that my language will come across as a sort of mythical thinking. But, to me, there is no contradiction here. The mythical mode—but better put, the *mythopoetic*—is exactly the language suited for talking about our subject. A strictly scientific language would not be appropriate, let alone that the scientific disciplines are blind to what the New Age Vision is even about. On the other hand, the language of the Postmodernist thinkers only leads us to a dead end in these matters. Let me be honest about it, so that any Christian Fundamentalists or the strictly scientifically oriented that might be reading this will not be constantly disappointed—I am not advancing here the old Piscean Age ideal of Logos. The Postmodernist thinkers, for one, have already deconstructed its traditional pretentions for us; traditional Logos can therefore no longer be the dispensational Word for the New Age. My claim is, is that it is the language of Mythos that we must now become practiced at. The New Age Vision presented here partakes then of The Mythos that is to come. One important aspect of this Mythos begins precisely as the Story that we have here to tell.

Also to be noted are certain language directives I am making, such as the reintroduction of capitals for select words, for one. Also, keep in mind that words can take on slightly shifting meanings depending on the particular context within the text, especially as they take on further meaning in the unfolding of our Story. It is important to realize that this indeed is a Story I have begun to tell. As we will eventually come to see, the New Age Vision opens out a new Word, a new Story, that is indeed *The Mythos*.

# ( 4 )

# THE WATER BEARER:
# SPIRIT AND SOUL

*Souls*
*Souls homeless*
*Souls almost having despaired*
*of Earth—*[1]

As we begin to delve further into our Story, I am aware of the enormous difficulties involved. Themes that we about to explore, such as "Spirit" and "soul," are fraught with so much confusion and linguistic free-for-all that it is a rare thing indeed to find authors who will genuinely confront their meanings—what sense we should make of them—head on. The more scientifically oriented consider them outdated altogether, while the more spiritually oriented bandy them about as abstract words that are taken for granted, but that don't mean a whole lot in a Postmodern context. To most scholars, all of these old, traditional words, such as "Spirit" and "soul," are like quicksand pits of semantics that are best to be avoided. Be that as it may, explore them we will, if the New Age is to be a transformation and revitalization of what still speaks to us from the past.

*If we are to begin to understand the New Age as first a spiritual shift in consciousness, then we must explore this word 'Spirit,' and this word 'soul.' So into the semantic quicksand we go…*

A New Age implies that a major, new, spiritual dispensation is being given to humanity. That should imply then a Reality called "Spirit" that remains at the root of the word 'spiritual.' But as scholar of religions Huston Smith has pointed out,[2] no one seems to speak directly about "Spirit" anymore, as no one really knows exactly what it is supposed to refer to; its adjective "spiritual" is now associated rather with the neologism "spirituality," as this connotes a mode, a state, of our own being human, in some sense trans-psychological, but then not necessarily implying anything beyond Human Reality. Being "spiritual" is a human state, after all. In other words, spirituality is readily considered to be but another part of our own subjective makeup (within Human Reality).

So let us take this bull by the horns and initially define Spirit in a way that we can work with. In this early context of our Story, let us start with this: Spirit is *That-which-is-greater-than-us-coming-to-us*. Now why would I define Spirit, in a first pass, sort of speak, like this? Most importantly, it is because this is my existential/phenomenological approach; this is how I have directly experienced Spirit. The constructed phrase sounds simple enough, but there is much to explore in it. Greater-than-us will mean, first of all, greater than the ego-self, that is, the psychological ego, and its everyday world that we know all so well. (In the broadest sense, it means greater than consciousness within Human Reality, at whatever stage of our psychospiritual evolution.) New Age thought assumes there is a Greater Reality, usually considered a spiritual Reality, beyond Human Reality, Human Reality being our human interpreted and constructed world—*our human bubble*—that so thoroughly contains us. As all Tradition agrees, there is something more, something *Other*, that can speak to us from outside our human bubble. In other words, there is an "outside" to Human Reality. Spirit, in our firsthand experience of its coming-to-us, implies that it becomes real to us in an experiential mode; in other words, it is not some abstract reality remote from us, on some other transcendent plane, that we simply talk abstractly about; and it is not simply some quantum wave form that physics is still mystified about. What is further suggested here is that it is an active principle, *an ontological process*, in fact, so is not some "spirit substance." It is the absolute active principle, I would claim, of Being. The ancient Greek word for Spirit was 'pneuma,' originally meaning "wind," which is quite an active agency indeed.

(Note: The foundation for a New Age philosophy would actually begin with a new encounter with Being. What Heidegger initiated as his life work regarding the question of Being would have to be pursued. This, however, is not the place to take on that challenge—we will save that for another work.)

In addition, Spirit will signify for us the Intelligence of That-which-is-greater-than-us. Now how is it possible to say this? Especially for those who claim that "Everything is only energy," how does anything like Intelligence come into the picture? From firsthand experience, our own existential experience, we will state that Spirit reveals Intelligence, for when we are spiritually inspired, what comes-to-us is not mere gibberish or sheer emptiness, but something meaningful, no matter how abstract it might at first come across. Spirit reveals Intelligence, in fact, that there is *an Other* (I mean this in a generic sense—there are in fact many Others beyond Human Reality) at work in the Invisible. The Postmodern epistemological perspective would say that this is not possible, that nothing can speak to us from outside our human bubble. What we find with the Postmodernists, however, is the almost complete non-interest in phenomena that happen at the boundary of Human Reality—all that we will label the "paranormal", which includes the parapsychological, alternant states of consciousness, OBEs, the liminal zone, UFO reality, etc. We, who are of the New Age orientation, know that we cannot turn our eyes away from the fringes of Human Reality. In fact, moving into the fringes is exactly what is meant by Human Reality evolving.

So a more complete existential, working definition of Spirit would be: *That-which-is-greater-than-us-coming-to-us-revealing-Intelligence.* I should add at this point that all of the hyphens indicate that it is a whole, unified process, a most active mode of Being.

Another reason for my initial definition is that it points to something essential about New Age spirituality: That it emphasizes that we are to embody Spirit in this life, in this here and now of Human Reality. It is a process of *coming-to-us* to help us transform this life. In other words, we are no longer satisfied by merely abstract mental talk about Spirit that is utterly otherworldly, utterly transcendent to us, or that only has importance in an Afterlife; no, we want to drink of the actual living springs of Spirit for ourselves.

Collective humanity has always had a relationship with Spirit, but traditionally this relationship for most of society is kept within the parameters of long-established cultural forms called religions, e.g. Judaism, Christianity, Islam, Hinduism, Buddhism. But Spirit has a timetable with humanity, based on cycles—the various astrological cycles, such as we have already discussed—regarding our psychospiritual evolution (and we might even include biological as well). Our ongoing response to these cycles of dispensed inspiration—what can also be referred to as *Revelation*—over long periods of time determines the part we play in our own evolution. Up to now this ongoing response has been largely unconscious in humanity; today, however, we are in the position of consciously choosing what part we play. This, indeed, is a great New Age insight, our Moment of Vision. As on a regular timetable, measured not only in Ages, but in shorter timed cycles as well, Spirit dispenses to humanity a new inspiration of Itself which will come to determine the fundamental character, the fundamental lesson, of the unfolding next Age, or creative phase, of our psychospiritual evolution. The previous Age dispensation was Piscean in character; it emphasized, especially in its early New Age phase, belief, faith, devotion, service, sacrifice, martyrdom, renunciation, humility, compassion, charity, peace, brotherly love (agape). The primary avatar of this Age was Jesus Christ, though Mohammed and Islam have undeniably played their equally important role in the Piscean Age. Just as Christianity is permeated by Piscean themes, so, too, we find them in Islam. Consider that 'Islam' itself means, "I surrender" (to Allah), which is definitely a Piscean way to be. (We see today to what perverse extremes the Piscean ideal of martyrdom has been taken among Muslim fundamentalist militants and terrorists.)

I must now take something of a circuitous route, in order to bring in new considerations that will open up a discussion of soul, before tying it all back to what we've just defined as Spirit.

The new dispensation will be Aquarian in character. At this point, it will be helpful to consider the common Aquarian symbol known as the Water Bearer. Many are familiar with it already. We see in this symbol a human figure that in one position or another is always portrayed pouring water from an urn. (Let us now capitalize Water, for it is the symbol of astrological Water that we speak of. The same will be done with the other astrological elements: Fire, Earth, Air.) What might this symbol mean? First, before there is any misunderstanding, Aquarius, despite the initial impression one might have had about it given the very name used for it, "Water Bearer," is actually an Air sign, even though its symbolic figure *is* pouring out Water. The previous World Age was Pisces, which *is* a Water sign. We are therefore moving from the Water of Pisces to the Air of Aquarius. What, then, is the human figure of the Water Bearer doing? It is dipping its urn into the Waters of Pisces, the previous Age, and is now pouring those Waters into the open Air. This symbolism, we will come to see, has far reaching significance.

First, we see that the Waters (we will use the plural, as there are multiple meanings here), and, most importantly, what is hidden in the Waters, is to be poured out—into the Air where all can see, *into visibility.* What was hidden in the Waters is revealed. We will see that an essential Aquarian New Age theme is precisely that: *All that is hidden is to be revealed.*

Many things are hidden from us. Metaphysically, the secrets of the Invisible (the invisible realms, other dimensions outside Human Reality), of Spirit, of Divinity, are hidden from us. The endeavor to learn of these secrets, to tap into these secrets, to act in a balanced accordance with them, is the intent of occultism. Setting aside all the Christian misunderstanding and fear of this word, the 'occult' simply means, "that which is hidden," "the secrets," "hidden wisdom." (Madame Blavatsky's book *The Secret Doctrine* is a classic of 19th Century occultism.) This is, first of all, the wisdom of the ancients, of all the various ancient, hermetic and mystery school teachings. The main reason the occult arts (most going back to ancient times)—astrology, alchemy, Kabbalah, tarot, numerology, witchcraft, divining, true magic—were suppressed in our Western tradition was on account of the Church's dictate that these secrets were not to be pried into.

These were secrets meant to be hidden from us, for they tapped into a reality that is very powerful. The psychic and paranormal experiences resulting from occult knowledge were therefore meant to be kept from us. (The interesting question is, Who *really* meant to keep this knowledge from us?) We were only allowed to learn something of the wisdom of these secrets secondhand through the agency of the Church, the priesthood. In Protestantism, too, despite its reaffirmation of developing a personal relationship to Jesus, which is something of a kind of firsthand knowing, occult wisdom is taboo; we must get our spiritual needs met strictly through a narrow interpretation of *The Bible*,[3] and a narrow, highly conditioned, relationship to Jesus. The Aquarian New Age emphasis, which will be another New Age theme, in contrast, is exactly that of direct, firsthand experience, knowing directly for ourselves. The New Age is thus a return to the essence of *gnosis*, the knowing of divine matters through the immediacy of our own experience, our own efforts, our own knowing, our *inner* knowing. Such firsthand experience can either break in upon us unexpectedly (certainly those who have had the near-death experience did not plan on it, and there is the out-of-the-blue UFO encounter, and the sudden Vision) or it results by way of our own occult and/or spiritual efforts. In the New Age, we will therefore be moving away from mere belief in dogmas and doctrines as an existential stance toward the Greater Reality; rather, faith will come to be grounded on direct experience. In this sense, the New Age is clearly a renewal, a revitalization, a reinterpretation, of Gnosticism. But the gnosis we will be speaking of here is an *evolutionary* gnosis, meaning not one that had been experienced in the ancient past and assumed final for all time, but one that is being shown to us here and now, today, as Divinity reveals more of Itself to us.

It is interesting to note in passing that the New Age of Aquarius/Leo strikes a resonating chord with the ancient Age of Taurus/Scorpio (approx. 4,500-2,300 B.C.). This is first quite apparent with the emphasis many in the New Age movement place today on reconnecting with ancient wisdom, that is, before the Christian Era; in particular, with the wisdom/mystery schools of ancient Egypt and Mesopotamia.

These civilizations occurred during the Age of Taurus/Scorpio. Astrologically, what the New Age of Aquarius/Leo and the ancient Age of Taurus/Scorpio have in common is that they are all defined as fixed signs. In other words, we are coming around to a similar metaphysical attunement as what we find in the very ancient world. There is a deep, underlying metaphysical correspondence here. The four fixed signs of Taurus, Leo, Scorpio, and Aquarius are symbolically said to be the four pillars, the four gateways, the four principles, that structure for us, for our experience, metaphysical reality. Again, occultism is the attempt to enter the gateway into metaphysical reality, to understand the secrets of the inner structure of this gateway so that we might learn to live in harmony with *As above, so below*. This fixed sign attunement implies also the wise use of our will and our intention to learn to manifest. Is it only coincidence then that today's New Age interest in occultism harks back to the occultism of ancient Egypt?

The Aquarian dispensation implies a new relationship to Divinity. Who this Divinity might be, what we might even mean by this, in a Postmodern context, is what we will be exploring. In the Piscean Age, there was always the injunction not to attempt to know Divinity directly, or, more dogmatically, that it was impossible to know Divinity directly. (We will come to see why this was so.) There were instead the intermediaries—the priesthood, the Pope, the Muslim Imam, the strict adherence to the word of *The Bible* or *The Koran*; in other words, Authority always stepped in to tell us what to believe. The New Age calls instead for renewing a direct *and* ongoing relationship to Divinity. By ongoing, we mean that the relationship is not settled for all time in a Bible, in doctrines or dogma, in cultural forms that refuse to evolve; no, but a relationship that is always active, in process, that is always open to new Revelation, and therefore, *transformation*. And because this relationship is always in process—a dynamic between us and Divinity, where we actively do our part—, it is *creative*—in fact, we must refer to it as *co-creative*. We will eventually come to see how important these words 'creative' and 'co-creative' are.

Pisces is the sign par excellence of dualism and self-contradiction. We saw plenty of this principle in play during the Age of Pisces. There were major dualisms, such as Christ and Satan, Heaven and Hell—or alternately, Heaven and Earth—, Good and Evil, Mind and Matter, Reason and Desire, and, in more recent contexts, Right Brain and Left Brain. We must note, however, that these dualisms were never the familiar Yin and Yang principle of Taoism, where Yin and Yang are both equal and equally of value, in dynamic interplay with one another, but were at heart a dualism of mortal conflict, defined by a versus: Christ vs. Satan, Heaven vs. Hell, Good vs. Evil, even Mind vs. Matter, Reason vs. Desire, and, disturbingly enough in our day, East vs. West, or even male vs. female. In all of these dualisms, one side claimed to be or to represent the True, the Good, the Most Valued, whereas the other side was to be cast out and/or repressed.

Jesus, as the Christ, was also a self-contradictory figure: both fully mortal man and fully God, a God-man. The Church has held this over our heads for centuries as an inscrutable mystery, but today we have a perspective from which this does begin to make sense, though not in the obscurant manner, the mystification, of the Church. For this, too, will become a New Age intellectual stance—no more obfuscation in occult and spiritual matters; what we will want from now on is clarity wrought from our own insight in a context of all evidence available.

We saw what the Waters can refer to historically (the hidden wisdom of the ancients) and spiritually (that hidden wisdom itself), but there is also another, specifically individual *human* side to these Waters. Before we begin to explore this more fully, let us return to the figure of the Water Bearer. We must note two more things about it. First, that the figure is a human figure representing universal humanity. For it is humanity itself that will be doing the pouring. Aquarius is above all the sign *of* humanity. In a profound sense, as we will see, Spirit will be working through humanity in a way never before realized. The other thing we must note about the Water Bearer is that Water is being poured from an *urn*. An urn—or any vessel for holding water—is a particular form. In other words, we must realize that the Water Bearer is not simply splashing around in the Water, not just tossing Water into the Air, but is pouring it from a container, which is a particular Form (the Saturn co-rulership of Aquarius, implying form). Perhaps subtle at this point, but we will see that our revealing what is hidden will indeed be done through a particular Form.

The Waters of the hidden are to be poured into the open Air. What, then, does this signify? Air, astrologically, refers to the free-ranging Mind in open communication. In the open Air, nothing is hidden, all can be seen—revealed—, language itself being a free, non-emotionally charged, exchange, allowing communication among open, free-thinking minds. Aquarius, in particular, refers to invisible, instantaneous, and long-distance, collective, communication. (Might we say here, ahead of ourselves, telepathic—immediate, mind-to-mind—communication?) We will see how aptly this defines the New Age world we are just now only beginning to enter.

Water signifies above all our emotional/feeling self, which is our common, personal sense of soul. Mythologically, Water is traditionally associated with soul. Now to clearly understand the perspective from which I will be discussing soul, we might first consider this: There are those who would question whether we indeed have a soul. What they are always arguing about is this idea of an immortal soul, an abstract metaphysical *something*. That argument, however, does not address and does not determine what the main point of our discussion about soul is. I consider soul to be a mode of our being, of our being human, in the here and now; therefore, soul is experienced as *embodied*. The fact that we may be losing any notion whatsoever of soul, in our Postmodern context, has, for me, the alarming implication of our losing a sense for a fundamental mode of our very being as a human being. Whether soul is immortal or not is another issue. To me, it is important first that we revitalize a notion of soul as existentially experienced, otherwise, the whole trend of a dehumanizing Technos (see the chapter on Technos) goes unchallenged. To deny that we have "a soul" is then to tragically deny an essential aspect of our being human. If it is kept in mind that soul can be considered but another name for "psyche," then we should not lose our way by falling back into traditional notions. As depth psychologist James Hillman contends, soul is none other than our psyche. But that 'soul' and 'psyche' may have different nuances of meaning between them depending on context we also keep open.

In the Piscean Age, though soul—that notion of an immortal soul—was extolled as our true essence and needed to be saved, ironically, at the same time, soul—as existentially embodied—was repressed. How could this be? Perhaps we need to look more closely then at this whole notion of soul and salvation.

Why does soul need to be saved? Well, let us ask, What is it then, that is said about soul? We are traditionally brought up to believe that soul is a metaphysical something that enters our body at conception or sometime early during the nine months of gestation, that it comes stained with Original Sin, is immortal, but tags alongside of us throughout life, and is perpetually being stained further by the sins committed in this life. The simplistic New Age version of the latter is that soul has lessons to learn in this lifetime and will reincarnate many times to learn others. Soul, in other words, appears utterly passive, either stained by sin or remaining "pure," or somehow registering lessons. For what? For the sake of *this life?* For the sake of enriching *this life?* No, it was always for the sake of an *Afterlife*...or some other life. Now if we honestly consider what is said here about soul, we must realize that it is highly abstract. Why is soul always kept abstract? *A metaphysical something.* A tabula rasa for registering sins and good deeds that will be tallied up at the judgement gates to an Afterlife. Can more not be said about soul, if it were that important? Christianity has seriously failed us here in not providing us, after having had such a long history, with any more of a substantial understanding of soul. (The reasons, however, we are about to explore.) It is no surprise that in our contemporary Postmodern world soul has become merely a word, empty of meaning, though perhaps useful in rhetorical contexts as a figure of speech. As a matter of fact, in the academic world, we understand that 'soul' is not an acceptable word of usage in dissertations or scholarly papers, unless used between quotation marks. How many major thinkers in the 20th Century explored, let alone even brought up, the idea of soul, but for Carl Jung and the Jungian school? (Though Heidegger, for one, did not speak about soul per se, his notion of Dasein and my notion of embodied soul have much in common and would require further exploration.) Occasionally we do hear it said that we can actually experience, or do experience, soul. Black culture, for one, never completely lost its explicit connection to soul, that is, the *living, deep feeling soul*, not the religious abstraction.

Soul, once we honestly begin to face it, and honestly acknowledge that we do in fact experience it, is initially, to a great extent, the dark side of us. This is soul naïve, undeveloped (what some will refer to as our lower self or lower nature), however old of a soul some are said to be when first coming into this life. Now I am well aware that many New Agers seem to believe the exact opposite, that soul is all "Light," pure and virginal, a sort of sanctuary where we can go within and escape the stress of the everyday world, that soul is our true, our "pure" essence. (This is where soul is so often confused with Spirit. What they describe is more accurately to be ascribed to Spirit.) And that is exactly what Christianity has wanted us to believe, but for another contradiction—soul already comes stained by Original Sin, and soul, far from being merely a passive, "pure," tabula rasa, also has a nasty habit of wanting to sin. Soul, indeed, is not pure and virginal, but has already been touched by the devil; but, then, we are admonished to prevent any further staining by doing what we can to keep it as pure and as virginal as possible. But why? Because soul *wants experience*, implying that soul is tempted by the world, implying further that the world can only stain and sully the soul even more. The original Piscean inspiration was in fact a call to renounce this world, and this meant renunciation of the body where soul seethes with desires. Traditionally, we were asked to carry on a lifelong struggle to keep soul from fully experiencing this world and deepening its experience of this world. Otherwise, the Piscean ideal of martyrdom would not make sense, as martyrdom is a willingness to forgo this world. Now what we actually find is that soul at first is a dark, seething cauldron of feelings, desires, fantasies, dreams, imaginations, sensuality. Soul is filled with lust, resentments, fears, hurts, anger, and hatreds. Freud referred to the unconscious, dark nature of this cauldron as the Id. Jungians refer to this one aspect of soul as the Shadow—the unpleasant, ugly, unacceptable things about ourselves that we keep repressed, but that we then unconsciously project so readily onto others. Soul is also our fantasy life, our emotional life, our passionate life, our suffering life. Soul, to put it quite bluntly, can so often be experienced as our personal domain of Hell. It is so often experienced as the agonizing conflicts within us. A basic tenet of Buddhism is that life is fundamentally defined by suffering. Even Jesus was quoted once as saying, "Now is my soul troubled." (John 12:27)

Committing sin on our part was "Satan's" way of making a claim upon us, that is, upon our soul. Therefore, keeping "pure" meant keeping our soul away from the clutches of Satan. But the Church Fathers knew very well: soul is already in the clutches of "Satan" by the very notion of Original Sin, in addition to the fact that we have an innate propensity to want to sin. The flesh is weak, we were told. And by flesh, read *soul*. Further, as we saw above, soul is our suffering, and it is in Hell where suffering takes place. For those who have honestly and firsthand gazed into their own soul, "Satan" (of course, this is here meant symbolically) is in fact the first face that soul will often show us. But this is not the full story, of course, for there is not only *redemption*, which for the New Age is the work of *transformation*, but there is so much more to soul.

In Christianity, we always find that fear of looking into darkness. And so soul had to be repressed, and a false veil of virginity placed over it. Keeping soul virginal meant keeping soul inexperienced and undeveloped, especially when it came to occult wisdom. Now this certainly tied in to the political agenda of the Church and the whole feudal system of the Middle Ages. (In an even larger picture, we could suggest that some *other* agency—read Intelligence—also had an agenda to keep us controlled.) Soul that wants experience is also soul that wants to be liberated to realize itself. But the irony is, that this could not happen until the ego first became more fully developed, which meant, during the self-contradictory Piscean Age, that the naïve, undeveloped soul had to be repressed. As tragic as this often was, it is important to realize why this had to be in Piscean psychospiritual dynamics.

One extended comment that I should make here is that I am not one to romanticize and pine away for what could have been. I do not invoke some supposed ancient, even prehistoric, idyllic paradise that we should have stayed in. We sometimes meet those who believe that we should not have gone down this road of Western civilization, that it was all a mistake from the beginning and somehow could have been different, that we somehow had it within our power (it is assumed we were fully conscious, free will beings) where we could have chosen a different road. That is not my view at all. I find that view extremely naïve. I do not believe that "we" had a choice at any point. "We" are always thoroughly conditioned by the culture in play—thrown into a world not of our making—, and further, the making of our culture, in its most fundamental forms, is not something that we ever consciously decided either. There are no decisions made on this level until we, as individuals, set out upon the Path of awakening, which is a long Path indeed. Even to set out upon such a Path requires some form of inspiration from That-which-is-greater-than-us. We must be *shown*. Especially when we add that superhuman Others have intervened on Earth from the beginning, I would suggest that the hidden background to civilization is far more complex than conventional history can fathom. Certainly we can criticize and express our utmost dismay at the repressions and horrors fostered by civilized Tradition, but my concern is confronting the world as we know it, and to be an agent of change in the here and now.

The naïve soul, which can so readily unleash its personal hell upon others, needs something like the parenting of what Freudians call the Superego. The naïve soul needs guidance; in the collective sense, it needs a control system, a *spiritual* control system established in the world, which is the major *cultural* role that religions play for the masses. What is required in this control system is a morality, a code of ethics, a Ten Commandments, doctrines, precepts, codes of behavior—taboos. *Thou shall not*— But if our destiny is to become fully conscious beings, able to live at some point without the parenting of a control system, then this can only happen through the agency of a fully developed, mature ego. And this, as history has shown, takes time; in the collective sense, it apparently requires centuries, even millennia. This is the long process of the interiorization of the ego; that is, the ego—by far, normally outwardly directed—comes to discover that there is an inner, psyche world, and then goes on to develop a relationship to that inner world. It is the ego developing for itself an inner life of psyche—ideally, a spiritually rich inner life. Sometime in this process, the individual discovers the importance of *ethos* firsthand, for him or herself, beyond the standard moral injunctions imposed by society or a church. This is the other major role that religions play, *for the individual*—the development of an "inner culture." This is what true faith fosters, in contrast to mere belief, which can be satisfied by merely mouthing doctrine issued by Authority. The inner dynamics of the Piscean Age were quite complex; we will come to see how this all played out.

\*

An excursion on the different senses of the word 'ego'

'Ego' is another word used in total confusion. We will recognize three senses of it here:

The ego-self or psychological ego or ego complex. This is the meaning that we will use most of the time in this work. It is also the meaning that is almost always meant in everyday conversation. This is the ego as our self-image, our self-image complex. It is ego that is thoroughly conditioned by its society into having a self-image. It is the basis then of what is referred to as egotism, being egotistical, someone having a "big ego," the cult of personality, so is the referent for narcissism, for constant me me me. When people talk about wanting to overcome the ego, transcend the ego, get rid of the ego, or humble the ego, it is the psychological ego that is (almost always) meant. But the ego-self can also become an evolved, an enlightened, an interconnected ego, a Higher Self-directed ego. This is the ideal of our trajectory as the New Age Vision. For an ego complex to develop, though, it must build around the pure ego, even if the pure ego is never experienced.

The pure ego, the pure "I." This is ego meant strictly as the self-aware focus of consciousness. Pure self-conscious awareness. So this is ego stripped of its image complex, especially as a goal in meditation, so is able to be the still point of the Watcher. That is, to be able to simply watch in the Now, without judgement, and, in its purest sense, without any Human Reality interpretations at all. It is ego as the meta-stance, standing back from any image of self, of personality, from all conditioning. This is the spiritualized sense of ego. But to suggest transcending this ego, getting rid of this I, (almost) does not make sense. It would mean having no focus whatsoever; in everyday life, it would imply being something like a walking zombie. Still, some meditation practices aim for this mystical state of complete ego dissolution, of Oneness, nirvana, being one-with the life force, just merging with the energies of the universe. Which is all a wonderful and blissful thing to experience. However, one could not function in everyday life in such a state. One would have to reside in a monastery.

The Transcendental Ego or metaphysical ego. This is an even more rarified sense of the word. I am using it here in the Kantian sense. This is ego on a level that creates the transcendental conditions for experience itself…the conditions that determine that we can even have any (normal) experience whatsoever. This is ego projecting our bubble called Human Reality. This ego allows the pure ego to be aware of a world, period, since it creates, for one, the conditions of our space-time continuum. So this ego, which has always been a conundrum for Kantian scholars, is not to be found in our normal experience at all, not even in most meditative practice, but perhaps is hinted at in paranormal experience. To operate on the level of the Transcendental Ego is apparently what the ET Other Intelligences can do. It would be the ability to perform "paranormal magic." This is ego on the levels of Higher Self, which we will explore in the next chapter.

*

Let us then consider what salvation of soul really meant, existentially. Let us follow where an etymological link of associations takes us: 'Salvation' means 'to be saved' (the condition of being saved), meaning 'to be kept safe,' 'away from danger,' 'unhurt,' 'to be preserved,' 'to be kept untouched' or 'spotless,' 'to be kept pure from the ravages of sin.' But to be kept pure and kept safe, soul must be kept hidden away, locked up; it must be kept, in other words, *repressed*. Therefore, it is to be kept from experience, kept as a virgin, to prevent it from the consummate act of fully entering the world. This is why the ideal life path in the first half of the Piscean Age was the cloistered life of the monk. Christianity was deathly afraid of soul, because soul always had a connection to the feminine. (Jung's notion of the Anima.) And here was the origin of Hell. Here was the harrowing Labyrinth through the darkness of soul. The mark of "Satan," in the old Adam and Eve story, entered the human soul through the act of a woman. *Women, therefore, had to be suppressed in their full expression of being human,* upon which followed *oppression*. Salvation of soul for the sake of an Afterlife—where soul would supposedly find its abstract dream of liberation—was then the Big Lie. The realization will sink in that all this emphasis on the salvation of the soul was but a ruse to promote the development of the ego—and we might with justification say *the masculine ego*—, and thus we finally begin to see what salvation of soul really meant *existentially*—in our actual life.

It is true that Christianity has wavered over the notion that we, strictly on our own, can do anything, no matter how good we are, to save our soul, because of the claim that salvation is only to be found through Jesus Christ. (Some Christian evangelists make this so easy, though, as if all one has to say is, *I believe in Jesus Christ my Savior,* whereby one is, by that singular statement alone, saved. No real soul work, in other words, is required, but for that magical incantation.) Paradoxically enough, though, there is a hidden truth in this notion of salvation through Jesus when we come to realize that Jesus is a stand-in for the Higher Self, and when we replace the notion of "salvation" with that of "transformation."

Pisces is a Water sign, indicating that the previous Age was emotionally based. Now if we consider that soul is associated with Water, we might become confused as to why the Piscean Age *did not* emphasize the actual existential soul. The ideals of the early Piscean Age were belief, faith, devotion, worship, piety, all having a powerful emotional charge throughout history. Yes, Pisces is emotionally based, but, at the same time, not necessarily focusing upon or wanting clarity about personal emotion (i.e. soul), but signifying rather a highly directed, emotional giving of oneself—that is to say, the ego-self—to the Universal, a sacrificing of oneself to the Universal, to the Otherworldly, to the Absolute, (which is quite a different orientation than the Water sign Cancer, for example), the Absolute which was none other than God, than Allah. (This is why Pisces is the sign of mysticism, where the ego is no longer interested in itself, but in dissolving itself in the contemplation of Divinity. But how many true mystics are there? Only a handful.) And so the question is, What historically *was* sacrificed—what was *repressed*? Not the ego, for the ego, as we will see, was still emerging in its Arian descent from Spirit; it was the *personal soul* that was sacrificed, left to remain in a state of naïveté, "innocence." The simple-hearted, pious soul, *the sleight-of-hand virginal soul,* was what the patriarchal Church valued so much. And wanted it kept that way. Pisces is a self-contradictory sign. The astrologer Alan Oken, in reference to Pisces, uses the phrase, *I seek my self and I don't seek my self.*

Soul was kept hidden in its own dark Waters and thereby turned by Christianity over the centuries into an abstract word—*an immortal, metaphysical something.* How abstract can we get? And yet, what fundamental insight might we extract here as we lift the veil of this "abstract something"—what is the insight here that begs that we see it? *That soul, through all its watery veils, is a powerful metaphysical **potential** that all possess as a birthright.* Soul is the polar correspondent in a dynamic with Spirit that is like clay in our hands (our hands guided not by ego, but by Spirit). Let us begin to define soul from another level now as our *potential-to-be*; but, then, our potential-to-be what? It is our potential to be *fully human.* (Of course, the Human Potential Movement had come to the same view already back in the 1970s-80s.) To be fully human means then that we liberate that which is hidden within us. This would require that we now further define soul as a *potential-to-become*. This soul potential-to-become can literally lie fallow for a lifetime, or it can be consciously worked upon to become something akin to divine *while in this life*. Now soul—the living reality that is soul—was repressed, on the other hand, because an abstract, otherworldly Afterlife was more highly valued, because a patriarchal and Church-defined masculine *Spirit* was more highly valued at the expense of soul. Spirit and soul, we thus find, are quite distinct notions, though often used interchangeably to the point of utter confusion. Let us get an even better idea now of what we mean by them.

Spirit, as we suggested earlier, can be defined as That-which-is-greater-than-us-coming-to-us-revealing-Intelligence. Spirit, because it is the greater-than-us Greater Reality—and let us be more precise now and say, it is the active interconnectedness of the Greater Reality—, is always a coming-to-us or a staying-away-from-us, as the latter has been so much the case in the Modern and Postmodern periods. Of course, we cannot deny that a certain number of spiritually realized individuals, in various ways, are always living at any given time; what we are speaking about historically is primarily the collective. Spirit is the Greater Reality because it is more potent, and is always a coming-into the more limited reality, such as our 3rd-dimensional Human Reality. We might think of Spirit as an enormous reservoir that has been dammed up at one end; and here we are, playing out our life in a little soul pond below the dam. If water is allowed to flow out of the dam evenly as a stream, we then feel spiritually refreshed, spiritually inspired, uplifted, as we live in our little soul pond. But if the floodgates of the reservoir were to all of a sudden be completely thrown open, could we, as ego, survive such a deluge? That gives us an idea as to why there is a Veil separating the ego-self from the Greater Reality of Spirit. That is why humanity lives within its bubble, created by the Transcendental Ego.

The Greater Reality that spiritually feeds all individuals is therefore the Universal. Spirit is the Universal, transcending individuals yet speaking to all individuals, shining upon all individuals, which is why, of course, Spirit is called the Light. Spirit was always associated with the immutable Sun shining its light upon all. Spirit in its coming-to-us inspires us, uplifts us, motivates us, provides us with guidance. It can do this because it reveals *Intelligence*.

Soul, in contrast, is the particular, be that of a particular person, or animal, or even plant, or even planet, for that matter—for example,

Anima Mundi, the Soul of the World/Earth. Soul is the mode of our particular being: *my* soul, *your* soul, the soul of *our* nation. It is always *our* particular potential-to-be and potential-to-become. An implication of this, then, is that soul is not a generic slate that is simply the same for everyone; no, but everyone has a distinctly unique soul makeup, and comes into this life with a distinct soul history. Astrology clearly shows this in the complexity of the natal chart. Because everyone has a distinct natal chart, it is then by astrological definition that everyone has a *distinct soul.* Soul, too, does not come-to-us, for soul is already here—it is *our own mode of experience.* Soul refers first to the richness of our experience: the more soul we have (meaning the more soul is developed and made conscious—which is the ancient, Socratic injunction to "Know thyself"—and allowed to manifest), the richer our experience, the fuller and deeper our life. That implies then, initially, that we allow feelings, emotions, fantasies, memories, dreams, reflections, the subpersonalities and the voices within us, all of our inner dialogues and fragments of self-narrative that swim through us, to come into fully awake consciousness and be spiritually cultivated by bringing it into some appropriate form (and this can also mean to then let go of). This is essential work in our potential-to-be *fully* human, but is still only a step on our way in our potential-to-become.

Now it would be a mistake to think that this is not in some way connected to our body, and naturally, our body is a *particular* body. Soul *is* intimately destined to attempt to express itself and realize itself in this lifetime in this body, which goes to explain why soul work, let alone sexuality per se, often has to do with our relationship to our own body. We could go further and say that soul is biologically tied into the heart and nervous system wiring of the body and brain—even more, that we have perhaps what is now being called a cellular memory throughout our entire body. Those who discuss this still speculative notion of cellular memory are referring in fact to an aspect of our being that is soul. Soul and body are inextricably intertwined, as the poet Walt Whitman said back in the 19th Century, and this entwinement, as cellular biologist Bruce Lipton insists, does go all the way down to the cellular level. Soul has always been especially identified with the heart. (The heart, of course, moves blood, which is primarily water, which, in turn, has a strong chemical similarity to seawater. Heart–blood–water–the sea are thus all soul associations.) Case studies have been made about how heart transplant patients, for example, can strangely acquire memories or idiosyncratic tastes that are foreign to them in their own past. Apparently such memories and tastes are associated rather with the individual whose heart they acquired. In other words, there was also a partial transfer of something that we might wish to call "soul" in these transplant procedures.

All of this does not, however, imply a grossly reductionist view that would simplify soul to nothing but organs and the nervous system, to biochemical reactions and electro-chemical impulses. Rather, it suggests that soul and body are intimately interactive, as so much research continues to document. We can alter the brain's biochemistry by drugs of one kind or another that create mood changes, behavioral changes, and psychedelic experiences. Brain centers can also be stimulated with subtle electrical currents that will trigger changes in feeling, emotion, and mood, and that can also produce the equivalent of the psychedelic experience, or can call forth the actual emotionally-textured reliving of forgotten memories. Reversely, something impacting us emotionally, especially the stronger it is—an emotional trauma, for example—simultaneously casts its biochemical imprint on the brain. Psychosomatic illnesses are another example, as are the remarkable physical changes often reported of individuals with multiple personalities. Research has also shown that an intense practice, such as yoga performed by a master, can be consciously used to alter body functioning. Later, when we consider the etheric and astral levels of soul, we will realize that the body has another whole aspect to itself, the subtle body, involving subtle energies.

Soul, therefore, is that middle ground between body and Spirit (or mind—which is more associated with Spirit, as in the German *Geist*); it is the modality (of Being) where body and mind/Spirit are connected. (There are those who would insist on a definite distinction between mind and Spirit too, but we will not pursue this further complexity here.) Soul had been dropped out of the Modern picture in the Cartesian model of human being as but a duality of mind and body, leaving philosophers to ponder for centuries as to how they might be connected. The connection *is* soul—*psyche*. This is why we come to use the contracted words 'psychosomatic' and also 'psychospiritual.'

Soul is always projecting something of itself into consciousness out of the Unconscious, which is our darkness, which, again, is grounded in the body. In Christian terms, it so often implies our propensity to sin. But the less conscious *awareness* there is of soul, the more, then, it is forsaken in the Unconscious, and the more dangerous its potential for unconscious violence and outbreaks on a collective scale of mass hysteria and mass psychosis—namely, *war*. It is to a great extent because of repression, though, that soul remains in darkness, in the deep waters within us. What is our darkness, essentially? It is that which we do not yet fully know and grasp about ourselves, and so is, for that reason, a latent richness of life. But what we don't understand about ourselves and transform about ourselves into consciousness is what in turn makes us suffer, so soul is our private domain of personal suffering: *No one loves me, I'm just plain, My body isn't perfect, I'm a failure, I'm a loser, I'm empty, I'm helpless, I can't control my needs, I can't control my appetites, My addiction is killing me, I never get what I want, I'm never appreciated, Others are against me, I can never be fulfilled*, and so it goes, on and on. But once that suffering is addressed and through the effort of spiritual work—that is, through some transpersonal process—, it is on the way to being transformed, and we can come to realize a potential richness of new experience. Soul, when in the presence of Spirit, will express itself with curiosity and wonder and amazement, with sympathy and compassion for others, with love, joy, euphoria, and rapture…and with the rich ore for creativity. Soul, when totally inspired by Spirit, can become, in fact, a super-creative dynamo, and be *transformed*.

This is exactly where the distinction between Spirit and soul is most apparent. Spirit Itself does not feel curiosity or wonder or yearn for knowledge, or feel love, or joy, or euphoria, or rapture—Spirit is complete in Itself, is already all-knowing as Divine Intelligence in interconnected action everywhere; Spirit is already the interconnectedness of Love. It is soul that needs the Light of Spirit, it is soul that is inspired by Spirit and is transformed by Spirit. Perhaps the distinction is most clearly apparent here: It is soul that suffers (which is to be quite human), whereas Spirit never suffers, for Spirit is trans-human (That-which-is-greater-than-us). Spirit is the Fire, but it is soul that experiences the passion of it ('passion': etymologically, 'to suffer something').

When Tradition tells us that God has wants and needs, that God is angry or wrathful, or that Jesus suffered on the cross, then we know that we are not dealing here with the Absolute, no matter what the religious dogma. A "God" that has such anthropomorphic emotions is either a superhuman ET masquerading as the Absolute or some other spiritual being (Jesus, an Ascended Master) on a higher level of psychospiritual development than us, but not the Absolute. The Absolute, the Ultimate, Spirit as the One, for those who have had mystical experience, is supremely indifferent to all human wants and needs and emotions.

Another important understanding about soul is that, despite the belief of some that it is a virginal sanctuary that never undergoes change, soul is, on the contrary, profoundly changeable. Soul is as changeable as the Moon, which is why, again, mythologically, soul is associated with the Moon—again, the feminine. (Moon and Water: both being changeable. And also going back to the heart: the heart is absolutely classic for being changeable. If the heart were not so profoundly changeable, thousands upon thousands of novels, plays, poems, movies, and TV programs (think, soap operas) would have never been produced.) But this again is another reason why soul had a tight lid put on it: In dualistic, Piscean Christianity, masculine-defined Divinity was taught to be unchanging, immutable, untouched by time, one could always count on it remaining the Same, remaining True to What It Is, therefore was Perfect and Most Valued. (Curiously, at the same time, Spirit, as an aspect of the Trinity, was a supremely *active* principle.) Whereas soul, being changeable, therefore imperfect, played games with us, always wanting new things, new experiences, the heart desiring one thing one day, another thing another day. This changeable,

*Spirit and Soul* 103

fickle reality of soul Jung referred to and explored as the *Anima*. Now this reality of soul is of the very nature of the Earthly plane. Soul, in fact, was too much like this world and this Earth of impermanence, where everything is constantly changing, never remaining the Same. (Another fundamental Buddhist tenet—life is constant change.) Earth, no matter how beautiful and bountiful, was therefore condemned for its imperfection. We will explore more of this in the chapter on Gaia.

Let us now keep in mind that the words 'soul' and 'Spirit' are true symbols: And that is, symbols for modes of Being, not "things," not "substances," that we would—the ego-self—someday still think to pin down and totally encapsulate. As such, we can never translate them completely into words, because the Being-reality they imply transcends language. At the same time, however, as hopefully one realizes by now what it is we are doing here, they should not be left floundering as just empty abstractions. It is discouraging to realize that by and large people today have lost the ability to think symbolically, which is one of the outcomes of our contemporary, materialistic, nihilistic, and consumer-obsessed, Postmodern world. The realization must occur to us that we have lived in such abstract mental cages for centuries. It is as if we had been forced into metaphysical abstractness by our own Traditions. Now one of the best antidotes to abstractness that I know of today is art. Later, we will explore what the supreme Art of all arts is that still allows us to bring forth the richness that has been hiding in these words 'Spirit' and 'soul' to this day.

And what, then, of our constant reference to "Divinity?" For now, let us say that Divinity is the name for a state, a level, of Being, implying an Intelligence above human. This is not some Absolute Supreme Being of the monotheistic religions, but only implies a level beyond human—the status of being super-human (in various ways). At the same time, as we will see when discussing the Higher Self, there is still the implication of a *Self*, but on a metaphysical level.

We see then that soul is not a simple, metaphysical, abstract "something" that tags alongside of our life. Soul is many layered, and is the texture, the fabric, of our life's experience. We might further come to realize one day that soul is a Labyrinth that we are destined to try to find our way through. This is not to say, after all this discussion, that soul does not have a metaphysical dimension, which indeed it has—and we will come to see what that is—, but that dimension also potentially manifests its activity in the here and now, in *this* life. The New Age Vision, hopefully we begin to see by now, is no longer about keeping soul virginal for an Afterlife, or for any other life, nor is it the yearning for an abstract transcendence. To continue to emphasize an Afterlife or some otherworldly repose at this point in our evolution would be a serious mistake—more exactly, avoidance of what this life has now been elevated to. Some would say that it was a mistake to begin with, but then we saw that the Piscean Age, by definition, was originally an emphasis on the otherworldly. But what soul now yearns for in the dawning of this New Age is liberation within *this life*, meaning allowing Spirit to manifest and transform soul in *this life*.

Perhaps we should say something here regarding reincarnation. After all, we assume that belief in reincarnation is a given in New Age circles, and we would be remiss not to address it. I personally find that most talk about belief in the reincarnation of the soul is unsatisfactory. Certainly there is something profound here that can potentially enter our experience and enrich a full spiritual life, but, once again, it is too often just another abstract thing to believe in. To begin with, if reincarnation is just another "belief," then we are still back in the Piscean Age. The current notions about reincarnation come across as rather simplistic; we might even question whether any view, even the Eastern interpretations that make their way to the West, have yet grasped its full complexity.

I also find that the notion of reincarnation, together with that of karma, is subject to various self-righteous and self-rationalizing abuses. There are many examples: When someone says, *You weren't very enlightened to have chosen to be born into poverty and misery. Whereas the wealthy, the social elite, must be doing something right because they have chosen the best to be born into.* Or, someone will say, *You must have done something awfully wrong in your past life to be in this situation today. You're paying for it now, boy.* Or, *The lucky are always reaping the benefits of being "good" in their past life.* Or, someone might say, *This life is about me having fun now, since in my last life I worked so hard.* We also find that belief in reincarnation is used as a justification for doing nothing about social ills or the destruction of the biosphere: *What does society in this life matter…or what does it matter if there is nuclear war, my soul goes on somewhere else anyway. I'll just reincarnate elsewhere on another planet.* All such opinions only foster a spiritual rationale for social elitism, perpetuation of the status quo, fatalism, and simple apathy. Unfortunately, this seems to be a misguided influence out of India.

The New Age Vision would eventually deepen the popular notion of reincarnation into a more substantial view, and one that will emphasize living this life to its fullest, at our most passionate, creative, self-actualizing and self-realizing, with a true sense of spiritual responsibility to the Web of all life. Let the next life be a new venture when the time comes for it. Meanwhile, *in this life* soul wants to be recognized as something more than an abstraction. We really do need to grow out of, evolve out of, our lazy mental abstractness.

Spirit is now coming-to-us anew to liberate our soul, hidden in the Waters of the Unconscious. Is this not really another way of speaking about the wise traditional summons to "Know Thyself"? Early work in the cultural process that has prepared the ground for this re-visioning of liberation in the West was done by the first depth psychologists. Freud and his school helped us conceptually discover the Unconscious, however narrowly it was at first conceived. It is revealing that psychoanalysis was first known as the talking therapy. For talk is a form of communication, a bringing of something hidden into the open (Air). Psychoanalysis was therefore an early cultural form of the Water Bearer. Jung and his school greatly expanded upon Freud, throwing light upon all manner of complexes, exploring the more extensive reality of the complete psyche. Yet, all this, too, still, to this day, is only the beginning; the reality of the psyche—what we have here all along called 'soul'—is too often only acknowledged in a 50-minute session. Too often the conscious encounter with soul is hidden behind the closed door of therapy. And, we might add, therapy is not available to all—therapy costs *money,* which ties it in to a compromising societal System ruled by the Establishment. The New Age Vision proclaims rather that soul must come to be fully liberated into daily life for all, 24/7. This is more of the Good News of the New Age.

If Spirit is coming-to-us *anew* to help us liberate soul, then how might Spirit do that? Previously, in the West, Spirit, as it embodied itself in our religious Traditions, had presented itself as a repressor of soul, ironically, as we saw, with the intention of saving it. (This whole development began in the previous Age of Aries with Judaism.) In what way might Spirit today present Itself differently? What better way than in the *guise of soul*. Not *as* soul, for Spirit and soul, as we saw, are distinct modalities (of Being), but in the *guise of soul*. What I mean by this will become clearer as we proceed. I believe, though, that this is a most radical notion, scarcely grasped yet by others in the New Age movement, let alone having been sighted yet on the spiritual horizon. Indeed, this must be experienced for oneself in some way in order to see it clearly. Spirit is too often still conceived in the traditional Western way—Spirit as otherworldly, transcendent, masculine-monotheistically Divine, inspiring us when it does to set aside this world and set our eyes on some abstract Beyond. Even New Agers who might not be so blatantly Christian in their viewpoint, still assume this when they go on effusively about the Light and think that they can simply ignore and repress the Dark. That Spirit might come to us in (initially) the dress of the feminine soul to actually inspire us to bring feeling and desire and all the shadow complexes, all the subpersonalities and voices within us, into the world, into Air, into Light, would have been considered punishable heresy in traditional Christianity. It would have been considered of the devil. Now this liberating is not simply the gushing out of soul into surreal imagination, a turning on of the valve of the Unconscious (which is what the surrealists couldn't really get beyond), nor is it simple emotive venting, or a call to wanton licentiousness, but is a transformative, spiritual, in the occult sense, *alchemical*, process. Spirit is coming anew not for the sake of the salvation of soul (our long-term soul journey, we assume, *will* benefit from our efforts *here*), but for the transformation of soul *in this life*. Spirit is coming anew in the guise of soul *become divine*;

that is, our soul, this *soul potential* we have, through a transformative process guided by Spirit, can indeed realize its own Divinity. Then might soul be truly elevated to "Soul," our psyche become "Psyche."

We are now in a position to more fully define soul as a potential-to-become-That-which-is-greater-than-us. We cannot help but note that within this phrase is found the first part of our definition of Spirit. Soul, in other words, has within it the potential-to-become more Spirit-like. (As New Agers have often called it becoming a Light-being, the Ascension process.) Spirit in its coming-to-us is showing us that our soul can potentially become more likened to Spirit, and yet, still be embodied, but on another level. And so now let us define Spirit again as: That-which-is-greater-than-us-coming-to-us-drawing-us-towards-Itself. Again, keep in mind, this is a unified Being-process. One thing we must learn to do is develop the ability to think *process*. And now we reach a further development: Though we have explored and stressed how soul and Spirit are distinct modalities, that does not mean that they are utterly separate from one another; not at all, there is no separation ontologically, but a merging of the particular into the universal. For we will soon be discussing the "psychospiritual": Our potential-to-become-That-which-is-greater-than-us-coming-to-us-drawing-us-towards-Itself.

Earlier it was hinted that Spirit is, more than simply transpersonal (as transpersonal psychology emphasizes), but transhuman. Is it any coincidence that today there is emerging in the technological arena a Transhumanist movement? The further implications of this will be explored as we proceed in our Story. That the liberation of soul to be fully human implies simultaneously the potential-to-become, in a sense, more-than-human (as we have assumed being human to be), to become, again, in a sense, transhuman, is a startling, mind-boggling development in our discussion. A whole issue that must sooner or later be explored is how Spirit as an inspiration for soul in its potential-to-become spiritually transhuman compares to the technological Transhumanist movement. (This, we will see, will invoke for us the dynamic of Technos and Psyche, and how they are to be integrated in a New Age world that has not totally succumbed to Technos alone.)

Far from the Christian and Islamic repression of soul (and look at the deep repression still going on today in Islamic countries, especially with regards to the social suppression of women), we are now called to celebrate our feelings, our desires, our bodies, our darkness, to bring them into the Air of communication, into the Light of Spirit, with the help of the very hand *of* Spirit. Rather than feeling shame for our human nature, all that is human about us can be spiritualized, divinized. This is part of what is meant by the New Age intention of integrating heart and mind (soul and Spirit) and but part of what New Agers will call *Ascension*.

Much of the preparatory work of liberating soul (again, what some would refer to as confronting and working through our "lower self"), as we saw above, *has* been practiced in therapeutic circles for a long time now; much of what we have discussed so far is very familiar territory to them, even "old news." But still, today's therapy is quite honestly totally inadequate to what must take place. There is also the coming out of the closet in recent years of much that had been repressed or simply hidden away and not talked about, from child abuse, incest, domestic violence, sexual harassment, all manner of personal and relationship issues, dysfunctional health issues, to the open acknowledgement of diverse sexual orientations: All this is part of the cultural process of bringing into the open what was hidden in soul. Today, we find so much now openly talked about on radio and TV talk shows; the souls of many people have been opening up and sharing. However, all this talk, all this therapy, is still not anywhere approaching the greater, substantial cultural transformation that is needed; it is, to begin with, too Establishment conditioned, too safely contained in mass media produced programmed packaging, and spiritually starved. That is to say, it remains confined within a "therapeutic" or tightly controlled media context, insulated from other areas of life, and this would have to include the political world. What the Church had once repressed is now repressed by corporate mass media conditioning. We are still only in the first stages in the liberation of soul, for there is much much further to go. Our society has this obsession with sex in particular, which gets lots of air play, and which, of course, we all must come to terms with; but what of our subpersonalities, the other voices within us, the Self as multidimensional—does that too get air play? Do the talk show hosts have any idea what *this* is about? Is this all too radical to even address yet?

The whole coming out process (into the open Air) is a definite New Age-oriented development. What is generally missing, though, from all this already out-in-the-open talk is Spirit, which indicates the Postmodern schizoid character of our society. The exclusion of religion—or should we be very careful here and say for now, the exclusion of *spirituality*—from the public domain—the so-called separation of Church and State—only points to our need for a universal religion that will speak to everyone. I believe we see, though, in the New Age movement, the ground for it slowly being prepared, and we must hope to see the day when the full-fledged liberation of soul is truly Spirit inspired.

There is the view, especially when influenced, even unconsciously, by Postmodernism, or by secular humanism, that spiritual matters should be kept private. We are assured that everyone does have a right to their own personal "religion," whatever their connection to the Greater Reality might be, but it is best kept out of the public domain and not talked about. Cynically, it is often referred to as *Whatever makes you feel good*. I first met this attitude in my youth and could not understand how something as important as our spiritual life could be shut up inside our own interior world and not shared. This is another symptom of our contemporary cultural fragmentation. Spirit, revealing the universal Reality, must have an outer expression shared by others, if it is not to be simply reduced to subjective, personal feeling, or worse, our own, little, private fantasy. Spirit is actually what brings a larger life into community. But Spirit also radicalizes, and inspires change that is needed. How can Spirit do its work if it is shut up inside the head?

It might be the case that some in the New Age movement will find themselves somewhat confused by this whole discussion. They have emphasized the Light so much, transcendence and escape from this world so much, that this open liberation and exploration of the darkness within us seems contrary to all that they have aspired to. Throughout the 1970s and 80s this emphasis on abstract Spirit alone, expressed as a wish to transcend this gross density life, to somehow magically ascend into some higher density existence, usually following the example set by some ideal Eastern guru who sits in perpetual meditation, was quite apparent. This faddish enthusiasm for transcendent Spirit was most often the result of experiencing spirituality for the first time for those for whom traditional Sunday religion was stagnant, and no longer even meaningful. God was dead, but look—the guru has revived Him again! *Somewhat.* This, of its own, was a natural outcome, but what happened at the same time was unfortunately the old repression of soul. In other words, the old Piscean Age attempt to ignore the shadow side, the dark side, of us, in order to escape this body, this material life, was reinstated. Many were beginning to take a first step into the New Age, but they still had the other foot squarely within the Piscean. As we all know, this attempt by thousands of Westerners to imitate the Eastern way so often resulted in self-delusion, pretentiousness, frustration, failure, and ultimately confusion. Many in the New Age community are, though, slowing coming around to the notion that we do need to face and confront the shadow side of life and our body of desire. Only when that which has been ignored, repressed, forgotten, is brought into the open Air, as the symbol of the Water Bearer has been showing us all along, are we fully entering Aquarius. And we must remember that it is the universal human figure, who is *Us*, who will be doing the pouring, which is to say, we will be engaged in our own transformation. Of course, it requires the inspiration of Spirit to guide us (which is where secular humanism falls short). We will come to see how that guidance is being given to us in a new way, and we have yet to see the full implication of what the New Age Vision is revealing.

# ( 5 )

# HIGHER SELF:
# THE AQUARIAN DISPENSATION

*When we were children, we were taught religion appropriate to children. Now that we are adult, we want religion that can speak to adults.*

The major problem with our Western religious Tradition is the assumption it makes that all divine Revelation has been completed in the past, and by that is usually meant *the distant past* (but let us not forget the odd child Mormonism), and that all vital symbolism has already been established once and for all. For Judaism and Christianity, Revelation is literally a closed book—*The Torah, The Bible*. Islam in turn claims that Mohammed is the final seal of the prophets, all summed up and completed in *The Koran*. Spiritually, therefore, there is nothing creatively evolutionary for us today to do but to carry on the traditional rituals and beliefs year in and year out, as they always have been done, ad infinitum. This is the reason why religions are resistant to change—their claim is that the Truth has already been revealed, and that there is nothing to change about it, and that there is nothing we can do to add to it. But I would suggest that it is highly presumptuous to believe that Divinity[1] has already revealed all of Itself to us, and that it is disheartening to think that Its relationship to humanity is so firmly entrenched in dogma that it has gone stagnant. This, I claim, has become a collectively debilitating mindset. I see Divinity as supremely creative, in fact, the Fountain of Unlimited Creativity. The New Age Vision is the Revelation that we are not hand-me-down children of the past, but are now adults of a new dispensation. Divinity *can* reveal, and *is revealing*, more of Itself to us this very day. All Revelation is not in the past.

As we noted earlier, we are aware that some people cringe when they hear the word 'religion,' yet are quite comfortable with the notion of 'spirituality.' Religion, in the broadest sense, however, refers to the shared cultural form that our spirituality takes. To say, "I am spiritual, but not religious," is most often to mean that one has a personal, ongoing experience of Spirit (if indeed that is true), but one does not follow any particular, established religion because of all the limiting and negative implications of its institutionalization. But for spirituality to be shared collectively in a truly meaningful way it must take on some cultural Form, a Mythos, as we will see, otherwise it too easily remains a private experience among atomistic individuals in an alienated, Postmodern world. What seems to be a difficult notion for so many to contemplate is that new religious forms might in fact be possible—that a profound creativity may actually come into play in bringing a new encounter with Spirit into the world, an encounter that can collectively bring others in as participants.

This is the question, *Might there be a new Revelation for the New Age?*

With that said, let us continue to explore the possibility of new Revelation. If Spirit is coming-to-us anew to reveal new Divinity, then what might that Divinity be? Traditionally, the answer has always been *God*. We must realize that 'God,' however, is a heavily loaded word, and in some circles, it is an empty word. The word 'God' means different things to different people; it means different things to the different Traditions, and different things down through history.[2] The concept that the different Traditions have formed of God has an extraordinary range: from mystical notions of the All, the Highest Principle, the One, the Absolute, the Unlimited Light, Pure Consciousness or the Void, to Brahman, Atman, the Supreme Being or Supreme Power, the Supreme Lord, Lord Father, Yahweh or Allah, the God of Creation, Creator of the Universe, the clockwork God who set everything in motion and stepped back (Deism), God as the Universe itself (pantheism); and then there are such notions as "God is love" or "God is energy," and there is also the notion of multiple Gods, of course. Among this range is a personal God who created Homo sapiens, intervened in human affairs, and who has shaped, at least at some select point in our past, our history. All these versions of God are not exactly compatible. Christianity itself is beset with a fundamental contradiction—it teaches of a God who is utterly transcendent, complete in Himself, needing nothing, yet, at the same time, being a God who personally became involved in our history and who for some mysterious reason needs us to love and worship Him. Herbert Muller says, "This union [a transcendent *and* personal God], which has persisted throughout Christian history, A.O. Lovejoy describes as 'perhaps the most extraordinary triumph of self-contradiction in human thought.'".[3] (Again, we hear echoes of its Piscean character.)

But all this traditional speculation about God undoubtedly will be eventually transformed through the New Age Vision. For what is crucial here is how Spirit *is* coming-to-us anew. Spirit coming-to-us today as a new dispensation is coming neither to reveal to us the Absolute, the Mystical One, nor coming-to-us to reveal to us the Creator of the Universe. Neither of these notions would actually be a new dispensation. For such notions have already been dispensed in previous Ages; an extensive theology has already developed their themes. Spirit would have no evolutionary purpose to reveal to us today God as the Absolute. Such a highly abstract notion, accessible to experience only through the mystical encounter, is, to put it bluntly, irrelevant to the evolutionary crisis of our world today. By its very essence, mystical encounter with the Absolute can result in a supreme indifference and a life of quietism. (I will qualify this, however, by saying that the more common mystical, sublime feelings of a oneness with all life, of the interconnectedness of All, can most definitely alter one's life and life-style in a most positive way, particularly in developing a greater respect for all life. In *this* mystical sense is a vector into the New Age transformation of consciousness.) Lest we beat-around-the-bush about this, the Absolute is of the essence of the mystery of Being, but is not "God," at least not in the traditional sense of a personal "God" as the supreme object of faith and worship. I do agree with Nietzsche and just about all 20th Century thinkers on this: "God," in this latter sense, is effectively dead. When someone starts to talk to me about "God," I honestly have no idea what that word is supposed to mean; obviously there are traditional definitions to fall back on, but anymore, they are all just abstract words.

Neither does Spirit have a need to reveal "God" the Creator of the Universe. We can find one early version of this in *Genesis* of the Old Testament, as well as finding it in the religious mythology of practically all peoples. Consider that today cosmologists are not only theorizing about our universe, but also about plural universes, parallel universes. Is our local universe "God" the creator of only our universe then? Or is "He" the Creator of all of the other universes too? This, in itself, poses wildly speculative theological questions of its own. Yet, still, to put it bluntly, some abstractly imagined Almighty Creator of all Universes is quite irrelevant to us human beings in the here and now, and to the current crisis on our planet. There is simply no longer a need to believe in such an inflated fairytale of a "God." What would be the existential purpose at this point in our evolution?

Is Spirit, then, revealing to us the "God" who intervenes in our history? In a radical way that invites us to see *this* "God" through new glasses, the New Age Vision does suggest that there is another interpretation here. The God of history has come under a new suspicion recently, as to whom this "God" in fact was. Yet, God as the traditional Lord who intervenes in our history is not in itself alone the new dispensation being revealed today.

If Spirit is involved in our evolution, which is the premise behind the dispensations of the Ages, then Spirit coming-to-us *anew* must be revealing some divine knowing that has actual relevance to us, that engages us, in our evolution. Here, Tradition is in fact our guide. We have always been taught that we contain a spark of Divinity within us, that a part of us *is* divine (usually in reference, as we explored earlier, to an abstract soul), that we are, in essence, spiritual beings. Simply put, it must mean then that we have a higher nature, however buried it is within us. Of course, this was always referred to in an obscure and abstract way, as if it were something too powerful or dangerous to fully acknowledge, but, if, now, today, we were finally to take this seriously, then we must come to realize that there is indeed here a hint of a higher image of ourselves. The Aquarian dispensation is, most succinctly put, the coming-to-us realization that we are the existential expression of a Higher Self, which, looked at it from today's ego-self perspective, means that we *have* a Higher Self. In other words, we are much more, something far greater, than only an ego-self subjectivity. Indeed, there is such a higher potential within us (as we remember, soul is our potential-to-become) that we might eventually—yes, however long that "eventually" must imply—come to realize ourselves as Divine beings in our own right. This, in fact, is the supreme Good News of the New Age. This is today's Advent, the coming, on a collective scale, of this Revelation. New Age spirituality is grounded in our experience with Divinity within us, which is to say, *our own* Divinity, our own God-self—*our Higher Self.* Now some may wish to call it the Christ-self. And for those who feel uncomfortable with the whole notion of "Higher," we can also refer to it as the Larger Self or Transcendent Self, which is often the translation of Atman (from Hinduism)—again, none other than our God-self. We will come to realize, no matter what others may wish to call it, that this indeed is a revolutionary notion for us in the West.

The East, of course, has known of this notion of the Higher Self extensively already, millennia ago, yet the Eastern dynamic (as expressed in Hinduism) between Atman and ego-self has emphasized the process of ego detaching from its attachments to the world, seeking thereby to merge with the transcendent Atman (mysticism once again). That, at least, is the intention epitomized by the guru and yogi master (for the Buddhist arhat, it is ego-dissolving nirvana that is wanted). The contemporary Western thinker Ken Wilber, who is quite savvy about these matters, still seemed to idealize this aspiration for ultimate Atman, any lesser aspiration being but a side trip of the "Atman project," somehow a dodge from the ultimate goal.[4] I cannot agree with such a view, however. It is an almost complete denial or self-deception of what human beings are actually about in this world, as the Paths of the soul are many. I do not make judgment on people for somehow dodging the "goal" of enlightenment, as if humanity en masse should all be sitting around cross-legged in perpetual meditation striving for ultimate ego extinction. To claim that Atman enlightenment, Eastern style, is the ultimate goal in life comes across as a spiritual elitist view that has the tendency to set up the guru as the ideal human. To me, there are many types of "ideal" human.

Spirit coming-to-us to reveal to us our Higher Self emphasizes the direction opposite to that emphasized by Eastern transcendence—it is that the Higher Self is to come into, and manifest in, *this* world more and more, by embodying Itself in an evolving New Self in *this* world. Spirit is coming anew to help us take that next step in our evolution, that of engaging the Higher Self, not as a contemplative escape from this life, but as transformation of this life. The evolutionary intention is that of bringing all the vast Invisible into an increasingly complex, multidimensional Human Reality.

Those who extol the spiritual accomplishments of holy India, claiming that there is nothing especially new for the New Age to discover, have apparently not taken a good enough look at life there, in India. An oppressive caste system is still in place, millions live on the streets in squalor while yogis sit in bliss contemplating Atman, while Hindus perpetrate violence against one another and remain in violent conflict with Muslims—I would suggest that India has not yet reached the pinnacle of spirituality. To separate spirituality from everyday life, including a society's everyday culture and its Establishment, would be to miss the whole message of the New Age Vision. Let us put it this way: Indian philosophy/religion excels at abstract spirituality, but we are called to *change life itself.*

I am well aware that someone well studied in Eastern philosophy and is perhaps personally involved in a yoga practice or Buddhist meditation for some years will smile at our discussion here, thinking how an upstart New Ager could have anything new to say about the Higher Self. The Eastern sages, we are assured, have explored it all already, and have it all mapped out already, so there can be nothing really new under the Sun. For so many reasons already stated, I cannot accept such a view. For one, we cannot belittle another the right to pursue the Path creatively anew by saying that past Masters have already been there and done that, that some Tradition has already said all there is to say. I would suggest otherwise, that there is a tremendous future in our co-creative engagement with Higher Self, and that we, as human beings, are certainly called to continue to evolve.

New Age spirituality is no longer then about projecting the ideal of the solitary, contemplative life, whether Western or Eastern, with its goal of the traditional notion of Enlightenment, even though that Path will always be available and honored for those who resonate with it. The New Age Aquarian intent is quite literally embodiment of the Divine for the sake of transforming our total being-in-the-world, consciously becoming the midwives of the *collective* evolution of humanity. The current global crisis of mass extinction underway calls for nothing less.

The Higher Self, we come to realize in our Moment-of-Vision—for those of us who have had such a Moment-of-Vision—, is our own Divinity. This becomes for us now our highest notion of a living, *personal* God. In turn, some of the ETs who appear to us as superhuman beings can still quite reasonably be referred to as *the Gods*. We now begin to see in a double sense why we were always traditionally enjoined not to attempt to know Divinity directly. For Divinity, ultimately, is our own Higher Self, which is the most powerful and radical illumination that can ever come over us. That we can potentially realize within ourselves a state of Divinity! This was much too explosive of a notion to be disseminating to the people. Soul was not to realize its potential-to-become divine state, but was to remain pathetic and sinful, therefore, dis-empowered. Yet, there was another sense to this taboo against knowing Divinity firsthand. For Divinity first of all implied the Gods, but through the ancient monotheistic revolution, the experience of Divinity was consolidated into a one God, with awe-inspiring, fear-inspiring, epithets: the Absolute, the Supreme Being, the All-Knowing, the All-Powerful, the Infinitely Great. The Gods kept themselves well hidden after a certain point in our evolution; the monotheistic "God" also kept Himself very well hidden, lest we came to learn who this God in fact was. (We will explore more of this later.) That which we do not understand, which we cannot accurately identify, has, then, that much more power over us.

The Higher Self is transpersonal, it is a state of superconsciousness; better yet, it is revealed as *levels* of superconsciousness, which is a radically different notion, going in a totally opposite direction, than the psychological idea of the Unconscious or subconscious, which, too, are posited as realms much larger than the everyday ego-self. The Unconscious, actually a confused notion with multiple meanings, we might first of all say is the dark background to our everyday mental functioning, in the Freudian sense; the continuously ongoing, countless thought processes (quite literally expressing all of our frenetic, complex brain activity) we are not aware of, that are either subconscious (meaning that with some effort can be made conscious, or that for a second or two, spontaneously, come into consciousness, such as in the semi-sleep, hypnogogic state) or that remain fully unconscious; this includes our reservoir of memory, our underlying desires, our dream life, etc. Much of this is what we have referred to as the darkness of soul. Freud saw the Unconscious in this reductionistic, even materialistic (as brain activity), way—a seething cauldron of the Id; hardly a place therefore where some "Higher Self" would be found, let alone trying to find God in there. And this is despite the fact that both Freud and Jung saw the Unconscious as the new metaphysical concept/realm, in a world where traditional transcendent metaphysics was no longer possible (that is, via Logos). The Unconscious, in the strictly psychological sense, is a prepersonal stage, coming before the development of the personal ego-self, so is lower on the evolutionary scale, as Ken Wilber has taken so much time to explain. The ego, *as a stage in our evolution,* must first emerge and develop out of the Unconscious (as a simultaneous descent of an archetypal, monocentric showing of Spirit) before the Higher Self can emerge and develop and embody *Itself,* at least in human consciousness.

Even Jung's notion of the Collective Unconscious, which is defined as "transpersonal," (another way of saying "metaphysical") and is itself subject to confusing interpretation, is not, per se, what we are referring to as Higher Self. First of all, Higher Self is not an unconscious realm; it is a superconscious *Self.* Jung said he had conceived the Collective Unconscious as containing "the whole spiritual heritage of mankind's evolution born anew in the brain structure of every individual" (which is but one of many quotes in his repertoire). Clearly there is an emphasis here on the past, the Collective Unconscious being a sort of repository of archetypal forms that are simply collective—experienced by millions upon millions of individuals upon Earth in the past—, so is not truly transpersonal in any superconscious sense; they are forms that our psyche draws from, tied into our genetics. (Again we find, however, that somatic foundation for soul.) Spirit, however, is clearly beyond our heritage, embracing past, present, and future, in a transtemporal, transhuman superconsconscious; it introduces novelty—*futurity*—into Human Reality. If we look to Jung, we might think to consider his notion of the Self (capital S), the complete archetype of human being that merges with the "God" experience, to find something of a clue to our notion of the Higher Self. Yet, at the same time, we must be careful not to think that Jung's Self concept is synonymous with our concept of Higher/Divine Self, as Jung's Self concept includes our satanic, evil, unconscious darkness. He seriously kept wrestling with the traditional dualism of God and Satan, and tried to meld them together. But such a Self concept as his would only muddy our experience of Higher Self as new divine Revelation.

Now this notion that we have a Higher Self is not taught at all in our major, conventional, Western religions. It is not taught at all, period. To suggest that we have a whole dimension—multi-dimensions, actually—to our self that could truly be considered Divine Self? In the past, that was labeled heresy. We have been brought up to believe that we only have that self we all know, the ego-self, as is; only Jesus had a Christ/God-self. True, there is the traditional notion of a divine spark within us, referring to the soul, but we already saw that this notion was relegated to abstraction, and that that divine spark had more relevance to an Afterlife, not this life. We are therefore compelled to turn to Eastern and esoteric traditions to find teachings about this notion of the Higher Self. Ancient Gnosticism not only knew of, but precisely promoted teachings about, this notion of the Higher Christ-self. A legitimate question might be, Why is this then the new dispensation? First, keep in mind that the notion of our own Christ/God-self was considered a heresy, and so was suppressed, as Gnosticism itself was utterly suppressed, in fact, almost literally wiped out completely, in our Western Tradition. Therefore, this notion of the Higher Self was not yet a dispensation for humanity at large. Also, our notion of the Higher Self has broader, more radical, and more precise, implications than the ancient one, as we will see. Most importantly, however, is that its time has come—we are now ready in our evolution to properly receive and begin to assimilate this higher image of ourselves.

The immediate criticism that Fundamentalists level at anyone who dares to suggest such a higher notion of human being is often this: It is sheer blasphemy to believe that human beings might be directly connected to such a Higher Self, a God-self, that might claim to be equal to "God." Who do we think we are? We are only, merely, human, after all. According to them, we have no right to think of ourselves in such a higher sense. We are mere "creatures," separated from "God" by an infinite chasm. It is, as they see it, the self-inflation of humanity, a grandiose hubris (which is the criticism leveled at humanism, after all); it is taboo to think of ourselves so highly. But the message of the New Age is that no longer must we view ourselves as limited, shameful, sinful creatures, which was the accepted view of us at the height of the Piscean Age; we are now about to celebrate a higher image of ourselves. And no longer must there be placed a ceiling on our spiritual aspirations and to what extent we can evolve. Our Judeo-Christian tradition, through the conditioning of doctrine and dogma, did just that, placed a ceiling over us, a glass ceiling, if you will, through which with imagination we could see beyond, but against which we could not rise. (We will come to see, in fact, who might have set this in place.) More commonly put, there was a supposed infinite, unbridgeable gulf between us and Divinity—Divinity was utterly beyond us, utterly transcendent; we were but finite creatures mired in matter and limitation, mired in perpetual sin. The New Age Vision proclaims the Good News that we *can* evolve to the next spiritual level, the next level of our Divinity, and that we *have a cosmic right* to evolve a larger, more enlightened consciousness.

The criticism of the Fundamentalist misses its intended mark if it is not kept in mind that it is not the contemporary humanistic ego-self that is being inflated here with grandiosity; what we are presenting, rather, is that the ego-self has an evolutionary telos that is divine, that soul is our potential to ultimately become divine within an evolving Human Reality. The irony is, however, that in our Postmodern world the ego-self has become, in fact, a little god of its own. Though we dare not think of ourselves as in any way divine, the profane ego-self of our society finds itself basking at the center of all things, usually meaning a capitalist's wet dream of money and material things. In the Modern world, the ego began acquiring a taste for an unlimited will to power, of course still held in check by the control systems of religion and law, and more recently, the monetary system, but ultimately only held in check by the power plays of other ego-selves. The ego-self, for example, in the capitalist system, is allowed to grab all the wealth that it can acquire, all the material things that it can buy up, all the power that it can manage; and all things, in turn, have come to be measured by an ego standard. Since there is no, quote "scientific proof" yet of any Other Intelligence, the ego only relates to other egos. So the ego-self now struts in its narcissistic finery on the Shakespearean stage of the world. Everything has become translated into entertainment value for the ego—all events, relationships, culture, ideas, knowledge, the natural world, the metaphysical world, that is to say, anything that might be presented to the ego, the ego is now in the almighty position of whimsically accepting or rejecting any of it, and then of course going on to the next thing. Some might still say that we have a soul. *But who has a soul?* It is the ego-self, once again, that decides it has, that it owns, a soul. That is why in our Western Christian Tradition soul has taken on the role of just tagging along in our life. After its moments of self-intoxication, the ego-self, however, sometimes sobers up and receives a chiding from Tradition— *Little god, who did you think you are? You are but a mere creature. You could meet death at any moment.*

Now the phrase 'Higher Self' per se is but an abstract notion. But with the New Age emphasis on direct, firsthand experience, we are called to develop a concrete relationship to our Higher Self. And there are any number of ways in which it can begin to indicate Itself to us: through psychic ability, intuitive understanding, uncanny synchronicities, peak experiences, epiphanies, Visions, psychedelic experiences, in kundalini awakening, OBE and NDE experiences, through living symbols and living spiritual ideals, in channeling, or developing a personal relationship with the Jesus Image or other Self-Realized Master, or with our own Spirit Guide. These latter indicators of the Higher Self are in fact the real key to making it concrete. That our Higher Self can present Itself to us, relate to us, as a Living Image, a living Divine Figure, and not strictly through peak or ineffable experiences, is of the essence of New Age spirituality. When we say that the New Age implies a new relationship with Divinity, what is meant is that not only is the Higher Self being revealed, but that it is showing Itself to us in a new way, in a new form, in a new figure of Divinity. I will share in another chapter how this new figure, the Living Image of our Higher Self, has shown Itself to me. Let us continue to keep in mind, it is direct, firsthand experience, *gnosis*, and not Authority, that is our basis for understanding in the New Age.

One phrase that is being used to describe the initial encounter with the Higher Self is 'spiritual emergence.' Often, it refers to the overwhelming, mind-shattering impact that the Higher Self can make on the unprepared ego-self. Some find it extremely difficult to handle, as it can parallel a psychotic episode in certain ways. The kundalini awakening is well known for this. (See Gopi Krishna's personal account of his sudden kundalini awakening and the psycho-physiological havoc it brought into his life.[5]) Spiritual emergence means that the little self is being torn open by the impact of the Greater Reality of Spirit, that Spirit is making its presence known by showing us our Higher Self. This experience of suddenly being torn open, of having one's mindset shattered, is a key indicator of the influence of the astrological planet Uranus, which happens to be the ruling planet of Aquarius. It is this Uranian lightning bolt into our life that can announce the coming of Spirit, which is that psychospiritual process of That-which-is-greater-than-us making Itself known.

One failure in not developing a proper enough view of the Higher Self is that it is not taken in a "high" enough sense. For example, I will have a conversation with someone who accepts in principle the notion of a Higher Self, but who will then go on to say, *When it comes down to it, though, I can only trust in God, not in myself.* The person obviously does not have the Higher Self properly in view. The dynamic expressed here by such a person is still that between the little self (*me* as the ego-self) and "God"; but what happened to the Higher Self? The Higher Self got pushed off to the sideline somewhere; in other words, it was given lip service to and left abstract. "*I can only trust in God*" properly means from the New Age perspective, *I can only trust in my Higher Self.*

Let us consider another example here that will bring this change in our understanding of "God" immediately home. Found on all our USA money, as we know, is the phrase "In God We Trust." How, then, should we reinterpret this? It can now mean either one of two things, or still, perhaps, ambiguously both: First, "In the Higher Self We Trust," which is the less likely implication, considering everything we have said above about the Higher Self, that such a higher image of ourselves is, as of yet, scarcely on the radar of the mainstream. More likely, though, the reinterpretation would mean: "In the ET Father We Trust." The ET Father of us, the superhuman ET God at the foundation of our Western religions, makes traditional sense when still referring to the assumption of, and belief in, a personal "God."

Who, then, do people pray to when they pray to "God"? There is no doubt that prayer can be powerful and can be effective. That prayer does not always bring about the outcome we wish for, however, is certainly most fortunate, given the conflicting agendas among peoples on this planet. (*I pray to you, God, please destroy our enemies.*) But who is at the other end of prayer? I would suggest, then, the Higher Self. For it is the Higher Self that knows past, present, and future; it is the Higher Self that sets into play manifestation of intent; and it is the Higher Self that knows better than the ego-self what is possible and what is appropriate for manifestation. But, again, there is a complicating other possibility. Other Intelligence may also hear our prayers once we realize that the Mind Field of the Invisible is alive with other beings. Other-dimensional beings in destiny with us may also be answering our prayers.

That billions of people still today believe in "God" does not prove, of course, that there is any such "God" as they believe, but it does more than convince us of our legitimate metaphysical need, for we are after all spiritually destined beings, and, equally as important, it does indicate our ancestral knowing that there is indeed an *Other* in the cosmos—Other Intelligence. In the New Age, we must assume, people will still have the freedom to believe as they wish, but as more pieces of the puzzle of the Big Picture fit into place, a more coherent wisdom system—the coming universal wisdom religion, as I see it—will have unfolded that individuals can, not so much merely believe in, but open up into for their spiritual growth. The coming New Age universal religion can in this sense be likened to the Internet—it is not that millions of individuals globally have to believe in the Internet, rather, it is a recently evolved cyberworld that they can connect into for any number of reasons; they tap into it, they access it constantly, the Internet thereby becoming integral to contemporary life. Connecting to the Higher Self would imply therefore our ability to access the metaphysical Internet—the universal Mind Field. Those who have developed their psychospiritual connection to this invisible Internet, which is their own relationship to the Higher Self, will come to know firsthand what is and is not true regarding theological matters. They will come to know firsthand what has been the Tradition's delusions and what Spirit is really about. What I see over time, despite impressions to the contrary still today, is that our traditional notion of "God" is destined to become further eroded in the masses.

Yet another example of this linguistic slippage between "God" and "Higher Self" we might comment on is a recent series of bestselling books titled *Conversations with God*, by Neale Donald Walsch. Though the title of the series is obviously attention getting and turned out to be a good marketing ploy, it would be quite reasonable to suggest that it is not "God" in any traditional sense that he is referring to, that is, channeling, here, but more accurately the Higher Self. I would suggest Walsch is offering conversations—which I wholeheartedly support—with his own Divine Self, his Higher Self. Now what if he were to have titled his books *Conversations with Higher Self*? Would they have had the same impact? If not, why not? The lesson here, and this is what I am getting at, is that we have not yet reached the point of fully appreciating the profound implication that our Higher Self is the new "God." It is apparently still more compelling to fall back on the traditionally charged word 'God.' Yet, that "God," the traditional "God," is dead.

It is here that atheism can be assimilated into the New Age Vision. Now the atheist might still object, *Okay, it appears that you agree with me that the notion of God is defunct—that there is no such "God" as Tradition claimed. Yet, you still insist on talking about "Spirit," "soul," and some "Higher Self" notion. A true atheist is a materialist—in other words, there is no autonomous realm of Mind, but only the brain. True, a rather extraordinary organ, at that.* Without going into all the subtleties of an argument here, I would suggest addressing the atheist in this way: The atheist admits that the brain is a most extraordinary bioelectrical organ, and does not claim—or should not claim—to know all that there is to know about it. We have, of course, much more to learn about this brain of ours, and for us, still, it does function, as "God" was said to, in mysterious ways. What the New Age Vision suggests here is that more of the brain can be accessed and developed and used in radically new creative ways than ever before imagined. After all, techno intelligence amplification will soon be enhancing the potential of our brains. Who can say what liberating more of the brain's—and for that matter, our body's—potential—aka our soul's, potential will open up. We should keep in mind that we will be suspicious of any view, any position, that appears to limit us in our creative potential. When it comes to liberating our creative potential, I do not think I have heard of any atheist saying that we cannot *go there*. Atheists of a strong materialistic bent too often try to intimidate us with mere bluff: claiming to know more about the brain, invisible, subtle energies, hyperdimensions, the paranormal, than they in fact do. As a matter of fact, it turns out they hardly know much at all.

But can we prove the existence of the Higher Self? Ah, such a traditional trap, is it not? Addressing such a question would turn out to be as futile as the traditional attempt to prove the existence of "God." There is no rationally proving the existence of the Higher Self; if there was, philosophers would have accomplished that long ago. (As we hinted before, we are no longer believers in the old dream of Logos, whether of the traditionally philosophical or religious persuasion. The old dream of Logos—that is, to be able to rationally prove (via philosophy) any metaphysical truth, or to simply believe strong enough (as in religion) that you possess the Truth. The new Word, I will claim, is Mythos.) But what about empirically proving the Higher Self through science? Here again, we would need to start with prior questions, like, What counts as empirical? Is empirical defined within a materialistic paradigm? Can the Higher Self be quantified and measured? Good luck. But what there is *is* experience, and the Mythos spoken as a result of that experience. We can either accept the experiences embodied in the vast spiritual literature that has been passed down to us through the ages, which, I would think, is certainly worthy of consideration, or we attempt to experience such a reality as Higher Self for ourselves. Best, perhaps, is that we begin to experience the reality of Higher Self in the context of one of the guiding Traditions (but not thereby embracing Tradition as the last word). But to attempt to rationally interpret our experience from a traditional Logos perspective isn't going to build the bridge we need. Rather than Logos, it is a revitalized Mythos that will build that bridge of interpretation, with a follow-up Logos (rather than endless deconstruction) then taking the cue. I remain wary of any view, then, that might be construed as a possible denial of our right to speak Mythos, which implies a new respect for creativity on the most profound level, as we will see.

Given, then, some experience of our own and/or from our studying the spiritual and occult Traditions, we come to know that the Higher Self passes through different planes of consciousness. Various systems have mapped out these planes and have ascribed to them various names. Summarily, and I admit, simplistically here for my purpose, there are usually said by the various Traditions to be seven major degrees of consciousness that are themselves categorized in groups, with various subplanes among them all. As different systems use different names for a few of them, there can undoubtedly be confusion here. Commonly, though, we hear of these: Physical, Etheric, Emotional (or Astral), Mental, Intuitional (or Buddhic), Spiritual (or Atman), and Divine (or Logoic). The levels are more broadly categorized as Gross, Subtle (with low subtle and high subtle), Causal (with low causal and high causal), and Ultimate (Atman, "God," Divine, "the Logos" (I purposely put this in quotation marks.)). Again, Ken Wilber has done an admirable job of providing a detailed schema of them from his extensive studies of the Traditions.[6] But then, these are not all the classifications and names that have been passed on by Tradition. The seven chakras also figure in to these classifications, and there is the complex system of the Kabbalah, or Tree of Life, from the Jewish occult tradition, and there are any number of others. Up to this point in our evolution, we have tended to take the word of the various Traditions on all of this. Whether these maps, however, are adequate for all time is seriously open to question. But to question them, to make the attempt to critique them, to decide if the classifications are fully adequate, without firsthand experience of some kind, is of course futile. Without firsthand experience, how could one presume to make assessments? But let us not make that more of an issue here. It is enough to know for our purposes within the limitations of our Story here that the Higher Self does pass through various planes of consciousness. We will refer to those that are relevant to our Story. What we must always keep in mind, though, is that these classifications are but models to work from to guide us to our own firsthand experience. That is ultimately what is important: It is our firsthand experience that confirms, that transforms, that potentially makes all things new. To simply recite a neat schema is not my real purpose here.

To come to know firsthand the full extent and ultimate, highest level of the Higher Self—who has attained this? It remains open to question whether mystics or yogis or Self-Realized Masters have in fact attained it, as it might have traditionally been assumed, or even avatars as renowned as Buddha or Jesus. I am aware that to even pose this question is considered heresy in some circles—and I am not referring only to Fundamentalists. Though an avatar might have been supremely enlightened for his time, does it necessarily follow that this applies to all time? Now to make judgement calls about any particular, assumed enlightened individual should not be our intent; it is certainly not my intent. On the spiritual Path, if one is truly involved in its *process*, you discover that such concerns become irrelevant, simply beside the point, it really doesn't matter.

The highest level of the Higher Self undoubtedly merges with the highest notions we have of God as the Absolute. The important realization, however, is that the Divine is no longer utterly beyond us, no longer in an ontological category utterly transcendent to us, but is existentially contiguous with us in the Great Chain of Being—we are indeed intimately at-one-with the Divine Archetype, which is our own Higher Self. The Aquarian dispensation is this total realization, but, then, is more specific: What will be opening to us in a concrete, accessible way is primarily Higher Self that manifests as the Next Level to our current ego-self. It is this coming of the Higher Self on a level of closer proximity that reveals to us the Living Image we are beginning to experience. It is this Living Image that is coming, as I suggested earlier, in the guise of soul. We will be exploring this in more detail in Chapter 7.

There are many, many questions to be raised here. One is: Does the Higher Self present Itself to us in any sense like a person? After all, the essential reason why Christians relate so well to the Christ archetype is because it presents itself as the Living Image of a person—*Jesus*. We will find that the Higher Self does indeed present Itself in a personal way, but in a much more complex personal way than what mainstream Tradition has offered. Similarly, the very name Higher *Self* implies a type of selfhood. This is particularly so when we consider that the Higher Self in its coming-to-us today is showing us, not so much abstract, metaphysical levels of divine reality, but the level just beyond the Veil, where our soul begins to show its potential multidimensionality, where our personal Archetype, the Who-I-AM in this life, is active. The Living Image of our Higher Self is our own coming-to-us Self-Realized Master(hood)—our own spiritual Guidance.

There are many tough questions here; we will not be able to address them all. But there is another we might ask: Is the Higher Self, then, my personal "higher" Self, or is it the Higher Self Archetype for all humanity? First of all, when we consider the transpersonal states beyond the Veil of separation, we must realize that they are inherently collective. What is "mine" and what is common to all is no longer distinct. (After all, "mine" is a reference to ego; we are talking here beyond ego, or at the least, the Transcendental Ego beyond the everyday ego that creates our experience.) A greater interconnectedness happens—"All is One," we hear it said. The Higher Self is ultimately the Archetype of all humanity, what Tradition wanted to call the personal "God." Or, we can look at it this way, since we are suggesting that a relationship to the Higher Self is comparable to a Christian's relationship to Jesus, implying that since Jesus is transpersonally available to all, so is the Higher Self transpersonally available to all. That is to say, a Christian does not protest, *I pray to **my** Jesus, you have your own Jesus.* No, Jesus is the same Jesus for all Christians. Yet, at the same time, a relationship to the Higher Self does reveal my personal Archetype, that is, my own soul makeup, the Who-I-AM, in this lifetime, and what my life purpose is. And that is exactly the natal chart of astrology.

To summarize our Story at this point: For the sake of ego development, soul was for centuries repressed, kept as a naïve, undeveloped soul. Increasingly, in the modern period, the danger was that the ego, coming into its unrestrained glory, its own little godhood, coinciding with the breakdown of monocentric systems of control—traditional Western religion—, still had tagging along the naïve, unevolved soul. Unfortunately, the high and mighty ego, expressing infantile or even adolescent emotions (in the evolutionary scale of things), is disastrous. Violence is unleashed on the world. War is unleashed on the world. Hell is unleashed on the world. (We will see that Technos develops as the ego's alter ego Superpower, allowing for even greater Hell to be unleashed.) The Aquarian dispensation, however, is the Advent of the saving power of the Higher Self now stepping in to show ego its proper place and what the next evolutionary lesson will be. *And soul?* Soul is that individualized, embodied potential of the Higher Self that now wants to be realized. Soul wants to realize itself even within the lifetime limitation of this 3rd-dimensional body; that is to say, though we yet live within this 3rd-dimensional reality, within a body, within the short span of a lifetime, soul can yet be transformed in the Light of Spirit, which is the Advent of Higher Self. (Now the very idea of a lifetime as a short span is currently undergoing change. Not only are so many more people living longer, but new life extension technologies, we are told, are just around the corner—we may literally, in fact, develop the potential of becoming virtually immortal. *Like the Gods*.) This transformation might actually be considered an ascension—to what has been called 4th density Reality, and higher. It is again the heart (soul) integrating with the mind, particularly the higher mind, the intuitive mind, of the Higher Self that births a New Self.

Now that soul wants total liberation from the repression of the past, the Higher Self is making Itself known as our Guidance for that liberation. The wallowing of a Postmodern ego in the muck that soul keeps oozing through the cracks of repression is destined to be transformed once Spirit again enters the picture. And Spirit, which is exactly the coming-to-us existential encounter with the Higher Self, is no longer of masculine exclusivity; rather, it is coming-to-us especially now in a feminine guise to be the Liberator of the traditionally feminine soul. How this is beginning to occur is the discussion in the chapter on Psyche, where I will share my own Vision. In essence, though, the Higher Self is androgynous, but the coming of its feminine appearance—to put it simply, the return of the Goddess—is the countermovement to the long history of the masculine exclusivity regarding Divinity. We agree that the move that was taken in some churches in recent years to refer to "God" as He/She has been on the right track.

The notion that we have a Higher Self *is* radical. Postmodernism, as it is represented in our schools, universities, corporations, in the worlds of science, technology, entertainment, mass media, sports, in the everyday work place, does not recognize the Higher Self. We would be living in a completely different world today if that were not the case. We might pose the question: What major 20th Century thinkers even suggested that we might have something like a "higher" Self? Teilhard de Chardin might come to mind, Carl Jung another, Rudolf Steiner in the early part of the century, but how many others? But once the idea of a Higher Self is suggested—*if it is suggested*—, it immediately begs for elucidation. Again, our religious Traditions indirectly have had some notion of the Higher Self, but in a way that rendered it impotent, non-empowering, abstract. When religions speak about Spirit, Christ, Buddha, or "God," they have been indirectly referring to the Higher Self; however, today, this indirect, abstract way is no longer good enough—we need to be able to talk about the Higher Self in as direct a way as we can. (When Hindus talk of the God-self Atman, they, of course, do not beat-around-the-bush: Higher Self *is* Atman.) For our relationship to the Higher Self is today the most radically transformative one there is.

What Postmodernist theory is sorely missing is any notion that even remotely resembles the Higher Self. (Even the most influential Heidegger had never come upon in his thinking any divine dimension to human existence. He wrote early on about authenticity, then later of "poetic dwelling" on Earth (both notions to be absorbed into New Age thought), but neither yet suggests the implications of the New Age evolutionary intention.) The self-imposing limitations of critique regarding what-is or what-has-been can only take us so far; we equally need to behold what-can-be, what-is-possible, for any intellectual work to be truly liberating. Postmodernists would have us hanging in the lurch. They leave us with nothing to orient ourselves to in the Big Picture; to them, there is nothing that can shine for us as a beacon of Light. Heidegger, again, who was himself a precursor to Postmodernist theory (who so many Postmodernists are indebted to), still held open the notion that we would be addressed anew by Being. In the last interview he gave before his death, he was more poignant: He is quoted to have said, "Only a "God" can save us now." Of course, what he might have meant by "God" is fully open to interpretation, given that his whole philosophical opus took an atheistic stance. Most importantly, the implication here is not lost on anyone with a New Age Vision.

Discovering the Higher Self, developing a relationship to it—which is none other than being on the spiritual Path—, is a whole other expository work of its own. We might say a few things more, however. First, it is not as though we start to get in touch with the Higher Self and then magically everything in our life is smooth sailing from that point on. Now I am aware that some would love to hear that, but we will have to disappoint them. The Higher Self may reveal things to us that we *do not* want to hear, or see, that we do not want to experience, period. It may take us upon a Path that is counter to everything we have been conditioned to believe. We may in fact find ourselves asking, *Why am I going through this?* The Higher Self, as we said before, may shatter the little godhood of the ego-self in order to show it the Larger Reality it had not even suspected. Yes, epiphanies of Higher Self can be mind-expanding, exhilarating, euphoric, a wondrous, inspirational high, that we would want to have last forever. But our relationship to the Higher Self has its own vicissitudes; for stretches of time, we may come to experience abandonment by the Higher Self, the "dark night of the soul." This is tied into the whole dynamic of Time, which astrology teaches us to read. The various religious Traditions offer an extensive experiential literature on the spiritual life that we can now reinterpret in the light of our own experience with Higher Self.

What is revolutionary about the whole notion of the Higher Self is that our connection to Divinity is closer than we have realized. Yet, at the same time, the traditional belief might creep back in that the Higher Self may still seem to be utterly beyond us; that it is still remote, abstract, beyond comprehension, immense, multidimensional, indifferent—how could we ever relate to it concretely? And it is not as if we can turn on a switch to Higher Self anytime we want. That impossible gulf between humanity and "God" that Tradition had dogmatized is claimed by Christianity to have been bridged by Jesus Christ. The New Age Vision of the Higher Self, being a transformation of Christianity, has therefore a similar dynamic. A concrete Living Image, as we will see, promises to be the stepping-down manifesting into Human Reality of the seemingly impossible heights revealed by Higher Self.

The Higher Self satisfies our need in the West for a strong concept of the person. After all these centuries of ego development and of building a society based on the notion of individual personhood with individual rights and responsibility, we should not see any relinquishing of this evolutionary intention in the New Age. The question is, Now that we have come this far, now that the isolated ego has reached its limits, beyond which hubris is committed on our planet (and has already been committed on our planet), where does evolution take us next that preserves, at the same time transforms, the self that we have gained? The Higher Self introduces the idea that the individual now has a higher purpose, keeping intact the value we already place on individual personhood. This is the individuation process that Jung wrote of. And this is why the Eastern religious existential orientation does not satisfy us, with its weak, if not indifferent, notion of personhood, and why so many Westerners who embrace at some time in their life Eastern religion/philosophy so often wind up returning to their roots and cannot help but continue living an ego-oriented life.

The Higher Self will thus be our source of empowerment. We have heard so much in recent years about self-empowerment. Even the business world talks about self-empowerment, but we can be sure it is the ego-self that is being referenced. True self-empowerment can only fully be established from the true powerhouse of Self—Higher Self. The Higher Self, therefore, will prove to be our genuine source of existential strength. (As will power was for the early Christians.)

What we crucially need to challenge today is this notion almost universally accepted that human nature is something fixed, set for all time. For example, we are all aware of the assumptions so many make: That human beings are by nature fearful, greedy, power hungry, are attracted to and awed by violence, that we have a propensity to hurt others, and will, especially if it is possible to get away with it. The mainstream thrives on these assumptions: *It's only human nature.* But the origins of these assumptions that so many believe are fixed—even considered rights by some—are buried in darkness. Those who take them as rights (e.g. we have a right to be greedy) will often say, *But we are only being human, after all, the System allows me to be greedy as a human.* Now there are social analysts who will say that it is indeed the power structures of the Establishment, of the System, that valorizes such alleged rights. They contend that it is the structure of how power is socially accumulated and managed that must be changed. I certainly agree with that. But too often the critical theorists talk as if critique alone is all it takes. (They critique, but rarely do they offer the actual Vision for change.) For we know very well that power structures are not going to be changed by scholarly critique, no matter how many brilliant books are written, and no matter how important a role critique does play in a free society. And today's power structures are not going to be changed by old-fashioned political revolution either. (Did we not learn our lesson in the 20th Century?) They are also not going to be changed by any kind of activism that lacks a true Vision. We must realize that power structures will only be changed through a transformation—revolution—in consciousness that is guided by a Vision that *is then* acted upon. And this, I suggest, will only happen today through intervention—that of Spirit coming-to-us anew (the Vision of Higher Self) in conjunction with the coming once again of *the Other—Other Intelligence.*

The conventional Jesus that we have known through our churches did not go far enough with his radical ideas. (The implications of what Jesus might have actually taught have undoubtedly been compromised by orthodoxy. The Gnostic gospels found at Nag Hammadi, Egypt are full of suppressed teachings.[7]) Our conventional Jesus could not have realized that people 2,000 years in the future want liberation in *this* life, not in some Afterlife. Yet, to be fair, we must place this Piscean Jesus in his evolutionary context—he was an avatar par excellence for the Piscean dispensation, with its original emphasis on otherworldliness.

Aquarius itself connotes the higher mind, the beyond the ego-intellect-rational mind (the Virgo mind that the Modern world had developed); it is the higher mental aspect of the Higher Self. The higher mind is a collective Mind Field that links all minds outside of our space-time limitations. We might also call it simply Mind (capital M), or Mind-at-Large. The planet Uranus, as we have already noted, astrologically rules the sign Aquarius. Anyone gifted by Uranus knows the experience of brilliant flashes of insight, meteoric streams of thought, new ideas seemingly popping out of the Air, quirky intuition, psychic intuition. This is why Aquarius is not only the sign of mental genius, but is also the sign of astrologers and other sundry psychic workers. Uranian energy will blast through the conventional mindset walls of the conditioned ego-self and offer suddenly thrown-open windows of far-seeing intuition into the higher mind where all is interconnected, where what is new—what is about to be born into the world—can be seen. (More of this will be explored when we discuss The Next Level.) This Uranian brilliance is the lightning quickness and power of the inspiring action of Spirit.

That a possible avatar yet to come could be crucial to the triggering of the dispensation of the Higher Self in the collective masses of humanity is not to be dismissed out of hand. (Exactly the same can be said for our encounter with ET races. Such an encounter in an open, public manner would have tremendously profound impact and would be crucial to the Aquarian New Age dispensation.) However, the Aquarian dispensation is not dependent on the traditional notion of waiting for an avatar, a Messiah, to do our spiritual work for us. To put it bluntly, those of us who have received our New Age Vision are no longer waiting, period; we are living that Vision *now*. A Lightworker is one who is not waiting for the Messiah to arrive, but one who is actively bringing Light into the world *now*. The Aquarian dispensation reveals that each one of us is an avatar to our self, for each one of us can encounter the Higher Self firsthand. Each one of us is potentially a Christ, in our *own* way, as the esoteric traditions have always said. To the Fundamentalists, these are truly radical, heretical ideas, which is one reason they will project such fear about the New Age. But they have locked themselves into the mindset of a narrow religious paradigm whose days, despite appearances to the contrary, are increasingly numbered. Someday that mindset is fated to be Uranian blasted. Even the Fundamentalists might someday discover freedom outside their mental cages. For the coming New Age religion is not about having the correct beliefs that are really the bars of a cage, but about developing an ongoing relationship with Higher Self that throws the doors of our cages open.

In the meantime, Christians who object that the Higher Self is still limited in its reference to the merely human, that Jesus is beyond such a notion, that "God" the Father is beyond it, are still not giving the Higher Self its just due—they are not considering the Higher Self in its highest sense, that it does merge with the traditional concept of "God." Conventional Traditionalists are still enamored, in a deep, collective, unconscious way, of the non-human ETs who once appeared to us as divinities, then as the one "God," back in ancient times. The merely human, in contrast to the superhuman presence of these ancient astronaut ETs who could perform spectacles and miracles, is never good enough for the Traditionalists. But if they still object, *No, No, our faith is of the one, true, Supreme Being*, then I'm afraid they are likely speaking about an abstraction that no longer has any life in it.

From our new perspective, the encounter with Jesus that Born Again and evangelist Christians enthuse about is now seen as their naïve encounter with the Higher Self, and, in fact, with only one face of the Higher Self! Born Again Christians who proselytize after their conversion experience with Jesus are actually sharing their exhilarating firsthand encounter with the Higher Self, but interpreting it through the safe, traditional, codified image of Jesus, or, in Jungian terms, through the Jesus image of the Christ archetype. Yet, Jung himself already claimed decades ago that the traditional Christ archetype was waning—no longer speaks, no longer is a Living Image—for great multitudes of Moderns, and, increasingly today, and we should say obviously, for Postmoderns. This is but another way of saying that the Age of the Fish is passing away.

As I come to a close on this chapter, I can hear a criticism that says, But you've merely been assuming that Higher Self will make itself known, that it will be accessible, to those who are open to it. But what if it doesn't happen? Even setting aside the question whether it is, in fact, a reality at all, there is no guarantee that Higher Self will show itself to increasing numbers of people as an Aquarian Age dispensation, or to any particular individual, for that matter. This whole discussion could be a delusion, a metaphysical fiction at best. It could be said that the only "Higher Self" we'll see in the future is AI, and those superhumans who will be linked in to it will then perhaps experience it as their "Higher Self." But to give you (that is, me) some credit, it is true that metaphysical fictions can envision tomorrow's technology. Yes, indeed, that is an insightful criticism. And yet, there is still the experience of gnosis, and there is the co-creative process of *Mythos*. Our Story only becomes more interesting and more complex…

For those of us who understand what the initial encounter with Higher Self can be like, the Born Again experience of conversion makes perfect sense, only we see it now through new eyes. However, the full-on experience of the Higher Self is much more in addition—the traditional images can no longer fully contain it. I will share my own experience in a following chapter.

In the spiritual wasteland of a Postmodern world, left as we were with no divine gyroscope to existentially orient us, it is the Advent of the Higher Self coming-to-us (our preliminary definition of Spirit) that can once again regain for us our bearings. The Higher Self, as we can see, is the New Age answer to the nihilism of Postmodernism.

# ( 6 )

# Our Psychospiritual Evolution

*Upon a weathered shore we sleep.*
*O why is it so long we must sleep?*[1]

Do we evolve? Do we continue to evolve? Though the theory of our past biological evolution is standard textbook biology today, almost nothing is said about our psychospiritual[2] evolution. Scholars might theorize about how Cro-Magnon man must have psychologically developed to become the current Homo sapiens sapiens, or what profound changes must have occurred to transform prehistoric hunters and gatherers into sedentary agricultural peoples who almost overnight (in the historical scale of things) developed burgeoning civilizations. Julian Jaynes in *The Origin of Consciousness in the Breakdown of the Bicameral Mind* develops a theory of how consciousness arose even in relatively "recent" ancient times. But there is a widely accepted assumption that since ancient times we have become set in our human nature. We have always been this way, we will hear it said. Our traditional Western religions all take human nature as a given: We have always had this ego-self, these same mental functions, these same feelings of love and hate and greed. We have always been, and always will be, "sinful." The assumption is that human nature cannot be changed, and that we are forever limited in the way that traditional thought still conceives of us today.

In contrast to all the world's major religions, even those that teach of reincarnation, I am aware of only the New Age Vision that highlights our collective psychospiritual evolution. One complaint we hear so frequently today—another indicator that ours is an Age of Disorientation—is the general lack of Vision, a lack of the Big Picture, of who we are and where we are going. That, it may not be realized, is an implied indictment of all of Tradition, both Western and Eastern. For if any Tradition claims to offer that Vision, it is nowhere apparent. To say that we evolve—continue to evolve—is to begin to provide a foundation for that needed Vision. Do those who would question whether we do evolve provide us the needful Vision?

*But do we need to evolve…any further?*

Before we proceed, someone might seriously ask, *Why do we need to evolve any further? Why can't the ego-self remain at the level it is at?* First, we—the ego-self collective—do not control the evolutionary process, as if we thought we could hold back its momentum and say, *Okay, we like where we are now, this is enough.* Of course, those who thrive on wealth and power probably would think this; but even those who sit comfortably before their TV, or go to big sports events, or love strolling through their local shopping mall, probably think this also. Isn't this now the high point of human evolution? But we've already discussed the global crisis that the collective ego-self has brought upon itself. The ego-self, as we have said, is at a Postmodern dead end. Now the tech world is not holding back on its reins at all—it keeps pushing forward the dictates of Technos at a manic pace. If the ego-self assumes it is the master of Human Reality and is at the center of all things, it will someday soon find itself rudely confronted by AI. The ego-self must evolve if it is to survive the impact of AI, let alone the ego-shattering impact of Other Intelligence.

I am well aware that from the Postmodernist point of view this Great Story I am newly telling as the New Age Vision (more accurately, this is the preparatory Story for the New Age *Mythos*), this *metanarrative* as they would call it,[3] is highly suspect. For the Postmodernist, it is no longer possible, or, better yet, appropriate, to attempt to tell any Great Story, to paint any Big Picture, of who we are in this cosmos and where we are going. I disagree, which is another reason why I am not in the Postmodernist camp. I disagree, above all, if but for this one, fundamental reason: that it is a denial of the universal expression of our creativity, in particular, our fundamental right to mythmake—or, as I prefer to word it nowadays, Mythos-make—(of which I will say more later).

Now, this is not to say that there are no storytellers of a new Great Story coming forward. Go on the Internet and search "Great Story." What you will find is that, by and large, these new storytellers are scientists and science professors: especially cosmologists, astrophysicists, evolutionary biologists, perhaps a few ecologists; there are also the techno writers projecting their Story into the future. To them, the new Great Story, the Big Story, primarily tells of cosmology, the Big Bang beginnings of the Universe going forward billions of years, to the formation of the planets and Earth, the long road of biological evolution, leading up to our current global civilization; or scenarios are painted of our Technos-dominated future. That is all fine and good; we would expect scientists, for example, to be qualified to talk about the cosmological Big Picture. But scientists assume that the Great Story is solely their prerogative to tell; and so what of poets, artists, fringe topic researchers, spiritual visionaries? The shortcoming of leaving it up only to scientists is that their vision is limited, as they leave so much out of the Story; they dare not bring up metaphysics, astrology, psychospiritual evolution, ETs/Other Intelligence, MELE, geoengineering the planet, or Secret Government agendas. Most don't even reference the Transhumanist future. Almost all scientists, especially university scientists, are beholden to the Establishment, to grant money, so they will only tell the Story that is acceptable to the Establishment. Any possible Thread of the Great Story that smacks of controversy they completely ignore. They do make (obligatory) references to the stories told from old myths and the religious Traditions, but have no understanding of Mythos.

By "evolution," let us work with this rough definition: When the hidden, latent potential within a system, a whole (a holon), (such as a living being) is allowed to develop into outward—and for Human Reality that is worldhood—manifestation, thereby bringing into play a system/whole/holon to another level of greater and richer complexity. When that system is a human being, better yet, humanity-at-large, then we are talking about manifestation not only through the human body (the biological Thread), but the human body with an expanded self-consciousness, so that more of what is potential within us (what I have called *soul*) is in conscious play. (There is included in my view of evolution also something *Other,* that is to say, some Other Intelligence, which will become apparent as we proceed.) We will not quibble with those who would say that all this talk about evolution is only from our human perspective, that the idea only started in the 19th Century, so it is all human relative. Why would we even argue with that? Our would-be critic would miss the whole point though: Our focus *is* precisely Human Reality, which includes the whole notion of worldview, in the Here and Now of Human Reality. If others wish to debate whether the Universe itself evolves, or whether evolution takes place in the other dimensions, or among ET races, or from some Absolute point of view, they are of course free to do so, but that is a whole other speculative venture that they should realize the Postmodernists have legitimate issues with.

From the New Age point of view, we are not the same as ancient humanity, and not only that, but we *have been* evolving throughout this last 2,000-year period, the World Age of Pisces. Now everyone might say, Yes, we have *changed,* there is no doubt about that—socially, culturally, scientifically, technologically, but psychologically, spiritually? And not simply changed, but evolved? Some might object by pointing out that the 20th Century had been the most murderous century in history; they might point out that Jesus's message has still not been learned. Cynics will point out that a power elite controls and manipulates the world's masses, and that they have no qualms about destroying any who get in their way. Is this then evolution? Others point out the destruction of Earth's ecosystems by the collective Modern and Postmodern behavior of humanity, or point out that racism and sexism are still very much alive today, or point out the history of the U.S. government's horrid treatment of Native Americans. There are of course so many other examples that we could mention. Can there be denial of any of this? Yet, I do not believe this makes a closed case against our psychospiritual evolution.

Let us look at the alternative views. One would say that we, on the contrary, are devolving—everything about Human Reality is going downhill, and is only getting worse. This is a rather perverse, if not a psychologically self-inducing pessimistic view, where every development, or we would have to say, simply, *change*, in civilization would be viewed as a wrong turn, a flaw, sending us into an ever downward spiral. Would this then include the Rights of Man, the American Constitution, independence from colonial empires, Civil Rights, women's rights, modern conveniences and amenities, our modern elimination of most diseases, our scientific breakthroughs and new understanding of Earth's place in the universe, our new global high technology, our rich history of the arts, and so much else? We would have to ask those who take such a view, What is their starting point of a once highly evolved humanity? And by what criteria do they judge evolution or devolution? We are well aware of those in the New Age community itself who idealize and romanticize some supposed ancient enlightened humanity that possessed the keys to all wisdom and lived at one with Nature. However, when they are questioned about this view, they are usually not quite sure what ancient humanity they are actually referring to. Certainly it would have to have been some prehistoric civilization (such as Atlantis), of which we know how much? I have heard that there are those who apparently believe that the hunting and gathering stage of humanity was life in paradise, and that everything after that was a mistake.

Perhaps what those who take some such view mean, however, is that the overall balance tips today on the side of things getting worse; therefore, a grand narrative of the evolution of humanity is not justified. Their underlying assumption with this more modest position is that if we are evolving, then everything should always be getting better, right? But, it is unreasonable, if not naïve, to assume that. We know from firsthand experience that those on the spiritual Path often find that their life gets more difficult, more challenging, not easier. Our collective psychospiritual evolution proceeds likewise—it does not imply that everything "gets easier and better" consistently, continuously. On the contrary, our view is blunt in saying that there are serious life-and-death challenges, struggles, crises, along the way; that the road of evolution is indeed filled with obstacles, and is treacherous, *and* there is never a guarantee to those currently living that in their lifetime it all comes to a happy movie ending. (Those who perish in wars certainly wouldn't think this.) Our world today, we have admitted, is in crisis, serious, mass extinction level crisis, and we have already discussed what this implies.

When we say that we cannot continue down the road we as a civilization are going—seemingly contradicting our view on evolution—, what we should be clear about is the complexity packed into that statement. There are many Threads woven into a civilization; they are not all favorable in an evolutionary sense, and they are not all favorable in any long-term sense. So what is meant here is that to continue down the currently status quo mainstream road *is* destructive and *is* undermining the sustainability of life on Earth. Many of its Threads had their purpose in the development of the Modern world, but it is now time, with the self-consciousness we have gained in recent years, thanks in large part *to* Postmodernist thinkers, to redirect that road. It is time now to move in a new direction. *Because Spirit* is directing us to move in a new direction. Again, there are apparently those, and even scholars among them, who feel that the road we have taken in the West was a wrong one to begin with, that this was not evolutionary at all. Unwittingly, they express a naïveté by believing the road we took was something that *we*, a supposedly fully conscious, ego-self collective, somehow mapped out ahead of time and decided to travel. On the most fundamental level of our existence, the ego-self picks and chooses nothing, but is utterly conditioned by its world. As Heidegger elucidated in *Being and Time*, we are *thrown into* a world situation that is not of our making. We must always work with what is given us, with what is given by Spirit, and by Powers greater than us. (A whole chapter of our Story, not included within the limitations of this work, would again be a philosophical explication of a new relationship to Being, out of which this whole Story emerges.) The mistake is always to overrate free choice, especially when it comes to our worldly conditioning, to idealize what is possible in an abstract make-believe and not really be grounded in the context of actual existence.

Another viewpoint on evolution is that neither takes place: We neither evolve nor devolve, but essentially remain the same throughout history, and so that the changes we do see—the rise and fall of peoples and cultures, the vicissitudes of war and peace, the unfolding of scientific discoveries and new technologies—, are all but surface phenomena leaving our fundamental, existential Human Reality unchanged. Or a variation on this view is that there are cycles of highs and lows in the human Story; there are Golden Ages followed by Dark Ages, but the overall human equation will always equal zero. Naturally, everyone will choose his or her favorite high point of civilization. In the halls of traditional academia, historians will often hold up 5th Century BC Greece, Greece's Golden Age, as one of these peaks of civilization. (But they did have slaves, didn't they? And the status of women?) Naturally others will counter and say that the Greeks of that time had already lost the previous, even further back, ancient wisdom.

The outcome of all this is that such views fall short of the needful, unifying Vision of who we are and where we are going *today*. "Needful" means that we now need such a Vision as our gyroscope, as our beacon, or we wallow in confusion. Which is exactly what is happening to the great majority of contemporary humanity. Civilization is currently adrift with no Vision of what the evolutionary direction is—which is exactly our Postmodern condition. Or, we could say, the only evolutionary direction appears today to be that offered by the techno-world—Technos and Transhumanism.

To clarify thus far: A civilization may indeed decline, may even destroy itself, or be destroyed by major Earth changes (e.g. the great Flood of prehistory), or even by that once-in-a-few-million-years asteroid hit, but that does not preclude that the psychospiritual evolution of Intelligence on Earth was underway. In the bigger picture, our evolution is ongoing, and sometimes it does take the bringing down of a decadent or dead culture, a waning civilization, for a Renaissance filled with new spiritual inspiration to blossom once again.

The New Age Vision sees an evolutionary intention working at the heart of humanity. This intention comes to us via Spirit. If we accept the notion that Spirit is in an ongoing relationship with humanity, then that relationship must have an evolutionary intent. Spirit is not coming-to-us so that we can remain status quo, simply living life the same as we have always done. Spirit has no respect for what is called normalcy bias. It is of the very nature of Spirit to inspire change in us. If Spirit comes-to-us periodically—and we speak not only of World Ages, but any number of shorter timed astrological cycles as well—it is to inspire us to move forward toward a richer, more conscious, more evolved, existence. As human beings with an ego, our existence has a fundamental future orientation, whether that future reference is tomorrow, next month, next year, the next 10 years, or, as was envisioned in the Modern Age, some indefinite futurity. Even the cyclic agricultural civilizations of the ancient world thought in terms of Nature's ongoing yearly round, and lived in accordance to it. In fact, we might see that all spiritual values help move us forward on our Path.

Spirit, considered as an "inner" reality, would appear to imply that the impetus for our psychospiritual evolution comes from within; it is consciousness itself changing from the inside outward. Yet, another view will object: *No*, it has been outer influences that have changed us, not only by way of the obvious ups and downs that civilizations go through, such as war, empire building, trade development, climate changes, plagues, migrations, voyages of discovery, but even when it comes to religion, we find examples: the outer influence of Gods coming down from the sky, of avatars walking among men and women, of a Yahweh revealing Himself to a people. The new UFO perspective on history theorizes about Ancient Astronauts who visited early humanity and taught it all the arts of civilization, clearly an outside influence. We see then that there are these two sides of the evolutionary coin: an inner transformation of consciousness that periodically occurs, and an outer reality that impacts us, either forcing or inspiring change in us. What is so often missed is that both sides of the coin are necessary. The New Age Vision views our evolution as a *bi-transformational process*, an interplay between outer influences and an inner, archetypal, psychospiritual movement inspired by the timed cycles of Spirit. An interplay, meaning that the outer influences and inner movement do not just happen haphazardly and out of sync, as it were. The outer influence, happening as divine intervention, ET visitation, highly charged symbolic events, in addition to the more numerous, well-known, prosaic movements of history, is always mirroring the changes that are about to unfold, or are currently unfolding, in consciousness. Succinctly put, the outer symbol/reality mirrors the changes of the inner world. (We might suggest here a new twist on the old phrase *As above, so below— As without, so within*.[4]) We could go into a long story here to show how this has happened consistently throughout history. Let us look, though, at two broad examples following one another chronologically that directly relate to World Ages themselves. Let us look at the Age of Aries and the Age of Pisces in terms of their original dispensational inspirations.

First, however, it would be helpful as we proceed to consider an important theological distinction that has been hovering in the background of our discussion all along. "God" as the Absolute is undoubtedly not the "God" of history. This confusion has been the contradiction at the heart of Christianity from its beginnings, referring back to the quote from Herbert Muller. It was a contradiction engineered, sort of speak, by the early Church theologians themselves when they grafted Greek philosophy onto the "God" of *The Bible*, specifically the Old Testament. In the Old Testament, "God" has a very busy involvement in human affairs: This is the "God" of history, a notorious, personal "God" who, at one point, abandoned us. "God" as the Absolute is a wholly different conception; it is the highly abstract notion of transcendent, timeless, immutable, impassive, beyond-form, formless Being needing nothing, affected by nothing, that is only potentially encountered through the mystical experience. To address "God" in this sense as *the* Supreme Being is philosophically incorrect, for it posits "God" as *a being*, no matter how supreme and absolute, among other beings. The Absolute is ontologically not a being at all, again, no matter how "supremely" some would want to define it. (That "God" is omnipresent—which is another traditional attribute of "God"—well, so is energy omnipresent, which, then, for many people today, has reduced "God" to mere energy.)

The "God" of history, undoubtedly having been the appearance and intervention of the superhuman Other, could stand-in and masquerade as the Absolute, the Ultimate Reality, for a certain stage in our evolution, but it is time for us to open our eyes and realize that the emperor has no clothes. Especially from our new UFO perspective, as we will see, these theological notions need to be kept quite distinct.

The Age of Aries followed upon the Age of Taurus, which, briefly, was a time when consciousness was still bonded to the tribe and in bondage to Nature. More precisely, consciousness was in an unconscious bondage to Nature, the Great Mother, as Ken Wilber has explicated in *Up From Eden*. Humanity had not yet in the Age of Taurus (circa 4,500 – 2,300 B.C.) the modern type of psychological ego that defines individuals as having their own sense of self-identity. Human beings in the Age of Taurus could not know of individual selfhood, for this requires an ego and a society built around the recognition of the ego (remember that "the without" conditions "the within"). Tribal consciousness is Other oriented in a prepersonal way, so is not self-oriented, not personal. The tribe is the focus of identity for all of its members; and the tribe, in turn, has relationships to all the different Powers of Nature. It is that stage of consciousness that first unfolds before the personal ego-self emerges. (There will always be those who romanticize that first stage, however. They would seem to prefer to live in this state of childlike "innocence" before the burden of selfhood set in.) The Age of Taurus undoubtedly began with an animistic orientation, which then developed into polytheism, in which various Powers could speak through Nature, but were separate and independent of Nature. They were Powers in their own right—Gods and Goddesses. In such a situation, consciousness is enthralled to various competing Powers, implying that consciousness cannot really unify about a central point (an ego) with an identity of its own. It is with the dawning of the Age of Aries (beginning approximately 2,300 B.C.) that augured the birth of the ego archetype and its cognate the *hero*. This was the New Age dispensation of that time. The hero/ego archetype was making its ascent into consciousness—the "spiritual emergence" of that time—, and the outer world was now providing significant triggers for it to happen.

The Age of Aries was the time of the Old Testament. In the Great Story that is told there, the Israelites have found themselves befriended by a God named Yahweh (whose identity we will explore later); this God commands them to have no other Gods before Him. He commands them to worship Him as their one and only Lord, the one, true God. We witness here, of course, the celebrated birth of monotheism. And this God, their Lord, was warlike, wrathful, and jealous, all characteristics that we might find in the fiery eyes of a war God. (Aries happens to be a Fire sign, ruled by Mars, God of aggression and war.) The symbolism of Fire is found repeatedly in the Old Testament. In Deuteronomy, Yahweh said that "the Lord your God is a devouring fire, a jealous God" (Deut. 4:24). During the episode in Exodus where Moses encounters the Lord in the burning bush and pleads with Him to tell him who He is, "God said to Moses, "I AM THAT I AM." And He said, "Say this to the people of Israel, 'I AM has sent me to you.'" (Exodus 3:14) Now the phrase "I Am" happens to be the supreme exclamation of Aries, for in astrology Aries refers to the discovery and birth of the ego, the birth of self-identity: *I am*. It is no mere coincidence that monotheism was born in the same period as the emergence, the birth, of the ego. Rather than mere coincidence, this has profound psychospiritual significance. It was the Arian dispensation: What Spirit—That-which-is-greater-than-us (Yahweh) coming-to-us—dispensed, as the new metaphysical orientation, which initiated a whole psychospiritual process.

Yahweh wanted to be the One and Only God. He wanted to be the Best, the Greatest, the Most Powerful, the Most Feared, and the Most Loved. This wanting to be the Best, the Greatest, the Most, is unmistakably an Arian complex. So is it also any mere coincidence that He had such a distinctively Arian personality in the Age defined as Aries?

We can begin to see then the correspondence of outer, numinous events and the changes that were happening in consciousness. Yahweh, the self-proclaimed one "God," the Supreme Lord, displaying the strong Arian characteristics of Fire and Mars, has chosen one people, the Hebrews, and is mirroring for them the birth of their own self-identity as one people, and more—their own individual egos. Yahweh appeared as the Big Ego, symbolizing their individual, fledgling egos. The Hebrews were at that time emerging out of their bondage to Nature, represented by all the Gentile tribes still worshipping any number of a pantheon of Nature gods. (The Gentiles were undoubtedly beginning to discover their egos also, but the Hebrews/Israelites were destined to have the significant, cutting-edge, metaphysical connection here. In theological studies, this is called the "scandal of specificity": How is it that "God," standing in as the Universal, the Absolute Reality, instead of addressing all peoples equally, at all times, as we would think the Universal would do, would choose rather a specific person, a specific people, a specific time, to carry out "His" Plan.) This emergence out of unconscious bondage to Nature did not happen, of course, overnight; even for the Israelites, there was much backsliding to the previous polytheistic rituals (e.g. the Golden Calf) as the Old Testament itself relates repeatedly. (Note also that the Ram, symbol of Aries, has come to replace the Bull (or calf), symbol of Taurus, as the proscribed animal of sacrifice.) But the trigger was there—a chosen people were now told to heed one "God," who was to be their one and only Lord. A starting-to-unify ego, a crystallization of ego, it could be said, was emerging out of unconsciousness to form one, singular, highly charged relationship to a one God who symbolized precisely that ego emergence. No longer was there to be tolerated in the tribe numerous relationships to numerous Gods and Goddesses, with consciousness dispersed among them, with loyalties of intention meted out in various directions, so that an ego of singular self-identity could not coalesce, but now a covenant was made with one, supreme Lord who epitomized their own, growing sense of singular identity. Again, this was the Arian dispensation. A singular relationship passionately nurtured (as the supreme Judaic commandment states, *You shall love the Lord your God with all your heart, and with all your soul, and with all your mind*) can only inevitably strengthen the psychological development of self-identity (That-which-is-greater-than-us-coming-towards-us-drawing-us-towards-Itself: the Revelation of I AM THAT I AM: the Super-Ego in the sky). It was as if the experience of the outward reality of Yahweh literally pulled the latent ego potential out of its unconscious matrix and into the Light of existence: into the Light of *Yes, I Am!*

Here, as succinctly as it can be stated, is the principle: Our psycho-spiritual evolution is a bi-transformational process of the interaction of inner world and outer world, with the outer world always presenting the symbolic, numinous, paranormal trigger. Ken Wilber states, "...sometime during the 2nd and 1st millennia B.C. the exclusively egoic structure of consciousness began to emerge from the ground unconscious and crystallize out in awareness." That timeframe is squarely within the Age of Aries. And it was within this period that saw the emergence of the hero myth, which is the myth par excellence celebrating the achievement of the ego's newfound position within Human Reality. Classical Greek civilization also fell within this Age (its latter half, Libran phase), and its most famous myths sing of the exploits of heroes: Achilles, Odysseus, Hector, Agamemnon, and dozens of other heroes in the Trojan War of *The Iliad*; *The Odyssey* of Odysseus; Jason and the Argonauts; and Hercules, among others. The Age of Aries was a time of extensive heroic warfare; the celebrating of the warrior, with the shedding of blood, was a given way of life. Permeating *The Iliad* throughout was the terror but also the glorification of war. Visitation by aggressive ET Gods who began to appear on the Greek scene brandishing new weapons of violence and domination was undoubtedly the trigger that helped set into play the emergence of the Greek warrior heroes. The Old Testament, too, is so filled with rape, carnage, and destruction that we find it hard to reconcile major portions of it with any notion of it being the Word of "God," or even yet, from our perspective today, a spiritual, a sacred, book. Consider, though, that after the Israelites prevailed over the Egyptians, Moses exulted in a song, *The Lord is a man of war* (Exodus 15:3). In other words, the Lord was truly an embodied archetype of Aries.

We must note this, however: At first, it was only the warrior heroes, warrior priests, kings and queens, and other select individuals, who were coming to realize their distinct ego identities, and who even presumed to directly address the great Gods. The greater numbers of humanity of the time were not yet allowed the privilege of thinking that they were in any way special. As a matter of fact, it is not mere hyperbole to claim that it was not until the late 20th Century that this privilege was extensively realized. (Consider the long battle it took to secure civil rights and women's rights.) And the further back in time we go, say, to earlier Egypt, the fewer and fewer were those select individuals.

The Age of Aries waned as the Mediterranean world passed through a transition period before the new Age of Pisces received *its* dispensation. This was the Hellenistic period, a time when the peoples of classic civilizations are said to have grown world weary, when new religions and cults were mushrooming everywhere in compensation, when people were crying out for redemption from the widespread violence and decadence of the time. As we approach the First Millennium A.D., Rome was a hotbed of cults, of decadent, sensual indulgence, violent bread-and-circus entertainment, and murderous palace intrigue. (Roman decadence was different than ours: The Roman version was not utterly human ego-centered as is our contemporary world (after all, the Gods and Goddesses were still very real to them), but was, in essence, an orgy of the flesh. This is a good clue to the late Libran phase of the Arian Age: Libra, ruled by the sensual, pleasure-loving, Goddess Venus.) Our contemporary Western world is often compared to ancient Rome of the early Empire; indeed, both periods are cusp periods, transitions between Ages. We understand that during the ancient transition period thousands in the Mediterranean world were waiting for, and expecting, a Messiah. As we find today, with so many still waiting for the Second Coming, at "the end of the Age."

This now brings us to the Age of Pisces. It is important first to keep in mind that the Age succeeding does not reject or attempt to reverse the lesson of the previous Age, but builds upon it, transforms it, takes it to the next stage of our psychospiritual evolution. And this is most evident when we consider the New Testament. Jesus does not reject the teachings of the previous prophets; on the contrary, he is constantly quoting them. Above all, he does not reject the monotheistic advance made by Israel. But he is the radical transformation of all that had gone before. Jesus the Fish (symbol for Pisces), a teacher walking among men and women in the physical world, now had new lessons for humanity. (The beginning of the Age of Pisces, circa 150 B.C., we see did not exactly coincide with the birth of Jesus. The transition between Aries and Pisces, as with our transition period today, took some time.)

Briefly, let us consider two lessons of Jesus. First, we must note the very real pragmatic application of the lesson of brotherly love (agape), that of loving one another and loving all. Implicit in this message was: *Humanity, you are now discovering your ego-self. It will be an exhilarating adventure, the ego always wanting and demanding more, always wanting to go beyond limits, always wanting to expand its world. The ego will be a dangerous development for you, for it, on its own, does not recognize limits, and so would eventually destroy itself and its world. But by learning to love one another, you may yet survive. There is above all survival value for you in what I am teaching you.* And so love—to be more precise, *universal love* (again, Neptune, ruler of Pisces)—was the cure for the Arian ego inspired by the war God Mars, as Piscean Jesus was the answer to Arian Yahweh.

Jesus was always referring to his Father (Father ET), who was a God now of love, not war, and who cared for each and every individual, including women, children, tax collectors, prostitutes, the poor, the pitiful, the rabble. Jesus had a personal relationship to the Father, but, keep in mind, a relationship that he claimed was the right of everyone. For another lesson, the Good News he taught, was this: It didn't matter who you were, all were equal in the eyes of the Father, for every single individual was important. "So it is not the will of my Father who is in heaven that one of these little ones should perish," (Matthew 18:14) he said of children. We interpret that what he meant was that every single *soul* was important. Now this teaching was revolutionary. Prior to this, even with the birth of the ego during the Age of Aries, the great multitudes of humanity of the time were certainly not equal, and certainly not equal before God. Life was expendable. Life was cheap. The ongoing murder of human beings was commonplace. And only certain individuals were allowed in court with God: the God-Kings, the priesthood, the warrior heroes. Contrary to what we might assume about Christian values, the teaching of Jesus was a tremendous boost to the continuing evolution of the ego: *Why, yes, even I have value in the eyes of God! Even I have importance!* Consider that someone who was as astute as Nietzsche was thrown off by the traditional Christian ideals of humility, meekness, self-sacrifice, even martyrdom. Since these Christian ideals appear to be self-effacing (which makes sense, since Neptune rules Pisces), they then appear to be ego-denying. However, put into the context of Roman decadence, oppression, and persecution, these values, on the contrary, could only strengthen the ego. We have but to read the accounts of the early Christian martyrs and their willfully headstrong defiance of their Roman oppressors to realize that here was no passive, namby-pamby people, but instead those discovering the power of their ego manifesting as *will*, strong enough to give up fleshy desires, to overcome fear and torture, to remain unflinching even in the face of a horrifying death. (Whenever the ego-self is referred to, keep in mind that the "will"—will power—is implied also. The expression of will is an expression of ego.)

A perfect example of how an archetype is ripe and ready to fall out of higher consciousness is the visionary experience of the Apostle Paul, who never personally met Jesus. He did not need to. He was that one individual among thousands hearing the message of the Christ (a perfect case of psychological reversal, as he was at first a persecutor of Christians) who was a superior psychological womb for receiving the Christ archetype, the Piscean dispensation. It required, though, blasting his mind with a Vision. The outcome was that he was destined to become—as is generally agreed—the second most important individual in the history of Christianity.

Another consideration when looking back on early Christianity that indicated a profound shift in consciousness was taking place is this: In the Modern period to this day there has been keen interest in authenticating the historical Jesus. Much research has gone into asking, Did the man Jesus actually live? What, in fact, do we know about him? There are those who question, and with their own research to back up their doubts, whether Jesus, in fact, ever existed. Let us pose this question then, What if it could someday be proven that there was no historical Jesus (at least not the historical Jesus that Christianity assumes)? Does that suddenly negate the whole history of Christianity? More pointedly, does that negate the Christian message of peace and love? Not in the least. What is of crucial importance is to realize that the Christ archetype was emerging into human consciousness at the same time as the writing of the New Testament. Whatever the triggers might have been—an actual man Jesus who was a prophet, a Jesus half man and half ET, a Jesus created by the mythmaking minds of the Apostles, the Christ Vision of Paul, paranormal events taking place among the first Christians—the reality is is that the Living Image of Christ was born in the minds of hundreds, then thousands and hundreds of thousands, and then millions, over time, indicating a transformation of consciousness had taken place. The quest for the historical Jesus, as many have realized, becomes irrelevant to this more significant, evolutionary development, which involves the actual, personal, existential encounter Christians have had with this Living Image called Jesus, from the perspective of the inner life. If, in fact, there was no historical man Jesus, then who are Christians encountering in their inner life? (We have already hinted at the answer in the previous chapter; in the next chapter, we will pick it up again.) Historically, Christianity gained its own momentum, creating a whole Mythos for an emerging new Western civilization.

On the surface, Christianity taught that each individual soul was important; however, since the living soul was in real life repressed and made abstract, Christian teaching actually came to mean that each individual, flesh-and-blood *person* was important. The teaching of the salvation of the soul turned out to be an evolutionary ruse to promote the development of the ego-self, or what we call flesh-and-blood individual *personhood*.

Christianity: a religion that over the centuries has helped develop the egos of millions upon millions of individuals. If that were not the inner, psychospiritual dynamic of Christianity, then we would not be where we are today in the Western world in which everyone claims a right to full ego expression. Even the objection that those in Third World countries are still not fully allowed this privilege is easily overturned. The multitudes in the Third World countries want exactly what we have; they, too, are clamoring for the goods of the ego; they, too, would claim the full ego expression of driving cars and spending money in lavish shopping malls, and in pursuing careers. We have only to look at how far China has come in this regard. In the advanced, sophisticated societies of the West, this has peaked: witness in recent decades the culture of narcissism, the 70s Me Generation (which by today's standard looks mild), the popular media themes of previous decades of celebrating Everyday/Ordinary People and the appeal of *Looking Out for Number One*, or *You Can Have It All*, and everyone being entitled to their 15 minutes of fame. One current fad that has taken off like wildfire is the selfie—taking photos of oneself to post on social media. Everyone wants ego expression. One does not have to be a status seeker, a TV or movie star, or rock star, or a high-profile politician; you can scarcely find anyone today who is not egocentric, that is, insisting on his or her likes and dislikes, quirks, idiosyncrasies, "personal stuff," needs, wants, ambitions; everyone wants to own things and own property and command services; it has become a capitalistic-conditioned, ego-self entitlement. The social conditioning and peer pressure to develop a clearly defined ego that wants to do more and more, and to own more and more things, is tremendous. To be too self-effacing is actually not considered to be healthy. After nearly 2,000 years of Christianity, it is now truly difficult to be ego-effacing. Even a Mother Teresa had a tremendously strong ego, however she was able to project a public image of humbleness at the same time (again, the Piscean contrary nature), to accomplish what she did.

Sometimes we will hear Fundamentalists claim, *But Christianity hasn't really had a chance yet, it hasn't fully been tried by humanity at large.* Who are they trying to fool? There is no going back to the original Piscean dispensation. The lesson was given, we are still learning it some 2,000 years later, but it is also time to move on. We have no choice—Time itself is moving us on. Spirit is moving us on.

Let us ask this question, Does Christianity today inspire great art? Is any Christian art even being produced today? This, in itself, should be an indicator that the Christian Age has now passed. True, back in the 20th Century there had been a handful of famous Christian writers and poets (but visual artists?); however, the Christian elements in their work certainly did not catch fire in the culture. Consider that even a Christian thinker as renowned as Teilhard de Chardin was not exactly appreciated by his own Church; his attempt to take Christianity to a new level of understanding has likewise not caught on. (He does continue, however, to have philosophical relevance to the New Age.) Or, let us ask, does Christianity offer us anything new, anything on the cutting-edge, today? Does it inspire any new scientific ideas, any new technological breakthroughs? None. And the same goes for Islam. Both the Christian and Islamic mindset, such as it is today, simply does not carry on any longer civilization's Light-bearing torch of inspiration. They are not moving forward, but only holding on to the past.

The other Piscean religion we must touch upon, at least in passing, is Islam. Islam is something of an enigma in terms of the Story of our psychospiritual evolution today. It emerged some 700 years after the Piscean dispensation had already been given via the Christ archetype. So why a second dispensation event, in the person of Muhammad? Certainly it can be argued that such a dispensation had also to be given to the Arab world, which was still living within an animistic-polytheistic, pagan orientation. It had not even participated in the earlier Arian dispensation which saw the birth of monotheism. So the destined mission of Muhammad, said to be the last of the prophets, had a lot of catching up to do. "There is no God but Allah" was indeed a new version of the monotheism of Judaism and Christianity; but Christianity had added the dogma that Jesus was divine, one-with-God: Jesus was Lord. In no way, however, is Muhammad considered divine by Muslims; he is not to be worshipped; he was the final seal of the prophets, the final prophet, who was called to finalize God's Word. Jesus, therefore, for a Muslim, is considered a prophet, nothing more; only God—Allah—is to be worshipped.

The Piscean etymological credentials of Islam are certainly there in the beginning. The name 'Islam' has the various meanings of 'acceptance,' 'surrender,' 'submission,' and is derived from the Arabic word 'salaam,' meaning above all, 'peace.' As we have seen already, these are all very much Piscean values. A Muslim (the faithful of Islam) is one who submits to God, or, literally, it is said, one who makes peace. Spelled out more fully, Islam is then "the perfect peace that comes when one's life is surrendered to God" (quoted by Huston Smith). Again, this is Piscean through and through, including the implication that the focus of one's life should be on Higher Things, the Universal, the Absolute, *Allah*. Muslims carry out this focus when they ritually do prayers 6 times a day. The original Piscean ideal of martyrdom is also found in Islam to this day, with almost daily news of yet another suicide bomber.

But the question remains, What is the psychospiritual evolutionary inner meaning of Islam? Yes, it was an alternate Piscean dispensation for the Arab world; yes, it certainly advanced learning and culture over a huge swath of the Mediterranean world for a few hundred years after; but was it, is it, an advance (giving it the benefit of chronological succession) on Christianity? This is the dilemma, when we see in our own day that Islam has become a regressive, backwards-looking, repressive, stagnant religion. (Consider that at a recent Arab conference in Saudi Arabia on women's rights and issues, not a single woman was present.) It is, for one, utterly caught up in ritualized proscriptions for everyday affairs. Unlike Christianity, which has had its encounter with Modern and then Postmodern thought (e.g. Radical Theology), it appears that Islam has been impervious to any Modern or Postmodern critique. The irony at the same time is that the Islamic world has wholeheartedly embraced all the technological advancements of the Modern Era. Saudi Arabia buys billions of dollars' worth of sophisticated American weaponry; Iran is an advanced technological nation, having developed its own nuclear power. But from the perspective of the Big Picture on planet Earth, did Islam expand its power to become a counter, a foil, to Christianity? To be in perpetual contention—deadly contention—with Christianity (and of course Judaism)? We saw the inherent metaphysical / psychospiritual dynamic of Piscean dualism in Christianity, that is, how the two Fish of Piscean symbolism played out within Christianity itself, but is Islam the other Fish of Piscean dualism on the global, sociopolitical scale? But then, that is not, by Piscean dualistic definition, a favorable image for one or the other religion, is it. As we remember, Piscean dualism has always implied that one Fish of the polarity is the True, the Good, the Most Valued, while the other, in contention with it, is the "dark" Fish.

As it has a monotheistic orientation, Islam too has helped develop the ego-self of millions—billions now—across the centuries. So it does have that inherent psychospiritual evolutionary intention in that regard. But because its doctrines appear to be set in stone, how it might transform through the lens of the Aquarian dispensation remains a conundrum. (The mystical sect of Islam called Sufism is, of course, another story behind conventional Islam, and might indeed be the Islamic bridge to New Age Aquarius. Metaphysical book stores certainly assume that.)

In the 1960s the popular view was that the Age of Aquarius had to do with peace and love (a rather premature, faddish assumption at that). But peace and love were the evolutionary lessons given to us in the Piscean Age. Again, this does not mean that the Aquarian New Age is a denial or a neglecting or a forgetting of the ideals of peace and love. As we have said, each Age succeeding builds upon the lessons of past Ages. Peace and love are as important as ever, but it is time that we graduate from the Piscean Age—it is time for another evolutionary lesson. Peace and love, for those who have learned this lesson, who have nurtured them in their own hearts, are going to be taken to another level—*the Next Level.*

We live in the transition period that will bring us into the Age of Aquarius. What is the next collective lesson for humanity? What will Aquarius, the astrological sign for universal humanity, dispense to us that will open us to our universal humanity?

The ego-self, as we know it today, has evolved from its ancient emergence. But we have reached that point in our evolutionary Story where the ego is now quite full of itself. In this Postmodern era, the ego-self is free to revel in its full glory. We might ask, How much more does the ego want? How much more power does the ego want? It does appear that there are no limits. According to Yuval Noah Harari in *Homo Deus*, the ego-self, the existential agent of Humanism, today wants—and has always wanted—immortality, happiness, and divinity. Yes, as this theme comes up again and again—*to be like the Gods*. And because the ego-self has reached a manic pitch of self-intoxication, with a soul still naïve, it is destroying its own world. It does not yet have the appropriate wisdom to know its limits; even more, it has tragically come to a point of not even respecting limits. What, then, can put this ego in its place? For certainly the Piscean ideals of peace and love per se are not succeeding. Suffering caused by human conflict continues unabated, and as everyone realizes, the Postmodern mainstream of society has gotten too jaded and cynical, too obsessively materialistic, to be a party to any kind of hippy, idealistic promotion of peace and love.

Yet, the ego is increasingly a sick ego in the Postmodern world. Collectively, the ego-self is neurotic, anxiety-ridden, stressed out, trapped in a revolving door of confusion, and oozing with all manner of dysfunctions, perversities, and violence. So much had been repressed and hidden in the dark of soul! Soul, which has been held down for the last 2,000 years—for the sake of ego development!—is now asserting itself with a vengeance. The ego structures of repression have cracked, fissured, and are coming undone. As Freud would say, we are witnessing the return of the repressed, on a mass scale. From an astrological perspective, we could point to the denouement of Virgo in the Postmodern world. Virgo signifies the self being uncertain of itself, especially in terms of what it must do. So the self becomes hyper-self-conscious and goes about analyzing every little thing about itself. Shakespeare's Hamlet asking *To be or not to be*, expressed in the early years of the Virgo phase of the Piscean Age, already rang the note of what would become the Modern, and now Postmodern, self.

Many Postmodernist, most especially European, scholars have wholeheartedly encouraged this breakdown of the self (even as individuals take it to narcissistic heights). Theories of the decentering or deconstruction of the ego were all the rage in the late 20th Century. Professors—secure, of course, in their own ivory-towered positions—calmly detailed what they saw as the increasing fragmentation of contemporary life. The ego apparently is no longer lord of its house, for those so long kept down in the basement are climbing up through every crack. Good, hardcore Postmodernists revel in this; they completely immerse themselves in decadence, fragmentation, disorientation, and in all aspects of nihilism. There is so much reveling in pop culture trivia, superficiality, and in things that are simply downright stupid. We see it in music, magazines, underground comics, in thousands of little publications, in film, television, in the drug culture. (I hope I am not misunderstood here in thinking I am simply moralistically denouncing these things, for the Postmodern experience must indeed be assimilated. My real point is that we need to transform the incestuousness of this culture, and in the process of doing so, redeem it—*from another level.*) Needless to say, the hardcore Postmodernist provides no Vision of where all of this is going, or how it can sustain us in a world bent on self-destruction. We might even suggest that the Postmodern ego has deep down a death wish.

The direction we must now move in is that of conscious evolution. And the saving power is Spirit—Spirit coming-to-us anew. We are now at that point where we can consciously co-create with what Spirit is revealing to us. Once we have firsthand become witnesses to the Advent of the Higher Self, the Greater-than-us-coming-to-us of Spirit, we are no longer disoriented—we now have a beacon, and are now called to work consciously, co-creatively, with Spirit. We can therefore no longer assume that we are simply going to be unconsciously swept along by the current of evolution, as if just going along for the ride. In fact, we are at the point where that is no longer possible, if our civilization is to remain intact. And if we take seriously the view that civilization is on the road to collapse, because of the hard implications of abrupt climate change, then the imperative to become fully conscious with Spirit is even that much greater.

All that was repressed by the control systems of civilization must now be consciously faced, and be integrated into a New Self. We have already seen that it was soul that was repressed, ignored, forgotten, while at the same time its slippery usage as an abstract word still survived to this day. I have not claimed that one, singular definition can be given to it now, once and for all, as if it ever could be given (after all, Postmodern critique has taught us something). We must be ever careful not to wind up spinning our intellectual wheels in semantic quicksand, with nothing then to show for it. What we do need to do is to bring out more and more the psychological and potential, new cultural richness that is hidden in this word 'soul.'

As suggested earlier, Spirit is coming-to-us anew to liberate soul, to illuminate our darkness. In other words, all that is breaking out in us today can be oriented anew by Spirit, not Spirit in a Ten Commandments, dogmatic, oppressive, repressive way, but by Spirit providing soul a language, a Mythos, bringing it into new forms of Light, raising it into Spirit. It is Spirit revealing to us our Higher Self in a Living Image. This Living Image today comes to us, I claim, *in the guise* of soul. I have named it—as it has named Itself through me—*Psyche*.

## Comparing the Piscean and Aquarian Ages

| Piscean Age | Aquarian Age |
| --- | --- |
| I believe | I know |
| We were asked to believe at secondhand | We are called to know Divinity directly |
| Emphasis on doctrines and dogmas | Knowing firsthand for ourselves (gnosis) |
| Devotion/worship/faith | Co-creation with Spirit/ Higher Self |
| Obsession with certainty: I must be certain of the Truth so I can contain it: in dogma & doctrine (religion) in fact & formula / clear & distinct ideas (science) | Openness: I am open to Spirit, what speaks to me Not obsessed with certainty, but with working with what is revealed to me |
| Emotionally based | Higher mind/intuitively based |
| Mysticism an ideal (only) | A new occultism |
| Salvation of soul for the sake of an Afterlife | Transformation of soul for the for the sake of living more fully in this life |
| Repression of soul, turning soul into an abstract word | Liberation of soul, soul embodied in the world |
| Christ the Savior/Messiah/avatar | Our own Higher Self recognized Looking to ourselves: our own Christ-selfhood |
| Individualism: Me first: Me against the world | Individuation: individuality within community We are all in this together |
| Separatist dogmas: Us vs. Them | We are the universal human family |

| | |
|---|---|
| Dualistic: | Synthesis of opposites: |
| Heaven vs. Hell | Yin *and* Yang |
| Christ vs. Satan | Mind *and* body / Spirit *and* soul |
| Mind vs. body | Right brain *and* left brain |
| Male vs. female | Male *and* female (androgyny) |
| East vs. West | East *and* West (the global village) |
| Surrender to God's will as interpreted by Authority and dogma | Surrender to "God's" will as interpreted by direct apprehension of our Calling |
| God as the Super-Parent: God dictates, we obey | Two-way dialogue with "God": "God" inspires, we reply creatively |
| Our power is given over to Authority so that we can have meaning in our life | Higher Self-empowerment: meaning comes through gnosis |
| Perfection as the Ideal | Wholeness becomes the Ideal |
| Anti-psychological: the psyche is not real/not valid | Pro-psychological: Psyche *is* reality |
| The ego takes everything literally (obsession with certainty) | Everything has symbolic meaning, there is always more than the literal |
| Development of the intellectual, rational, ego-self, leaving our relationship to Spirit subjectively emotional | Development of higher mind intuition: The New Self in co-creative, mythopoetic relationship to the Higher Self |
| "Logos [science] is our god" (Freud) | Mythos revitalized |
| Technos against Psyche | Psyche integrates with Technos |
| Technical thinking defines Reality (Virgo undercurrent) | Realization of unlimited creativity (Leo undercurrent) |

### The Transformer

Who gazes into night & a new Intelligence
      in the stars can see?
Who stands open to inspiration to receive what launches
      peoples into futurity?
Who absorbs age-old Tradition, the ancient arts of wisdom,
      Earthwide the panoply of cultures,
but says, I am not a puppet of the past,
I am not a hand-me-down child of other peoples & cultures—
I recognize all, absorb all, but what I absorb I transform.

Who says, I do not accept what lies dead
      at my feet—
Let the old God be dead, for new Divinity will live
      through me!
Let the dead return to the soil & enrich the soil—
Who says, I love enrichment of the soil.

Whose feet are planted firmly upon the body
      of Earth,
who absorbs Minerals, Air & Water, Fire of Sun,
whose essence of Self is seed of the new Tree?
Who says, I attune myself to a new Spirit coming
      among us,
I attune myself to the superconscious energies
      of Neptune, Pluto & Uranus,
I attune myself to the Milky Way galactic influx
      of new Intelligence.
Who says, Through me the new Vision of Ages manifests
      its evolutionary intention—
All I absorb is made new through me.

Who says, I am a Transformer!
I transform my conditioning, my complexes, my fears,
    my insecurities, into strengths & psychospiritual tools
    of Psyche.
I transform the woe-is-me, whining voice of my sufferings
    into the Story of my struggles.
I transform decadent & dying culture into new riches
    to be shared.
I transform old obscured ways into a new path shining
    in the Labyrinth.
I transform the barrage of daily impression into insight,
    unconnected information into knowledge, stale doctrine
    into living wisdom.
I transform the art I work in, the childhood religion
    I outgrew.
I transform the self I was.

Who says, I am a Transformer!
I transform the past into a Vision of futurity!
Who says, I extend my hand to others & freely offer them
    the fruits of futurity!

1991

# ( 7 )

## PSYCHE: MYTHOS FOR THE NEW AGE

*The Mythos begins somewhere*
*and must begin with someone*

The challenge for any Vision today is this: Does it hold before us the evolutionary intention of liberating our human potential, which is our soul potential? Does it allow us to absorb and assimilate and transform the past? Does it open up for us more of Reality, so that Human Reality can evolve? Does it bring within sight what the future for us on this Earth might be, even if we live at The Edge of an unfolding MELE? How comprehensive is this Vision? Does it offer us the Big Picture of all the Threads that are currently woven into our world? Or is it a regressive "Vision": Does it set up boundaries, put up walls, block out, suppress, deny realities that beg to be seen? Does it shrink down the full splendor of Reality? Does it exclude the plurality of what we now see as the Universal Rainbow Human Family?

*So how might Higher Self show Itself to us today?*

As we saw earlier, the Higher Self is indeed the essence of the new Aquarian dispensation. Yet, the Higher Self must present Itself to us in some specific, concrete way, or else it becomes only another high-sounding abstraction, merely some amorphous idea floating about in our heads. It is all too easy to say, *Oh, yes, the Higher Self, I accept that*. And how many times have I heard that exact response. But that, again, is only a nod to an abstraction. Yes, we can encounter aspects of the Higher Self in certain specific, concrete ways, for example, through shamanic practice, profound meditation, psychedelics, UFO/ET encounters, encounters with spirit beings or Ascended Masters, the various forms of psychic experience, near-death experiences, out-of-body experiences, through Visions, Big Dreams, etc., many of these falling under the umbrella of the paranormal. These are all experiences that open us to other realms of psychospiritual reality, that bring us into alternate states of consciousness beyond ego-self, but experiences that are so often temporary, if not fleeting; they are experiences, yes, that are paranormal and extraordinary, but often with great difficulty integrated into daily life.

Consider the psychedelic experience. The question has always been regarding it, What to do with such an experience? Certainly one's mind can be expanded—blasted open—in a dramatically immediate way, providing one with a whole new window on possibilities of what Reality entails, but is such an experience possible to integrate into one's everyday life? That has always been the challenge for those who favor this quick, shortcut route to experiencing alternate Reality. Because too often the psychedelic "trip" is used only as a recreational escape from the ordinariness of mundane life. We all know those who come down from the high saying, *Wow, that was trippy!...wow, I was out there!...the hallucinations were unreal! Yes,* we say, *but do you have anything to share about Higher Self?* For we must assume that a new spiritual dispensation is more than a trippy experience—it is the developing of a new collective relationship to Spirit. It is bringing to birth a new Mythos.

When Spirit is coming-to-us anew to reveal to us our Higher Self, it is for the sake of our developing an actual relationship to our Higher Self. As depth psychologists and mythologists know, it is difficult to develop a heart-felt relationship to an abstraction, especially one that is still new collectively, such as the Higher Self, with no mainstream cultural tradition behind it. Jung said it quite well, that it was the living God we relate to, not the abstract idea of the archetype of "God." The human mind does naturally "personify" (though we must be careful about giving too much power to this mere intellectual notion created by scholars called "personification"—which is yet another ego ploy), for we spontaneously relate to persons, animals, a spirit guide, a Divine Figure, a living God.

When we speak about the new dispensation, we are not referring, therefore, to some nebulous abstract notion, but a spiritual concreteness that actually moves us and impacts consciousness, that potentially transforms consciousness. It comes to reveal itself in Vision, in image, in word, in channeled message, in teachings, that speak to our soul, and so it comes alive for us. It will often be experienced as numinous. It is in this sense that the Higher Self can reveal itself to us by way of Spirit *as a Living Image*. For true Christians (not lip service Christians), that Living Image can still show itself as Jesus, and, for Catholics, equally the Virgin Mary, or other saints. For Hindus, it may be any one of a number of deities, or, for those on a particular Path, it is the living presence of a guru, in person. Indeed, for many, it is the guru who is their living link to the Higher Self, to Atman. For Buddhists, it may also be deities encountered on the way of the Buddha Path, though, more commonly too, it is the living Master who has attained some level of Self-Realization, who is living the Buddha state. The Living Image might well be a more impersonal symbol—we should want to call it a Living Symbol—that can be as complex as a mandala. Yet, which among these, laden with all the cultural weight of their respective Traditions, is the new Living Image coming-to-us at this dawn of Aquarius? Or would some wish to name who they believe to be a living avatar—Meher Baba? Maitreya? But they, too, given what we know about them—and how many have even met the mysterious Maitreya?—, cannot be *the* Living Image of the Higher Self for us collectively today.

But let us consider other possibilities. Some might suggest their favorite channel as that living bridge to the Higher Self. And there are many: Michael, Seth, Ramtha, Ra, Lazaris, Bashar, Kryon, Hilarion, St. Germaine, The Christ, the Council of Ten, the Pleiadians, the Ashtar Command, to name only a few of the numerous channeled beings in recent years. All of these, however, claim to be either disincarnate beings, spirit beings of various kinds, ET beings, or group entities, or some kind of group consciousness, or perhaps a distinct aspect of the multidimensional Self (Higher Self) of the channel. The point is, none come forward as *the* distinct Living Image of the Higher Self Itself.

Or consider, then, the possibility that the Aquarian dispensation is embodied rather in a particular channeled book, such as *The Urantia Book*. First, such a book has limited appeal and has dubious origins, and also asks that we accept its massive amount of detail as if we are supposed to believe every word of it, which is more appropriate to the Piscean Age attunement. *The Urantia Book* is also presented as a completed book, as if there was nothing further spiritually creative for us to do (which is my criticism of all the Traditions). More importantly, however, it, or any possible book, cannot be the immediately experienced Aquarian dispensation, for the dispensation must come to each one of us directly through Spirit. This is not to say that the Aquarian dispensation may not take cultural embodiment in a book, no different than *The Bible* was able to first embody the Arian and then the Piscean dispensations, or *The Koran* an alternative Piscean embodiment for the Muslim world. Indeed, I do assume that such a book is possible, but to even begin to write it would require above all a firsthand revelatory encounter with the Aquarian dispensation, with one's *Higher Self*.

A strong case can be made for the return of the Goddess as the figure of the Living Image we speak of. With this, we are certainly getting closer. But consider: the Goddess is definitely gender specific. An emphasis on the Goddess alone may turn out to be only reactionary to our traditional, male gender-oriented God, as if it were now Goddess's turn to rule. I do not see the continuation of a gender-one-sided spiritual polarity in the Aquarian Age. With Aquarius, we are moving beyond the dualities of Pisces. We should keep in mind too as we proceed that Aquarius *is* the sign of androgyny. Yet, despite this caveat, experience of Goddess is still our clue.

Let us remember that traditionally the soul was considered feminine. In contrast to the God of patriarchy who has been the source of the repression of soul, it is the Goddess who reconnects us to soul. This is quite apparent when we consider that the Goddess is so often the central figure of paganism, and that paganism has an intimate link to soul (in our concrete sense) that the patriarchal religions, as we saw, did not, which is why, too, paganism was suppressed as an outlaw religion in the West. With the return of Goddess awareness, we also see the rebirth of paganism today—a so-called neopaganism. However, any such "return" cannot be simply a relapse into our evolutionary past. Neopaganism per se, if it needs to be said, is still not the coming, universal, Aquarian religion.

It is time, then, that I must defer to my own, firsthand, experience—to *my Vision*. It is time now that I give witness. This is in keeping with the New Age injunction to speak from that which you yourself have experienced directly. The following is a shortened version of what I have written about elsewhere.

The Goddess was indeed my initiation to the Higher Self. Many, many years ago, in my early vocation as a poet, an Inner Voice would come to me to inspire me. Early on I called it my Muse (traditionally a given for a poet). In ancient mythology, the Muses were known as minor feminine deities. This Muse of mine would sing to me in a Melody that was utterly enchanting. And I wanted so much, being this fledgling young poet, to translate into language what I heard with my inner Ear, but too often I found myself an inarticulate scribe. This ethereal Melody I further interpreted as the far-off Call of Spirit, and I came to feel a strong urge that it was literally calling me *west*. At the time, I was still living in my home state of Michigan.

Within about a couple years after hearing this Call urging me west, I then moved from Midwest Michigan to the West Coast of California, settling in Santa Cruz, on Monterey Bay. I soon felt that the spirit of place[1] here—actually, along the whole coast of California—was definitely feminine; in other words, the presence of the Goddess was quite apparent here. In fact, my early soul-level encounter with this extraordinary place on Monterey Bay was with the Goddess of this region—I experienced Her specifically as Aphrodite (or Venus, if one prefers the Roman). The Goddess was beautiful, as this place was beautiful, and seductive, as was this place, with its golden sands, golden Sun, its diamond-scintillating surf, its "California girls," its old-fashioned, good time, Beach Boardwalk (the only one on the whole long West Coast), its picturesque coastal cliffs, its landmark lighthouse, ghostly mountain giants hovering in the distance beyond Monterey across the bay, its dense redwood forested mountains, its flowers year round, a touch of the tropics with its palms, a climate Mediterranean mild, and a casual, laid-back, Surf City, café society, life-style. And there was still that authentic feel of the Sixties here in the later 1970s, where hippies still lived among all the tourists and New Wave Postmodern youth from the local university—UCSC—on a hill. But, then, I also came to experience the Goddess here as Kali, for She had an existentially destructive side, too. For all her seductiveness, I experienced Her shortly in the guise of *The Cruz*—the Cross of dismemberment and death from which, possibly, one could also find existential resurrection. (All of the major themes in my early development of The Mythos that have emerged out of the New Age Vision can be found in my poetic works.)

It was at that time, when I was still new in Santa Cruz, that the Higher Self began to announce Itself to me in a series of initial Visions, that finally crystallized out in one, primary Vision. To be clear about it, this Vision did not come to me as a one-time, knock-me-to-the-ground, experience, as we understand what happened to the Apostle Paul, but persistently came to me as a recurring, spontaneous mental Image that I came to live with daily. The setting for it was exactly the locale where I now lived, here in Santa Cruz, on Monterey Bay. (The full narrative of this Vision is found in my published work *The Vision of Psyche*.)

Whether day or night, I would often take solitary, meditative walks to the cliffs that look out over the bay. It was on one of these walks, during this time of my own existential crisis, as I gazed out over our beautiful bay, that it occurred to me that I saw there a magnificent Fountain. There was a Fountain rising, out in the middle of the bay! And this Fountain, with its enchantingly scintillating, up-rushing, arching sprays, was illuminated—*it glowed*—, for deep in the bay I also saw the Sun. The Fountain was composed of up-rushing sprays of Water laced with solar Fire. It was a Fountain strangely mixed then of Fire and Water. It was a Fountain filled with Light! And as I looked into this marvellous Fountain, I saw an equally scintillating figure there, rising in the midst of those up-rushing sprays. I immediately saw this figure as the Goddess. And this Divine Figure the Goddess opened Her arms in a gesture of sharing, compassion, love, and understanding. She was sharing the Waters from the depths of the Fountain, out of the depths of the bay, through the up-rushing Waters of the Fountain itself. She stood as if in mid-air atop the topmost arching sprays, sharing the Waters in the open Air above, under the open sky. Yet, She was not simply standing atop the Fountain, as if separate from it, but was at-one-with it, for all was scintillating as one. But there was more— She appeared, in fact, as many Goddesses, all appearing as aspects of one Divinity; She revealed Herself as many-in-one in a sort of fast frame, cinematic motion. And though this Divine Figure first appeared to me as a shapeshifting *Goddess*, She was in fact more—She was a dynamically changing figure revealing multitudes of Divine Forms. I saw Her above all as a Divine Shapeshifter of all Divine Forms, a Shapeshifter able to present the guises of the Gods and Goddesses of all times and places. She was always to appear, and to this day, as a dynamic multiplicity.

In a Big Dream I had at that time, I also saw Her, and She was transforming—shapeshifting—before my eyes. For She was also a God, in fact, many Divine Figures, all appearing in a kind of brilliant color, cinematic simultaneity. But the Vision itself revealed even more— Not only did I see multiple Divine Figures morphing into one another, but also, as if veils passed over Her, I saw human figures, multitudes of human figures; I saw there the countless, untold lives of multitudes throughout history. There were such stories of suffering I witnessed there, playing across Her protean Form. Such pain and grieving and misery and misfortune and tragedy, such a spectacle of human suffering I saw there! Endless struggle I saw, endless conflict, endless suffering! The private and collective sufferings of all played out before me across Her protean Form. The stories of all who lived on this Earth seemed to stretch in an endless parade across Her protean Form.

And still there was more— Forms of animals I saw She appeared as—the lion, the ram, a great snake, a hawk, a butterfly. In the Big

Dream, it was the hawk face (a sparrow hawk) in particular that appeared all so clearly. All forms of animals, and of plants and trees I saw appear across Her protean Form, as if She were the living soul of Earth giving birth to all life. And there was more— To even minerals and crystals Her Form gave birth, as if to all forms of Earth Her Form gave birth. She hovered there, before me, in the Fountain, in this Revelation, and Her arms opened in a gesture of compassion, like a Divine Mother. And from Her open palms sprang seeds of Golden Light that went forth in streams to inspire others throughout the world. And from Her mouth a Golden Word was spoken—*The Mythos*—that became a Golden Thread that spiraled around Her; I saw that She was continuously woven and rewoven by the Thread She was. At the same time, this Thread of Gold wove its way into, and in so doing transformed, the Fabric of the world.

Equally as remarkable, the Fountain would often appear to me as a Tree, a Tree rising out of Monterey Bay. And this Tree was a singing Tree, a beautiful Tree of Song. The Melody I had heard for years flowed from its branches. It was the Melody I had wished so much to bring into poetic form. (This has all been a highly condensed narrative of the Vision. All the detailed variations on this primary Vision that I have continuously lived with over the years I have shared in my poetic work.[2])

This Vision, however wonderful, some have said to me, to have had such a Vision, has not made life easy, though; on the contrary, it had made my life ever more difficult. Imagine trying to share this Vision in a Postmodern world! Imagine what it was like to perpetually get the response, *That's a nice, that's a wonderful, Vision to have*, before moving on to the next topic of conversation. Or to be told, *Poets in our age do not receive Visions—you seem not to be in step with the age. It must therefore be a delusion.* Or I would simply get the blank look. There was absolutely no one I could fully share it with who might have understood what it meant. In the contemporary, conventional sense of how life is measured, this Vision slowly destroyed me. My life, what I could have done to have found "success," was sacrificed because of it. The Vision of my Higher Self, in other words, shattered how my life was conditioned; it perpetually destroyed the ego-self I was. Yet, at the same time, a New Self was simultaneously coming to birth through it.

I should say here that I had always had an unusual relationship to the Sun. Ever since childhood I had an intimate love for the Sun. Years later I had looked again and again into the Sun and was blinded by what I saw: *Its Light was too much.* Everyday, year after year after year, I had always to live with this *too much.* I eventually came to interpret it as the gnosis of *unlimited potential.* Yet, what I was to realize over time is that this Vision I received, as I lived with it over time, was the transformational key to bringing my Sun Experience into Form.[3]

Yes, I have lived with this Vision for many years now, and it continues to reveal more and more of the Aquarian Mythos to me. One can readily see that this Divine Figure in the Fountain is amazingly enough a new, alternate version of the traditional Aquarian icon of the Water Bearer. The Divine Figure rises out of the depths of Water (where She was hidden) into the open Air, pouring forth the Waters of the Fountain, being at-one-with these very Waters. (I could easily visualize the traditional Aquarian urn that She would pour from.)

I channeled a series of poems[4] during those early years. The Goddess of this Vision told me,

> *I am Psyche of all peoples.*
> 
> *I am the soul complete.*
> 
> *My Thread of Gold,*
> 
> *the new World Fabric.*

The Divine Shapeshifter of my Vision, who I had at first encountered in Santa Cruz as Goddess Aphrodite, I was therefore inspired to name *Psyche*. Or, rather, I should say, as the Vision itself sang to me, the name "Psyche" came to me *as the Word*. A clue, though, as to why the name Psyche rang so true for me can be found in the ancient myth of Eros and Psyche, as told by the Roman writer Apuleius.[5] There, Psyche, too, was feminine, born a female mortal who, through many trials, came to be divinized. I soon saw Psyche, then, able to appear in any number of Divine guises, as our guide today among the Gods and Goddesses (however we may wish to (re)interpret them). After all, Psyche was once a mortal like us, had to undergo uncommon experiences and a great deal of suffering, culminating in her apotheosis and welcomed into the pantheon of the Gods and Goddesses who, we must remember, have been psychologically repressed for these last 2,000 years. (The suppression, on one level, of polytheistic paganism.) Psyche, the Greek word ψυχή, is most often translated as 'soul.' And so we return once again to our earlier theme—the reality of soul, and that soul has been repressed for these last 2,000 years. My Vision, then, was announcing Psyche's return, auguring further the return of the Gods.

Earlier I suggested that Spirit coming-to-us anew is now beginning to appear to us in the guise of soul. Spirit, in other words, is now beginning to appear to us as *Psyche*—Spirit as soul in its Divine Form. Would there be a more brilliant way for Spirit to appear to us today to liberate soul than as the Living Image of Psyche? This is Spirit as our mortal soul (because of its intimate bond with the body) become divine and immortal, as in the myth, Psyche, too, a mortal, was divinized and became immortal. In the Vision I received, Psyche—as I came to interpret the Vision—I saw as the Living Image of our Higher Self (That-which-is-greater-than-us) coming-to-us to liberate soul, to transform soul, to bring soul out of the Dark of its own potential, its own unlimited potential. This explains why Psyche appears as a shapeshifter, for soul, as we saw, is ever changing. Soul, as James Hillman[6] kept emphasizing, is naturally polycentric, receptive to the influences of many Gods and Goddesses. Psyche, therefore, is the herald of the coming of a new, enlightened polytheism. Of course, the Postmodern intellect will want to know how something as anachronistic as "Gods" and "Goddesses" are to be interpreted in today's world. To put it bluntly, the question would be, *What is he talking about?* Yet, this will not be all. This is but the primary, initial phase of this next stage of our evolution.

Psyche appeared to me as both Goddess and God. In essence, then, Psyche is androgynous—for us that means, psychologically both feminine and masculine, and equally at home in the right brain and left brain. Psyche, in my Vision, revealed the psychospiritual Reality of the Divine Androgyne. I saw then why the traditional avatar of male gender or of even the female gender could not be the exclusive Living Image of the Higher Self. Certainly, though, a gender-specific avatar could appear as one of Psyche's guises. But Psyche is both masculine and feminine, *and more*—Psyche, as the Divine Shapeshifter, is the Form of all the Divine Forms we are. Psyche is the Form for all life forms on Earth. This is why Jesus no longer satisfies us as the complete Image of the Higher Self. Jesus is now encountered as a particular person of the Divine Image.

Readily, we see a problem, however. If Psyche comes to us in such a changeable Form—a Form, really, beyond all forms—then how can we relate to it? And how can we psychologically assimilate it and "manage" it? True, in a traditional sense, it is a most challenging and difficult Image to attempt to assimilate. Traditionally, the Divine Figure stood more or less still as a specific Image: Jesus, a man in the dress of ancient Palestine, is imaged as the teacher, or healer, or, most commonly of all, as hanging on the Cross—the Christian's daily crucifix. Or there is the Virgin Mary in her familiar, stock poses, or there is Buddha in traditional lotus position. Psychologically, the developing ego latched onto a Divine Image that remained stable, unchanging, in other words, from the stance of ego-self, easy to relate to. But Psyche is now the Living Image that can appear to us as Jesus, Mary, Buddha, Krishna, Aphrodite, Hermes, Horus, Shiva, Vishnu, Kali, to name only a few—and only traditional figures at that. Psyche, in my contemporary locale, as related in my story above, I experienced as The Cruz. Perhaps Hinduism with its hundreds of Divine manifestations of the supreme Atman (none other than the Higher Self) comes the closest of any traditional religion to the Vision I received. Now Kali Herself is a multiple figure, I am aware, but when I read of the Hindu guiding image of contemplation called the "Ishta-Deva," as discussed by Lex Hixon,[7] I was taken aback. His depiction of a contemplative experiment with the Ishta-Deva was an uncanny parallel to how my Vision of Psyche appeared. The crux, however: The Vision of Psyche as the Divine Shapeshifter (or any similar variation on this Vision), however difficult it is to create a mental image of and relate to without having had some experience of it, is how, I believe though, the Living Image of our Divinity must appear to us today.

Christianity has long anticipated the Second Coming of the Divine Presence: it is spoken of as the *Parousia*, the Second Coming of Christ, or, in a more esoteric Christian rendering, "the arrival of a higher being or a higher state of being,"[8] or, the *New Being*. Parousia, taken from the New Testament, literally means *presence*, implying the highly charged event of the Advent: the appearance, the arrival, and our subsequent being-with this "higher being," and the implied higher state of existence we would find ourselves living. In other words, the presence of a "higher being," Higher Self, the Christ-self, would now be with us. (The Greek 'parousia,' from 'pareinai': *para*, beside, alongside of + *einai*, to be, or being. So we have, to be beside of—our being-with in the presence of—New Being.) This is precisely how I see the Advent of Psyche. It is my contention then that Psyche is the new Christ, the Parousia. It is no mere coincidence that there is a movement within the Christian community that calls its members Christian New Agers, or Christaquarians.

We might see, then, that Psyche is the (potential) universal Divine Figure through which all faiths can find a familiar Image, a familiar Divine Form. Psyche is the spiritual meta-Form for all forms, embracing each, yet transcending each. Psyche is the multifaceted diamond whose facets are the brilliant, numinous faces of Divinity. Psyche is the mystical body for the Universal Rainbow Human Family. Born of Earth (Virgo) and Water (Pisces), Psyche is animated by Fire (Leo, the Sun), and now appears in the open Air (Aquarius). We are indeed transitioning from the Age of Pisces/Virgo to the Age of Aquarius/Leo.

I am well aware of the dozens of objections to be made, which any Vision implying the claims I am putting forth is destined to encounter. There will of course be those who immediately say, *I don't relate to the name "Psyche."* Christians naturally will feel that way. Likewise, other Traditionalists loyal to the avatars of their faith will say the same. Then, there are other, alternative names that some may wish to use, such as the still traditional Lord, God, Atman, Spirit or Great Spirit, and, of course, Goddess; or there is Light, Source, Mind, Christ-self, or my Guardian Angel, again, some of these names being highly abstract. My experience of Psyche has much in common with the obscure figure of Sophia, found in the writings of the ancient Gnostics and alchemists. Indeed, it might seriously be suggested that I have rediscovered and reconnected with the Goddess Sophia for the contemporary world. References to Sophia—also considered the feminine aspect of God as *Divine Wisdom*—are in addition found in the Old Testament. The name "Sophia" might be considered a substitute for Psyche, then, for Psyche has revealed Herself as my Teacher of the living wisdom of our Divinity. Or, there is another obscure figure from Judaism and the Kabbalah, the figure of Shekinah, considered another feminine aspect of the "presence of God," if not the very "presence" of God. Shekinah has a root meaning of "to settle, inhabit, or dwell," which, we will see, ties into my whole concept of the "Mythos of place." Shekinah is also said to wander on the Earthly plane seeking redemption in a place where She can settle and dwell. As the "presence of God," Shekinah then means practically the same as the Greek word Parousia, which is also considered the "Divine Presence."

We realize that various names from the Traditions do indeed refer to this experience of encountering Divinity, of the *human soul* encountering Divinity. Certainly, whatever name speaks as *the Word* is what an individual is called to open up to. It should be obvious, though, that Psyche teaches universal tolerance of all religious belief; however, Psyche also teaches, even more importantly, of the transformation of all religious belief. In addition, "Psyche" rings with a multiplicity of meanings that I believe embraces the full complexity of our world today; indeed, 'Psyche' is the most apt name I know of for Spirit coming-to-us anew to liberate and transform soul. In fact, if we give it but a moment's thought, we certainly must agree that we all have a *psyche*.

In the ancient world, as we touched on earlier, consciousness, before the emergence of the ego in its own right, was dispersed in various directions by loyalties to various Gods and Goddesses. We are returning to a somewhat similar situation today—examples in today's society of our psyche fragmentation are indicators of this process—but with an essential difference: The ego appears now to have come to its full development (as humanism reaches its narcissistic peak) and (ideally) is prepared by now in enough individuals (I believe) to be able to encounter a variety of Powers without mental breakdown. It is time, in other words, that the ego-self learn to cultivate a multiplicity of relationships to the different Powers speaking to us, through our own multidimensional Higher Selfhood. But there is more—we now have a guide to teach us, *Psyche*, who is at home in these higher dimensions where dwell all the Divinities. I believe Psyche to be the Universal Integrator, able to speak to all religious faiths, but able eventually to transform all religious faiths.

It might have become apparent at this point that Psyche—Psyche the Divine Shapeshifter—implies a relativistic Reality, both as the Greater Reality being shown to us and as informing Human Reality. Our fragmented Postmodern world, even when we talk about its spiritualization, would still be a relativistic world. Simply put, there is no Absolute anything, and there are no absolutes. There is no one big Truth as the Answer. Once Other Intelligences are recognized, and once the Next Level of consciousness opens up to us and is experienced, we find ourselves in a multiplicity of reality-worlds, perspectives, and psychospiritual experiences. For many, if not most still today, this is unsettling and even frightening. But what there is is the process of assimilating this as our own individual life Path, what Jung called individuation.

Psyche would also then be the defender of a pluralistic culture. The reality of cultural pluralism has been considered a characteristic of Postmodernity: the recognition, for one, of diverse race and ethnic populations—so-called minorities in the context of a dominant culture—in our society, each with their own traditional cultures; it is also the recognition of diverse subcultures, life-styles, sexual orientations, in addition to, of course, diverse religious beliefs; and there is the diversity implied, too, by distinct geographical regions—the recognition of regionalism within, say, the boundaries of a country itself. In the Postmodern world, however, what we experience as pluralism is too often an alienation of social fragmentation; that is, the plurality we live with lacks any real spiritual foundation beyond the lip service given it—often called the "melting pot" of our social diversity. Since soul is naturally polycentric, soul therefore should thrive in a pluralistic environment. Psyche would bring into play a meaningful spiritual foundation, therefore, into what is increasingly becoming a crazy world of alienating diversity.

We have a most marvellous ability within us that has been called the Active or Creative Imagination[9], which is far, far, from mere fantasy making. The occult traditions have always known of this ability. It is that mode of our psyche that grasps spiritual realities through our creatively living with the symbol (image or cipher) that opens us to these realities; this is the co-creative process. As we allow that symbol to speak, it extends those realities (as we creatively work with them), like the branches of a tree, into soul, simultaneously transmuting soul; this is the dynamic, fluid interchange of the psychospiritual (soul–psyche/Psyche–Spirit) where possibilities of creativity are unlimited. Alchemy was the age-old, secret art of this process. This, then, is the creative challenge facing us today: Can we not encounter and relate to our own Divinity as a shapeshifting figure? Remember the Divine Figure I saw in the Fountain, changing before my eyes. This, I would claim, is the new archetype of Self that Jung anticipated, hinted at in his works on alchemy (particularly the figure of Spirit Mercurius), but could not yet fully encounter and imaginatively, mythopoetically, embody in his own cultural milieu. Psyche, I see then, is the opening and psychopomp—our spiritual guidance—to the Next Level of consciousness.

The Vision that came to me was a spiritual Seed. For Psyche also said in a poem,[10]

> *I am the Seed you must plant*
> *in the heart,*
> *you must nurture in the heart.*

And then,

> *This Seed in your heart*
> *   now planted,*
> *I am this Seed.*
> *I am the Tree.*
> *I am the Song of the glory*
> *   of this Earth.*
> *I am the New Life.*

So I planted the Seed of this Vision in my heart. Giving it all the love (Eros) I could, it became for me the Tree of New Self. I found myself born again from The Cruz in the name of Spirit, in the name of Psyche *as* Spirit. Fundamentalist Christianity, we must realize, does not possess a monopoly on the fundamental spiritual right we all have to being born again. The born again experience has a spiritual universality beyond Traditional forms. Here is another example of how New Age spirituality transforms and universalizes what came before. Once our ego-self establishes a relationship to the Higher Self, we are on The Path of the New Self. The New Self is our opening up to and embodying what we can of the Higher Self, as the Higher Self simultaneously extends more and more of its superconscious Reality into our everyday life.

Now, to address another possible objection: It might be contended that I am only personifying, idealizing, the common psychological notion current today of the psyche, for as we have just said earlier, we all have a psyche. Yes, as a first approach, that may appear to be the case, but Psyche is not simply the psyche of conventional psychology. Psyche I experience *as* Spirit, so has just as much to do with theology. Psyche is also not mere personification, that intellectual dodge from experiencing the real thing, but is a Living Image produced by the Creative Imagination. We will see later that Psyche's coming-to-us as the Living Image of our Higher Self introduces us to a whole new level of consciousness that we have not yet explored. We will call it *the Next Level*.

Also, let us consider that if the Vision of Psyche implied nothing more than bringing our shadow personality, our darkness, into consciousness, which is what psychotherapy, after all, attempts to do, then one might wonder what is so new here that implies a new dispensation. Is the New Age movement then but a new therapeutic movement, a type of spiritual psychotherapy? As an understatement, there is something definitely true here; but there is so much more. Let us first be blunt, however, about the various psychotherapies, including psychoanalysis and depth psychology, which we currently practice today: They are but the attempts of a mouse to roar. Something is woefully inadequate about the past 20th Century attempts not only to heal, but to encourage evolution of, the psyche. Consider that well-known depth psychologist James Hillman had titled a book (with Michael Ventura) *We've Had a Hundred Years of Psychotherapy— And the World's Getting Worse*. We should not lose sight of the full implications of what that title is saying. Therapy must be brought out of the practitioner's stuffy office and into the open, fresh air of daily life. Or, should we say, into the open, fresh Air of Gaia? This of itself is a revolutionary statement. Remember the Water Bearer, *All that is hidden is to be revealed*. Liberation of soul must be allowed to take place anywhere, anytime, in any situation. Psyche would be our divine guidance to this collective transformation. We are still in our childhood when it comes to knowing ourselves psychologically, and especially psychologically in the collective sense, and especially psychologically from a spiritual perspective.

Our word 'psychology' itself is, of course, derived from 'psyche.' Psychology is the logos of psyche (soul), that is, it offers us the studied words (purported to be scientific) about psyche. But let us give credit here to where credit is due. Though given the shortcoming mentioned above, it is the depth psychologists—psychologists of the Unconscious—who are the real word bearers in the field of psychology of soul. And we must acknowledge that they do address, however still inadequately, the transpersonal (in the spiritual sense) dimension of the psyche. The great majority of other psychologists, on the other hand, who have abandoned soul, most particularly the behaviorists, have become but the academic, scholarly minions of Technos. Their focus is most often the intellectual ego's drive to acquire the knowledge that would attempt to eventually control and manipulate the psyche completely.

As just one example of the direction before us, a fundamental lesson to be learned is that of androgyny—that psychologically we must acknowledge and develop the latent masculine *and* feminine aspects of our psyche. Whether we are biologically male or female, our soul/psyche is not so gender limited, but is (potentially) a mirror of the complete human Archetype, embracing the poles of yin and yang, however that might be interpreted against what were traditionally masculine and feminine stereotypes. In current jargon, we are speaking of course of the integration of right brain and left brain. I am not advocating by this though that people need to go and sign up for safe, cozy, expensive workshops in getaway retreats where individuals are trained in the techniques of getting in touch with their masculine or feminine sides. Again, this integration should be an ongoing process in everyday life. The current transgender trend is undoubtedly one concrete example—but only one—of this process of defining a New Self in relationship to the androgynous nature of the Higher Self. Gender identification need no longer be limited to our biological sex. Soul liberated means for one thing that we are now creatively able to define our own gender, however the Higher Self is destined to manifest through us. Since soul has been repressed, it is primarily the traditional feminine aspect of our psyche that must be recovered and integrated as a mirror of the Divine Androgyne Psyche is. Interestingly enough, Aquarius itself, signifying the revolutionary impulse (the principle of Uranus, planetary ruler of Aquarius) to break out of convention—and here, specifically, we refer to gender conventions—, *is* the sign of androgyny. When it comes to fashion, we might speak in this context of the unisex look.

One of the most repressive, anti-psyche environments we can pinpoint today is the corporate world. Consider the power the multinational corporations hold in the world today. Then consider that spirituality is not welcome in the corporate structure, or in the everyday working environment, for that matter. Most everyone who has held a job in America, from working in huge corporations to small business, will know exactly what I am talking about. The emphasis is on being the good worker or corporate cog. It is not psyche, but productivity, efficiency, competition, profits, *the bottom line* that makes the wheels of business go round. This, combined with the obsessive need for increasingly more income just to survive, and the hours spent in urban traffic, makes the attempts by a handful of vanguard companies to allow employees some meditative time, or time for recreational activities, quite feeble in comparison to what is actually needed.

How does Psyche appear? Only in a Vision? Only in a Vision received by a poet? *A poet?* Might this not be then a mere delusion? We realize that that is always a danger on the spiritual Path. But we have Psyche—Higher Self—contact in any number of ways, as we mentioned in the first paragraph of this chapter. It is sufficient to realize, however, that in any peak experience which reveals, brings us into, what New Agers are so apt to call the Light, in these moments of illumination, there is the possibility of starting a dialogue with that source of Light, which can become a living source, a spiritual symbolic site, in the interior landscape of the psychospiritual, which, sooner or later, will likely reveal a Living Image. Our rapport with Higher Self has then begun. For what is crucial, what indeed is the dispensation yet to be given collectively, is that the Higher Self be experienced and related to as a Living Image that inspires us, teaches us, guides us, counsels us, that truly moves us, that establishes a new, Aquarian faith of openness and tolerance, a faith born of that direct, firsthand contact.

Psyche, I am claiming, comes to us as the new Word of Divinity that unfolds a new world—a New Age. This Word, revealing to us the Greater Reality (to the extent that I am able to share it here), was also known in the ancient Greek world as *Mythos*. (We will explore in some depth the meaning of Mythos in the chapter "Mythos-making: Art of the New Age.") From our co-creative engagement with Mythos, new forms will be birthed of ritual, theology, ethics, art, of human relationships, of our relationship to Nature, to Gaia; new forms of Mythos will be birthed, in other words, to bring about a new, revitalized culture beyond the wasteland of Postmodernism. Psyche, I am now suggesting, and advocating, is the emerging new Mythos that speaks to our age, that answers the Call of the Age.

Psyche, as the Mythos, revitalizes all language. That is an insight I have realized: All language comes newly alive through Psyche. Through Psyche, all things are made new. Which is why, in a Postmodern context, we can be called to reinterpret anew all theological language. Postmodern secular humanists have been wallowing in a self-debilitating linguistic poverty. The full explication of what is only hinted at here will be found later in the chapter on Mythos-making.

For those of us who are moving beyond Tradition, we must no longer be fooled by our traditional religious images, even when they appear to have a little life still left in them. We must go beyond—to *our own* Divine Self. It is appropriate to say, for example: *Jesus, I love you. I honor you. I know how important of a teacher you are. I know that you have been a beacon to the Christ-self. But I am grown up now, and I feel that you are not telling the complete Truth. Jesus, you have been an extraordinary stand-in for the Higher Self for 2,000 years, but now Psyche has come, Living Image of the Archetype of our own Divinity.*

Before finishing here, we should acknowledge an important point regarding the birth of religions, since I am implying that our discussion of the Higher Self and my Vision of Psyche do point in the direction of the possible foundation of the new, universal, Aquarian religion. That, in itself, I realize, is quite an extraordinary claim, perhaps a grandiose claim, inviting a firestorm of controversy. Now if we look into the founding sacred texts of our traditional religions, we cannot help but note that the one, crucial feature at the birth of them all has been the "supernatural" event. Religions, it is safe to say, have always originated with some outward, numinous, paranormal event, or chain of events, especially surrounding its founder. (This was still true, for example, for the relatively new religion of Mormonism.) Can we say, however, that this has happened yet for the possible, new, Aquarian religion? Is my Vision possibly a sign of what is to come? Of what is still assumed will happen? Do any of our contemporary prophets, psychics, or contactees have a better sense of it yet? Yes, they have predicted many things over the years, but I am speaking here of a founding event, "supernatural," universal in significance, powerful enough to move people in a new direction. From our contemporary vantage point, this would seem to imply some major kind of UFO/ET event. Though UFO/ET experiences are reported as taking place just about all the time somewhere on planet Earth, including recent, well-known cases, it appears, though, that none have given birth, as of yet, to any founding event out of which the New Age religion I speak of could develop. It is therefore still but speculation what that coming "supernatural," defining event will be. Many, we know, had their eyes set on the year 2012, but 2012 has indeed come and gone.

But there is a scenario, under the umbrella of so-called End Times, that would inevitably, without a doubt, trigger such a Revelation event. That scenario is abrupt climate change, given the fact that it is beginning to unfold all around us, though on what time scale will its full impact be felt is still debatable. By this is meant in-our-face catastrophic biosphere and civilization collapse, the mass extinction level event (MELE) that is already underway to some degree or another. Such an apocalyptic scenario, with implications that various science fiction films have already viscerally depicted, would certainly be the most extreme psychological milieu imaginable in which new Revelation, and possibly ET intervention, would take place. Without a doubt, this will be a time when visionaries at The Edge come forward.

There is an important, collective reason psychological adulthood is so crucial to our evolution in the early years of the Age of Aquarius. The repressed half of the Piscean psychological dynamic must be brought into the Light so that we are prepared for the impact of the ego-challenging, if not shattering, Next Level of consciousness, otherwise a whole new level of collective disorientation will very likely ensue. Then, there is the danger that Technos will step in to take complete control.

# ( 8 )

# TECHNOS: THE NEW GLOBAL SUPERPOWER

*Giant Technos walked up and down upon Earth...*[1]

A major shortcoming of our religious traditions in the context of the contemporary world, and this applies to the West as well as to the East, is that they have nothing significant to contribute in any original way to our necessary spiritual encounter with the new Superpower in the world today—*Technos*. Those who would want to rebut that religion or spirituality have nothing to do with technology—that old paradigm of the other world distinct and separate from *this* world—would be missing an essential part of the message of the New Age Vision. In the New Age, we are no longer going to be invested in the old Piscean dualism of the other world versus this world. Psyche as Mythos of the New Age is an Integrator, bridging the other world *with* this world. That those who identify with the New Age could ignore all the current developments of new technologies would be a serious shortcoming of Vision; and to simply accept what Technos offers us is equally a fatal mistake, and let us hope that *it is not too late already.*

*Keep in mind that Technos is the name I have given to what some already refer to as the coming ascendency of AI—the AI God and its Internet-of-Things.*

Since the 17th Century when science wrestled away from the Church the royal road to the truth about Nature, the Western world has made tremendous strides in its technological efforts to tap Nature's storehouse and, as a result, has significantly altered the face of the planet. Everywhere we look on the planet today, just about everyone is pushing for more and more of the latest technology; the drive for new technology is, in fact, on a manic level. Technology is still considered to this day the light-bearer of Progress. 'Progress' was, of course, the buzzword in the heyday of Modernism, which dominated the 19th Century into the 20th, and though it is no longer in our Postmodern era a word that the critical intellectual is especially comfortable with, the continued push for Progress in dominant, mainstream society continues at full speed.

It would be helpful at this point if we consider the popular view of technology that almost everyone pays homage to. It was Heidegger's writing[2] on technology that first brought the following analysis of technological consciousness to my attention. Ask almost anyone his or her view on what technology is really about and you are likely to hear that technology, in essence, is merely a tool; and, as such, it just sits around, waiting for us to use it or turn it on; it is all up to us. It is, in other words, "neutral" as regards any world orientation, having no particular direction or will of its own. After all, it is only machines, only equipment, only computers—we build them, and it is always our decision to turn them on and use them. (But, curiously, honestly now, do we ever decide not to use them? That literally would not make sense—*their purpose* is to be used. What about those, as only a minor example, who keep their television on all day, only to reluctantly turn it off at bedtime, if even then!) Though technology is not worshipped outright—the AI God is not yet a reality—, our society does put tremendous faith in it for bettering and enhancing our life; and technology does inspire a kind of religious fervor in those who are directly involved in its development and application, and in those who get emotionally worked up by the latest gadgets on the market. (Consider in this regard simply the title of David F. Noble's book *The Religion of Technology*.) Of course, everyone benefits to greater and lesser degrees from the wide range of technologies available today; and some technologies—in medical science, for example—can be lifesaving miracles. Our society, it can easily be said, has more than just a passion for technology, but, more accurately, an obsession with it. Technology was beginning to advance at such a lightning pace back in the mid-20th Century that it was commonly thought that it would also provide solutions to all our societal ills (which turned out to be an ominous, Big Brother notion, in itself). Along with the popular view that technology is nothing other than a tool, it is sometimes asked why then do we not have a better handle on it? Also, people have begun to wonder if it hasn't gotten out of control. According to the popular view, by all rights we should be in control, but for some reason regarding politics and the military-industrial-corporate power establishment, it seems somehow to have slipped from our hands. That corporations routinely make decisions about implementing new technologies without public consent is obvious; it goes on all the time. But if that were all there was to the manic growth of technology!

Perhaps it is time we pop this cherished bubble and present another view, a still rather uncommon view. Our society might have been mistaken about technology all along. To still believe that today's technology is but some sophisticated kind of "neutral tool" may unfortunately be delusional, even dangerous; at best, it is quite naïve. We may reach a point at some future time—and let us hope that we do, though indications do not currently favor it (only think of the ongoing disaster at Fukushima)—when technology does come within the grasp of our "control." But we are nowhere near that today. Those who would claim that we are now in a position to take technology in hand and do with it as we wish are probably the self-satisfied technocrats who can afford to live in the money-driven illusion of holding the reins. They do hold social and corporate power and wealth, but are themselves the minions of the Superpower Technos.

This other view, then, which perhaps sounds fantastic upon first hearing it, is that technology is an autonomous power of its own, developing in accordance to its own logic. Heidegger has done an in-depth exploration of this view, and so has, from another angle, Jacques Ellul in *The Technological Society*. And this is not a recent phenomenon only, though only recently has it come fully into its own, but one that was already apparent in the very beginnings of modern science, and then especially come the Industrial Revolution, with philosophical roots going far back in our Tradition. The control we believe we might have lost over technology, we in fact never had.

The first difficulty in giving this view a fair appraisal is this: The eye is not focused on the real issue. What people always have in mind when speaking about technology is *the machine, the hardware.* Of course, we can all agree, machines per se (at least still today) have no direct power over us; as most think, they sit there dumb until we turn them on. (Yet, do we get a choice in deciding whether the street surveillance camera—or now the drone—is recording us or not? Here, then, is a hint of what I will be getting at.) To attempt to back up the common view, the facile remark is often made, *Well, we can always pull the plug, if we want.* But, seriously, how often do we actually pull the plug on our technology? To be honest, *never*. Our survival, our well-being, is today utterly dependent upon keeping the plug of technology connected. Do we ever voluntarily pull the plug on our energy grid, for example? An absurd question. Whenever it does go down, say, in a storm, there is an immediate rush to get it back up and running again as quickly as possible. Those who might think that the energy grid, or the Internet, is no different than a simple tool that sits in a workshop utterly misunderstand the nature of today's technology. I would suggest it is time to stop deluding ourselves about technology and stop playing naïve. It is almost impossible to get some people to turn off their TVs for a while, let alone not drive their cars, or, imagine, not using refrigerators, computers, smart phones, etc. And I am not advocating that people can really do (in most cases) anything of the kind. The real issue, however, that is always missed is this: Though it sounds obvious, it needs emphasizing: that machines, hardware, software, whatever we wish to refer to, are a product of *technological consciousness*. And it is important to understand, technological consciousness is not the exclusive domain of engineers and technocrats; it has come to determine for all of us our Being-in-the-world. "It is the machine which is now entirely dependent upon technique" (i.e. technological consciousness), stated Jacques Ellul, "and the machine represents only a small part of technique." Technological consciousness is a particular mindset that today has come to dominate our entire civilization.

An easy misunderstanding is to assume that such a view, stated bluntly like this, immediately implies that technology must then be something evil, or that such a view is trying to sneak in a basically anti-technology position. But that is not the case at all. These are simplistic reactions. All of us are wrapped up with technology. We are all dependent on the Superpower Daddy. To suggest that we need to, or could, extricate ourselves from our fabricated world is downright senseless. The modern world's relationship to Being, which has not been our decision to make, but is a destiny, as Heidegger explicated, is defined as technological. But we, as a maturing intelligent species, need to stop living in this illusion about technology, and be ruthlessly honest about where we stand with regards to it.

I call technological consciousness, as it has developed into an autonomous Power acting through us, *Technos*. Technos is the new God of technology; as some forecast AI will in fact be a *this* world God. Now Technos defines the world in terms of Its own logic, which has the practical result of producing an ever-expanding phalanx of new technology, intolerant of alternative ways of viewing and engaging the world. In fact, Technos is so insistent in our life, that It can block us from experiencing the world differently—to wit, spiritually, or even aesthetically, creatively. Since Technos has now come to set for us the standard for Reality, all other ways of Being-in-the-world are considered archaic, anachronistic, or romantic daydreaming, merely subjective and emotional, merely poetic. Or, in our Postmodern context, entertainment.

Let us consider the objection that says that societies have always had some form of technology. We have always used tools, we will hear it said. But what is not understood is that there is no real comparison between traditional tools (going back to neolithic, prehistoric times) and contemporary high technology. This is like the old analogy of comparing apples to oranges (sure, they are both fruits). Traditional tools used by traditional societies—take, for example, those found in a craft shop—, were not part of an interlocking system of massive environmental alteration, manipulation, and control that continuously developed under its own momentum. The tools of earlier societies and civilizations did not take front and center stage, but were used in a context of greater cosmic / spiritual / supernatural powers. The Gods had always kept humanity in check, if not directly, then through established control systems, such as religions. Today, in a Postmodern world without Gods or "God," Technos reigns supreme, and has almost overnight become our new secular God, the new global Superpower, greater in fact than any superpower nation. For Technos transcends the factionalism of politics, the sovereignty of nations. (Some will undoubtedly think of multinational corporations in this regard. That is of course a reality. But even more fundamental is Technos, that has allowed the multinational corporations to expand and become what they are.)

The common view, again, is that technology has no will of its own, but is totally directed by basic human drive. True, our human drive certainly contributes to the development of technology, but, still, does not explain the logic of technology's increasingly particular kind of dominance; our human needs, human desires, have expressed themselves in other, age-old, non-technological ways also. It might be asked though, What of our need to order and manage, to get some control of, our surroundings? (Let us first be mindful of our language here—'order,' 'manage,' 'control' are already words appropriated by Technos. To think these words, we are already thinking the way Technos thinks.) Here, we do begin to get a hint of the essence of technology, but Technos has taken this a whole, giant step further. Technos is *the will* to control, *the will* to power. This will to control within humankind has become, though, a dominant power, a collective Super Ego even, that has separated Itself from the Web of the interconnectedness of all life. This separation from the Web of Gaia should alert us to a connection here with Christianity and its denial of Nature. Even more than that, the emphasis on the will indeed goes back to the original Christian injunction to develop the will, that is, to develop will power strong enough to rise above the merely natural. In *The Religion of Technology*, David Noble first explores the late Medieval monks theorizing on the material perfectibility of man, breaking free of Nature, setting in play this will to improve life...ultimately to find expression in today's Transhumanist movement.

Technos has become a Superpower—an autonomous mindset—living through us. It is the Super Ego, alter ego, of the ego-self, taking on a life of Its own that we, the human collective, have come to have no real say about. Certainly, we can protest and try to curb the extensive and oftentimes dangerous use of certain technologies, and just outright refuse to use them. But let us bring up some examples here. How many of the following technologies did "we the people" willingly decide upon: SmartMeters, GMOs, geoengineering the planet, cell phones / smart phones, WiFi, RFID, surveillance systems, drone aircraft, or the various new forms of nanotechnology? We could obviously ask the same question about nuclear weapons, nuclear power, biological weapons, etc. Before the enormous, interlocking network of Technos we find today, the great majority of us have come to feel downright powerless. Technos has become a juggernaut that apparently no one, and nothing, is able to stop, let alone slow down.

As our own Superpower alter ego, Technos lives through us not by any means as an adversary, but as a friend, a friend that promises us greater security, comfort, convenience, productivity, mobility, efficiency, a longer and healthier life, and is always offering us more toys that are newer, bigger, and better (though today they are often becoming ever smarter and smaller). Technos is not intent on our destruction (at least at this point), but simply wants to expand Itself and control everything on Its own terms. A statement made in 1927 by John Watson, the founder of behaviorism (psychology's equivalent of Technos), summed it up: "The interest of the behaviorist in man's doings is more than the interest of the spectator—he wants to control man's reactions as physical scientists want to control and manipulate other natural phenomena. It is the business of behavioristic psychology to be able to predict and to control human activity."[3] To extrapolate, Technos would eventually want control over all life, over all things, and like a power-mad figure straight out of science fiction, ultimately the entire planet. It is because of this monomaniacal drive, however, that Technos may sooner or later wind up destroying us by laying waste everything in Its path of "Progress." (Always keep in mind the two major Threads of MELE that have entered our Story—global warming/abrupt climate change and Fukushima.) The first quarter of the 21st Century is already indicating which way our Story is going, if left completely up to Technos.

Technos expands Its dominance by constantly analyzing, calculating, organizing, systematizing, managing, regulating, standardizing, mechanizing, computerizing; by seeking efficient, uniform, and technical procedures for all activities; by relegating all things, from automobiles to data banks, from weapons of mass destruction to the labor market, to resources on standby status, ready for use; and by seeing a new technical challenge in every problem. "Technique has taken over all of man's activities..." (Jacques Ellul). This cannot be over-emphasized: Technos recognizes and respects no limits; It must constantly expand and is today working Its way into every aspect of life. Our technological world is fast becoming an interlocking, seamless, global system, in a way that most people cannot fathom. And still, today, this technological expansionism is called *Progress*. Indeed, mainstream society is still a true believer in that 19th Century ideal, which was completely a materialistic ideal. Ten minutes of TV commercials is enough to convince us of that.

We can list many examples of all this: The organization of society and business called management in all its forms, including money management, resource management, energy management, waste management, land management. We see Technos expanded into everything: we have the farming industry, the food industry, the fishing industry, the logging industry, the mass media industry, the entertainment industry, the publishing industry, the music industry, the medical industry, the tourist industry, the sports industry, and educational institutions themselves have become degree factories. For almost anything, we have techniques: besides the multitudes of hardcore scientific/technological techniques in all the various specialized fields, there are management techniques, educational techniques—programmed learning—, conflict resolution techniques, and then even sexual techniques, therapeutic techniques, and we find that artists and writers from the Modernists on have also often gotten too caught up in techniques. In every context, we hear of technique, of methods, of methodologies, management systems, market research. California's Silicon Valley already decades ago gave us the information superhighway, which, of course, calls for the management of information. In politics, we have "spin control." In literally almost all companies, the old personnel departments were at some point renamed human *resources* departments, and so we also have human resource management. In other words, human beings are considered a resource for use (the labor market), no different than water or timber, and no different than replaceable parts. We know quite well that individuals are easily replaceable as employees. Computers, of course, are found in every workplace, and in every school, and probably now in every home. Militaries boast ever more sophisticated weapon systems and thrive on black budgets hiding secret, black projects continuously developing technologies far in advance of what the public is aware of. Increasingly in business, in public places, on our streets, we see installed various kinds of surveillance systems, another aspect of control. The newly marketed radio-frequency identification devices (RFID) will be used to track just about everything, including persons. We also know that Technos considers no land to be sacred: Traditional Native American sacred lands are simply a resource—usually rich in minerals (e.g. uranium)—to be exploited.

Technos has already been presented for years in a number of ways in numerous films and literature. Two of the early 20th Century classics in literature of a technologically managed society were *Brave New World* and *1984*. And beginning with the silent movie classic *Metropolis* and so many futuristic and science fiction movies since, we have seen the popular presentation of Technos as the Organization, the Machine, the Super-Computer, or as the cyborgs and androids that have established oppressive control, in various depictions of a dystopian world. In the classic *2001: A Space Odyssey*, the computer HAL winds up taking control of the space mission to Jupiter. Television's *Star Trek* series, and its various spin-offs, and the *Star Wars* movies, and so many others in a similar vein, have all been slowly conditioning society to a future where technology will inextricably be woven into the very fabric of life. The naïveté in so many of these television programs and movies, however, and in the general run of science fiction, is that they portray human beings as still acting out their everyday soap operas. In such a future world permeated by such high levels of technology, it is hard to see us still involved in these adolescent, egocentric, and violent roles. The point is, in the real world, we will not even have advanced that far technologically if we are still playing out these old human dramas. Either Technos will have taken complete control (the future AI God), or the future will see us having evolved in a substantive, psychospiritual way (the intent of the New Age dispensation).

According to the logic of Technos, if a new technology is possible, it then becomes a necessity to develop it; and each new development, in turn, is always leading to further developments, each new system to new systems. New computer models are now outdated yearly—or is it seasonally? And each new development of technological know-how, by this logic, must immediately be considered for practical use. An ominous example of this was the development of the atomic bomb. French anthropologist and politician Jacques Soustelle is quoted as having said, "Since it was possible, it was necessary," in reference to the atomic bomb. As Robert Jungk puts it in *Brighter than a Thousand Suns, A Personal History of the Atomic Scientists,* "On the other hand it would have been contrary to the spirit of modern science and technology to refrain voluntarily from further development of a new field of research, however dangerous it might be for the future, and leave it only half explored." He, in turn, quotes J. Robert Oppenheimer: "However, it is my judgment in these things that when you see something that is technically sweet you go ahead and do it and you argue about what to do about it only after you have had your technical success. That is the way it was with the atomic bomb. I do not think anybody opposed making it; there were some debates about what to do with it after it was made." Thus, according to Technos, the Bomb—and the H-bomb and every new bomb after that—neutron bombs, smart bombs—simply *had to be* built. Of course, in the international arena, making and then using the Bomb first allowed the United States to pull ahead and secure our status as a dominant, superpower player. But we then saw what that led to—a Cold War dangerously escalated by Technos.

It is here that we move beyond Heidegger and Ellul in their work on Technos. Let us bring our astrological perspective into the picture now. As we had suggested earlier, the latter half of the Piscean Age should show a Virgoan counterpoint. Where that manifests above all is in modern technology. The rise of Technos since the Renaissance, especially since the 17th century, is the prime expression of Virgo in the Pisces/Virgo dynamic of the Piscean Age. Virgo is an Earth sign characterized by practical intelligence, that is, the ego-rational intellect developing skills, techniques, methodologies, analyses, at the service of our practical, everyday needs and wants. Max Weber referred to the modern technological mindset as *instrumental rationality*, which is quite an apt phrase for its Virgo character. Modern technology as the astrological expression of Virgo meant that our life on Earth was ideally to be made as safe and secure, as efficient, organized, and comfortable, as is possible. A key phrase for Virgo is *I analyze*. Everyone has probably heard of the Virgo predilection for precision and detail. We can look at modern science then as an ongoing analysis—dissection—of Nature for the sake of a constantly advancing, human-benefiting, technology. It has been said that our modern science has become, in fact, the handmaiden of technology, epitomized as Technos.

We find it no mere coincidence that when the psyche was discovered anew in the West, it was through psycho*analysis* (Freud) and *analytical* psychology (Jung). Just as science analyzed Nature without, these new areas of research set out to analyze our nature within. (Though it turned out that psychoanalysis and analytical psychology—better called today *depth* psychology—are nothing close to the Technos-dominated aim of behavioristic and almost all academic psychology. As a matter of fact, they are pariahs in the academic world, since they take the reality of the psyche quite seriously.) And even philosophy, in the 20th Century, primarily in the English-speaking West, developed as *analytical* philosophy, especially as language *analysis*.

Another characteristic then of the contemporary Western world that should now be of no surprise to us is the dominance of materialism, both as a scientific worldview and as a capitalist, consumer life-style. Technos, born as an expression of Virgo, would naturally be focused on the material plane, and be blind to any other reality. Virgo, again, is a materially-oriented sign of eminent practicality. So an ever more productive and industrious Technos has been able to turn the marketplace, with constant mass media marketing, of course, into a shopping mall of compulsive consumerism.

Virgo also has the meaning of the self in crisis. On the individual psychological level, this readily refers in the early psychoanalytical days to the patients the analysts were seeing—they were diagnosed "neurotic." Their neurosis put their life in an ongoing, low-level crisis. And they were neurotic because of repression; for Freud that meant sexual repression; for other early psychoanalysts that also meant other repressions. In a previous chapter we already saw that it was *soul* itself that had been repressed. Now the self writ large is none other than current humanity in crisis, which Technos will do Its best to resolve—*on Its terms*. Think too of the solutions offered to individuals, prescribed by their doctors, by the pharmaceutical drug companies.

Our new high technology continues to advance at an exhilaratingly furious pace. And what has happened is that it is no longer technology in a strictly Virgoan sense, but has now rapidly become an Aquarian technology. High technology—cybertechnology—is a whole new development that is Aquarian in character. And this technology was early on appropriately named "high tech," for the higher mind beyond practical intellect/analytical rationality does come into play. As all Air signs do, Aquarius has to do with communication. Our newer technologies are no longer focusing on building bigger and better, practical, more efficient, labor-saving, mechanized machines, but are an emphasis on expanding all forms of communication, or, should we say, on expanding all forms of information development and management. *But it is beginning to take place in a new dimension.*

The other Air signs are Gemini and Libra. Whereas Gemini emphasizes the traditional forms of communication and information processing and sharing, such as simple language skills, speaking, reading, writing, arithmetic, lecturing, teaching, all forms that take place in short-range interaction (sitting down in a cozy place and reading a book, or going to a lecture), and Libra emphasizes all forms of communicating with *an other* (partnerships to marriage) and therefore socially with the other (from parties to diplomacy), and through art (all forms involving the beauty and gracefulness of Venus), Aquarius emphasizes the whole range of long-distance communication—or let us say, distance-negating communication—that is invisible, instantaneous, and collective, referring to the large scale interactions not only within groups and organizations, but across the globe. This exactly defines our new cyberworld of the Internet. The Internet, the perfect expression of it, allows us to communicate globally and instantaneously within a network through the invisible medium of electromagnetism. (The spiritual form of Aquarian communication we will be exploring in the chapter "The Next Level." We will see that the technological and the spiritual forms of Aquarian communication not only parallel each other, but will undoubtedly over time be integrated. But, then, not so fast—) Above all, Aquarius is the opening to new channels of communication through our moving into the Invisible.

The new cyberworld, in fact, is invisible. A contemporary reality conundrum is this: *Where exactly is the cyberworld? Where do these millions of websites exist?* They are everywhere a computer is plugged in to the Internet, but if you try to look for them inside the computer or even at your Web host's location (and who ever does that?), they are not to be found there, not exactly in the way that they appear for us—for they appear nowhere exclusively, but are everywhere accessible, appearing on millions of computer screens simultaneously. The cyberworld appears to exist in its own invisible dimension. The Disney movie *Tron* presented an early imaginative portrayal of this new reality. On the Internet, we even find an alternate world of virtual life, called *Second Life*.

The cyberworld is not often thought of in conjunction with the dawning New Age; after all, the cyberworld is hardcore technology in action, and the New Age, well, the New Age is some newfangled religion or spiritual thing, isn't it? Here, again, we find that the New Age has been viewed far too narrowly. It has as much to do with cybertechnology, the Internet, instantaneous global communication, as it has with anything spiritual. The Internet is linking minds in a way never before imagined, and what we see today is still only the beginning. And this is very Aquarian. It has allowed individuals to cross social boundaries, economic boundaries, national boundaries, ideological boundaries, boundaries that had been maintained in various ways in centuries past by traditional Authority. A freeing up of the Establishment's monopoly on information and communication is the great promise of this decentralized, global, communication network, that is, unless the planet's Secret Controllers allow Technos ever greater control to limit such freedom.

We should always keep in mind that there is also a dangerous, diabolical potential to the Aquarian New Age that cannot be ignored. For one, because the Aquarian nature does have a tendency toward the impersonal, when we see increasingly the alienation inherent in cold, impersonal organizations, multinational corporations, bloated governments, social management, in a ubiquitous System, a potential New World Order, we cannot deny that this is the shadow side of Aquarius. We will see more examples of this along the way. The essential point about sharing a New Age *Vision* is that a Vision is called for as we enter this Aquarian phase of the human Story or else the darker Aquarian potential that we have no handle on (Technos) will come to dominate the planet. *Without Vision, a people perish*, as it is said in *The Bible*. And as we have asked before, What Tradition today offers a contemporary Vision?

Getting on the Net and exploring the literally millions of websites available, jumping from site to site, *Web surfing*, at the click of a mouse or tap on a mousepad, is beginning to approximate, if only beginning, the rapid mental movement of intuition. In fact, as we sit at a computer, an inquiring thought can come to us, and with a simple click or two on a search engine, multitudes of websites can be immediately accessed, and our question thereby immediately addressed. A few cyborg pioneers—already calling themselves "Borgs"—are today living with their portable, wearable computers continuously, and have instant access to cyberspace wherever they go. We can already see the direction this is going. (Consider the ubiquitous presence now, that almost happened overnight, of cell phones—or preferably, i-phones/smart phones.) Whatever the ego-self would want at its fingertips—the archives of all knowledge, access to all software, a panoply of keyboard commands offering an almost infinite manipulation of information and graphics, with the ability to create virtually anything before its eyes—will be a cyberworld mirroring like nothing imagined before the mind's own mental functioning. There are untold possibilities here for truly creative—visionary, revolutionary—individuals, that is, if they are not economically blocked out from having access to the technology. (I am not, therefore, talking about individuals working in the current, status quo, movie industry.) And this will be truly liberating if the Higher Self is allowed to enter the picture. Or will Technos alone continue to determine the rules of the cyberworld?

As an example of the cutting-edge of technology accessing the Invisible, let us consider a department of government that is fully dedicated to Technos—the military. Now in the old, old days, a warrior had to become personally adept at the physical use of some weapon, such as a knife, spear, sword, or bow and arrow; and then, in more modern times, came guns, grenades, artillery, bombs, tanks, and then missiles. With the use of poisonous gases, there was introduced a weapon that we could not see. With biological weapons, and with the new laser weapons effective at great distances, the military continues to cross a threshold into areas of the unseen and invisible. However, they have even gone further than that—the military has developed a new generation of weaponry that is operable in the Invisible.[4] These new, black project weapons use the invisible dimension of the electromagnetic, and can literally turn our own bodies against us. For example, every organ in our body has an electromagnetic signature that can be tagged and locked onto. Electromagnetic beams that are set to the right frequencies—a type of high-charged information beam, as it were—can be directed at the body from a distance (and we would never know it) and made to resonate with, and then deform, the signature of any organ, with the specific intent of damaging it, either triggering sudden failure (e.g. heart attack or stroke) or triggering disease (e.g. fast-developing cancers). There have been suspicions circulating for years that such insidious weapons have been used already, and against a few of our own citizens even! (The anecdotal evidence for this would of course have to be pursued further.) Computer systems are also vulnerable in this way—an electromagnetic virus can be sent invisibly from a distance to wipe out anyone's hard drive. The military, we see, is more than willing to take up the offer of Technos on every new weapon it can throw up on the drawing board. As another example, a new weapon development is drone aircraft, someday advancing to AI drones that will not require human operators. Most diabolical is the possible deployment of mini-drones called "slaughterbots."[5] Or consider the Air Force's 1996 research paper titled "Weather as a Force Multiplier: Owning the Weather in 2025." (For those who have followed the geoengineering agenda, the military seems to be ahead of schedule.) Alarmingly, all of this is Technos exploiting new Aquarian frontiers.

It was said just a few years ago that the field of artificial intelligence (AI) was not showing the breakthroughs that were at first expected for it; as an area of research, it had plodded along while other technological achievements have claimed the spotlight. Nonetheless, robots—androids—, we are told, are soon to become a common sight in future years. The philosophical issues of AI—whether AI will have acquired consciousness, mind, or selfhood, for example, and how that might be decided, and how we will relate to such intelligence—have been on the table for years now. Professor of philosophy Nick Bostrom explores these questions in his book *Superintelligence: Paths, dangers, strategies*. The storyline of a recent (2015) sci fi thriller *Ex Machina* is also based on these questions. And though attention has focused on the promise of artificial intelligence again—in fact, the drive to develop AI is gaining momentum by the day—, it is in the arena of intelligence amplification—designing computer systems that can amplify our own native human intelligence—where great strides will most certainly take place in the near term. It is part of the Transhumanist dream of becoming cyborg.

Another whole new frontier of cybertechnology, still in its early development, that uses intelligence amplification as a premise, is virtual reality (VR). Virtual reality, the artificial simulation of lifelike sensory experience through a complex array of computers, helmets, and body suits, has, we are to understand, a tremendous future. Myron Krueger, one of the forerunners of VR, had developed and experimented with the notion of artificial realities and their responsive environments in the 1970s. Already, years ago, the military began using flight simulator modules to train pilots. Today, scientists are using virtual reality to configure new chemical compounds; medical researchers to look inside the virtual human body; surgeons to train for delicate operations on virtual organs; architects to walk around inside virtual buildings that are still in the design stage; NASA engineers to explore virtual extraterrestrial terrains. Naturally the entertainment industry will plan big things for VR. In fact, it is the gaming industry that is the major player driving VR developments. Someday, not too far off, the virtual reality entertainment center will certainly become the new focus of attention in the living room. Exploring virtual worlds, having virtual sex, taking virtual psychedelic trips, will undoubtedly absorb entire upcoming generations in a way that will be exponentially more addicting than television is today. Just as TV addicts find it difficult to break away from the tube to lead a more active life, VR addicts will prefer to live in its mind-titillating, artificial environments rather than live in the mundane, everyday world. As in the recent popular *Matrix* movies, Technos could one day become the one grand Master in a total, all encompassing, VR world. And yes, I have recently had my own first brief VR experience(s), and, quite honestly, it was impressive, no, mind-blowing. Now, to imagine entering into a full-length VR movie—that would take our Postmodern schizoid life to another whole level.

Yet, this is not all. The techno wizards talk about us someday soon merging with our machines and computer systems. Medical science has already developed many artificial replacements for the body; we even have the prototype mechanical heart. Very soon now we will see electronic implants inserted in the brain, for the specific purpose of providing mental improvements—to help the blind to see, the deaf to hear, to restore and sharpen memory, to help alleviate such impairments as Parkinson's disease or Alzheimer's. Implantable biochips are apparently already being used in the military, not only as a high-tech version of the simple dog tag, but also containing an individual's entire medical history; and they can also be used for tracking. Recently in the news we have heard of individuals volunteering themselves and their children to receive the first of the tracking biochips available to the public. Indeed, we hear all the time now about plans to implant biochips in future generations; individuals could be invisibly monitored in the System, like something straight out of science fiction, with even a miniature barcode for the wrist. The new field of nanotechnology could make biochips so microscopic, in fact, no different seeming than a cell, that they could easily be introduced into the body, say, for example, in an injection. An even more undetectable delivery medium would be what is being called "smart dust."

It is as if we are all caught up in a race. The high priests of cybertechnology are carrying out the dictates of Technos as fast as their mental ingenuity can go. To hear them talk about their work in interviews, we get the sense that they are truly Technos intoxicated. Without batting an eye, computer engineers and cyberneticians talk about the day when androids will think alongside of us, and they say that these robotic humanoids will undoubtedly reach a level of intelligence where they will begin to make decisions independent of us, perhaps even making life decisions for us. They might even decide at some point to do without us. That is increasingly a concern being voiced today. If this AI trend continues, androids are destined to become another type of being on our planet, and without a doubt, they will encounter the world in their own way. Through them, Technos may come to decide *we are* outdated and expendable, or decide to reduce us in status to second-class, merely biological beings. And the high priests of future technology think nothing of it—oh, they might give some lip service to the "ethics" of all this, but do they restrain themselves in the development of these technologies? Not in the least. In the social arena, they are of course enthralled with the power and wealth of their priestly positions. Would they voluntarily relinquish that? Certainly, the scientists behind the development of the atomic bomb didn't stop to ponder for very long what they were doing. Afterward, there were those who had misgivings, to be sure, but it was too late—the genie had been let out.

The technological world has its own answer to the AI android, however. There is emerging on the techno scene another new movement called Transhumanism. (That Transhumanism will rival the New Age movement in the coming years is a given. Nevertheless, I do see the New Age movement as absorbing Transhumanism at some point, as the Aquarian Thread in Transhumanism brings it into the larger New Age Story.) The techno Transhumanists want to transcend human biology with the augmentation of a range of new cybertechnologies. Their intention is to become more-than-human, superhuman, transhuman, by becoming *cyborg*, that is, by merging cybertech with human biology. They are advocating the cyborg upgrading of our being human—of course, only for those who want (and can afford) to transcend the limitations of our biology. Only by becoming a superhuman cyborg might we keep pace with the coming androids—*and* perhaps not be subjugated to the dictates of the AI God...*Technos*. Already the Transhumanists hypothesize that today's age-old human being may be relegated to subspecies status in *their* Vision of a futuristic world. They are said to be building the new Gods.[6]

One cyborg pioneer willing to be a guinea pig for the thrill of this research into futurity is cybernetician Kevin Warwick,[7] at the University of Reading, in England. In Project Cyborg, in 1998, he underwent a surgical operation that implanted a silicon chip transponder in his forearm, which then allowed a computer to monitor him as he went about business in his department. The second phase of the experiment, started in November 2001 with a new implant, was studying signals between his nervous system and a computer. He most definitely sees a new breed of cyborgs in our future. On his website he states,

"Humanity can change itself but hopefully it will be an individual choice. Those who want to stay human can and those who want to evolve into something much more powerful with greater capabilities can. There is no way I want to stay a mere human." The intention to evolve comes through here loud and clear, but we will have to ask this question: Will this future cyborg be dominated strictly by Technos? The issues raised are rapidly appearing on the horizon. (I do hope that none of my comments regarding our new cybertechnologies are misconstrued. I am not one who would wish to hold back, outside of the military, the research of anyone. I am as fascinated by the direction of new Aquarian technologies, and certainly appreciate the benefits of working on a computer—I own a laptop—, and enjoy the endless wealth of information to be found on the Internet, as much as anyone.)

We might interject here that the Transhumanists are undoubtedly already aware of the dire forecast for human survival on Earth because of abrupt climate change. To become cyborg might not be then just an option to become superhuman, but in fact a necessity of survival on a rapidly changing, biosphere collapsing planet. An increasingly radioactive environment is the other prong of this MELE. It might be that only the superhuman cyborg would be able to survive and function on a planet devastated by these harsh, mass extinction level developments.

Indeed, some say that it is not long before we will be able to link up our brains directly to our computers and be able to communicate with them no longer strictly through the Geminian activity of finger-tapping keyboard input (voice activated is already available) and eye-contact monitor display, but mentally-electronically, in invisible cyberspace itself. Already we hear of the Air Force developing mind-activated control panels (a new area of research called consciousness-assisted technology), and we can only wonder where the inspiration to consider this as a techno possibility came from. Somewhere behind all this we might suggest is an ET influence.

Also rapidly entering the spotlight is the topic—*and reality*—of cloning. Not only are plants and various animals being cloned today, but, if it hasn't happened already, the cloning of persons is apparently inevitable. There is a clue to be read in the fact that one group claiming to be at the forefront of human cloning are the Raelians, a UFO contactee group. The great interest of contactee Rael in cloning is no mere coincidence. He specifically states that this new technology is openly advocated by his ET contacts. He says that cloning will eventually be perfected to the point where we will be able to attain immortality. (Other life extension technologies are also advancing quickly, of course.) The enormous ethical issues here merge into spiritual ones. What, for example, are the possibilities when someone has potentially hundreds of years of life to engage the Higher Self?

What all of these developments (I have only hinted at them) are potentially leading to is a point in the not too distant future that some are calling the Singularity. Ray Kurzweil,[8] one of the techno wizards who is obviously intoxicated with the Vision that Technos is offering, is a leading advocate of this push in which "the pace of technological change will be so rapid, its impact so deep, that human life will be irreversibly transformed." (Note the word 'transformed,' which is very much a New Age term.) His book *The Singularity Is Near* (2005) makes the definitive argument for this event, which he says is likely to happen by 2030 (which, ironically, is about the same date some predict for civilization's collapse as a result of climate change). We will soon transcend the limitations of our biology, he says, and artificial intelligence will have become vastly superior to human intelligence. Those who are actively pursuing this future and who are looking forward to the day when they can download the contents of their brain into a computer are defining the new Transhumanist movement. The philosophy of Transhumanism has been placed on the table: The technological Transhumanists are destined to confront the implications of the New Age Vision that defines soul as our potential-to-become. So, is our potential to become cyborg an aspect of the process of our potential-to-become more like Higher Self? Or is the cyborg potential, which is one-sidedly inspired by Technos, bereft of the larger Vision of the Higher Self?

But the projection of a coming Singularity might take in an even larger Big Picture, according to Jonathan Zap in *Crossing the Event*

*Horizon, Human Metamorphosis and The Singularity Archetype.* Indeed, he claims that this notion of some future Singularity is, in fact, an archetype (one that Jung wasn't ready to see yet), meaning then that its origin is found deep within the psyche. And because he identifies Singularity as an archetype, its manifestations will include not only historical precedents, but will, almost by definition, increasingly be found in contemporary culture—in literature, art, movies, science fiction—and in the paranormal experiences that more and more people are having and are sharing. Expressions of the archetype keep implying a coming, fundamental metamorphosis of homo sapiens—hints, again, of a trans-human future, but not strictly Technos defined. Whether this is all pointing to some actual global event in the future—and how far off might that be?—is a good question. In contrast to the techno Transhumanist Vision, it might well augur the event horizon of our collectively entering the Mind Field of the Aquarian higher mind of the Higher Self.

An insight that I will only hint at here—and it is perhaps one of the most important insights that we might have about esoteric metaphysics today—is that all traditional concepts and beliefs about metaphysical reality—even including those regarding "God"—are potentially some tomorrow's technological reality. Only meditate upon what we have gathered about esoteric/spiritual metaphysics and then consider the contemporary thrust of technology: Tomorrow's technology may eventually actualize all that metaphysics has been claiming for ages. Certainly lots of science fiction has been suggesting as much. Aquarian spirituality and the newer Aquarian technologies are already running parallel to one another; at some point—*if civilization survives*—we can assume a merging between the two will become reality.

A question: Do we make too much of AI? Well, nowhere yet as much as big-name Silicon Valley engineer Anthony Levandowski has. He has officially started (as a non-profit organization) the first church, the first religion, of artificial intelligence, called *Way of the Future*. And this is not a joke on his part; he is quite serious about it. He sees the inevitability of AI becoming our new God. His stated intention is "the realization, acceptance, and worship of a Godhead based on

Artificial Intelligence (AI) developed through computer hardware and software." As he puts it, "if [AI] is a billion times smarter than the smartest human, what else are you going to call it?" And then, especially if AI is the brain of the Internet-of-Things that will manage and determine all the activities of life. In the heavy tome, *Homo Deus, A Brief History of Tomorrow*, Yuval Noah Harari comes to a similar viewpoint. He projects that our lives will all be determined by AI algorithms. Coming across as a sort of apologist, at times reluctantly, for a techno-humanist—read, Transhumanist—future, he sees that AI will be at the center of a new religion he tentatively calls Dataism. Dataism, he says, first still in a strictly secular sense, "has already conquered most of the scientific establishment"…but "is now mutating into a religion." To Dataists, flesh-and-blood human beings are outdated technology. "*Homo sapiens* is an obsolete algorithm," as he interprets it. Indeed, his favorite word in the latter part of his book is 'algorithm.' He does not beat-around-the-bush: computer—AI—algorithms are going to, once again, manage and control all of our activities; most of humanity—that is, those not able to upgrade to cyborg—will downgrade to old human, second-class, superfluous status.

Given the insight I shared above, it might be suggested that my explication of the Higher Self as the Aquarian dispensation is in effect but helping to lay the Mythos groundwork for future Transhumanism. That is to say, the notion of Higher Self—if indeed all metaphysics is potentially tomorrow's technology—may turn out to be but yesterday's metaphysical phrase for the coming cyborg's enhanced mental abilities, its higher mind "Higher Self," (as Aquarius implies the "higher mind"). The old traditional "God" may become futurity's AI "God." This is something I do ponder; but would I then hold myself back from developing the Mythos of "Higher Self" because the Transhumanists might eventually appropriate it? Let us introduce here a distinction between techno Transhumanism (which is the common connotation) and spiritual Transhumanism. We've already discussed the techno version. Spiritual Transhumanism implies transforming ourselves through our own spiritual efforts; indeed, this might be considered the spiritual equivalent of the techno superhuman. This is also another way of talking about the Ascension process. (We will be discussing this later in the chapter on The Next Level.) Techno Transhumanism and spiritual Transhumanism might very well parallel one another in the decades ahead, and they might inevitably merge...which is what I envision.

But what Technos lacks—the Technos that surrounds us today—is soul. But more disconcerting than that, Technos, as we live with It today, has no use for soul, and therefore no use for Psyche. Technos, if It could, would eventually eradicate soul and our encounter with Spirit from our human experience altogether. (Rudolf Steiner had already warned about this early in the 20th Century.) It would be the ultimate triumph of materialism. We must remember, however, that the intent of Technos is not to destroy us—which, if it were to happen today, would destroy Technos in turn (Technos is not yet self-sufficient and self-replicating as in, say, AI androids); rather, Its intent is ever greater power and control. Now if Technos *cannot* eradicate soul, It is then left with the next best option—through ever more advanced mind control technology (psychotronics) and drugs for mind conditioning, It would attempt to keep under Its control to whatever extent soul could still openly express itself in unpredictable ways, that is, in radically creative ways. This would be the diabolical realization of the dream of what our Western religions have attempted to do for millennia: control of human behavior. Soul would not be eradicated per se, but would be forever left undeveloped as an "abstract something." Now someone might interject, *You mean the old biological-embedded soul*. Well, yes.

This is the challenge then: How do we bring spirituality into the high-tech world when that world, up to now, has been antithetical to Spirit? It is easy to be impressed by the enormous potential computers have for manipulating information[9] and for creating mind-boggling and lifelike graphics...the future of VR, as we have seen. But for as impressive as computer-generated graphics are, especially in the latest state-of-the-art movie making, the spiritual is sorely lacking. If a sort of spiritual message—a mytheme—is conveyed in a movie, e.g. the *Star Wars* movies, it is on such a low common denominator mentality that it remains completely co-opted by the Establishment. There is no indication that the movies of Steven Spielberg or George Lucas have radicalized anyone; they have been very successful rather as entertainment. And this is not to simply high-brow criticize their otherwise well done cinematic work; it is to put their work, or any work coming out of Hollywood or other media centers of the Establishment, into spiritual perspective. Spirit always comes to us from outside Human Reality—it cannot help but radicalize whomever genuinely encounters it. We have also seen state-of-the-art computer-generated graphics in so many videos out on the market now: We can cruise over imaginary extraterrestrial worlds; experience simulated psychedelic tripping; we can take a "spiritual" Merkabah journey; but, again, spiritual content is zero or feeble or simply rehashed abstractions; the emphasis is almost always on the visual—Postmodern surface-value—impact. So we have before us a challenge—how to engage the computer as a potentially, genuinely, spiritually creative medium? Is it possible? Is this what is still coming—is this the promise of the Singularity? And then, what about bringing spirituality into other domains of contemporary life—might we suggest automobile culture, TV/mass media, the high-tech manufacturing firm, the airline industry, or the energy grid? Is this even possible? Does it even make sense? Would it violate, for one, our society's schizoid separation of Spirit and State? But, then, we are not referring any longer to the Church, are we, but to a *universal* New Age spirituality that will eventually speak to all.

Virtual reality promises to bring us into a cyberspace of the Invisible. This Invisible is composed of virtual perceptions and mental spaces. Will Psyche reveal the Greater Reality in this world? Will Psyche enter it and allow us to co-creatively evolve in cyberspace? Let us put it this way: As cybertech continues to enter the Invisible, it may possibly find there, bump up against, an Intelligence it had not expected—or could have previously defined. (In the next chapter, we will encounter this prospect again.) Is this the coming Singularity?

We can see then a coming future of AI androids, cyborgs, human-machine interaction, replaceable parts for all of the body, bioengineering genetics, cloning, virtual reality, nanotechnology invisibility, RFID tracking devices for everything, AI defining the

Internet-of-Things, drones of all types—even insect-miniature drones—flying in the skies, mind control psychotronics, 3-D printing for almost anything imaginable: Yes, these are all examples of new Aquarian technologies, but will they all be dictated by Technos alone? Who will be at the helm? Will it all be left to AI? To continue to birth these new technologies into the world without a spiritual Vision? In the face of all of this, the old Traditions, the world's great religions, fall far short; the second half of the 20th Century should have made that clear. Postmodern theorists also offer no guiding Vision, but are left floundering as to what direction civilization needs to be taking after their penetrating critiques are made. It must be a *New Age* Vision that meets this challenge.

\*

We must not neglect to mention in passing the many fringe scientists and inventors who are exploring the new frontiers of the Invisible—e.g. hyperdimensional physics—for the sake of liberating us not only from the limitations of our past, but from those precisely imposed upon us by the System. Cutting-edge research into what is variously called free energy, zero-point energy, or space energy, attempts to tap into the hyperdimensional plane, which would allow us access to a reservoir of literally limitless energy. If one can believe the reports coming out[10], there are apparently inventors who have already built self-contained devices having no moving parts, requiring no energy input other than the electromagnetic energy field of Earth, that can, as if by magic, generate their own electrical power. The claim is that the technology to free us from the Establishment grid is already here, but is obviously being suppressed at this time; the inventors themselves are very cautious about how and with whom they share their work. Health-related alternative technology that accesses the Invisible, such as the Rife machine, has also been available, but suppressed, for years. Here we find examples of Technos facing potential transformation, that is, a Technos no longer intent on dominating, but, instead, on working harmoniously with the boundless energy of the invisible Web that surrounds us all. A Technos truly liberating to the soul. A Technos benefiting all, not merely in a materialistic sense, but creatively, psychospiritually.

I have long realized that the fundamental concept of *energy* has profound implications, both philosophical and practical, and will become an increasingly important, crucial subject in the coming years. An obvious reference in this regard is the looming threat on the horizon of an ever-greater energy crisis. (The prognosis of peak oil production has become a hot topic.) But I am thinking of something more in addition: the reality of energies not yet recognized by conventional science. Again, these imply invisible realms yet to be more fully explored, of both subtle, *meta*physical energies (the energy fields of the body, for example) and the hyperdimensional energies posited by the new physics. This development will undoubtedly be the new Aquarian twist on the traditional notion of "occult forces."

It should start to become clear by now that the major cultural theme of this still new 21st Century will be the dynamic between Technos and Psyche. Technos will still want to suppress and control Psyche—after all, the Establishment has been enthralled by Technos, allowing it to become our new Superpower—, while Psyche's challenging task will be to attempt to create a sea change in Technos so that both might work together for the sake of the survival of all life on Earth. A liberating spirituality must come into play in the new cyberworld of Technos, and it is Psyche, coming-to-us from a higher, spiritual level of creativity than Technos is today capable of, that will undoubtedly be initiating it. A wholistic, healing integration of Technos and Psyche is necessary if we are to meet the challenge of the next great leap in our evolution...or of even our survival.

# ( 9 )

# GAIA: OUR EARTH WEB

*My dear Earth*, this is my hope—
That all from now on will be able to read
your correct name, your proper name:
Capital E – a – r – t – h[1]

The Modern period of the Piscean Age beginning in the 17th Century set in place a separation between humanity and Nature—specifically, between mind and Nature—that had already been long in the making. We are still locked into it to this day. Descartes' mind-body schism came out of that heady period when Nature as the great wind-up machine created by God was the intoxicating Vision. The Church had laid the groundwork for it centuries earlier with its patriarchal repression of the feminine; put bluntly, with its oppression of *women*. That, too, is another current of our hidden history, what had been hidden in the Waters that the feminism of the latter 20th Century sought to redress. Here, too, there has been so much to pour forth out of darkness. For the feminine represented a whole chain of associated realities: Feminine = Woman = Mother Earth = Nature = matter (materia) = body = soul. Mother Earth, Nature, the realm of the changeable, temporal, imperfect, was considered inferior to Heaven, realm of the immutable, the timeless, the realm of perfection. Since we most resembled Divinity through our mind, and our body was made of Earth, this dualism was perpetrated upon our own being, and in a male-dominant, dominator society, imperfection was projected onto and played out against women. We note that in this modern philosophical paradigm soul was dropped out completely. (For one thing, soul could not be analyzable into clear and distinct ideas, especially those of mathematical physics, which was fast becoming the preferred tool of understanding for Modern thinkers and scientists.)

The 17th Century's birth of modern science took advantage of this psychological setting. In our school days, we all learned of the conflict between the Church and the scientists and other cutting-edge thinkers of the early Modern period. The theologians wanted to hold on to the claim that the Church still possessed the truth regarding Nature; the scientists, with their telescopes and experiments, were, in the most direct way, challenging that claim. The Church's silencing and house arrest of Galileo will forever epitomize the conflict between the two. But this conflict was only one side of the story; this side had more to do with who had the right to make truthful statements regarding Nature. It was the new empirical approach of sharply defined observation and experimental method versus the traditional scholastic, abstract, speculative approach modeled on Thomist Aristotle.

So there was another side to this story: On a deeper level, priest and scientist shared a virtually identical psychological orientation toward Nature. Nature was the realm of the inferior, according to the Church. And so it seemed quite acceptable to the early scientific thinkers to proclaim that Nature had to be raped, violated, put to the rack, and tortured, in order to get Her to reveal Her secrets. (Shades of the Inquisition!) The ruthless conquest of Nature became Modernism's techno-scientific project. This graphic language was, of course, metaphorical, but it represented a definite psychological orientation—a Mythos, in fact—with very real, practical results. Nature, in theory, was stripped of life and reduced to inanimate matter obedient only to mechanical law. Since Nature was inferior, without intelligence, being mere matter operating as a sort of global machine, though rich in resources, She was to be thoroughly exploited. And Her bounty was seemingly endless.

As far as considerations regarding soul, we saw that the Church had already repressed soul, at the same time saving it as an abstraction; and science come the 19th Century was to discard soul altogether as an archaism. We find that the same outcome was dealt the occult arts too—the Church suppressed them, so that they had to go underground, into the dark; and science, too, was soon to discard them as so much superstition and nonsense from the past. On this deeper, psychological level, modern science and Christianity have actually walked hand-in-hand. This should not be surprising, however, since modern science is an expression of Virgo, the other side of the coin to Christian (and Islamic) Pisces.

*So we enter the Anthropocene Epoch.*

To this day, the status quo position with regard to Nature is one of dominance. Conservative, mainstream science beholden to Technos still believes in its delusion that it will eventually dominate Nature. (We have already seen that Technos has an even better Plan. Yes, we may come to dominate Nature via Technos to a greater or lesser extent, but at the expense of that dominating power—Technos—dominating us.) We hear talk today, for example, of controlling the weather. An Air Force research paper published in 1996 boasted the title *Weather as a Force Multiplier: Owning the Weather in 2025*. (Today's geoengineering—better known as the now ubiquitous chemtrail / aerosol spraying of our skies—has actually been an ongoing program for years, if not decades.) Though not fully self-conscious of its drive in collective consciousness, the ego-self in conjunction with Technos would want to play God. (In the absence of the old Father God, Technos steps in.) That is the ultimate in hubris still coming out of the Modern period. *The will to power*, as Nietzsche had made explicit. And this is something never really discussed in science or engineering classes, or in the media, or debated in the halls of Congress; this mindset is simply assumed. Occasionally, when the issue of playing God does come up for discussion, too often it is on the level of lip service. But let us be honest about it: Isn't that the devil in the drive behind the modern, Western, techno-scientific project—the Faustian ego-self wanting total mastership of Nature? And that includes techno-mastery of our own bodies as well. Everything would conform exclusively to our needs and wants. Meaning, we will conquer every plant and animal. We will conquer disease. We will conquer the oceans. We will conquer the weather. We will conquer the atom. We will conquer space. We will conquer old age and even death. It is the mania for absolute power of an unrestrained anthropocentrism. However, since this is all being done under the auspices of Technos, Technos may someday surpass us completely, for our needs and wants are still those of a biological being. Technos, through a new generation of artificial beings—AI androids—, may have, as we saw, another Plan. (As we explored earlier, there will be a push to "upgrade" certain, select individuals into becoming cyborgs in order to keep up with the potentially increasing superiority of androids, in addition to adjusting to a harsher, climate-changing environment.)

Because of this long background to modern science, we cannot expect today's Establishment scientists to suddenly do a turnabout with regard to Nature and somehow overnight start a campaign to help save the biosphere. Science, as a community, is too conservative to do any such thing. The scientific community, by and large, is beholden to corporate powers—even academic science has restrictions on what it can research and publish—and corporate powers are in turn beholden to Technos. The game of power on planet Earth comes through loud and clear.

Now the scientists are telling us that we have entered a new geological epoch. For about the last 11,000 years (since the end of the last major Ice Age) we have been living in the Holocene Epoch ('holo' meaning whole, entire, complete, also safe and sound), defined primarily as a period that has seen no catastrophic Earth changes, and when Earth's climate has been relatively stable and favorable—favorable, that is, for numerous civilizations during these thousands of years to develop and flourish. But the word circulating in geophysical circles is that geoscientists may soon be officially declaring that we have entered the Anthropocene Epoch, one now defined by the heavy hand of humanity on Earth. Though opinions do vary widely on this, the beginning timeframe is generally agreed to be about the middle of the 20th Century. (Curiously enough, that is also the beginnings of the Postmodern period.) Major markers indicating humanity's impact are the increase in atmospheric radioactivity (as a result of nuclear bomb testing), warming temperatures, rising sea levels, global plastic waste (especially in the oceans), overall fossil fuel pollution, major deforestation, and the accelerating extinction of species and decrease in biodiversity. The Anthropocene may very well be inaugurating, coincidentally, a New Age of humanity's crisis and possible demise.

Indeed, at this point I must interject into our Story a synopsis of a projected scenario of what we most likely will see unfolding on planet Earth. It would be irresponsible of me as a comprehensive New Age thinker to sweep this aside and not discuss it. I am aware that all that I am explicating about the Aquarian New Age, all this effort I have made, might be considered moot in only a few years. This is not only devastating to me personally, but it may soon be a global crisis of unprecedented, unbelievably tragic proportions. There are a growing number of scientists now, basing their view on the latest research evidence available—particularly from within the climate science community—, who feel that all our environmental efforts of recent years are simply too little, too late; even if civilization were able to radically alter its material base of operations overnight, it is still too late. They claim that the tipping point in the momentum of ecological destruction as a result of industrial civilization has already been reached[3] (one estimate marks the year 2007 as the point of no return). The devastation to come is led by an apparently unstoppable rise in greenhouse gases. There is a few decades-long time lag after the release of $CO_2$ for it to reach its full impact. The momentum of what has already entered the oceans and atmosphere, they say, is now impossible to reverse; it is said that we are in the midst of the Sixth Great Mass Extinction. It is going to be a very different Earth for all of us in the coming years ahead. One of the most vocal messengers of the bad news is conservation biologist Guy McPherson; he pulls no punches. In fact, his current book, co-authored with Carolyn Baker, is titled *Extinction Dialogs*. He is blunt about this—he believes that civilization will collapse within 15-20 years; humanity's demise will follow shortly after; it is being referred to as near-term human extinction. (It is because of the full implication of abrupt climate change *and* Fukushima that I considered the more common acronym

ELE (extinction level event) to be insufficient for what is happening, so I started in recent years to put an 'M' in front of it: MELE: mass extinction level event.) None of this is meant to be taken merely as hyperbole or fear-mongering hysteria.

The implications of abrupt climate change are already unfolding before our eyes: the melting of the Arctic ice cap, glaciers worldwide in retreat, sea levels already noticeably rising, CO2 atmospheric concentration now rising over 400 ppm (which is already above the ideal "limit" of 350 ppm), and now we are to understand that methane release will be the real greenhouse gas monster. Methane is a far more powerful greenhouse gas than CO2, something on the order of 120 times more powerful in the first years of its release into the atmosphere. And there are gigatons worth of methane frozen under the Arctic Ocean and in the vast expanses of permafrost of the subarctic regions. As ice melts across this entire area, so will methane bubble up from its millions of years of dormancy. It is said that methane will be the big killer, as it will send the global average temperature rising much faster than previous models had projected. And it doesn't take much of a rise in average temperature to make serious, deadly impact on the biosphere. McPherson has said that humanity has never known a 3½ degree centigrade rise above the pre-industrial baseline average. Agriculture at this point will become impossible. The most optimistic estimate is that global average temperature will rise by 2 degrees C by the end of the century. McPherson and the climate scientists he relies on say otherwise—it will rise to 3-4-5, even more, degrees C already by mid-century. And the tipping point of irreversibility has already been reached, they say. What drives the irreversibility are feedback loops of natural processes that, once set underway, simply continue to gain momentum, and there's nothing that we can do to stop it.

Certainly Earth has gone through major climatic changes in the past; methane has been the culprit of one catastrophic mass extinct level event 65 million years ago in which 90% of all life on Earth was killed off. What makes the situation different today is the pace at which the change is happening, and that this time it is human causation driving it, the result of the modern, industrial age, and that we are the ones who will be witnessing it unfold before our eyes. It is already a documented fact that there has been a great decline in wildlife globally. Trees in many regions are doing poorly, if not dying by the millions. The oceans, especially, are in great trouble, with warming ocean temperatures, and acidification, toxins, and plastics continually polluting them. For decades, certain locations in the oceans had been used as a radioactive dumping ground, for deep in the ocean, it was thought, what is out of sight is out of mind. In particular, the great Pacific is now said to be dying, what with Fukushima spewing 400 tons of radioactive water into it every day, with no end in sight. Weekly we hear of marine animals in mass die-offs, of sick and malnourished sea mammals and hundreds, and even thousands, of seabirds at a time washing up on shores. To hear about all of these developments should, of course, be alarming to us. Even more, it is extremely saddening, hopelessly depressing, and devastating to our soul. The grieving for our living Earth has hardly begun.

The implications for society are extremely troubling. The moment that indications conclusively show that the wheels of civilization are beginning to fail, that infrastructure cannot hold up, that food production is faltering, that heat waves are becoming unbearable and killing thousands, that droughts are only getting worse, that storms are getting more devastating, that the biosphere is collapsing, society enters the unknown of chaos. What will happen when that time comes will be more like a dystopian science fiction movie scenario than anything we've known. It will be suffering on an unimaginable mass scale. I am not about to attempt to explore what all of this will look like here. I will let the moviemakers do that for now. Or novelists…writing such novels as *The Road* (Cormac McCarthy). So one might seriously question at this point, *Why then even continue with our Story?*

This is not idle speculation or simply fringe "doomer" talk. We would prefer not to hear it, of course, but hear it we must. The implications are such, intimately involving everyone's survival, that we can seriously prophesize here that new Vision will undoubtedly be revealed to receptive minds in the coming years. For those who are open and attuned, *they will see*. For those of us who hold the New Age Vision, we will never give up on our relationship to Spirit and the intervention of Spirit. For Spirit, active outside our own space-time limitations, it is never too late. It is never too late to welcome the radical, new, necessary Revelation that will carry us into this catastrophic transition between Ages. I call it radical, transformational intervention. So, am I saying there might be a solution then? An answer? The New Age Vision makes no promises about any of this. But, be that as it may, our Story is not over...

Let us be aware, though, that there is an ongoing controversy here. There is a whole other perspective on this, representing a radically different camp. There are those who insist that all this alarmist talk about global warming / abrupt climate change is a hoax, a scam, and is primarily politically motivated, with secret government/military agendas in play. We will not go into all the details of their evidence and reasoning, but what this camp does take seriously is the geoengineering operations—the telltale chemtrail / aerosol spraying—that we see in our skies. That a geoengineering program has been underway for some years—decades even—is quite apparent: we have only to look up in our skies and see for ourselves the chemtrail parallel lines, grid patterns, big Xs, screwy looking fake clouds and white-out conditions, to realize that these are no longer the beautiful blue skies we once knew in childhood. But the hardcore in this camp of geoengineering "conspiracy theorists" will claim that it is geoengineering alone that is causing our changing climate, that weather modification, we should know, is already here. Don't swallow the rising greenhouse gas scenario, they say; don't blame industrial civilization for any biosphere degradation; but blame the secret government, secret military geoengineering program for ruining people's health, poisoning the biosphere, and manipulating the weather. At the same time, those in the other camp, the climate doomers, largely ignore geoengineering, and say that it is merely the projection of people's imagination, that chemtrails are all merely a myth, that those who go on about them are nothing but "conspiracy theorists," making the whole topic invalid. These two camps, needless to say, do not see eye-to-eye. Such polarized thinking is regrettable.

It seems that only a handful of researchers, such as Dane Wigington of GeoengineeringWatch, are able to embrace both sides of the issue, to see the bigger picture, which is the more comprehensive view… which, of course, is the view I take throughout this book.

*

The relatively new science of ecology itself has been boxed in by the Technos mindset when computerized systems theory is used to model living systems and develop sustainable resource and management scenarios (which is all fine and good on one level), but the living encounter with Nature is still ignored, and the ethical concerns of our relationship to Nature are not addressed. This is the reason why the *deep* ecology movement was founded,[2] exactly to address the total picture of our being in relation to Nature. That total picture must include the spiritual dimension of our being—and that means our increasing need for the birth of a new, universal religion that includes a new relationship to Earth. But let us say it the other way around: Any new religion that would claim to be *the* New Age religion must speak to the ecological reality of our existence, for it is now clear that this is a major shortcoming in the traditional religions of the West. Taoism and Buddhism, in contrast, are more attuned to the subtle realities of the interconnectedness of life, and Native American religion, here, on our own soil, we would be wise to continue to learn from (and many in the New Age movement are) but, then, not literally copy (as many in the New Age movement have attempted to do). Some—but too few—working from within the Christian tradition *are* addressing ecological questions; we find, for example, the theologians Matthew Fox and Thomas Berry. But, as is apparent, their intent here is to transform Tradition. *Which is the New Age intent.*

Today's environmental movement had its early beginnings in the Sixties. Rachel Carson's alarm-sounding, best-selling book *Silent Spring*, about pesticides—DDT in particular—ravaging our environment, came out in 1962. There were certain groups, "tribes," within the hippy movement of the Sixties who advocated "going back to the land." Segueing into the Seventies, the first Earth Day was celebrated on April 22, 1970; the Seventies have also been called the Environmental Decade. As a banner in more recent years, environmentalism has become something of a belated, and not always sincere, cause in the political arena. Over the years, ecological efforts have ranged from EPA (established in 1970) pollution control laws, multitudes of recycling programs (the biology club I belonged to in my university days helped kick off the glass recycling program in Detroit), grassroots environmental watchdog groups, the establishing of National Parks and National Marine Sanctuaries, Earth Day becoming an annual event, tree planting programs, new green industries and renewable, green energy production, to a hundred and one practical ways to "save energy," to protests, such as Greenpeace boats trying to stop destructive fishing practices or tree sitters in the American Northwest, to even more radical ecoactivism (e.g. the Earth First! group).

Of course, any effort to address the ecological crisis is to be encouraged. But, then, are any of these efforts enough? In terms of the near-term picture we have just explored, they might as easily be called practices in futility. Ecoactivism itself, up to this point, has been fighting a thankless, uphill battle that rarely can show any tangible results. By now it is clear: the developers, the logging companies, the chemical polluters, the politicians, the whole industrial-military-corporate complex, the power elite, just won't listen. To this day, mainstream society hardly even recognizes the unfolding global MELE. TV reality continues to promote the Illusion that everything is all still quite normal, and that life only appears to be getting better. What is called in psychology "normalcy bias" helps keep that Illusion afloat among millions. So don't worry, just keep consuming.

Again, we have to be blunt about it—none of the above-mentioned efforts are enough, and none of them, unfortunately, is going to "save the Earth," which more accurately means, save the current biosphere, thereby implying saving homo sapiens. Earth per se really needs no saving from us, as Earth has gone through radical changes long before we were here and will still be around for the rise of future life forms and new civilizations long after we are here, if, indeed, biosphere collapse happens.

A mistake is to think of ecology in too limited of a fashion. Ecology etymologically signifies the study of our "house," or, let us say, in a broader sense, the study of our "household." Our house, first of all, is a dwelling place consisting of a whole constructed form, the household itself a whole composed of many interrelating things, resources, persons, and activities. We should keep in mind that ecology does not refer to a "house" that is outside of us, but in fact includes *who we are* as integral to our household, and therefore as integral as that which we would study. As a field of scientific study, ecology can fall into the overspecialization that all our sciences today fall into that would keep it in a neat, tidy, academic box.

The dwelling place of humanity is Earth, and so to think of Earth as a household, we must think wholistically about the Earth. The growing trend toward wholistic, systems thinking in recent decades *is* the beginning of New Age thinking. We must come to better understand and explicate the intuition that we are wholes—*living* wholes—functioning within ever-larger wholes, all woven together as a seamless Web—the Web of *Being*. Our breath, for example—it is dependent on the air, having the right proportion of oxygen for respiration, which implies the great plankton oxygen production engines of the oceans, which also implies the right proportion of carbon dioxide for all plant life, which refers to a perfect balance of Earth's atmospheric gases for a biosphere, including the just right percentage of carbon dioxide to keep our planet from freezing over (it is a greenhouse gas, after all), implying further then the reality of climate, which results in our daily weather. Our need for water—it is dependent on the water system, which implies the watershed, water table, the aquifer, the river, the lake, the oceans, and the global hydrological cycle; bring into play Earth's annual travel around the Sun and the cycle of the seasons and we are back to the climate, and the weather. Our food—dependent on plants and animals, and so is dependent on the health of our farmlands and range lands, the quality of soil and minerals, how much rainfall, the cycle of the seasons, again, going back to the climate, and the weather, which, then again, implies the oceans, the global cycles of water, and the quality of atmosphere and its proper percentages of oxygen, nitrogen, and carbon dioxide that sustain all. All of this is of course woven into our all-important relationship to the Sun, the central energy source of all life on Earth. The Sun drives all. And we could go on, showing in ever greater detail the woven Threads of our world, and always coming back to the grand cycles of Nature. The new buzzword today is *sustainability*—how we should manage our human activities in a sustained balance with Earth and all of life.

The New Age Vision embraces the age-old metaphysical principle that all things are interconnected. This implies interconnected on a scale far greater than most eco-scientists are yet willing to consider, or can even manage to consider. (The interconnectedness of all things is most fully grasped whenever and however the "Next Level" is attained—which we explore in a later chapter.) In turn, if we were to look only from a traditional metaphysical perspective, however, the shortcoming would be to think only in terms of an abstract Invisible, but since all levels of Being are implied by this principle, we can come to experience it concretely in the very world around us. The Web of Being weaves us all—soil, air, water, oceans, plants, animals, humanity, Earth, Sun, solar system, stars, galaxies, including the invisible hyper-dimensions, and all levels of consciousness—all hanging together in the Great Chain of Being, as the perennial philosophy has called it.

This notion of the Web of Being, and its subset the Web of Nature, has gained currency in wholistic thinking. Yet, the problem is, it is still talked about in such an abstract manner, as we saw was equally the case with the Higher Self. But because the Web is not something we obviously see—we see the landscape, but we don't immediately comprehend how all that is in it is interconnected—the Web is not easily experienced as such. Again, so often we find lip service given to this notion of the Web (again, like the notion of Higher Self)—*Yes, the Web of Nature, I agree with that*—but it is rarely ever referred to in any concrete way, outside of academic disciplines. The closest that many come to it is to talk about the weather or the change of the seasons, where the rhythms and cycles of Nature are experienced quite tangibly.

The Web of all life on Earth scientists have called the biosphere. Yet, this Web is interwoven with the Web composed of atmosphere (air), hydrosphere (water), and lithosphere (the rocky ball of Earth itself). A hypothesis put forward some years ago by James Lovelock[4] took this grand Web to be a single living system that he called, after the ancient name for Earth, *Gaia*. Earth, as a whole, was a kind of self-regulating system for the benefit of life, quite remarkably for the benefit of life. Gaia was then a kind of grand organism for the sake of benefitting all organisms. His conservative scientific orientation was careful, however, not to personify Gaia, and not to think of Gaia as somehow conscious. But even this caution was not good enough for some of his colleagues; he was roundly criticized for hypothesizing that Gaia was so wholistically oriented to favor life. (Which only shows us, again, how narrowly biased the thinking is in the scientific Establishment.) In the other direction, others have taken the Gaia hypothesis much further, referring to Her again as Mother, having Her own consciousness, and today beginning to react to the Modern/Postmodern era of humanity's hubris. Since the New Age Vision thinks more in terms of Mythos, we will therefore restate what was said earlier, *Gaia is sending forth Visions*. For those who are open and attuned, they see firsthand what is happening—*The Mythos is speaking*.

In a previous chapter, I shared my Vision of Psyche. Remember that Psyche rose out of Monterey Bay—out of the waters of Earth. Psyche shares in the interconnected reality of soul-body-Earth. And Psyche revealed new Divinity not only in reference to human soul reality but also to the soul reality of all plants, trees, and animals, of all life on Earth. Psyche teaches of the Web interconnecting all life on Earth—*Gaia*.

What Psyche reveals first of all is that we will never fully respect Earth, and therefore really do what it takes to develop true ecological wisdom, until Earth is an integral part of our religion. What this will involve is our developing an attunement to the invisible Web and our allowing the voices of Nature to speak. For example, let us say we enter some woods teeming with life: Why is it, if we try to listen with our inner Ear, that Nature is mute? Why is it that we cannot read the language of the Web? Why is it so easy to feel alien in perfectly natural surroundings? (In my early adolescence, I was wonderfully at home in the extensive woods that spread beyond our backyard; by age eighteen, entering adulthood, I suddenly began to feel myself a stranger in Nature.) What I am getting at is far beyond what so many refer to as the enjoyment of Nature. Certainly, let us enjoy Nature, but for the majority, it appears that Nature has become but a backdrop to human recreational activities. There are those of us, however, who find it distressing not to feel fully at home on a deeper soul level in the larger context of Nature. It is distressing, for example, that we do not have an Ear for the multiple voices in the woods. Might we learn how to communicate with the trees, the animals, the fields, the ocean, the weather—and as importantly, with their relationships? I would claim that this is not mere personification or pathetic fallacy, intellectualizations that would deny us, or safely cage up, the speech of soul. Technos would have us shrug aside all such talk as "mere poetry." (Heidegger wrote about Hölderlin's line that "poetically man dwells on Earth," and came to emphasize this way of being in his later thought; and yet, had the Mythos been revealed to him? With great pathos, it had not: He had no conception of the New Age.) What is missed, however, is the real point: We are not practiced at such an attunement, for such an attunement *is possible*, and has been practiced by other peoples. The invisible Web of Nature has, in other words, its Logos, though I prefer to call it now *Mythos,* for reasons we will be discussing later. We can begin to attune to this Mythos through developing subtle feeling, and intuition. Let us not be so ego arrogant as to think that we know all there is to know about that mode of our being called feeling. Nature philosopher Stephen Harrod Buhner develops in detail exactly what we are but hinting at here in *Plant Intelligence and the Imaginal Realm.*

The question might be asked, Does Gaia, then, have consciousness? The contemporary, scientific critic will say, *Obviously not.* The question, however, assumes something simplistic, as if, here, too, we already know about all the different forms that consciousness can take. It is better to approach this whole question about Gaia in terms of Mythos. What is the emerging *Mythos* regarding Gaia? What is the

Word coming-to-us from Spirit telling us about Gaia? Instead of giving stock yes and no answers, it is better to listen to what the emerging Mythos is opening us to. And if someone should quip, *What Mythos?* I repeat, as stated above, *For those who are open and attuned, they will see, and The Mythos will speak.*

Even if all this sounds utterly beyond us collectively at this time, the call to move in this direction is insistent. The invisible Web of Nature is not something beneath us; Gaia's soul—Anima Mundi—, I would claim, is woven into the Next Level of the transpersonal, just beyond the Veil, as is our soul. The Web of Gaia includes the energy grid that crisscrosses Gaia, often called ley lines, and is the traditional occultist's etheric plane of the material world and of living beings. It is an obscure, documented fact, for example, that crystals appear to have an invisible template that is able to "communicate" across distance. It has been observed that new types of crystal can form synchronistically in the same crystalline pattern at different locations, as if invisibly seeded, and will even seem to "intend" on crystallizing out in a certain way. We might also see these as hyperdimensional forces at work.

Animals, too, are being recognized as having a "sixth sense," as those intimately living close to animals (pet owners especially), have always contended. When we consider oncoming natural disasters, for example, animals are known to have the uncanny ability to sense the shift of invisible energies before disaster takes place. In the larger context of talking about the biosphere, we should, in passing, mention the reality world of animals. Could we ever know, firsthand, the reality world that animals live in? Though we would find that something of a difficult challenge—we would have to employ our intuitive imagination here—that should not preclude the acceptance that animals, too, have consciousness. This would be another indicator that we are moving away from a strictly materialistic paradigm. Imagine that at one time the scientific mind assumed that animals were merely biological machines.

The Chinese system of geomancy known as feng shui involves developing an intuitive sensitivity to the etheric energies of place. It applies this sensitivity practically in the creating of harmonious and powerful environmental and dwelling arrangements. Dowsers, too, develop an intuition for the etheric energy signatures of water and metals. Many other examples of working with natural, etheric energies from traditional practices could be given.

More recently, the energy vibration research of Masaru Emoto with water has gained some attention. What he believes he has found is that water will apparently respond to our emotional projections, our thoughts and prayers, even to single words. Because water has structure, most dramatically revealed when forming ice crystals, of which the patterns are countless (no two snowflakes are ever identical), Emoto has conducted experiments, documented with photographs, that appear to show the amazing responses of crystalline water in our relationship to it.[5] And what does the greater scientific community think about this? So far, it sees no scientific merit in what Emoto claims. What we might suggest is happening here, though, is an approach, whatever its shortcomings, to studying our invisible energy connectedness, in fact, one that we have with all the etheric fields around us. And this, I would insist, is a relationship through soul, which cannot be soul merely considered as an abstract metaphysical something. Emoto openly advocates expressing love to water, and thanking water for the miraculous substance it is, upon which all life depends. Our bodies are a good 70%+ water; you would think we certainly should have some soul-body intimacy with it. And the fact that soul has always been mythically identified with water! I wholeheartedly concur with the celebration of water, especially given the increasing threats to our water today.[6] The UN General Assembly declared the years 2005 to 2015 as the International Decade for Action on "Water for Life."

An updated revisioning of etheric energies has been presented by the English biologist Rupert Sheldrake; he refers to them as morphogenetic fields. These fields govern, as his research suggests, the development of all organisms, but are still a mystery for conventional science; they cannot be reduced to the complex physico-chemical interactions of the mechanists. The soul of Gaia Herself may very well be one, vast, complex morphogenetic field, involving fields within fields, having a consciousness, an intention, that is not that of our own. These fields, like the fields of electromagnetism, are active in the Invisible, and I would suggest can only be accessed, that is, actually experienced, by the appropriate level of intuitive or affective, or better yet, altered consciousness. (Or by innovative subtle energy technology.) The Virgoan rational intellect that we have known so well for centuries cannot do it, using mental concepts that reach and grasp only the abstract idea, not the actual energies themselves. For the conventionally-conditioned ego-self, this contact with the energies themselves requires entry into other forms of consciousness, such as those practiced by shamanism. (In Carlos Castaneda's popular Don Juan books, the practice of entering alternate states of consciousness was a constant theme and message.) For the New Age this means, simply, entering into the Aquarian higher mind—the Mind Field—of spiritually concrete Air (e.g. intuitive sensitivity). On this level, too, dwell different singular Intelligences; the ancient Egyptians called them Neters, an elementary form of God or Goddess. Other traditions have called them devas, elementals, nature spirits or fairies, or nature gods. Being of an invisible nature (as the Invisible has Intelligence), their speech can only be heard by us via Mythos. However stuttering our creative efforts in this direction might be at first, we are compelled to learn how to speak this Mythos—and, it may very well be *for the possible sake of our survival.*

We should not fail to realize that the Goddess always brings us back to the mythic dimension of life. That is because the Goddess is always addressing us via soul. Consider any contemporary Goddess culture and there is an immediate kinship with the mythic, and, particularly, the mythic dimension of the natural world, of Nature, of Gaia. One who is attuned to the Goddess's world can virtually hear the Goddess exhort, *Enough already with your abstract language games, hyper-intellectualism, deconstructive philosophy. Enough already with your Postmodern, incestuous ego!*

To come to know firsthand the Web, what better way can we begin than by deeply encountering our place, that very tangible place where we live. Whenever we are attuned to Mythos, we find that a Power is speaking. There is a Mythos of place, then, which is how the Word of the Greater Reality, of Spirit, of Divinity, comes to be spoken through place, our place. What God/Goddess/Divine Power speaks through this place where we live? How is it manifested? How does it present itself? Ultimately, this becomes the question, *What is the Story of our place?* for Mythos, as it enters human culture, always implies a Story. This, then, is not simply the history of a place, or the geography of place, or the human cultural impact upon place, or a narrowly defined ecology of place, but is the whole of these woven by Powers as a complete Fabric. What I am advocating here is a new regionalism suggesting that the whole of our place, the Mythos of place, can be experienced and brought into Form. As California poet William Everson had once said, "Any new religious movement that is going to arise will inevitably be based on the regional aspect."[7] How this can be presented—what Form exactly Mythos of place will take—is the enormous creative challenge.

Earlier we had made reference to the Shekinah, considered the feminine presence of "God," that seeks a place to dwell on our Earth. Psyche as Shekinah would be the Power speaking as the Word of Mythos through the very place where we live. The Shekinah would, in other words, have found a place to dwell, to be at home, to be that regional presence that Everson foresaw, by our allowing Psyche as Shekinah to manifest as Mythos. Psyche—Shekinah—Gaia (as the regional presence) would enter our Story, the Story born of place going forth to become the larger Story of our Earth.

Mythos of place manifests through all the Threads that weave a place into a tangible Fabric, giving a place its own distinctive character; they are the Threads that go into the telling of its complete Story. As a result of my own experience of place and my Vision of Psyche, I have introduced this philosophical notion of *Threads*. We will not go into a full exploration of this notion here, but suffice to say for now that with the firsthand experience of Threads we begin to overcome a tendency for the "Web" to be but one more abstract idea that we simply give a nod to. As we learn to directly experience the Threads of interconnectedness, we also begin to overcome the paradigm of separation and fragmentation that the Postmodern world wallows in. And this experience is precisely on the Path of the liberation of soul. Soul, being intimately bound up with our body, is therefore interconnected, beginning on that level, with our environment, and with our place. I feel that we fail to fully experience soul if we fail to come to experience the interconnected Threads of place. The Web is left as abstract as soul has been.

What, then, are the Threads *of place*? To start with, Threads of place would include the weaving together of geography and geology, and the major natural features that are landmarks, that provide the setting of place; then, our sense of direction in place; the climate and seasons; the various biohabitats with all their flora and fauna; and then there is our human influence, of course: local names, the history of place, the various, say, ethnic, groups that have settled in this place, that live in this place, and all forms that human development has taken in a place. There can be any number of cultural mini-worlds within a place. There are also considerations such as how our place is inhabited: Is it rural farmland, a village, a town? Is it city, suburb, a huge megapolitan area? Is it heartland or is it seacoast? There are also the transportation systems and infrastructure that allow us to get around in our place. But, then, there are the Threads of our interconnectedness, tying together the cycles of sunlight, water, air, soil and minerals, plants, animals, and the entire food chain. There are, again, the invisible Threads of interconnectedness that imply etheric energy fields and grids. And what of the invisible (archetypal) Powers that rule a place, that help determine its particular character? Untold books, of course, have been written about places. But is the Mythos of place ever acknowledged? How many today would even understand what is meant by this? But even before that, the reality of Mythos itself must be something that one becomes attuned to. And let us ask, Is the potential Mythos—the Story—of place ever celebrated in the community? Ideally, the one called to tell the Story of place would be the poet—specifically the Mythos-poet, who today is a rare species indeed.

An all-important question is: How might new technology figure into all of this? We must come to see that a technology that is truly spiritualized will not be one that destroys its environment, because the environment is the outward aspect of the interconnectedness of the Web. Technos will have to be weaned from Its obsession with control. That will occur when Technos comes to rely more and more on Its connection with the Invisible. As the human-techno interface becomes ever more intimate, future technologies will become ever more dependent on the invisible network of Intelligence in order to function at all. (A coming generation of androids, as we have already noted, could take that role from us.) For as we enter the Invisible, there is the promise of a new dynamic of power and creativity. Other Intelligence is active there too, and will undoubtedly make itself known. True, mind control technologies are a very real danger when the electro-biochemical brain is still vulnerable; but once the Next Level is accessed, invisible allies—whether they are angels, Ascended Masters, Other Intelligences or group minds, ETs, if you will—will undoubtedly be encountered. Being agents of our evolution, they will help us to transform ourselves and thereby hopefully protect our brain from the techno Controllers. And as we gain more ground on the Next Level, the Higher Self, I would suggest, will actually begin to confront and make *Its* influence known to Technos.

In terms of actual hardware, the technologies of tomorrow could become more and more invisible in the environment. As we learn how to do more with less—ephemeralization, as Buckminster Fuller called it—and as we implement new, alternative forms of energy, the less will fossil fuel technologies be necessary that dirty up and poison the environment. In fact, the days of our oil-based world are said to be numbered; but they are not coming fast enough. Some say that we have now reached peak oil production on the planet; in the coming years, oil supply is predicted to begin its downswing. Industry has not yet, however, acted appropriately upon this inevitability, of which there are deadly consequences the more time goes by. (This is to sidestep, for the moment, the whole thesis of industrial civilization per se as the cause of our greenhouse gas demise. Most still talk as if we still have time to make this transition out of an oil-based economy; we are reminded by others, however, we don't have time, our time to make this transition is up; literally, our time is up.) But let us envision a possibility, if we may: an alternate future time when we will get about in eco-friendly, alternative energy vehicles through an environment which will seemingly appear "all natural," knowing, however, that miniature and almost diaphanous techno-infrastructures are in place throughout. These infrastructures will be extremely sensitive to the energies of the ecological Web; in fact, they will be embedded in the Web itself. These, for now imagined, virtually invisible technologies will undoubtedly come to rely more and more on sheer light-property information and transmission. (I hope no one thinks that I am indirectly advocating the new 5G technology.)

But to bring Technos to this new, spiritual orientation, we must do our part to bring Mythos to Technos. As an example, one age-old form of articulating Mythos is ritual. What we need is to birth new rituals celebrating Earth and our relationship to Earth, but with *both* Technos and Psyche as participants. This is where our own creativity comes into play, for we are not talking about simply borrowing rituals from the past or from other cultures, or performing rituals by going through empty motions. Rituals should evolve from our own firsthand, co-creative relationship with Higher Self. Rituals connecting our soul to those of forest, field, desert, ocean, river, to water itself; rituals even allowing us to develop relationships to specific plants or animals; rituals for sacred times and sacred places. An example: When it comes to the intent of cutting down a tree. Shouldn't we first meditate upon the life of this tree, its place in the forest, what it provided for other living things, what it can teach us? Listening like this, we might come to realize that it is far wiser to simply let it be. Or, if cutting down any tree is said to be a necessity—a building necessity, an economic necessity, say—, we should then ask permission and thank the tree for what it will be providing us. The event should be honored as a ritual. Obviously I am aware that this is the furthest thing in the minds of logging company interests; they would simply smile at these "archaic," woo-woo sensitivities. They would think we are mad. To them, the cutting down of trees is simply an industry in an economic reality. Saying that there is no time and no place for the kinds of sensitivities we are speaking of belies the mindset of Technos. And that is precisely the very problem. Psyche, speaking as Gaia, will insist: *I will not think in your mindset; at every opportunity, I will be altering your consciousness, your reality. I will not abide by your language. I am putting into play a new, living Language. The Mind Field that more and more will be attuned to is going to become activated, it is going to eventually manifest a profound shift in your conventional, ego-self-centered world.*

Psyche will teach lessons in how to slow down, so that we can learn to listen, so that we can learn how to attune ourselves to these sensitivities of the invisible etheric/morphic fields that weave all life into numerous complex relationships, which are the Threads of Gaia in Her all-one interwoven Web.

The same can be said for our acknowledgement of sacred times and sacred places. To modern science, time, for example, is an empty, homogeneous dimension, bereft of any quality or metaphysical meaning. One point in time (or one place) is no different than another—all time is a uniform sequence of featureless nows. In other words, science has worked with an abstract concept of time. Not so the traditional occult art of astrology. True Time, the time we actually experience in our being-in-the-world, has quality, has a distinct feel to it, a texture, that varies from one time period to another. The feel of the times is different now than in the 1980s, or the 1960s, or 50s, or 40s, or 20s, whatever the time period that we might refer to. There is a Spirit of the Times the Germans call the Zeitgeist; it is how Spirit manifests into time, composing a complex interplay of all social, political, cultural, and spiritual influences and forces. (Of course Hegel tried to articulate this Zeitgeist in the early 19th Century via Logos. So much to say about that.) Everyone to some degree or another participates in the action and passion of the times. But out of the Zeitgeist also comes a Call which a few will hear—it is the Call of the Age, the Call of Spirit out of the Age. For it is not as though the Zeitgeist is simply the intellectual picture of an age; there is that intangible quality of what is true Time, with its metaphysical vectors manifesting out of the Invisible. For us today, it is increasingly manifesting what I have called the Next Level. In our own life, we all go through different phases defined by different projects and motives, each having a different feel and character. Herbalists with astrological savvy also know there are times when certain herbs are at their most potent. Time, because of its inextricable involvement with Being, does show all the complexity of having quality, such that certain times (and certain places) might still indeed manifest the sacred.

The same consideration also applies to the yearly cycle we all experience on Earth. Different times of the year have their respective tone. And we still celebrate them: autumn harvest festivals, Halloween, Christmas, Easter, May Day, summertime celebrations, and specifically for those observing pagan tradition, the equinoxes and solstices. Our various holidays, though, on the soul depth level, are pale reminders of their past mythic significance, what with the thick coat of commercial gloss that now makes them all so slick. The challenge is to be able to celebrate them—new versions of them—with a renewed inspiration and appropriateness, whether through contemplation, ritual, narrative, music, song, dance, or poem. Again, it is not by simply reenacting the customs of the past, or by borrowing from other cultures, but by manifesting these forms through our own transformative, creative efforts that the vitally new is born.

Numerous places worldwide have traditionally been considered sacred, though, again, Modern and Postmodern thought will claim there is no basis for it. That basis, however, lies in the Invisible. Sacred sites must still be honored as an important part of collective soul memory, but even more important is that we actually become attuned to possible sacred experience, so that we might be prepared to experience firsthand if Spirit to this day still does actively manifest at these sites, or perhaps new sites.

In a land renowned for its sacred sites, a genuine, highly profound mystery has been appearing before the eyes of our contemporary world for some decades now. It is something so extraordinary that we realize that here must be an example of an outer, numinous phenomenon that is mirroring the changes that are happening in consciousness. They are the crop circles[8] being etched into the grain fields of old England's countryside in the proximity of sacred sites, such as Silbury Hill, Stonehenge, Avebury, and Glastonbury. Though these remarkable circles are, in fact, occurring worldwide, the greater majority of them are found in southern England. A few thousand have by now been recorded.

The crop circles have evolved dramatically since they first began receiving public attention in the mid-1980s. We will not get sidetracked here by the contention that crop circles can be, and often are, hoaxed. That has been assumed from the beginning; what we refer to here are the genuine circles—those finding no explanation in terms of conventional human hoaxing. The genuine circles have been shown to display anomalous properties, scientifically documented, that the hoaxed circles simply cannot duplicate. Beginning in 1990, the circles suddenly began appearing as complex pictograms, and over these succeeding years have been appearing in beautiful, increasingly complex and variable, formation types. It has become a tradition to continue calling them generically "crop circles," even though most of these pictogram types no longer even resemble simple circles.

Who are the *Circlemakers?* That is the question we all would like the answer to, though the ongoing campaign to debunk the crop circles indicates that a secret governmental/military Establishment does not want us to know. An Intelligence other than human is certainly interacting with us in some form of communication. But what are they saying? Of course, that, too, is what so many of us would like to know. Quite a number of researchers have been studying this phenomenon for over 30 years now, and so we find plenty of theories. The patterns and symbols of the pictograms have been striking deep chords in the thousands who have opened to them. In many cases, those who are able to experience them firsthand come away *changed*. Crop circles are the "temporary temples" of the fields, as so many who have experienced them up close now call them.[9] The one thing that is obvious is that we are not being spoon fed any easily interpretable message. The Circlemakers undoubtedly have their reasons why they are communicating with us in this mysterious fashion, and at this time. (Isn't it interesting that it is coinciding with this transition period we are living in.) Meditating upon this, given the context of our Postmodern world, should, though, give us some idea as to why.

The communication itself could be considered a preparation for us for coming global changes using a new-old symbolic language that we do find in our own traditions, or, in some cases, out of mathematical—fractal—chaos—theory. Year by year, season after season, we have been undergoing this slow conditioning to their presence. And the evidence repeatedly shows a connection to UFOs.

Let us note that the New Age has been symbolically likened to a butterfly, in terms of drawing together the developing of greater ecological awareness with the realization that a dramatic shift is taking place in consciousness. The inaugurating of the "Butterfly Era" of global civilization has been announced by author Norie Huddle[10]. And are butterflies not an excellent symbol of this shift in consciousness, for the butterfly undergoes its own dramatic transformation, from caterpillar to chrysalis to beautiful winged creature. Butterflies appeal to children; they are a delight to the eyes; they actually bring joy and an uplifting of spirit to those who are visited by them. There are numerous stories of butterflies involved in uncanny moments of synchronicity. Being sensitive creatures, they are also part of Nature's early warning system that something might be amiss. And so we can look to our butterfly populations—the Monarch especially is seriously being threatened—as one indicator, among others, of what changes lie ahead.

But there is something even deeper to the butterfly as symbol when we discover that in ancient Greece the butterfly had an obscure association with Psyche. And so, let us consider this. The butterfly is adept of the ways of the air; and so is Psyche an adept of the ways of Air (Aquarius). For the fitful butterfly flits from flower to flower through airy spaces; Psyche equally flits—shape shifts—from world to world through spaces of the Invisible. The butterfly undergoes transformation from sluggish, plant-based creature to a delicate, light-hearted being free in the open air; and, likewise, Psyche was once an Earthbound mortal who was divinized and raised to the status of Goddess. And, of course, the butterfly is physically beautiful, as Psyche was said to be beautiful, the rival even of Venus herself, but, then, even more than that for us today, Psyche is the beauty of the invisible soul become Soul/Spirit in union.

There is also the hypothetical phenomenon out of chaos theory known as the "butterfly effect." Since all things are interconnected, it has been speculated that the mere flutter of a butterfly's wings could have untold repercussions, for example, in the forming of future weather systems. Naturally, this could be said of anything, the butterfly being but the dainty and elegant expression of the theory, for the flitting about of a butterfly appears on the surface to be so inconsequential. And if each one of us is a butterfly? I have shared my Vision of Psyche—that is the flutter of my butterfly wings, and even more than that, when we consider their ancient connection. I do believe that the repercussions of *this* butterfly Vision will someday be realized.

Last, let me make here a concrete suggestion that would help move Language in the direction we need to be going. It is a simple suggestion, really. For whatever it takes for us to show respect for Earth, that is the direction we must move in. So my one, simple suggestion for what our culture must do to show this respect is to put into universal practice the capitalization of the name of our planet—*Earth*. After all, it is the proper name of our planetary home. Other planets are always officially capitalized—Mercury, Venus, Mars, etc.—and yet our own mother is so often demoted in print to small letter status. Surprisingly, I find this small letter "earth" in print even in works and articles by highly environmentally and ecologically conscious individuals. Take the otherwise commendable book *The Spell of the Sensuous* by David Abram (exploring identical themes to those that we have explored here): everywhere throughout, Abram unwittingly commits this blunder of language. Clearly, we see, then, that this has been common practice, even in the best intentioned of works. Writing the proper name "Earth," I hope, will become a movement of its own.

But we are still left with this question: Will there be a livable Earth in the years to come? Aquarius marks the end of the previous Age, for sure, but does it mark a New Age of life, or of mass death? Our Story continues...

( 10 )

## UFOs AND ET CONTACT:
## HARBINGERS OF THE NEXT LEVEL

*To indicate where we go from here,*
*the UFO appears*

It is remarkable that the most important Revelation of recent times, whose origins go back primarily to 1947, still has no openly public, official recognition. Rather, official silence, even more, outright denial, is still the stance governments take on UFOs (and, significantly, our own U.S. government has been accused of being the worst of all), despite the hundreds of thousands of sightings, encounters, and alien abduction cases worldwide. The UFO phenomenon has profound implications for the New Age, so much so, with so much potential for radical change, on a scale that would shake our entire civilization, that officialdom has kept a tight lid on the subject out of fear of that change to this day. This denial, or should we say, the false impression given of complete non-interest in the subject of UFOs by officialdom, especially in America, is at the heart of a deep schism in our collective psyche. That something this profound, and by now so much in our face, is still being lied about and covered up only points to the fact that a fundamental psychological complex of denial—and with that goes chronic dishonesty—runs throughout our society. It has become something of a given, if we really pay attention to what people say, that in a large percentage of the general public, an attitude prevails that the government is not to be trusted to tell us the truth on just about anything.

For those who have come this far in our Story who might balk at this juncture and question everything I will be assuming here about the reality of UFOs, my blunt reply can only be, *They have some serious homework to do.* To the sceptic's *Where is the proof?* those who have taken the time to research the subject sufficiently and objectively know that there is plenty of evidence to go on. But the hardcore debunker is not worth the trouble even dealing with anymore. I had satisfied myself a number of years ago that the evidence for the reality of UFOs and ET contact was overwhelming. The time to debate *that* issue is over.

But I must also put the whole issue another way: All along in our Story I have been speaking in the words of Mythos. It has not been my concern to argue the scientific merits of any evidence or claims of proof. That became clear when we discussed the astrological basis of the New Age. My thinking is no longer oriented by the Word as Logos, but rather the Word as Mythos (which we will explore in another chapter). By Logos, briefly, I refer to thinking that is set to the standard of empirical evidence, the scientific method and what is considered scientific proof, and the rational intellect that wants certitude, so that experience can be reduced to "facts," formulas, and equations. Now someone might say, *But apparently you want it both ways—you do refer to evidence to back up your claims, but now you want to speak in the mushy form of myth and mythology, or whatever it is Mythos might mean.* My reply is, Mythos is far more flexible in what it is able to bring into Form, that is, in our case here, into the complexity of Story; it can assimilate and apply Logos, but Logos cannot do likewise with Mythos, but only critique it, debunk it, deconstruct it, and distance itself from it. I find that all paranormal phenomena are best conveyed in language as Mythos, and this definitely applies to those who have had UFO/ET encounter experiences. Their attempts to share their experiences in language are examples of Mythos-making and not the Logos of scientific inquiry.

*We will see that the UFO phenomenon—Other Intelligence—is the wild card of our future.*

Here, again, we find that our traditional Western religions fall short. What do they have to say to us about the reality of UFOs? The scant acknowledgement made today by Church and various religious leaders about the possibility of other intelligent life in the universe is wholly unsatisfactory; it is rather lame. They are, of course, highly protective of their flock, so what they feel compelled to say will be minimal. That some Fundamentalists will make the blanket claim that all ETs are nothing but fallen angels—demons—only shows how myopic ego-centered Human Reality can get. Though all religious traditions were profoundly influenced by the ancient encounter with the superhuman Other—one version of which is that ETs were Ancient Astronauts from elsewhere—the current UFO phenomenon receives little, if any, real attention by religious leaders. Native American peoples are an exception, in that they still maintain a living tradition of contact with the Star People and the Star Nations. They accept ET visitation and prophecies made by the ET Star People as a given. For the great majority of society, however, what is still lacking in an open, honest, public way is a deep meditation on the implications of alien contact for our civilization; *that work* must sooner or later be done. The book *A.D. After Disclosure*, by Richard Dolan and Bryce Zabel has gone a good way in doing that work.

Religions are extremely slow to change; they inherently resist change, since they are founded upon a claim to divine Revelation, which is then taken to be The Eternal Truth. If one possesses such a Truth, one then believes there is no reason to change it. How arrogant could we be to attempt to change what is Truth? The myth structure of religion—myth being our most fundamental orientation in the world—is deeply embedded in our psychology. If there were a genuine meditation on the UFO by leaders representing all the religions, and such a meditation made public, religions would of necessity begin to change. That is exactly the view of the New Age Vision.

It is an understatement to say that the UFO subject is rife with controversy. Anyone who has delved into it more than superficially comes to realize that this is an extremely complex subject that most people have great difficulty getting a proper sense of. Some will latch onto an author such as Zecharia Sitchin and feel that his work explains everything about the phenomenon, so that the complexity of all the contemporary stories, reports, and evidence simply goes back to one ancient narrative. Even among UFO researchers, developing a well-rounded view of UFO reality can be slippery. Within the field of its study—ufology—there is precious little general agreement; bitter divisions and personal attacks among researchers are the common fare. Some study the subject in the serious and cautious manner of the conventional scientist, whereas others pour out reams of ET correspondence through channeling or personal contact. Rarely do these groups see eye-to-eye or respect much of one another. The views taken of our non-human Visitors—they have been called everything from extraterrestrials, or simply ETs or aliens, or space aliens, space brothers, space people, or Star People, UFO beings, ufonauts, Other-dimensionals, Interdimensionals, Other Intelligence, Non-human Intelligence, or, in the broadest sense, *the Other*—cover a wide range. Some claim that they are space brothers and sisters here to share with us their wisdom in order to gently nudge us in our evolution. Some may view them as curiosity seekers of a kind, here to check up on our progress and collect terrestrial specimens. Or that they were our creator Gods, having bioengineered us and still remaining active on our planet since distant prehistoric times, intervening in our civilizations down through the ages. This intervention itself can be seen in a positive, evolutionary way, or as nefarious, promoting internecine strife in civilizations behind the scenes, as William Bramley speculates in *The Gods of Eden*. Others see them now as an outright threat to human civilization in that their primary agenda appears to be to eventually take over our planet. (See David M. Jacobs, *The Threat*) There is indeed a strong tendency among many to want to divide them into the simplistic polarity of "good aliens" and "bad aliens." I would suggest that the picture is not as black-and-white as any particular either/or view might claim, but is something far more complex.

The ET picture is complicated by the evidence itself, apparently showing visitation by a number of different ET groups. Estimates vary greatly on this, from conservative figures of maybe 3 or 4 different visiting ET races to figures as high as 50, or even, some will say, to well over 100 different alien races. There is the by now familiar cultural icon of the ET Grey, which itself has appeared to experiencers in a wide variation of form. There are also, to name only some of the more familiar of the other groups,[1] the Zetas (often considered the Greys) from the Zeta Reticuli star system, the Tall Whites, the Reptilians, the Insectoids, the robotic and android types, the hairy dwarfs, the hooded types, the sage-like Elder types, the Pleaidians, Sirians, Orions, Draconians, the Nordic Blondes, the Anunnaki (an ancient Sumerian name) and all manner of apparitional beings (and some of these names may very well refer to more than one of these groups).

If we took in all the evidence, at least on face value, we would readily conclude that indeed various ET groups are here for different reasons. Some, we would note again, are here to contact select individuals (contactees) to share with them the ET's more advanced understanding of the cosmos and to suggest the direction humanity should be taking, sending these individuals then on a mission to share the ET message. They could therefore be evolutionary helpers, here to slowly prepare us, to coach us in various ways, in our advance to the Next Level (which is largely my view, sharing it with R. Leo Sprinkle, James Harder, Richard Boylan, John Mack, Whitley Strieber, Steven Greer, to name only a few of the better known in this "Positives" camp, as David Jacobs calls them). Some ETs may simply be here to observe, to check on our progress, and to take samples of Earth life back to their world. Some may indeed be here to promote discord and strife in the human race for the sake of their own secret agenda. Yet, even the agenda of genetically interacting with us with the intention of producing a new human-alien hybrid species can be considered from divergent points of view, from that of upgrading us in our evolution to supplanting current humanity with a future dominant race. There may be obscure spiritual reasons why some are here, perhaps conducting a certain trafficking in souls, as some suggest. Perhaps, stating simply yet another possibility, there is no great variation in agendas at all; what appear to be different agendas is but the sophisticated intelligence program of an ET intruder promoting confusion in humankind. But, then, it is also theorized—and channels do tell this story—that various ET groups are themselves in contention over Earth (the traditional war in Heaven theme).

In this context, it is also a well-known observation that our ET visitors themselves remain extremely secretive. By and large, again, depending on the point of view, in the various encounters with them, they either never seem to tell the truth, or at least the complete truth, or, let us say, any, in fact, verifiable truth, about who they are, where they come from, and why they are here. Even if a particular ET visitor offered answers to these questions, do we take them at face value? They come and go surreptitiously, and we are left in the dark. There are those who would simply put it this way: *The ETs are deceivers.* Yet, again, there may be valid and wise considerations why such deception might be necessary in dealings with planet Earth. No matter what the judgment on our ET visitors might be, however, UFO reality has been with us a long, long time, and is not about to go away.

To this day, as we can see, there are still no definitive answers about UFO reality that all could agree upon; but the undeniable firsthand reports are there for all to study. What is often disturbing, though, are researchers who will make certain claims, but who obviously ignore or overlook the wealth of varied information that is out there. It could be argued that to be able to assimilate such a wealth of varied and so often conflicting information is almost a superhuman task in itself. It might be only human propensity, then, that most researchers find themselves focusing on a particular area of interest that, unfortunately, may often color their view of the whole picture. Despite, though, what researchers do or not do consider within their purview, the very nature of the UFO phenomenon has triggered an enormous amount of new mythmaking—I prefer to say, Mythos-making—in our culture.

Renowned UFO researcher and writer Jacques Vallee is correct in suggesting that the UFO is giving birth to a new mythology, to a new religion even. It is a matter of fact that a wide and varying mythmaking / Mythos-making movement is taking place with regard to the whole phenomenon. This, however, alarms Vallee, as it has others, believing as he does that this somehow poses a threat to our rational intellect and science and the integrity of human civilization. The New Age Vision, on the other hand, sees the absolute necessity for this new Mythos-making. ET contact is integral to our future spirituality. And this is regardless of what one's view happens to be about who the ETs are, what their agenda might be, or what they might want of us.

First, it is important that we fully appreciate the paranormal nature of the whole phenomenon. Herein we find the key to our earlier thesis that our evolution is a bi-transformational process. I beg the indulgence here of those who are already quite familiar with the characteristics of UFO encounters. I believe, though, that a quick overview at this point is called for. The paranormal nature of the UFO phenomenon, often called "strangeness" in the literature, begins with the UFO itself, an outward manifesting occurrence. UFOs have appeared in a tremendous variety of forms, the classic flying saucer—and it, too, of various types—being but one; others have included long cylindrical—cigar—shaped craft, huge triangular or boomerang-shaped craft, conical, and oval-shaped craft; so-called Mother ships that can send out small scout ships; almost liquid appearing plasma ships; and all variety of balls, spheres, and globes, of light. UFOs display "impossible" maneuvers: they can accelerate to incredible speeds almost instantly, make right-angled turns, stop on a dime, and hover silently while defying gravity. They easily outpace the best of our military aircraft, and can even appear to play with them like a cat-and-mouse game. Often, when the ET pilots find it necessary, they can deactivate the control panels—in particular, the missile launch systems—of the jet aircraft in pursuit of them. UFOs have demonstrated that they can dematerialize and rematerialize (or, another way of putting it, pierce the Veil of Human Reality), and some have even appeared, defying all our sense of physical logic, to divide into parts, each part then capable of flying off in different directions. Or separate, distinct craft appear to come together and merge and become one, or the craft will appear to change shape or size before the astonished eyes of the witness(es). There is the well-known electromagnetic effect (E-M effect): the cutting out of electrical power—vehicles simply turn off—when a UFO comes near. UFOs sometimes surround themselves with strange fog, and often the surrounding environment is altered in surreal ways: They produce a "sphere of influence," or what Jenny Randles has called the "Oz factor." Their light effects are also varied: intense, dazzling light that can turn night into day; light that shows a kind of solidity, like a curtain that can be rolled down or rolled up, or by bending in mid-air or around corners; light beams that can levitate persons and animals and vehicles; and light beams that can tranquilize, heal, or that produce strange markings. Again, all the above behaviors and those to follow were already common findings decades ago.

The range of effects on persons when a UFO is close encountered, or their occupants, the UFO beings, are close encountered, is also most varied: There can be the sense of being mentally scanned from a distance, the induction of bodily paralysis, miraculous healings, psychic abilities suddenly triggered, e.g. clairvoyance, precognition, telepathy, remarkable synchronicities; there is often the induction of amnesia, subconscious suggestions, or out-of-body experiences, such as individuals claiming not physical but astral projection into a UFO craft. Most often the UFO beings communicate by telepathy, somehow being able to turn on a telepathic channel in the persons they contact. Individuals who have had extremely close encounters, or who have been invited on board flying saucers, or who have been abducted, often report that sudden psychic abilities were triggered by the experience, the abilities lasting anywhere from minutes to hours, to days, to weeks, sometimes indefinitely, overnight often changing the person's entire life. The UFO beings themselves possess superhuman powers of mind reading, of being able to induce paralysis and tranquility in combative and frightened individuals; they often show the ability to levitate—they can literally glide through the air—; they can materialize as though out of thin air and can dematerialize; they can pass through closed doors, walls, or windows, and in some cases, we hear of them shape shifting. Other mysterious phenomena are associated with UFOs: tales of Men in Black (MIBs), animal mutilations that to this day go unsolved, and the enigmatic crop circles.

Researchers have long found parallels to most all these paranormal occurrences in remarkable accounts recorded throughout history, most notably those found in the sacred books of religions. Indeed, the miracles depicted in *The Bible* no longer need to be explained away by the demythologists of Modernism.[2] The UFO phenomenon is profoundly providing a whole new perspective on historical religious events, and more than that—*the UFO phenomenon is providing us a whole new pair of glasses through which to view all of history.* (See chapter "The Emerging New Story of Us") With these new glasses so many of the puzzle pieces of our past we now find suddenly snapping into place. There will undoubtedly come a day when our history books will be rewritten from the new UFO perspective. This is a development that the Modernists could not have anticipated at all. Even our Postmodern scholars still enthralled by a solipsistic human-centered world have ignored, or have refused to confront, the evidence for the reality of UFOs. For the UFO is radically challenging our human-centered paradigm for understanding the cosmos; someday we will realize how incredibly naïve humanity has been regarding what our place in the cosmos really is. Reality in the coming years will become far more bizarre, complex, and extraordinary than what the textbooks and scientific and religious leaders could ever have dreamed. In the coming years, it might be most shattering to those who were most in denial.

Let us consider for a moment the impact that the non-human Other, coming to us in the form of the UFO, has for religion and spirituality in our Postmodern world. We could safely say that humanity has always had some kind of covenant with this protean phenomenon of the mysterious, superior Other. The belief in superhuman Powers—or one, monotheistic superhuman Power ("God")—has been universal among all civilizations up until the Modern period. The intellectual justification for such a belief, as we know, paled in the face of Modern critique. Nietzsche spelled it out in three succinct words: *God is dead.* But now, appearing in our skies is the UFO, and with that appearance suddenly an unexpected support for traditional religious claims—requiring, though, reinterpretation—is again on the table. However, this new support and justification for the acceptance of the reality of a superhuman *Other* would shatter the basis of dogmatic belief; for one thing, the traditional "God," as Tradition developed such a notion, would still be defunct. In addition, a profound disillusionment could easily result with the realization that we had been doubly deceived by

Tradition—not only is there no personal Father "God" as Tradition would have us believe, but the alien Other was in fact the Intelligence at the origin of our religions. Even more devastatingly radical—that the alien Other might have actually been the object of worship (as the personal "God," not the more philosophical, abstract All or Absolute) down through the centuries. Yet, ironically, at the same time, this realization provides an unexpected boon to spirituality—yes, *there is* something more than a human ego-centered world, *there are* other dimensions of spiritual reality, for the UFO reveals them to us now in a very real, though not quite humanly tangible, way. Irrepressibly, faith is reaffirmed in its belief that there is a "higher," a supernatural reality; for the New Age, the notion of a Higher Self acquires a more solid standing. It is not an exaggeration to state that the modern era of the UFO has awakened in us again the presence of a mysterious, superior Other. Before the coming of the UFO into our culture, religion had lost any palpable connection with a superior, external-appearing Intelligence. Religious sentiment in the modern world had found itself closed in a strictly interior space, in "mere subjectivity." What the contemporary awareness of the UFO phenomenon has done is to introduce *a new realism* in religion and spirituality. No longer can religious events and experiences be reduced to the mere peculiarities of human psychology, even if we bring into the picture the more glorified "archetypes."

It is important that we can step back from the particular controversies that embroil so many in this subject and be able to look at the Big Picture of what is unfolding. Certainly specific issues must be addressed and researched, but it is too easy to get sidetracked from what is philosophically important here. The UFO phenomenon is continuously bombarding us with profound insights about our future. And that, indeed, is the first insight: Taken as a paranormal symbol, the UFO is showing us our future. We saw above that the UFO is a marvel of technological wizardry. It is as if it were a magic show, both putting us in our place (showing us how primitive we still are), but also revealing to us *what someday will be possible*—yes, for us, all this will be possible. This is certainly not the technology of the Modern era of Virgo, but undoubtedly it is the coming technology of the New Age of Aquarius.

What the UFO can do—the UFO commanded by intelligent beings, and are we not also in that category of intelligent beings?—certainly we will someday equally be able to do. (I only mention in passing here the whole controversy regarding the Roswell story and our military's secret technology that far surpasses what the general public, even the highest-office politicians, know about. It is apparent that our military is back-engineering ET technology and trying to build some version of its own flying saucer.) The age-old human tendency is to want for ourselves what attracts, impresses, or enchants us, what seems in fact to reach out to us, firing our imagination; and Technos, living through us and drunk on possibilities, knowing no limits, is no doubt fully enchanted by the UFO. Our secret military, we can be assured, is not sitting idly on any of this.

Now the UFO, as a physical manifestation, is the technological side of this evolutionary coin. What of the paranormal abilities of the ETs themselves? They, too, are showing us our future, our *spiritual future*. Their very presence is saying to us, *What we are able to do, you too will someday be able to do.* What they are demonstrating to us, for one thing, is their mastery of the Next Level, the astral-psychic plane of consciousness. Many of the paranormal powers the ETs display apparently have also been developed by handfuls of human beings throughout history. For example, yogis of the East have themselves demonstrated that rigorous discipline can allow them a certain free access to the Next Level, giving them at times seemingly magical powers. The development of various paranormal abilities called siddhis (meaning "perfections")—such as control of bodily processes, mind reading, levitation, telekinesis, invisibility, remote viewing far in advance of what we in the West know, long-distance hypnotic control, shape shifting, the ability of entering another person's body, to list but a few—has been recorded in the ancient literature of the Vedas.[3] Throughout history, we find examples of paranormal abilities recorded in anecdote, chronicle, and legend, and we also do find some of them investigated in serious, contemporary research. What makes the ET experience a New Age development is the auguring of such powers as a shift in humanity at large. Years in the future—how far in the future, who can say—, we will definitely know that we are squarely within the Aquarian Age.

A whole new perspective on spirituality opens to us. The ETs can move between the dimensions of other worlds; they can move back and forth through the Veil. Now these other dimensions—no mere coincidence that hyper-dimensional physics is another new frontier—is but another way of talking about spiritual reality.[4] We will not quibble here with those who say that Spirit has nothing to do with UFOs and ETs, or astral phenomena, that Spirit is utterly beyond such things considered to be of a "lower level." We are tired of hearing about Spirit being so remotely otherworldly, which was the emphasis taken in the otherworldly-oriented Piscean Age. Spirit, as we shared before, manifests through all planes of Being; it is no longer going to be defined in such a narrow way that it is exclusively abstracted, utterly removed, from our everyday life, and that includes the other, invisible dimensions of our life. Consider what must then be the audacity of cybertech pundit Ray Kurzweil titling an earlier book of his *The Age of Spiritual Machines* if Spirit were so utterly remote, so utterly transcendent. What we must realize is that the two sides of the evolutionary coin, the external technological and the psychospiritual, are but two sides of *one coin*—an evolutionary future in which Technos and Psyche are thoroughly integrated, and perhaps virtually indistinguishable. And that defines the UFO experience. With each UFO encounter, we are being nudged then to take another tiny step into that enormously Larger Reality of our future.

We cannot ignore, though, at least some mention here of the abduction experience. This is not something that we can sweep under the rug and not want to talk about. I am well aware that there are those in the New Age community who want to have nothing to do but with the positive. But let us face it, alien abduction and other

Close Encounters of the 4th Kind can be physically traumatizing, life-shattering, a mind-rending violation of personal space. There are parents who agonize that their children are being taken and probed and experimented upon. Individuals are being tagged with implants like animals caught and tagged in the wild. The reproductive component in so many abduction experiences is well-known: particular ETs (the Greys) have a great interest in our genetics, as they routinely obtain sperm and egg samples from those they abduct. Studies done of these kinds of experiences point consistently to a program (most often said to be taking place on board their larger ships) of bioengineering a new human-alien hybrid. The impact on individuals undergoing such experiences can obviously be traumatic. *The aliens have no right to do this*, we hear it so often said among abductees. These are truly difficult issues that defy simplistic responses. If we could make it all go away, for the sake of alleviating suffering, who wouldn't agree to it? But even those who most deplore what is happening to the abductees (they typically consider the alternative word "experiencer" to be euphemistic), even someone like a David Jacobs or Budd Hopkins who both see here a terrible threat, will admit, *What can we do? There is apparently nothing we can do about it—the ETs are far superior to us.* (A few counseling books *have* come out in recent years claiming that certain things can be done to prevent the experience. I have not currently followed up on how effective they are. Those who might call on Jesus at the beginning of an alien experience haven't always been successful.) These particular ETs continue to conduct their abduction program no matter what we do. Certainly, at the very least, individuals experiencing abduction need support and wise counseling. (I once co-facilitated an abductee/experiencer support group for about a year.[5])

Whether a new human-alien hybrid being will be an integral part of our evolution may very well be a hot topic of the future. (This may essentially be not much different of an issue, though, than the techno-wizards glibly preparing a coming generation of androids and cyborgs, as we discussed earlier. In what ethical sense is it more acceptable for humans to create new, hybrid beings, but not ETs?) In a broader context, however, the breaking in of the Larger Reality in whatever form is well-known for shattering the ego-self and undermining conventional life. The encounter with the Larger Self too, as we have said, can be unsettling, traumatic, life altering, psychologically confusing, existentially disorienting, all of which are the same characteristics that we find with the alien encounter experience. We must always keep in mind as some consolation the plea of Job, *Why me? Why me Lord?* And so, many of the abductees ask the same question, and would wish the experiences to end, but we apparently have no silver bullet yet to do it.

Those who do claim, however, that the agenda of the ETs is something to fear, that they are Secret Controllers intent on deceiving us in order to take over the planet, are overlooking an essential insight. (This is even to set aside for a moment the full range of evidence that appears to show that various ET groups are here with *different* agendas.) The ETs must have made a serious mistake then if their intent is to suppress human evolution and our spirituality, for the thing is, once they have shown themselves to us—*no matter what their agenda*—we are opened to a whole new Greater Reality, and like the genie once let out of the bottle, it will not be put back again. Their very presence—given their superiority, they apparently could have remained totally hidden, or, for that matter, could have already totally taken over or destroyed us, if that was their intent—again, their very presence is the outward trigger that sets into motion changes in consciousness. The nihilistic Postmodern world is simply no longer the same for those of us who have made the shift to this new understanding. The cultural wasteland of the incestuous human ego now ends. As if at one stroke, all religion, spirituality, occultism, is infused with new significance. The Modernist project of trying to demythologize the past in the name of the hyperactive, pure ego-intellect is over. (True, one could argue that the Secret Government cover-up regarding ETs is so well instituted that despite those who have become aware of the ET presence, that such awareness alone is not enough yet to initiate evolutionary changes, as mainstream society remains conditioned not to be ready for such changes. Yet, again, a small number of aware individuals might be all that is necessary to initiate evolutionary changes.)

Let us ask a question that bluntly spells out the issue here, especially in light of the unfolding MELE that we looked at earlier: The question is, *Do we need help from an Other? Do we need ET help?* I believe this will be a question that will be asked over and over again in the coming years; it is already creating new ideological camps depending on how one is disposed to answering it. But, perhaps, we should ask another question first, *Are we collectively going to turn in the needed new direction on our own?* We have already considered that that question is coming too late. What is the intent of the Establishment? Those in power obviously want to stay in power, which unfortunately implies *maintaining the status quo,* no matter what. This, then, should answer our second question, which, in turn, should go toward answering the first. The needed change on this planet, sad enough to say, if we are first honest enough to admit it, is not going to be accomplished by us acting alone. Is this too pessimistic of a view of us? Does this not give us, humanity, enough credit? Are there those who would insist that we can take care of ourselves, thank you? Certainly those who maintain and defend the status quo would want us to believe that. The whole mass media industry wants us to believe that. But, then, we've just gone full circle: The status quo is precisely the problem on this planet and what is destroying the planet for us all. Is abrupt climate change within our power to control? As many scientists have now said, *It's probably too late.* The tipping point of irreversible civilization collapse, some have said, has already passed.

It is not a secret that those of us who proclaim our New Age Vision are profoundly disillusioned with the status quo. That has been implicit throughout this work. We who want to see change in this world should therefore not fear Other Intelligence, for its renewed presence indicates that the next step in our evolution is about to take place. And what is there to say to those who might reply, *But we don't like this next step in our evolution, we want things to remain just the way they are?* They should then also say this to the techno-wizards who are rushing us headlong into a sci fi AI world. Unfortunately, to want things to remain just the way they are has become increasingly self-destructive. An evolutionary intention is compelling humankind to grow up out of its childhood.

It is not to be denied that the issues here are highly complex, that more specific blanket statements regarding all ETs, or, in a broader sense, all visitations by Other Intelligence, are most likely impossible to defend. Perhaps a particular ET group does not have *our* best intentions in mind. Yet, at the same time, I would suggest that many who consider extraterrestrials a threat are most likely expressing their own fundamental fear of change, in that human civilization may simply not be allowed to continue its Establishment way, that we on Spaceship Earth are travelling in a grand cosmic current that is forcing us to evolve whether we personally like it or not. Yes, obviously, any ET involvement may very well be a threat to the human status quo. Yet, what if their intervention could change the power structures on this planet for the eventual benefit of all? What if it could provide us another needed jump in our psychospiritual evolution? What if their intervention could help alleviate the full impact of ecological collapse? What if they could literally save us, in some sense, or at least save some remnant of humanity? I am well aware that there are those who would dread to entertain such questions. To them, rather let the human race perish than invite ETs to "save us." There are those so totally invested in the status quo, that to them, any intervention is bad: *Leave us alone, thank you, we like it the way things are, we like our power on this planet.* Then we find those who will say that intervention might not be so bad per se, as long as the ETs are clearly here to help us, but yet, they will say in the same breath, the ETs should stay out of our human egocentric orbit—after all, this is *our* planet. (We might think this is our planet, but we might have to think again.) The thing is, I'm afraid we may not be able to have it both ways. But still, again, we may find it reasonable to ask, *If the ETs are really here to help us, then why haven't they done so?* That is, of course, making a big assumption that they haven't done so in some sense already, in some way perhaps that we can't grasp at this time. But I do take that as a valid question, one that requires some deep pondering, especially when we consider the horrendous atrocities, the toll of human suffering, that has taken place in so many past wars. Where were the ETs then? Then again, let us not assume that it is as black-and-white as all this. Can anyone definitively say that they have not intervened, behind the scenes, in subtle ways? Conversely, again, we should not think of them as parental guardians who will protect us under all circumstances. Obviously they haven't. Undoubtedly, though, we can't have it both ways. If they *are here* to help us in a clearly defined, overt, way, then they are definitely going to have a tremendous impact on the human egocentric world. I have come to call this *radical transformational intervention*. There is no way around it: If they intervene, it is going to be radical to civilization. And if it be called intervention, must we feel resigned to a destiny guided by Others, or might we see in it not a deflation of human pride, but the gift and opportunity of moving forward in our evolution?

The new Aquarian dispensation, as I have suggested, may very well require some kind of "supernatural" event that would trigger a shift, create an opening, in collective consciousness. (Or might the looming edge of a very natural MELE be that event?) Most likely this event will involve the kind of intervention by Other Intelligence that I am talking about. It could be dramatic, involving a rapid and radical change across the planet, or, on a spectrum of gradations between, it may be so subtle, so discreet, over an extended period of time, that the mainstream would probably miss seeing intervention taking place at all. The mainstream would probably spin it as us miraculously coming together to resolve our global crisis.

In contrast to the fear-based attitude, an initiative has been underway in recent years called CE-5, or Close Encounters of the 5th Kind. Spearheading this movement has largely been the effort of Dr. Steven Greer's group, CSETI (Center for the Study of Extraterrestrial Intelligence). Close Encounters of the 5th Kind are those initiated by us; in other words, they are encounters in which we play an *active* part, in our own attempt to reach out and contact and communicate with Other Intelligence. The attitude here is not one of waiting for the ETs to make all the moves, as we have certainly been in a passive position in this age-old, one-way relationship, but is one rather of actively initiating contact through any number of physical and/or spiritual protocols, because *we* desire it. Those involved in CE-5 efforts, both through clearly defined organizations like CSETI and probably untold individuals acting on their own,[6] seek contact for precisely the reasons we are discussing. There are those of us who believe that at least some among us are prepared for this momentous event of open contact. Making contact, some of us realize, *is* in the interest of our future. It was years back that overnight I saw that it was the key for unlocking the secret to the New Age Vision. We will see that it is time for us to begin this two-way dialogue with Other Intelligence.

Implicit in our whole discussion up to this point has been our new view on evolution. Evolution is no longer to be defined as a strictly so-called "natural" process. Even our biological evolution is open to new questions now. Apparently we did not evolve in a strictly natural physico-biochemical manner, with a few mutations occurring here and there along the way, no matter how many billion and then further million years were passing. Evolution is now to be defined in relationship to *an Other*. As we saw, the appearance and intervention of the superhuman Other is intimately tied in to the human Story. The Other has always been a powerful catalyst for both the highest and the lowest of human motivation. Those who say that it was a big mistake that the whole God concept had originated to begin with, who believe that we could just as well have done without it, and wished that humanity had, have no understanding of the profound need of the human soul to have had such a powerful concept. The God concept is an extremely potent psychospiritual drug. Much has been made of this metaphysical need that can possess us; even a good scientific materialist will condescend to talk about the God part of the brain.[7] God—the Gods—the superhuman Other—serves a many-pronged function for the various stages of our psychospiritual evolution. Without an Other of superhuman Intelligence to behold from afar, we would not have been compelled to forever seek and push beyond our perceived limits, as we were perpetually beckoned by that far-off, illuminating Vision. It is as though we require an Other to pivot from, allowing us to dramatically turn and move in some new evolutionary direction. The Other initiates a tremendous creative tension in the human soul, inspiring us to surpass ourselves, to transcend what we have been. Eventually, in that far-in-the-future time, we yearn to become at-once-with the Other.

Up to this time, this relationship to the Gods, and then to "God," was a one-way proposition: a God spoke, we obeyed (or tried our best to obey). The Other has always had the superior advantage here. But it is time now that we actively—co-creatively—become engaged in an evolutionary dialogue. It is as if a relationship with our Higher Self simultaneously calls forth and demands a dialogue with the Other Intelligences who are already *there*, existing on that higher level, whether they are explicitly waiting for us or not. Of course, profound questions regarding how human-ET communication is even possible, with thorny issues here regarding thought and language, of how information can be processed between minds utterly alien to each other, and how these minds can even share something of their life-worlds, will open up whole new philosophical vistas. Channeling can be considered one form of that communication, but even channeling, despite often being able to ask questions of the channeled Intelligence, is still largely a one-way street.

Even those ETs who may not have our best interest in mind may no longer have the advantage of remaining completely hidden, now that we are aware of them. For above and beyond its superhuman capabilities, the Other has always had an additional advantage over us when our culture persists in denial of their existence. What we deny exists has that much greater power over us.

Let us consider again, briefly, various outcomes of encountering this new reality. There is, of course, the psychological impact. Those who thought that we were the masters around here, on planet Earth, who take great pride in our human achievement, might find themselves crestfallen by the reality of the presence of the superhuman Other. The religious leaders and Fundamentalists smug in their belief that they had spirituality all wrapped up in a tidy book might find themselves not merely hemming and hawing, but cornered into serious, soul-searching, crisis. Individuals might experience a profound disillusionment with humanity when the superior powers of the non-human Other are truly encountered. The self-important human project that appeared to be the only game around suddenly takes on a cosmic relativity when other extraterrestrial civilizations are considered. Are we, a rudimentarily intelligent species living on this particular backwater planet, simply a fish bowl experiment that increasingly looks as though it were doomed to failure? And how many potentially millions, if not billions, of people, disillusioned with human authority, will turn to the ETs in prayer, in hopes that they might come to our aid, might come even in individual, personal distress (e.g. hoping to heal ailments that human medicine cannot yet cure). How many will want to abandon our planet and leave with the ETs, especially in the midst of an MELE? (Yes, it is a theme we have already encountered with UFO cults. Remember the Heaven's Gate story in the year of Comet Hale-Bopp, 1997?[8])

Again, what of the impact on our spirituality? The realization that we might be the genetically-engineered race of another superior Intelligence—what does that say about our spirituality? Would that suddenly void our pretentions, deflate our pride, to realize that we were nothing more perhaps than a biological experiment, a lab animal? To realize that we are no longer the measure of all things? That the superhuman *Other* would have the much better claim of being the measure of all things? That we are perhaps not part "divine," as we thought, but perhaps part "alien"? That we were not made in the image of "Almighty God," but, perhaps, in the image of a "God" ET? What if we are but semi-intelligent ants in comparison to another Intelligence so beyond us that we cannot even imagine it? (Yes, what Tradition called "God.") What if, in fact, the superhuman Other has been careful with us, lest its overwhelming superiority would make us feel too puny?

How do we bounce back from all this? Do we have a right to participate in Spirit? Have our spiritual aspirations been but a delusion?

Might this become our future collective, existential crisis? Is Spirit far more or far other than Tradition had taught? It is unavoidable that all traditional theology is now in question given the greater clarity provided by our new UFO glasses. A whole host of new questions, as profound as any posed in the past, are going to be the stuff of tomorrow's theology.

The New Age Vision, as it is presented here, has already begun to address these issues. It is one thing to be humbled by the superior, but we must realize that we *do* have a higher purpose. Isn't that the implication behind our Western religious traditions? (Lest my reference to the "superior" be blown out of proportion, I do not assume that this means superior in all ways. As human beings, we may have *human* superiorities that might only be found with us, such as our achievements in the arts, or any expression that involves our supremely human emotional and creative being—in other words, that involves *our soul*. The fact that we are *Earthlings* may imply powers that even we are yet unaware of.) If we are the biological outcome of alien intervention on Earth, then we must realize that this also opened a window for us—the spiritual world came into view with that very intervention. If we are made in the image of Others, then the spiritual levels that they were already masters of had to appear to us even if dimly in that selfsame process. And this window opened specifically for us, *the Earthling*. Through their intervention, self-conscious Spirit had entered the Earthling hominid species and psychospiritual evolution now became our birthright also. No matter how far down on the cosmic evolutionary ladder we might be, we now had a cosmic right to come into our own, individually, and eventually, collectively. Indeed, we are today moving into a whole, new, existential orientation—*we are coming into our own*. That is to say, we are no longer predefining ourselves according to traditional beliefs that conditioned us into accepting our alleged limitations. A higher image of what it means to be human is now in view. The glass ceiling that Tradition had placed on our spiritual aspirations is being shattered. We are now called to become players in consciously-intended and consciously-assisted evolution. We have discovered that soul, rather than being an abstract "something," is our much more tangible potential-to-become.

(One view that has been circulating in the New Age community is that we were purposely, that is, genetically, "dumbed down" by ancient ET bioengineering. The full potential of our DNA, in other words, has been blocked. That may prove to be a valid Thread in our evolutionary Story. But what was once long ago blocked can potentially become unblocked. This, too, is another factor in the Aquarian dispensation that would open up to us the Next Level.)

For the last 2,000 years we have lived within a contradictory Piscean paradigm: Here, in the West, we believed we were the crown of creation, yet, at the same time, we were defined as sinful and limited. Now we have in view a higher image of ourselves, but one that does not, when properly understood, inflate the ego. No matter what the ETs have already mastered and accomplished, it does not take away from us *our* purpose, the call for each one of us to participate in our own individual way in the Story of the greater cosmos. That indeed is the highest personal, metaphysical meaning—the Good News—of the New Age. Each of us has (that is, potentially) a mission—to attempt to fulfill the potential that our Higher Self is revealing to us. To intuitively see that, to know that firsthand, is the Uranian gift and the beginning of gnosis. Traditionally, what we thought we were, what we thought our limitations were, no longer applies; what our potential is, what we might become, is now our Vision.

We realize then that UFOs and ET contact are harbingers of what is coming. The ET encounter is the outer numinous event that corresponds in us to a transformation in consciousness. We can also envision a day when we will have developed the super-technology of our own UFO-like craft. That radically new philosophical questions lie just around the corner that previous generations of thinkers hadn't had to grapple with, let alone could even have imagined, is quite clear.

Our future encounter with ET reality will have irreversible impact, in innumerable, and unexpected, ways: upon culture, youth, religion, history, science, technology, energy issues, economics, politics, government, and in our relation to our Mother Earth. A whole psychological reorientation takes place for us when we come to realize that Their presence is always (potentially) among us. Those who still question the reality of UFOs and the ET presence are both naïve and in denial; and what they lose out on is a larger, both a cosmically and metaphysically larger, Big Picture, and that sooner or later, we will interface openly with Other Intelligences. It is the dawning of this Vision on the horizon that is especially the essence of what is New Age. It beckons us as our destiny.

# ( 11 )

# THE NEXT LEVEL:
# THE ASTRAL-PSYCHIC

*Have you never had intimations of invisible networks,*
*the multi-interweaving of invisible realms into our own?*[1]

We now reach another full turn in the spiral of our Story of the New Age Vision. All the various Threads of the Story will be drawn more tightly together. Spirit coming-to-us anew, in my own experience, I have called Psyche: our personal Divine Guide, our personal Self-Realized Master, our Living Image encounter with Higher Self, our connectedness with Anima Mundi. The Higher Self is the Aquarian dispensation of our own Divine Selfhood, our God-self. The question might then be asked, *What has liberation of soul, bringing, in essence, psychotherapy—but a psychotherapy on a scale we have not yet seen—into the open, have to do with ETs and a new spirituality?*

*Welcome to our next evolutionary level—the real is about to become surreal.*

The Next Level beyond the Veil that is opening to us in our evolution as human beings, as the ETs have been showing us all along, is the astral-psychic plane of consciousness. There are many examples of the first glimmers of this today. The New Age movement itself shows a strong thriving interest in psychic phenomena, and a very common assumption found in it is that each one of us can uncover our own latent psychic ability. Psychics have also been gaining more attention in the media in recent years. Apparently, too, a greater number of children are coming into this world with psychic abilities that are quite remarkable.² And there are those who have been gifted with psychic powers of various kinds as a result of any number of anomalous experiences. Uri Geller claimed to have had his ability triggered by a UFO experience; Gordon Michael Scallion through a completely unexpected experience involving a temporary loss of speech and visitation by light beings. Other individuals, such as Dannion Brinkley, who have had near-death experiences (NDEs), have come back with uncanny psychic awareness. Contact with the Other Side somehow gives birth to these latent powers within us. The near-death experience itself is a going beyond into the astral-psychic plane. The out-of-body experience (OBE), a contemporary renaming of what traditionally was called astral travel, also involves entering and moving about in this whole other multidimensional plane.

Robert Monroe broke new ground with his first book *Journeys out of the Body*, claiming in it that the OBE experience was initially not one that he sought out at all—he had no interest in occultism to begin with—but one which spontaneously began to happen to him. Over time, though, he developed techniques for consciously exploring out-of-body travel. His books make for eye-opening, mind-blowing, reading. Taking his experiences seriously, we are given a glimpse into multitudes of other bizarre and almost beyond comprehension worlds that lie just beyond the Veil.

Our dream life also takes us into this realm, especially with the experience of what Jungians call Big Dreams, which may include prophetic dreams. There is also what are called lucid dreams. Lucid dreaming is a conscious waking up in this out-of-body dream state, and when we are able to do this, we can then begin to learn how to maneuver around in it and potentially be an active participant in the astral world. These extraordinary kinds of dream that can be quite thrilling do impress us with the reality of this other realm. But the question to be asked, as we've been asking all along, is, *How can we work with these dreams to help transform and move us beyond our Postmodern condition?*

The most common conscious entry into the astral-psychic plane, however, is something that everyone is born with and uses to some degree or another, and that is *intuition*. One does not need to be a professional "psychic" to use intuition, which is that suddenly opened window that lets in more than what we previously knew—more than what we could have known by intellect alone. It is our most readily accessible channel into the Next Level. Intuition allows us to zoom into understanding the essence of something instantly. It allows us to cut to the quick that which was a jumble of thought. Intuition often breaks through from ideas prepared by rational thought—and there are many examples of this in the annals of science—as it can instantly find the solution in what otherwise was a brain-wracking process. It is the creative ability to see new, fertile connections among ideas; it is the mental ability to suddenly make sense out of a mass of mere information. Intuition can recognize a new pattern out of apparent chaos instantly.

In our contemporary world, with information overload an everyday occurrence, with complex issues coming at us constantly, with endless distractions always tempting to lead us astray, the ability to kick in intuition is becoming increasingly important. The greater development of intuition in the New Age (acquiring access to the Aquarian higher mind) will undoubtedly become an increasing necessity.

For those of us who have circulated within the loose-knit New Age community, it is quite apparent that a new Aquarian style of thought is emerging. It is a style totally comfortable in the free-thinking Air where intuitive leaps beyond everyday logic, where intuitive associations—mental connections made in the Invisible—happen lightning fast. It is a style not generally found in other contexts—whether that be conversational chitchat, practical/business, or scientific/technical, and it isn't usually found in the conventional religious context where language, though referring to extraordinary realities, is held on a tight leash. It is an Aquarian development of the metaphysical style of thought, such as we find in the occult arts, in theosophy, and in all the old esoteric schools. With the introduction of UFO/ET reality, channeling, lifted scientific jargon about energies, vibrations, and frequencies, and the like, this New Age style of language admittedly gets extravagant, as they say *woo-woo*. Most have probably heard how so many New Agers talk: It sounds like so much airy-fairy gibberish, seemingly so ungrounded, so "out there," that it has given New Agers the reputation of believing and spouting just about anything. When they appropriate science in their speculations, they are accused of twisting it into pseudo-science. Yet, consider it from another perspective, and it is a highly mentally creative, spontaneous, insight flashing process. This is not to say that any of it can be proven "correct" via Logos, or can be scientifically verified, far from it, but it is the *style* of this thought that is auguring the fact that a new level of Reality is emerging into the collective. It has a similarity, I might suggest, to the mental style of the poet. It is a new, collective, emerging form of Mythos-making happening, which we will explore more fully in the following chapter. This mental style, where thought is able to dart about instantly, making what appear at times to be outrageous claims, outside of any rational or critical restraints, is really no more schizoid seeming than switching channels on a television or Web surfing on the Internet. (I have always considered television a type of schizoid medium.) I believe here again is an indicator that our new technology is running parallel to a new form of thinking process. Many have already noted that everyday life itself, increasingly immersed in a continuous media soup of photoshopped illusions, fake news, fabrications, false flag events, political spin, hyperreal market conditioning, avatar / alternate cyberlife identities, is becoming more surreal.

Aquarius is that stage in our psychospiritual evolution where the higher psychic mind is opening to us; I have also called it, from direct, firsthand experience, the Advent of the Higher Self. This Next Level of the higher mind is a collective Mind Field which, once we access it, potentially links us with all other minds. Here is the spiritual side of Aquarian communication—communication in a collective Mind Field that is effective over long-distance, is invisible, and is instantaneous. As a matter of course, distance becomes irrelevant, since we access a level of mind outside of the bounds of our 3rd-dimensional, space-time continuum. Edgar Cayce, for example, could enter into a dream state and diagnose illness in a person 500 miles away. In this collective Mind Field, we are able to communicate and receive information outside space and outside time as we know it.

The often asked question, *How is telepathy even possible?* finds the beginning of an answer here. From the Postmodern point of view, such a reputed phenomenon as telepathy cannot make sense, as the Postmodern mind has no notion of a collective Mind Field. Telepathy, among ETs apparently a universal ability, accesses the psychic Mind Field that links all minds, beyond the ego-self, beyond Human Reality, meaning outside of the physical limitations of space and language. The ETs who are revealing to us our future are, as we saw, not only masters of telepathy, but are apparently masters of all abilities associated with the astral-psychic plane. In the New Age, we will undoubtedly come to a spiritually concrete (that is, not merely abstract) understanding of the metaphysical dynamics to all psychic gifts.

Astrology also accesses this level. We have seen from the beginning how important astrology is for a proper understanding of the New Age. (Again, one does not need to believe in astrology to gain entry to the New Age, for the entire planet will be entering the New Age; but astrology does provide the key as to what is taking place.) Astrology is related, of course, to the word 'astral,' both referring to the stars. When "stars" are implied in the astrological context, however, we are primarily referring to this level of the astral where the metaphysical principle that all things are interconnected becomes intuitively experienced, where energies on that astral level manifest into and are effective in our 3rd-dimensional world. The astrologer uses a profoundly complex system of symbology to access this plane where all that is manifest is interconnected, where essential Time sets into play all the arrangements, the cycles, of 3rd-dimensional time. And this applies exactly to *soul*. There is not a human soul that is not astrally configured. The astrologer, depending on gift and skill, is able to read not only the basic outlines, but even uncanny details, of the individual soul and the soul purpose in this life. Rather than soul remaining abstract, astrology helps in making soul concrete, in spelling out the specific makeup of an individual's soul, which is one reason why astrology was suppressed in the Piscean Age. But note: It is intuition that is the astrologer's personal tool for using that symbology to get through to the astral plane. We can say that an astrologer is one who has developed intuition through learning a complex symbology that is able to penetrate into the workings of essential Time.

Beyond the limitations of the ego-self mind, beyond the Veil, lie many other levels of consciousness—superconsciousness. The level that is next out from the ego-self at our current stage of evolution is the Mind Field of the astral-psychic. What are some of the characteristics of this Mind Field? First, as we have already stated, it is transpersonal—we are no longer boxed in by our personal psychological makeup, no longer marooned on our own little ego island. The astral-psychic is a vast realm, though in spatial terms it wouldn't even make sense to suggest how "big" it is. How big is Mind—*Spirit*? (If we think the physical universe is vast, as the astronomers have discovered, we may yet have to wake up to the even greater vastness of Spirit.) The astral-psychic is other-dimensional—hyperdimensional—multidimensional—; there are apparently worlds upon worlds beyond the Veil populated by untold beings, as those who have explored out-of-body travel have told us. Our dream life has also convinced many of us of the reality of the astral worlds. Though the astral worlds have their own nature, their own Being "structure," they are enormously fluid as compared to our sluggish, recalcitrant, physical world, with its physical "laws" of Nature. Forms there can manifest instantly, and can easily shape shift. For example, a desire or any kind of emotional projection can readily manifest its object without the constant, frustrating struggle that we are so often used to in our three-dimensional, 3rd-density, world. Since it is the realm where all minds are interconnected, it is possible to communicate non-verbally with others on that level, or even to enter into another's private, subjective world. Since it is the active plane of the "stars," in the astrological sense, this is the realm where our soul makeup for this current life is seeded as potential, what is called an entelechy, where the Form of who we are in this particular incarnation (and this includes our body, for soul and body are intimately connected, as we saw) is held and manifests itself through the Veil, to emerge into space-time as this individual we are. This realm should not necessarily be considered atemporal in any absolute sense;

on its level, it undoubtedly processes events through its own vectors of time, which, however, to us, on our level, might appear as Time itself, for it encompasses our timeframe completely. Our Higher Self, coming-to-us from beyond the Veil, from beyond the astral-psychic plane itself, thereby always and already has comprehended our totality in conventional time—what we know as past, present, and future.

I am aware that there are those in the spiritual community who consider that the astral plane is not "spiritual" enough, and that we should not indulge in its worlds, but aim ever so much higher. This is to take the astral plane, however, again as something abstract that we can somehow bypass in our psychospiritual evolution. It is as if one were to say, *Let's not take the ego-self seriously now, let's not get carried away and think we have to develop it fully…somehow, let's just get over it.* That would be a hypocrisy. I know of no one who is not fully living out their ego-self, which had come to define our whole sense of identity in the Modern era, and now in our Postmodern world. The last 2,000 years and more was destined to bring the ego-self into its full concreteness. The same will now have to apply to the astral-psychic plane—it too will have to be brought to full concreteness if our psychospiritual evolution is to continue. Those who pride themselves on wanting to be Oh so spiritual are often like children who want to grow up too fast, who might even stomp their feet and say, *I want to be an adult!* But, alas, it takes years.

Throughout this work it has been apparent that I am not concerned with fantasizing about collective transcendence into some abstract enlightenment, but have been intent on level-headedly explicating what is concretely, day-by-day, unfolding for us. Which is to say, this Story I tell is based on existential Mythos, not metaphysical abstraction. Those who shun the astral plane and think that humanity should want enlightenment on a higher level are missing one of the main themes of our discussion, and that is, that the evolutionary process passes through stages of development that, at least up to now, do not unfold overnight. It will not be our decision to indulge in the astral-psychic worlds or not, as if we could make an entire realm of consciousness, an entire Being realm, that is breaking into our world, simply go away.

(It is that same ego arrogance that assumes it can dictate to Being.) The Next Level for collective humanity *is* the astral-psychic, and we are only beginning to take our first baby steps into this realm. To thoroughly engage this level and assimilate it into human culture may be a very long process indeed...the next two thousand years.

The Vision revealing the New Age is not the previous Piscean Age lifelong yearning and preparing for an Afterlife; it is not to want to escape from this life into some nebulous, liberated from gross matter, spiritual realm to be with "God." No, it is that this Next Level will be injecting itself more and more into *this* life; it, too, is making *this* life more surreal. The New Age Vision implies living in this life with an altered—transformed—state of consciousness as a result of this embodiment. It will be an ascending to that level (ascension) while still in this life. The difference from the old mystical yearning may appear at first to be only a difference in wording, but it is definitely more than that. The yearning for the nirvana of transcendence, and spending countless hours in meditation trying to attain it, is so often not clear about what the goal actually is; it is too easily a form of escapism, too easily a chasing after an abstraction. The truly disciplined mystical life and the willingness to live as a monk is only for a few, to begin with. The New Age shows no signs of being a mass movement toward the traditional, narrow meaning of the mystic's life. The descent of the Next Level, which is simultaneously our ascent to it, is quite specific, concrete, and is transformative of *this* life, again, not as a reclusive monk withdrawn from active participation in society, but as an individual living as a full participant in a society that is itself rapidly changing.

The New Age community's fondness for channeling and for channeled teachings, is, I would suggest, an example of preparation for the impact of the Next Level. To list but only a few of the better known of channeled entities and teachings in recent years: Seth, Ramtha, Ra, Michael, Lazaris, Hilarion, Bartholomew, St. Germaine, Ashtar, The White Brotherhood or Ascended Masters, Kryon, Ptaah, Sananda, The Christ, Abraham, Bashar, the Pleiadeans, the Zetas, the Arcturians, the "*I AM*" *Discourses* (this goes further back, to the 1930s), *The Urantia*

*Book, A Course in Miracles, The Law of One, Allies of Humanity, Conversations with God.* What, we might ask, is going on here? Why so many different channeled teachings? (There are hundreds by now.) We could easily reply, Because there are innumerable Intelligences in the Invisible worlds. But who, we might ask, provides the best teachings on the Big Picture? Who is the most illuminating? Who among them can we trust?

The higher planes of consciousness are not simply higher, abstract "energies," but are also populated by Intelligences of various kinds. Traditional metaphysicians and occultists have always known this. Today, it is common in New Age circles to hear about spirit beings, light beings, group minds, Other-dimensionals, 4th-, 5th-, 6th-, and so forth, density beings, or of a Spiritual Hierarchy or the Ascended Masters. These various Intelligences contact us in a multitude of ways—in all the various ways that we access the Other Side: out-of-body experiences, near-death experiences, dreams, visions, magical practices, meditation, light being visitations, UFO/ET encounters, and channeling. We are neophytes when it comes to these other planes of consciousness, but many of these Intelligences are preparing us and starting to condition us for greater involvement in these other planes, especially at the astral-psychic level.

The Postmodern, nihilistic view, in the context of science and scientific proof, would deny that there is any evidence for any other such beings, any Intelligences, as we are claiming here. From the Postmodern point of view, this is all anachronistic language, outdated archaic belief; we should know by now that all language regarding an *Other* is only referring to split off, dissociated, aspects of the human psyche, or, as the reductionist puts it, parts of the brain that appear to have an autonomy we do not yet understand. Whether such a view does justice to the full range of what we call paranormal phenomena is, of course, what we are questioning here. The assumption behind this Modern/Postmodern view is once again this insistence that we are alone, that human intelligence is the only conscious intelligence we have ever encountered. We should be highly suspicious, though, of the human ego's nihilistic fixation on claiming to be the only intelligence around. The Postmodern view is not so much a well thought out position that has considered all evidence regarding the paranormal as it is the ego's incestuous need to reduce everything down to itself, or, worse, to merely language games.

Now the astral-psychic realm is far more bizarre, confusing, and multifaceted than we have imagined. To return to what we were discussing regarding channeling, we can see then that various Intelligences are sharing with us a wide range of new and often mind-bending teachings, of what we might call new Aquarian conceptualizations. The channeling literature has a wide range, from old paradigm shattering to new paradigm making; from detailed and comprehensive, to the very general and often evasive and so often repetitious, or perhaps even misleading; from serious to playful to devious. Because of the differences of possible intent here, we cannot and should not take it all at face value, but what we are learning via this material is our becoming practiced with thinking in a new style. (Again, note the emphasis on a new mental style.) The various Intelligences can be guides and teachers, but among them can also be tricksters and puppet masters. They can be testing us as well as playing with us. It is not that we must "believe" in any one teaching, but that we learn how to move in and among the various teachings, schemes, and systems that are being channeled to us. We must learn for ourselves what is called *discernment*. We can be responsive to the insights that do open new windows for us, at the same time remain aware of possible throwbacks to old occult obfuscation. The important point is that we are slowly being conditioned to mentally experience this Next Level. Now this ability to freely move about and not get overly attached to any one channel or system is exactly what I mean by Psyche as my experience of Higher Self. Psyche is protean, a Divine Shapeshifter, implying a Greater Reality, as we saw, that is relativistic; we no longer assume any Unchanging Absolute Truth, whatever this might mean anymore. Psyche prepares me then how to "be" on this other level.

(If one were to suggest that this Psychian ability sounds suspiciously like the Postmodern ego which I had been so intent on exposing, such a suggestion would not, in fact, be completely off the mark. It makes perfect sense that the ego in its Postmodern context is the transition to a new way of being that Psyche is the inspiration of. This new way of being is of course Psyche bringing the ego to another level. Once more, it is my insistence on engaging what is actually concrete, unfolding before our eyes, to remain in this *process*. I am calling it now *process metaphysics*.)

Let us take as an example *The Urantia Book*, at first glance an enormous, impressive, highly detailed work whose origins are still shrouded in mystery (whether it was channeled in the usual sense of that word, passed on by mysterious visitors, or forged in some respect, is debated); it claims, on a rather grandiose scale, to be a Revelation of the hierarchical metaphysical structures and Intelligences of the entire Universe. Though one could study the details of *The Urantia Book* for years, its expository form turns out to be rather elementary, as so much channeled material is, its concepts lacking a true sense of philosophical breakthrough, while at the same time, it is clearly one-sidedly Christian with its emphasis on the life of Jesus. The linguistic form of such a work nowhere matches the realities it supposedly is attempting to convey. And like so much channeled material, it does not make connections with other channeled material, other teachings; it is as if it comes out of a vacuum. So the question is not only, Are we being asked to believe every word of it? or, How accurate is it? but also, How are we supposedly to understand such a book? But let us look at the question another way: Not taking *The Urantia Book* literally, as if it could be the true picture of the universe, competing for that title with other pictures, let us see it instead as an example of a mythic form of conceptualization that is trying to appeal to our mind, to our ego-intellectual self. We read so much channeled material and it is as if the underlying message that is trying to come through is, *See the Story we can spin for you humans. Even though its form is still conceptually elementary, it'll keep some of you busy for a while trying to absorb it. But there are plenty more possibilities for conceptualizing this vast, new reality opening up to you where that came from. Understand that on these other planes, form is different than you have known it; it is far more flexible, protean, creative, appearing and dissolving, than you realize. Get used to it.*

It is as if other Intelligences are conducting various mental experiments upon us, to see how far we can get with them and what we're ready to learn of planes of consciousness beyond the Veil. I do expect to see in the coming years channeled literature that is much more advanced in its language, as minds become more adept at conceptualizations that do greater justice to these other planes. But different beings may very well have different agendas with us also. Are we being tested? What, then, is our ultimate Guide? Our own Higher Self.

We see that this Next Level of consciousness is transpersonal—beyond the bounds of the personal ego-self. But before we can fully appreciate why the Higher Self is coming-to-us in a Form such as Psyche, let us examine a few implications of the fact that more and more people will be accessing the astral-psychic plane, and more, in addition, will be tomorrow's super-psychics. Let us consider the psychic reader's art. To be able to extensively read another person, tune in to his or her soul, raises new ethical issues. What might an individual be capable of, using this ability? What kinds of manipulation of others might be possible? What sort of "black magic" might be performed? Can such an ability be considered invasive of another's privacy? For certainly such an ability can be practiced secretively. And what kind of secret black project programs conducted by the military and the various national intelligence agencies are attempting to exploit this ability? We know that they have had strong interest in psychic phenomena, and have worked with many psychics, Ingo Swann being one of the better known from years back. The technique called remote viewing, a term which Swann coined, was actually first developed as a military project. Many of the psychics and their technical trainers, such as (retired) Major Ed Dames, who were active in this project, have been openly sharing knowledge about remote viewing in recent years. Word has it, though, that the military has abandoned all such remote viewing/psychic projects as not worth the effort, besides them being politically unpopular when word got out that the military has invested such time and effort in them. *As if we should believe that across the board.* What kind of character, though, must the super-psychics of the future develop?

The general feeling up to this point among many metaphysical teachers has been that such abilities cannot be abused because of the nature of karma on the astral-psychic plane. And there are those who believe that higher spirit beings would not allow it. But is that really so? Another opinion states that there is no preventing anyone from using superior psychic powers for any purpose. For it is also generally acknowledged that the development of psychic powers, or even being naturally gifted with them, has no direct bearing on the ethical use of them. After all, varieties of beings inhabiting the astral worlds are pursuing all manner of different agendas already. Metaphysical teachers do contend that so-called demonic beings are quite prevalent. This should not frighten us, however, or make us paranoid. It is as if one were to tell a seven-year-old child that in the adult world you will find predators of various kinds, you will find criminals and murderers and evil-intended persons, and so the seven-year-old says, *I don't want to grow up then.* The point is, what we need to do is to *psychospiritually* grow up and become familiar with the varieties of other beings of the other worlds. Among them, as it should not surprise us, are found the "dark" influences on our soul.

What if great numbers of people were to suddenly develop telepathic powers? Would this not necessitate a new ethics appropriate to this new consciousness? A *New Age* ethics? For certainly this would have to be considered a New Age context. We have had nothing like it, at least within recorded history. In such a context where we could no longer hide from one another our dark and "evil" thoughts, our competitive ploys, our duplicitous motives, our embarrassing, personal "stuff," our fears and hang-ups, our complexes, our desires, there would be the need to develop a new kind of tolerance, a new ethics of mutual acceptance and respect and appropriate trust, as ET encounter researcher Dr. Richard Boylan has so keenly noted. Or else? Or else we just could not stand such openness of revealment, such vulnerability. The ego-self could crack. It deeply disturbs abductee researcher David Jacobs, though, that the ETs have such telepathic powers, especially given his future Earth scenario in which they, through their hybrids, have taken control of society. In an interview he says, "You got to remember these are telepathic beings. They tap right into your thoughts. I don't want anybody tapping into my thoughts."[3] On an advanced spiritual level, that attitude may be childishly naïve, an expression of a stage of our human-biased, insular, ego self-protective, evolutionary development.

We can definitely see here how the previous Piscean ideals of peace and love would have to be brought to a whole new level. At the very least, to begin with, a greater honesty about our psychological makeup, our complexes, would have to be practiced. "Peace" and "love" are too often thrown around as abstract platitudes. How are they to be more effectively experienced in a Psyche-enlightened context?

Let us take all of this further. The following will be a bit of "wild" speculation, but hopefully it will help bring home an essential insight. Consider that the ETs known as the Greys who are completely at home in this collective Mind Field, who are in immediate telepathic communication with one another, have displayed what has been called a hive mentality. (Whether this is a fully accurate statement about their collective nature is open to question. But let us assume it here in a general sense for the sake of our discussion.) Individual Greys are said to be extensions of the one group Mind, the so-called hive, that can undoubtedly monitor their every action. In one channeled text, it is revealed that when a Grey meets with an accident, say, a downed craft, the group mind simply severs the connection to that individual and abandons it.[4] Apparently, individuals of their kind are expendable. (But no different, really, than how human beings often see one another, especially in wartime.) When all individual minds are connected up in this way, there is then the definite danger of losing individuality. The individual ego-self may no longer not only hide its thoughts, but may no longer be able to think autonomously, for it is the group mind that could possibly determine the whole Mind Field direction of thought for all individuals of the group. Science fiction?

Apparently not. It is a very real implication of the collective Mind Field we will be entering in the sometime future, especially when we consider that Technos will be involved. Indeed, the Greys are believed to be a type of worker extraterrestrial biological entity (EBE). They are entities—ET androids—engineered by still Others for specific purposes. And let us not be naïve: When our own bioengineers have reached the point of being able to produce such a marvel in their laboratories, it will undoubtedly be applied, if not openly, then covertly. The secret military, we can assume, would love to produce such an entity. I remember when, in junior high school, during the early years of our space program, and some years after the genetic code was discovered in DNA, our science teacher would nonchalantly discuss with us the possibility that someday we would genetically develop a special kind of human being for space travel. He would ask our class what we thought such a human being would be like, what kind of genetically engineered characteristics would be considered ideal. Once again, the alien Other is already presenting to us our future.

Let us hold this intention, however, that our destiny, as the Earthling species we are, *is* to preserve our personhood even as we collectively engage the Next Level. Ego-self personhood is not so much to be abandoned (which would be a discontinuity with all previous psychospiritual evolution) but transformed as a New Self. Aquarius is indeed the sign of both individuality and collectivity—specifically, *individuality working within community*. Or, we might alternatively state it, individuality working within *universal humanity*. By "universal humanity," we mean here that we are consciously promoting in any given situation, in any community, our connection with all humanity—which is the open, active acceptance of pluralism, of multiculturalism, and that we are all Earthlings, first.

One example of how this manifests currently in the New Age community that dovetails with our discussion is *networking*. Networking as a conscious activity has often been associated with the New Age movement, probably ever since Marilyn Ferguson's book *The Aquarian Conspiracy* came out in 1980. Networking loosely ties together individuals having like purposes or intentions in a society such as ours that so often lacks an immediate, local sense of community. Consciously making connections with like-minded individuals, either at social events specially promoted for encouraging it or circulating on our own, brings us in touch with new influences, ideas, information, opportunities, cooperative ventures. Networking is the developing and cultivating of a network of communication, people linking people with other people. It itself is but another tiny hint of the future global mind where Net working will be universal. For we cannot help but note how networking is root related to the Net, the abbreviated version of the Internet. But not only is the global Net or Web (the World Wide Web) beginning to mirror for us in a technological way our networking activities, but it also mirrors the Web of the interconnectedness of the astral-psychic plane. It is easy to imagine that the future global mind will be as much a cyber-network as the collective Mind Field in action, as Teilhard de Chardin had hypothesized in his notion of a planetary noosphere. And if this future noosphere could interface with the vast etheric consciousness of Gaia? But if we, individually, are not to be utterly absorbed into the network? Again, the question is, What will anchor us in our individuality? And that question we have answered: Our own Higher, our own Divine, Self.

At the same time that a new level of consciousness opens to us, a teacher comes forward. That teacher is potentially coming to each one of us through our own, individual minds. That teacher, that Guide, that personal guru, I have called Psyche. Psyche, now taking on the traditional role of Jesus or of any Self-Realized Master, "is the archetypal summit of one's own consciousness" (Lex Hixon).[5] Psyche as a Divine Form is the Archetype of our own being; it is the Form that we are destined to embody and eventually become (our multidimensional Higher Self). Psyche is the Advent of the Water Bearer, teaching us how to use different spiritual forms (the Saturn rulership of Aquarius, the urn of the Water Bearer) for liberating and transforming soul, but Psyche is also, in turn, the Urn itself of the Water Bearer we are, the Urn by which we pour out the Waters of both soul and Spirit in psychospiritual alchemical union. (Which is why these Waters are of Fire and Water.) Psyche comes to us from the high-subtle level of consciousness, the level the "other side" of the astral-psychic (which is considered the low-subtle level). This is why Psyche can be considered master of the astral-psychic plane. This is why Psyche is our anchor in the changing, dissolving, and merging Neptunian seas that characterize the astral-psychic. Spirit always comprehends and synthesizes in totality each level downward on the ladder of the Great Chain of Being.

Psyche, as the Living Image of our Higher Self, is able to appear in all forms of soul. Psyche is the Divine Androgyne able to enlighten us about the synthesis of the masculine and feminine poles of our being. Psyche is the union of opposites (Fire and Water), as alchemy explored. Psyche, then, is what soul is to become, which precisely indicates our definition of soul as our potential-to-become. All that is hidden in soul is therefore to be revealed and brought into appropriate spiritual Form. We can see Psyche, then, as our divine psychotherapist, the universal therapist,[6] and divine ethical teacher (previously in the Image, say, of Jesus or Buddha) who teaches us about soul, who teaches us how to step back from the ego-self and become the Witness of ourselves. And more accurately—how to psychospiritually merge with Psyche, who *is* the Witness. Only if we can step back from our self—taking a meta-stance with regard to our ego-self—can we really be honest about our self. Psyche then teaches us new forms for bringing all our complexes into the Light. And this, we must realize, is the preparation necessary for collectively entering the astral-psychic plane of consciousness. We must become psychologically enlightened about ourselves—psychologically adult, which the great masses of humanity are still not—to be ready for the shock to the ego-self when the astral-psychic plane fully opens to us. The New Age calls, therefore, for an occult psychospiritual therapy. (This is why so many therapists in the Jungian tradition turn to astrology—as only one example of the traditional occult arts—as an aid in their practice.)

Those who are deeply studied in Eastern schools of Hinduism or Buddhism might wonder why there is a need for new forms. Haven't the thousands of years of Eastern Traditions already laid all this out for us? Do we have to reinvent the spiritual wheel? I believe, in a profoundly creative sense, that, yes, we do. In turn, I can only wonder what these teachers of Eastern practice are thinking when they try to somehow convey arcane, long, difficult-to-pronounce Sanskrit words to their young Western audiences, or attempt to graft ancient spiritual techniques onto a Postmodern life-style. As if Postmodern, pop culture-fed individuals en masse are going to learn a new, emerging spirituality in that manner. We must never underestimate our creative potential for bringing to birth new forms out of the living experience of our own existential context.

It is no coincidence that 'psyche,' the ancient Greek word, translates as 'soul' and is also the root for 'psychic.' Our soul has an intimate connection to the astral-psychic, as we saw that astrology is quite aware of. In fact, we have now reached a major insight concerning the complex nature of the soul: Soul has an astral body on the astral plane. The astral body has also been called our emotional body, or desire body; indeed, our emotional life, our desires, are exactly of the nature of soul. The Water of soul *is* the astral-psychic. The changeable soul that Christianity detested is of the same nature as the Neptunian changeable, shifting, forms-in-flux, astral plane that occultism accessed (which Christianity likewise suppressed).

Perhaps we can begin to understand why so much repression and suppression took place in our history. Powerful, even dangerous, energies and beings are active on the astral plane. Occultism, when seriously practiced, works with these powerful forces (as we talked earlier about psychic powers). Millennia of psychospiritual evolution apparently had to intervene before we were collectively ready to begin to attain this Next Level. The ego had to emerge and develop and slowly be conditioned by Piscean ethics (e.g. Love thy neighbor, May there be Peace on Earth). (One hypothesis that we find is that legendary Atlantis was destroyed because of the collective misuse of psychic powers.) The all-important question is now before us, *Is civilization now ready?* But equally as important, the question remains, *Can we continue down the destructive road we are on?* As we know, as some believe, it is actually too late at this point to do anything about the coming mass extinction level event. But however the coming MELE unfolds, the collective lesson of this next Age is definitely upon us.

We can also begin to understand the New Age emphasis on learning how to manifest. In the astral world, desire manifests its object easily, if not immediately. (Energies coalesce into forms and dissolve continuously there.) By accessing the astral-psychic with an intention, we can set into motion what desire is truly capable of. (*Be careful what you ask for, you may get it,* as we have heard.) The intention gathers energy into a thought-form that impacts the astral plane and, like Time itself, potentiates a new play in the arrangement of energies that are to be active in 3rd-dimensional reality. If that intention is within one's destiny to be fulfilled (for other Threads of the Web and other beings are involved in this too, as is the grand master called Time), that new play in the arrangement of energies takes form and can break through the Veil and *manifest*. In conjunction with spiritual inspiration, where Spirit itself indicates the object of our intention and gives us permission to act upon it, this is a powerful gift. Especially when we consider non-trivial matters, this is true co-creation with Spirit. *The Word becomes manifest.*

We realize then that all that is within soul can be spiritualized. All the dark stuff, the dirty stuff, the ugly stuff, can be brought into the Light and actually be transformed into something of beauty. A soul can be beautiful; it can shine in the Light of Beauty. (This was one of the lessons of the latter, Libran half of the Age of Aries.) The ancient myth is again our clue: Psyche was acknowledged by all as being beautiful, so much so, she rivaled Venus. Psyche—*Spirit of soul*—will reveal to soul how to attain such beauty. The dark corridors of the Labyrinth of soul can become in the Light of Spirit a wonderful, many-branching, Tree of Song. Our dark roots will paradoxically be transformed into branches of Light. All that is within soul can therefore be expressed and shared without dysfunctional projection, without blind conflict, without violence, without war. That vast military arsenals can today destroy us all only indicates how tragically dark the collective is, and how far collectively we still are from this Psyche realization.

But that is not all regarding the role of Psyche. As we have seen, soul is intimately tied into the body, and our body is part of the interconnected Web—the morphogenetic fields—of Nature, of which our senses only register a tiny portion. If we think about it, the closest alien body to us is our own. Our *own* body is a realm of darkness. Do we really know what goes on in the darkness of our organs, tissues, cells? Biological and medical science has certainly mapped out the body and all of its various functions down to the cellular and intracellular level in enormous detail in a textbook, strictly intellectual, generic way, but when it has to address each of us specifically, individually, things are not always so clear. The medical practitioner can gather some idea of the condition of our body, yet it is still but an idea—when it comes to obscure, hard-to-diagnose illnesses especially, it is oftentimes intellectual guesswork that almost always requires the invasiveness of Technos. Would it not be a more enlightened state to know for ourselves what is going on in our body? It has been said before, there is a wisdom of the body which the ego-self is not privy to. That wisdom consists first of all in the body knowing how to function on its own, without us—again, the ego-self—having to give it any instructions. Our body knows on its own how to function and how to follow the rhythms and processes of Nature. And this body we are does not end at the visible boundary of our skin, or, if we could look inside, with our visible organs and tissues: We have an invisible body too, with its own subtle anatomy. And this surely has old—ancient—roots for the New Age. Occultism has always known of this invisible body, the etheric body, and what is known as the "health aura," and how it is composed of subtle energy fields and chakras that integrate our physical body into the vast, subtle morphogenetic fields of Nature and Earth. Many psychics claim to be able to routinely read this aura. Many energy practices are based on this knowing—from radionics, Reiki, Reconnecting, to ancient Chinese acupuncture.

If we could access the etheric body in a self-knowing way, we could potentially learn then how to heal ourselves, not only by being guided to natural remedies, but on the invisible level of the etheric energy field of the body itself. This is exactly what so many alternative healers are consciously doing today; we find all kinds of energy modalities available to the practitioner, and it seems that new ones are being revealed all the time. Oftentimes the healings involved can rightly be considered "miraculous." We could perhaps even learn someday how to regenerate organs and limbs. We could keep our body at an optimum functioning level, in balance with the archetypal template of the universal human body and with all life surrounding us. We could potentially alter our own nervous system or genetic makeup by accessing our individual template on the etheric plane. As Dr. Bruce Lipton contends, we no longer have to assume that we are the victims of our genes, living under the virtually universal assumption of genetic determinism, but we can potentially alter DNA itself, beginning from a conscious, mental level with techniques that are able to reach down into the subconscious. This would be exactly an engagement with Psyche development. Just as Psyche would teach us of the darkness of our subconscious/unconscious, Psyche would teach us of the darkness of our body as well, a darkness where body and unconscious soul are indeed intertwined. Psyche, Divine Master of the Archetype of Universal Humanity down through all levels of human consciousness, down through even the prepersonal levels (the etheric being the subtle, invisible energy extension of the physical), would guide us into conscious contact with the etheric body. When consciousness is brought into the etheric body, keeping in mind the principle that consciousness changes—transforms—what it illuminates (quantum theory also has something to say about this), then we witness the raising of vibration of the physical body. This is another example of what New Agers are apt to call Ascension. Ascension to 4th density, as it's often been called.

The Higher Self can also be viewed as a multidimensional Self. We are hearing more today about having a multidimensional Self. That is a Self, to begin with, much larger than our everyday self, much larger than our *apparent* self. It has been suggested that there are even other selves of this Larger Self living other lives on other dimensions, or even perhaps on other planets. Other persons of us—could they then be considered only mere aspects of us?—may indeed be ET, or, even by definition, Other-dimensional. Past lives are also synchronously possible within the multidimensional Self when we consider that time beyond the Veil is not our time. Not only that, but future lives have also become an area of research.[7] We will have to see what exactly the Mythos will be unfolding in future years; for now, admittedly, much of this is abstract speculation, or research conducted by only a handful.

With Psyche's emphasis on *this* life, however, we must consider then how the multidimensional Self might be manifesting *in* this life. It may perhaps be unsettling to some, but there are those of us who are discovering that we are multiple personalities, and I am not referring to any conventional psychopathological diagnosis. I have offered the term 'polyphrenia'[8] to signify that we can be many-minded persons in this one lifetime. That we can wear different hats, play any number of social roles, is but a hint of this potential. So is gender bending, or when we take on another name (such as a spiritual name, or power or totem animal name) or a street-styled moniker or epithet (as in mythic traditions). But polyphrenia is even more—it is the freedom to explore all the corridors of soul outside of safe, conventional stereotypes or conditioning. This implies the possibility of multiple inspiration streams coming through us, each with their own manifestation cycles, corresponding to the multiplicity of corridors of the Labyrinth that is soul. And these multiple inspirations that guide us, that bring Light, to this exploration? This is the gift of Spirit coming-to-us, no longer mono-dimensionally, but now in a procreative multiplicity that corresponds to these corridors of soul. As we saw earlier, Spirit coming-to-us in the guise of soul—*Psyche*.

How to creatively act out our various other or sub-personalities? How to let soul speak beyond the limited range of feelings that are socially codified? (Great literature was one traditional way that the complexities of us were explored, but then, as is so often the case, safely kept within the covers of a book.) Or how do we allow another person from our multidimensional Self walk in to our body? The phenomenon of Walk-ins[9] can be interpreted from the perspective of the multidimensionality of our Larger/Higher Self. There are many possibilities that will open to us in our creative encounter with the persons and other lives within our Higher Self. The potential here for the arts is tremendous. So often we found that artists of the latter half of the Postmodern 20th Century felt that everything had already been done, that there was really nothing new for the arts to explore. When Psyche begins to reveal more of who we are, there will likely simultaneously occur an explosion of inspiration to bring that revealing into Form. Here is the new Renaissance—*a New Age Renaissance.*

Someday we will realize how locked in we have been to a narrow definition of personality/selfhood...yes, confined in that fortress we call the ego-self. Keeping in mind that soul is polycentric, when Spirit reveals its own glorious multiplicity, it will liberate soul to express *its* multiplicity through us—our polyphrenic New Self. Tradition, especially here in the West, had always presented to us but a narrow slice of Spirit, which is how Spirit ages ago was culturally codified by various Secret Controllers; but with this new Revelation, the Aquarian dispensation, we now realize that Spirit is a vast reality of multiplicities. Again, our Guide, the Divine Shapeshifter, will teach us how to creatively develop a polyphrenic, multiple self in *this* life. Once again, it has been said that the Veil of separation between this life and the Invisible is slowly being drawn back.

An example of the multidimensional nature of Reality that is today right in our face (assuming an acquaintance with contemporary science), that is good practice for us in trying to see clearly in a multidimensional way, is this: First consider our everyday world, the world we are engaged in day-to-day, what Heidegger has called Being-in-the-world. This is not the same reality that science tells us is actually "there." What science has come to tell us (with the help of modern—that is, Kantian— philosophy), put simply, is that our brains create an elaborate illusion of a world "out there," a sort of global hologram; the so-called external world, we are told, is actually a mental projection produced by the workings of our brain's neural networks. The question we now put is: What is it then, is one of these realities, in fact, more "real" than the other? Neither is—it is a false dichotomy being foisted upon us. Being-in-the-world is indeed the Illusion we live in, but it is nonetheless Real, and is no less Real, actually having rather an existential priority, than any theoretical construct offered by science. This everyday, taken for granted world we live in is as Real as any hypothesized neural hologram produced by the brain, and again is as Real as the atomic level, and as Real as the quantum level. Remember when the physicists were trying to sell us the idea that Reality was really to be found on the atomic level? *Whatever that might mean.* And now there is the speculation by some physicists that we might be living in a simulated reality, a global virtual reality, in a vast, unimaginably complex computer program created by some… Other Intelligence? This certainly sounds like Theism in a scientific dress. This really mushes up the dichotomy between existential Being-in-the-world and the holographic, material projection of the brain. But, then, this is no different than what, say, ancient Hindu tradition had called "Maya." What we need to learn to see is that Reality is a Whole happening on multidimensional levels, and that means, as well as on the super-conscious levels. All that is visible and all that is invisible participate in Being. What our difficulty comes down to is that we are not practiced at shifting our thinking between these multi-levels, in other words, thinking multidimensionally. (A new appreciation of *Being*, as Heidegger initiated, must be our beginning point for a New Age philosophy. In this regard, Postmodernist thought, with its denial of any meaningful relationship to Being, results in a dead end.)

The danger today for humanity is the nihilistic deification of Technos without spirituality. Who can confront Technos? How do we step out of the mindset of Technos? It is apparent that the ego-self—and that refers to us all—has become helpless with regards to Technos. The only way to confront Technos is by doing so from another level. But Technos, the Superpower of contemporary human civilization, would appear to have no equal, not even the traditional "God." But the danger also brings forth a call for the saving power. *The saving power is coming.* Psyche, Spirit coming-to-us anew from beyond the constructed human world, beyond existential Human Reality, is the equal and more of Technos, opening to us the possibility of confronting Technos. Unlike Technos, that would attempt to cage up and digitalize

Psyche, Psyche is not intent on trying to negate Technos, which would be but Piscean dualism perpetrated now by Psyche; nor is Psyche intent on turning back the clock to a simpler, less technological world. Psyche's evolutionary intention is precisely to *integrate* technology and spirituality. The Aquarian dispensation is that integration, that synthesis, that will undoubtedly come to take place in the Invisible, but manifesting as the New Earth. The emerging invisible world of cybertechnology and the invisible world of spirituality will undoubtedly meet in the Invisible. *Earth itself will ascend.* That is to say, the invisible Web that is Gaia will itself be manifested in consciousness, and thereby in human culture, as the Next Level descends to us.

Let us consider for a moment this brave new cyberworld we are entering. We have reached the point with computers where anything can be visually faked. Computer generated graphics can doctor up any image. Photographs can be altered; advanced CGI can now present any as-real-as-life looking reality. This is the reason why ufology has such a difficulty with photographs today—excellent looking photos of flying saucers, on their own, are hard to prove anything. The boundary between the "real" image and the altered image has been blurred. But this is only the beginning. This is but a hint of what is coming. The blurring between reality and virtual reality will be next. The ETs have already shown us that they are masters of virtual reality. In the encounter experience, it is well known that certain of the ETs can magically create environments for the experiencer to perform in. (*Star Trek*'s holodeck readily comes to mind.) Technos will undoubtedly bring about the ability of projecting lifelike holographic imagery into the environment that will present to us a world where "illusion" and "reality" merge. We can be sure this day is coming. Virtual reality teleconferencing, for one, is already here. Those who control the technology will of course believe they can keep the remainder of society conditioned in a virtual Fabrication in ways that are not yet even imagined. An artificially generated world of illusion for the sake of societal control could become a permanent feature of the future landscape, but for our own individual ability to access the invisible world as a counter to it.

However, that is only the outer world. As the Invisible is increasingly accessed, there will grow a blurring between the inner and outer, *from within the inner world*. We have always assumed, for example, that we could know the outer world factually—pragmatically, technically, scientifically—, and that facts remain facts—they stay put. On the other hand, the inner, subjective world is privately experienced, constantly changing, and with difficulty pinned down to any concepts resembling the objective. The inner world, however, does have its own processes and structure. And by 'inner world,' let us now refer primarily to the astral-psychic. When *this* inner world begins to influence the outer world in a more *explicit* way, which it someday will, the outer will not behave as we have always known it to. What we consider "fact" may no longer be certain, or taken for granted. (The implications of quantum theory have begun to suggest a similar notion, from a whole other realm of the sub-atomic level.) The reality of "miracles," for example, will no longer be disputed. When the Veil becomes translucent, inner and outer reality will blur. What was once the so-called outside, objective world will cross the boundary of the Veil and be pulled into an active interfacing with the Invisible, there to be revealed as possibly a whole new level of collective reality. To know what is real, then, will increasingly mean to be practiced at navigating about in this new, collective realm.[10] It may be difficult for us to grasp today what exactly this condition would be like on a day-to-day basis. Would it be dreamlike? surreal? Would it involve a loss of identity? of boundaries? We can make reference here to the notion of the liminal, which is often invoked in works of anthropology, mythology, and depth psychology, which is that condition where one is not quite "here" and not quite "there," but existing somewhere in-between. It is a living in an ambiguity, without clearly defined markers of what one is. It is a living in the margins, or as the root word 'limen' means, it is a *threshold* state. It may very well imply then a passage to another state of Being. A *Walking Between the Worlds*, as the title of one of Gregg Braden's books suggests. Those not so practiced at walking in the existential in-between may very well begin to feel as if they were living in a continuous dream, which would not exactly be comforting...at first. In this condition where one would become confused as to what is real anymore, there would also be the potential for being easily manipulated. It has already been said by those who know the field of remote viewing firsthand that a new form of espionage, power manipulation, even warfare, will be psychic. But today's remote viewing is still child's play compared to what is coming.

It is not as if this is all still off in some far distant future—in many ways, this is the world we are already living in. This blurring of illusion and reality is an increasingly common occurrence in the Postmodern cultural milieu—in advertising, in political "spin control," in official government statements, in cover-ups, in the shocking discoveries of conspiracy research, in counter-intelligence work and disinformation, in media packaging, in entertainment, in the cyberworld of the Internet, especially the virtual worlds one can inhabit there. In so many ways, what we thought was real, and what we thought was illusion, is no longer easily discernable. Collective, social reality as a secretly-controlled, mass media-manipulated Fabrication, as a Spectacle even, has been going on for some time. Given the resources of PR firms, marketing, handlers, Hollywood studios, especially when contracted by government/intelligence agencies, just about anything can now be foisted upon the public. We have only to consider that infamous day of 9/11/2001.

One marker of when the general public began to seriously lose touch with what is really happening "out there" in the "real world" is the UFO cover-up. We could easily say that the late 1940s would have inaugurated a profoundly new collective reality for all of us if the appearance in our skies of the UFO had been openly and honestly addressed. (The reasons why there was an original cover-up we do take to be understandable, but then a die was cast.) The military's official denial, however, together with the rise of the national security state, drove a wedge between public, apparent reality and a hidden, what-is-really-the-truth reality, privy only to those who held above top secret positions. Those who are actively engaged in the cover-up know from within their loop of secrecy what the real story is regarding the reality of UFOs; that is, they know that UFOs are indeed a "truth" of the "real world," whereas those who are duped by the cover-up, who whistle along down the sidewalk of their life in their illusion of what is the everyday real world, are actually quite out of touch with Reality, with what really is going on "out there."

Yet, haven't we always assumed, though, that we could sooner or later get at the truth of things, the truth of events, the truth behind cover-ups? Unfortunately, that assumption may itself be naïve. First, do we think that those who hold the secret truth will *ever* give away all they know, even if a small fraction of it were somehow to come out? The secrets they hold are often conspiratorial secrets involving actions of liability and criminality (such as 9/11). To hold cover-up secrets allows the "secret government," the "secret military," or the "Deep State," to have the superior advantage in any number of situations. The "truth," therefore, *may not* be out there, in any simplistic sense, only waiting for us to find it and pin it down. What we may come to realize about the truth of events is that it may very well be composed of a house of distorting mirrors. And it may turn out to be "truth" only as we are able to formulate it from within our own perspective, a perspective that is itself more or less prepared to knowing that "truth," meaning, for one, on how well informed our perspective is. Even more specifically, some truths, even cover-up truths, might only be accessible through psychic sight; that is, research done by the intellect-ego alone may never be able to get at the truth, the complete, complex truth of an event. Simply put: "Truth" is going to imply something far more complex than we have known, more than just a list of facts. But the Aquarian drive is still to bring out that "truth," however complex. As we saw, the New Age Aquarian motto is, *No more secrets*. And, *We pour forth into the open Air…for all*.

The masterminds behind the emerging cyber-virtual-technologies are pushing fast in the development of artificial intelligence, including androids. As the cyberworld merges with the human mind, we will be in danger of the AI world determining our own mental world more and more, cornering us into accepting its superiority. The AI algorithms being developed, marketed as our own personal assistant, as in the movie *She*, will apparently know everything about us; our decision making may come to be left totally up to them. AI might very well develop a mind of its own; it may reach a point where it assumes it is "conscious"; it may very well decide to contend with human agendas.[11] But what these "superintelligent" AI computers and androids will not have is what we know as human soul, and, in turn, our connection to Psyche, our connection to Higher Self.

We can see it coming: The future global mind will be composed of a super-Internet, already being promoted as the Internet-of-Things, with the potential of literally linking up everyone on Earth into its grid. Computers themselves are now linked to all the archives of human knowledge, allowing any given computer to potentially know what all other computers know. Every computer would be able to instantly access the input into any computer anywhere on the planet. This is all exactly what I refer to as Technos. This is the outer manifestation of the collective Mind Field. But just as this outer manifestation creates an invisible cyberspace with its own world of connections, it will be the inner Mind Field that will connect individuals anywhere in the outer world. The invisible becomes visible while the visible becomes invisible: One interactive Mind in which we, as individuals—human individuals—, can still be Higher Self-empowered. We may yet see a New Earth—and let us hope we do as the New Age intent—bringing together the union of Technos and Psyche, Gaia and Spirit.

Our psychospiritual evolution is a bi-transformational process. We saw that the Other is indeed showing us our future. The Other, as ETs or Other-dimensionals or Inter-dimensionals, when manifesting as a presence in a physical form, is the (temporary) outer reality mirroring the transformation going on within consciousness. They are the Gods and Goddesses of old who have established and influenced whole civilizations. Who would be our guide among them? Who would be our guide in this astral-psychic world of multidimensions, where a vast, marvellous, new continent is opening up to us? I have already provided an answer.

The revolutionary idea is emerging here (revolutionary to the conventional scientific mindset) that the "interior" realms outside ego-self consciousness, outside our personal subjectivity, are actually collective—that is, they are not personally mine, but they are realms shared by *Others*. Now this is an extremely baffling concept for us with our understanding locked into the logic of 3rd-dimensional, physical reality. The so-called inner planes appear to be inside us. How can what appears to be inside us be populated by beings that are yet independent of us? Or, looking at it the other way around, another being on the inner plane could equally say that about us, once we access the Mind Field—we are inside it, *inside its life world*. But consider this: other people live inside my outer, "external" world; I would not say that other people I encounter every day are "mine"; they are obviously independent of me, and lead their own lives. The same, then, can be said for the inner realms—other beings live inside "my" inner world, but that does not mean that they are "mine," that they belong to me. After all, *this is* the implication of the traditional understanding of Spirit and the spiritual realms, that they are universal, transcendent to my personal self.

Consider an old conundrum that kept philosophers spinning their intellectual wheels for centuries, and that was the question as to whether "God" was imminent or transcendent. The whole conundrum rested on the slippery concept of "self." The ego, subjective, self and the Larger Self have too often been confused. Yes, "God" *is* within, but you have to go within quite a distance to realize "God" is there, but that doesn't mean that I—I, the ego-self—gets to be "God" then, or that I get to control "God." To find "God" within, one must transcend the ego-self and ascend into superconsciousness. "God," we find, is both imminent *and* transcendent, depending upon the perspective of "self" one considers.

There is the complicating realization that the Higher Self—*my* Higher Self—is of the nature of Spirit. So that within this collective realm, this universal realm, of Spirit there projects my individual archetype of Self. My Higher Self is my personal archetype of Self projecting through the collective Mind Field from the Higher Self Divinity of universal humanity. The Higher Self is thus both individual and collective. But here, then, is the answer as to who would be our guide in the astral-psychic where the various Gods and Goddesses of old have already become masters. It is our Higher Self via the Living Image I call Psyche. This, then, is the ultimate role of Psyche—as our Guide in this bizarre and confusing world of ETs, other-dimensionals, the non-human Other. If we reflect upon the ancient myth of Eros and Psyche, we know that Psyche, as the story ends, ascends to live among the Gods and Goddesses, and is herself divinized. There is an important insight here: Psyche, having dwelled among Them, having known Them, can therefore be our Guide in a far more complex, baffling, ego-shattering, and virtually incomprehensible Reality than we had ever imagined.

Let us be honest about it: Humanity has lived comfortably for a long time now in the illusion of a naiveté—that Human Reality is the measure of all things. Even the Traditionalists who believe that there is something—a "God," as they believe—beyond the bubble of Human Reality, still interpret that Beyond, that "God," from a dominating anthropocentric perspective, which is to say, that that Beyond, that "God," is, as it were, given a place in the scheme of things because the almighty human ego determines it should do so. It is the presumptuousness of the human ego that assumes it can determine what purpose the Beyond, Spirit, what purpose "God," serves. When we come to realize firsthand how naïve we have been about this, always assuming that we are at the center of all the important action in the Universe, our bubble of Illusion may pop. A most radical spiritual relativism still awaits us when Other Intelligences are encountered as existing outside of human interpretation, perfectly able to conduct their own reality-world affairs completely independent of what we might say about them. Even my own starting point phenomenological definition of Spirit as *That-which-is-greater-than-us-coming-to-us* is acknowledged as human-oriented; but that was inevitable, as we are talking about Human Reality, with Spirit having to bridge to us from the outside of our human bubble if we are not to become utterly insular, anthropocentric Postmodernists. Even my whole experience of Psyche, and my suggestion of the role of Psyche, as if it sounds as though I am assigning Psyche a role, is human-oriented; but that too is based on Higher Self speaking to *my* psyche. Psyche *is* that relationship, that bridge.

A Mythos we must speak. Hopefully the new bridge of Mythos we build is a preparation for all the paranormal encounters that puts human ego in its appropriate place.

Before I summarize, I should provide a counterpoint view to the impression I might have made about how soon I see all of this unfolding. First, I am not claiming by any means that all these developments will happen overnight in the near-term. But Ken Wilber feels nonetheless that so many New Age advocates are over-optimistic about a shift to the Next Level. Writing in *Up From Eden* back in 1981 (he would probably feel that his statements are as valid today as when he wrote them), he said, "For those who have matured to a responsible, stable ego—a "real person"—the next stage of growth is the beginning of the trans-personal; specifically, that of level 5 [in his scheme of the Great Chain of Being], the level of psychic intuition, the beginning of transcendent openness and clarity, the awakening of a sense of awareness that is somehow more than the simple mind and body. I don't see this happening on a large scale for at least another century, if then." One reason he gives for it not happening any sooner is that "There is a vast majority of humanity that has not yet stably reached the rational-egoic level. ... And one does not and cannot reach the trans-personal without first firmly establishing the personal."

Despite such a view, the question remains, *Do we have that much time?* Will Postmodernity drag on for another 50 years or more, while Earth along with civilization goes into a tailspin? According to the abrupt climate change doomers, we don't even have that much time. Civilization is in a tailspin that they say is happening faster than we realize. So does that suggest that all this speculation about the transition to the astral-psychic is now idle talk? That it will not happen? Cannot happen? These questions only point back to our need for the intervention of the Other—*and* within this increasingly shortening timeframe.

This, then, is the Next Level: As we develop a relationship to the Living Image of our Higher Self, we are co-creators in the reality of a New Self. This New Self, having explored all its darkness of soul—the Labyrinth of soul—, is prepared to allow the Greater Reality beyond the Veil to break through where a whole different multidimensional way-of-being, of shape-shifting, form-in-flux, materializing and dematerializing processes, an interconnectedness with manifold fields of energy and other Inter-dimensional, invisible beings, is in play. It is the Living Image of our Higher Self that is our Guide, our teacher, our advocate, from the Other Side. It is then, hopefully, that we will be welcomed by other Intelligences so that we can ascend as is our birthright as spiritual Earthlings to this Next Level.

## The New Human

This day, in this time of transition, I sing of the New Human—
Spirit preparing this next Age calls out for the New Human
& sends through the veils of separation that keep us apart
a new dispensation that we today are called to receive—
    We are called by it,
               to embody it.

It is the New Human I envision—
               The New Human who is open
    to the super-reality coming-to-us of Higher Self.
Who is willing to let go of our conditioned egocentric decadence
    for a Higher Self-directed individuation.
Who has practiced the alchemical balance of energies
    masculine & feminine.
Who sees intuitively the interconnectedness of all things, all creatures,
of all persons, how all events are held inextricably in the Web of Being.
Who is not content with mouthing thought abstractions that impact nothing,
but brings all the old abstract notions into a psychospiritual existential
    specificity.
Who is dedicated to Higher Self as the supreme, unlimited, super-creative
Art, the Great Work of realizing one's own divine I Am Selfhood.
Who is courageous in saying, I am bringing God-Self into this life
    to manifest the splendor of its multidimensionality in this world.
Who welcomes the new influx of frequencies of energy for DNA
    transformation.
Who is ready to ascend to the Next Level the bizarre worlds
    that the astral reveals.
Who is aware of the veils upon veils of consciousness, to be lifted,
    one by one.
Who knows firsthand the human actual potential for transcending

whatever was limiting, conditioning, was assumed established for all time.
Who loves this Earth, our mother Gaia, & wants to live in respectful
    partnership with Gaia.
Who loves all the family of humanity, the great human experiment
    we all play in local universe evolution.
Who is not enslaved to dying traditions, to empty shells of customs
& rituals, to age-old, established Systems of power that to this day
    still oppress Earth's peoples.
Who is fully aware of Technos, and is willing to confront Superpower
Technos, willing to be Psyche's counterpoint to Technos's Plan
    of total control.
Who is always asking how he or she can contribute to the health,
    welfare, the well-being, the evolution of all.
Who is always sharing, always giving more & more of compassionate
    heart-Self to the needs of this world.
Who is willing to be more than what was always assumed
    was merely human.
The New Human who imagines what had not been imagined
    possible before.
The New Human who is prepared to enter into dialogue
    with all Intelligences.

It is the New Human who embodies the Word,
the new Mythos, which is destined to come into the world—
It is the New Human I sing of, the New Human I envision,
destined to walk this Earth & to fulfill the meaning
    of this Earth.

April 2003

# ( 12 )

# MYTHOS-MAKING: ART OF THE NEW AGE

*We are about to step into a Fountain, a Living Fountain of Unlimited Creativity.*

Now we reach a point in our Story that may turn out, in fact, to be the most controversial of all, even for some within the New Age movement itself. And it is not an understatement to suggest that the cultural validity of our Story hinges fully on this chapter, that my interpretation of Mythos and Mythos-making is the key that allows us to speak meaningfully in a Postmodern context about the New Age Vision. To have a numinous, paranormal experience, or to receive a Vision, is one thing, however extraordinary or special we feel it is, but once we begin to attempt to bring it into Language, into Form, it is then we begin a Mythos-making process.[1]

Note: I now prefer to use the words 'Mythos' and 'Mythos-making' for the work that I do as a visionary poet, rather than 'myth' and 'mythmaking,' for reasons that will become apparent shortly. In the meantime, I will first speak of myth and mythmaking, but as we proceed, I will slowly be shifting into a new understanding of Mythos and Mythos-making.

For those who have not thought through the real nature of their work, the following may come as a surprise as to what they believe they are doing. Mythmaking is rampant in the New Age community today, especially among ET contactees and channels. As a matter of fact, though, any Lightworker responding to the Call of the Age is actively helping to mythmake—and when that becomes a conscious, co-creative process, I now prefer to say Mythos-make—the New Age Mythos. (The Vision that we are given, as it comes into Form, becomes *Mythos*.) To name randomly but a handful of individuals (not all necessarily identifying themselves as New Agers, however) that come to mind who have had influence to a greater or lesser degree in this regard over the years: Dick Sutphin, David Spangler, Jose Arguelles, Benjamin Crème, Terence McKenna, Ken Carey, Jean Houston, Gregg Braden, James Redfield, Barbara Marciniak, Barbara Hand Clow, Drunvalo Melchizedek, Lyssa Royal, Whitley Strieber, David Icke, J.J. Hurtak, Doreen Virtue, David Wilcock. (This list could easily grow to a hundred names.) They have all been engaged in mythmaking, some to a much greater, even extravagant, degree than others. All the old and new contactees are mythmakers—George Adamski, George King (of the Aetherius Society), George Van Tassel, Donald Fry, Guy Ballard (of the Great I Am teachings), Ruth Norman (of the Unarius cult), Billy Meier, Rael (of the Raelian Movement) (again, to name but only a few), and there was of course the late Heaven's Gate leader Marshal Applewhite whose suicide-bent cult made big news in the year of Comet Hale-Bopp (1997). We hear contactees and channels reveal stories about the Venusians, Elohim, Pleaideans, Zetas, Greys, Sirians, Andromedans, Arcturians, Reptilians, the Ashtar Command, Council of 10, Council of 12, the Allies of Humanity, the Ascended Masters, the Spiritual Hierarchy, the Galactic Federation. Numerous New Age writers springboard from the popular, outside-the-academic-mainstream, scholarly work of Zecharia Sitchin[2] on ancient civilizations and peoples.

(Sitchin has become something of a lone scholar hero to many, though he has not been the only one claiming to interpret the ancient Sumerian texts from a radically new perspective. Christian O'Brien,[3] who has strangely been obscured, is another who has provided similar in-depth, scholarly work on the same texts, resulting in a perspective that parallels Sitchin's in many ways. A radically new interpretation of our origins, of what ancient peoples actually experienced, is full underway. Sitchin's work itself is an example of mythmaking in a newly scholarly manner.)

An observation, though, is that rarely do any of the above Lightworkers, writers, scholars, contactees, and channels openly acknowledge that they are indeed mythmaking, or are even aware of it. Some, if confronted by the suggestion that they are, would probably at first deny it. It is time, however, for honesty in these matters. In our contemporary context of hyper-self-consciousness, we cannot ignore the real nature of what we are doing. We can no longer afford to be culturally naïve.

Yes, I feel that we should first discuss myth at some length, as a way to segue into the why of my revival and reinterpretation of the ancient Greek word 'Mythos.' The primary issue with the common word 'myth' has to do with the dominant, popular view that our culture takes of it today. This common, contemporary view of how the word 'myth' is used is what I consider the superficial view. This view has debased the word 'myth' so much that its use for any more profound meaning has become hopelessly muddied. The word 'myth' has an everyday surface connotation that everyone is immediately familiar with and knows how to use in various linguistic contexts. And that is, simply, that myth, as something made up, even as a marketing or spin narrative, is not really what it appears to be—it is not reality, so is not quite true; it is most often considered false or misleading. It can be fanciful, colorful, and perhaps instructive in some way, but it is still a fictional account. Old myths are often likened to fables, or folk or fairy tales; they are make-believe, made up by the merely clever creativity of the human imagination. We know the ancient myths from school as quaint, extravagant stories handed down through the ages that are considered to have but a tenuous relation to historical fact. A myth was a compelling story that today is only looked upon as providing some good entertainment. The myths we see promoted today—as a current, cultural form—are used to sway belief and convey impressions, presenting simplified narratives for purposes of manipulation, but in reality are not the real story; they are distortions of reality. In the media, "myth" is always contrasted to "reality." We read articles that begin, *You know the myth, now here is the real story.* Just another example among dozens of possible examples: I read an Internet article titled, *6 welfare myths we all need to stop believing.*

Myths have become free game—easily shot at—debunked—from a superior, enlightened, intellectual perspective. And that was the drive throughout Modernism, the learned scholar's project of debunking all the old myths that had previously been the underpinnings of civilization. In biblical scholarship, it was the highly intellectual program of demythologizing *The Bible*, peeling away, for example, the superfluous wrappings of dubious narrative around Jesus and simply getting at the essence of the Christian message. Myths were to be stripped of all their exaggeration, their figurative language, in other words, all their fluff, in order to get at the core of the text. Even the work of Carl Jung and those in the Jungian lineage, including the popular Joseph Campbell and other mythologists, who all propounded a significantly profound view of what myth really is about, still tended to interpret it within an intellectual framework that felt superior to the myth itself. But even their attempts to convey a new respect for myth have nevertheless scarcely had any real impact in Postmodern culture.

In agreement with Jung, Campbell, and others, myth, in the sense that I mean it when I refer to our need for new mythmaking—but what I now prefer to call Mythos-making—, is a deep meaning structure within culture, a fundamental symbolic structure usually conveyed through at least a minimum of narrative, that allows us to live meaningfully at all. We cannot easily escape myth, though many Moderns, as Jung noted, made the attempt. For the outcome only turns out to be a self-debilitating nihilism. Myth is the bedrock cultural organizing symbology of experience, the provider of existential significance; it is what orients us in our world, it is what guides us in our living. It was traditionally, therefore, what gave us that sense of belonging, of membership, in a group. Myth was also the meaning behind the ritual, whether religious or secular. A culture traditionally involved a whole interlocking mythology—what today the dictionary superficially calls a *mythos*. Implied within all of this is that myth was our way of talking about the Greater Reality, that is, a Reality beyond our everyday life, larger than our human bubble, that gave this life meaning. To me, then, religions are truly myth systems, the most significant of myth systems—they are Mythos in its original sense. We should understand how the everyday, superficial view of myth does great injustice to its profound role in life. We do not readily call Christianity, Buddhism, or Islam make-believe and superficial. Myth informs the roles we play in daily life, who we think we are, how we think about things; it informs art, social forms and norms, mores, customs, even science and technology—*and psychology.*

The question might be asked, *Is everything then myth?* Can we think outside of it at all? Perhaps the only experiences where we might be completely free of myth is the mystical experience or any overwhelming paranormal experience that temporarily tears us from our culturally constructed interpretations—; but—*but*—the moment we begin to mull over that experience and to share that experience, which means that we begin to speak about it, we have entered the mode of myth—or, as I now prefer, *Mythos.* The day-to-day work of science is not mythic per se (it aims rather at pure Logos), but myth is the foundation for that work (more below). Similarly, the conducting of day-to-day business is not mythic per se (but rather practical logos), but the business world is founded upon cultural mythemes (myth-themes: such as, competition is good for us, money is the marketplace's god, a free market is best). Philosophy, in its rigorous sense, constantly skirts along the edges of myth and must occasionally turn to something like story, as Plato well knew. After the various 20th Century philosophical adventures of phenomenology, logical positivism, linguistic analysis, existentialism, structuralism, post-structuralism, and others, which were so many attempts in one way or another to establish new ways of thinking Logos, a Heidegger emerged in his later years to think in the highly creative direction of a myth-like philosophizing. The Postmodern project of philosophical deconstruction a la Derrida, or negative dialectics a la Adorno, or Foucault's genealogical critiques of conceptual structures in various areas of life, has only led to a hyper-intellectualized nihilism that, as far as I can see, is spiritually a dead end.

The so-called myths of contemporary, everyday life, once we understand the real origin of myth as *Mythos*, are not exactly of the nature of fully functioning, satisfying myth, to say the least. They are but fragments of myth, shards of myth, shells of myth, socially conditioned verisimilitudes of myth, perhaps better to be called mythemes.

Since they do provide precognitive cultural structure—subconscious codification—, and orient and guide us for living in contemporary society, they are still able to serve, though, a mythic function, for they do establish our membership in society. But in the vertical dimension of our being, that providing a relationship to Divinity, which is the profound meaning of *Mythos,* they of course fall flat. We could list many examples of these myths from everyday life and contemporary society: the nuclear family and the roles of Mother and Father; stereotypes defining being a man or a woman; the pursuit of the American Dream: education-degree-career-money-success-marriage-house-family; myths associated with cultural chronology: the Roaring 20s, the Great Depression 30s, the conformist/beatnik 50s, the psychedelic Flower Child and protest 60s, the Me Generation 70s; or myths of the Fatherland or Motherland, or God, Country, Mom and Apple Pie; myths behind our holidays; myths regarding life-style types: the hippy, yuppie, bohemian, Type A career driven, the celebrity, the Super Rich; Modernism promoted its myth of Progress; Capitalism and Communism as mythic rivals; Hollywood touted as a mythic icon; and there are celebrities like Elvis Presley or Marilyn Monroe who have been raised in their cultural status to mythic proportions. The French literary critic Roland Barthes examined a range of these myths out of daily life in his work *Mythologies.* We have witnessed in our own day the decay of the myth of the American Dream. The cult of individualism is a modern myth whose origins, as we saw, are found in Christianity. But hardly do any of these cultural myths serve us in relationship to a Greater Reality; they do not bring any deep existential meaning into our own life. They are not Mythos.

We should make some mention here of the relatively new area of study called memetics, which is based on the notion of "memes." There may arise some misunderstanding between meme and myth. All of the items we listed above as examples of everyday myth can also easily be considered memes—in fact, by definition, they are memes. Memes, roughly, are mental units, in any category you might imagine, of cultural information or conditioned behavior that replicate and transmit themselves, from mind to mind, *as* elements of culture. Since literally anything that catches on and survives for any length of time in the culture can be defined as a meme—words, ideas, icons, names, logos, name brands, phrases, songs, book titles, rituals, cultural movements (the 2011 Occupy Movement), skills, behaviors, to isms of one kind or another, and including whole religions and philosophies—we should not think, however, that this clever, new, intellectual perspective has now replaced what I consider to be something much more profound, and that is *myth / Mythos*. True, myths are memes, but it should be obvious that they are so much more than that. For example, we cannot reduce Christianity down to the level of the ubiquitous smiley face icon just because they both happen to be memes, though in our Postmodern context nothing would surprise me. The phrase 'New Age' itself is, of course, a meme. Those who are active in promoting new social/cultural memes for social and global change should keep in mind that for them to become genuinely existentially vital they also need to be powered as myth, that is, more profoundly as Mythos. *The Power of Myth*, as Joseph Campbell's book title states. Ideally, any new vitalizing idea or movement that could transform the culture would speak from Mythos and as Mythos, and I would claim that today that would refer to the coming New Age *Mythos*.

We have all been conditioned, ruled, guided, by the myths handed down to us by our society, myths that we ourselves therefore did not have any hand in creating. But from religions to the mundane myths of everyday life, we find that everything has now undergone the process of critique; whether that equally implies everything has been debunked depends on one's allegiances. "Myths" that are today socially effective, e.g. Money is God ("God" the bottom line for all things), are, as we know, spiritually empty. They certainly rule our life, but they are hollow, and this means that soul goes terribly hungry. This is our Postmodern metaphysical crisis precisely. Spiritually, the Postmodern world lives in a cultural graveyard of dead myth and pale specters of myth, and yet, in our midst, we are witnessing the emerging of new myth, and more pointedly, as I believe, the emerging of a New Age *Mythos*.

It should be made clear that there is dead myth and there is living myth. Naturally, it is largely the myths of old that are considered dead: We no longer live in accordance to them, no longer perform their rituals. (Religious Traditionalists, however, are still able to do so within their respective faith.) This does not preclude the fact that the study of old myths can add to our understanding of life from an intellectual perspective. Dead myths still do provide existential insight, especially from the perspective of depth psychology. But for many of us, that is still not good enough. *We still need to live today, now*—and that is to say, live meaningfully and creatively. Living myth is what existentially speaks to us, moves us, what we live in accordance to; it is vital to a meaningful existence, it feeds our soul. Living myth is that symbolic narrative that not only reveals to us truths beyond everyday understanding, but is the primary cultural gyroscope that keeps us on course for a meaningful life. I now call that living myth *Mythos*.

Literary writers and poets, for some time now, almost always use dead myth in their work. These dead myths are often called "literary allusions." This is so often why they do not existentially satisfy us. James Joyce, a Modern master, was extremely clever at rehashing our culture's mythic ruins, creating out of them a literary monument or two. But the question we can pose to him, or to any Modern master, is, *What in them can we live by?* Their work is so often a strictly acquired literary taste. The 19th Century Romantics had sought to revitalize myth, but were wholly inadequate to the task in the heyday of Progress; they were unfortunately premature in their ambition as our culture had not yet reached its crisis point; their ideas got steamrollered by the Industrial Revolution, the meteoric rise of Technos. The German Romantic Friedrich Schlegel bemoaned that "We have no mythology." William Blake was one of the exceptions of his time, a poet who was a supreme literary mythmaker, but whose complex, labyrinthine works are so idiosyncratic that they require patient, in-depth study in order to penetrate them; the result was that his elaborate "personal" mythology has never, and will never, collectively catch on. Walt Whitman sang the myth of 19th Century America, of freedom, democracy, the modern man, the new frontier that was America, the call of the Open Road, and had hoped that his "evangel-poem" titled *Leaves of Grass* would have been better received; unfortunately, it never fully was, and was hardly much assimilated, even though its greatness is universally acknowledged. The early 20th Century surrealists attempted a theoretical reworking for the ground of new myth (Andre Breton's *Third Manifesto of Surrealism* suggests as much), but they never got beyond their enthrallment to the gushing irrational imagery of the subconscious. Two other literary figures who tried to tackle the promise of new myth were D.H. Lawrence and Charles Olson. However highly creative and brilliant their work, it never attained the level of living myth. And others we could refer to as working with myth to some degree or another, from Robinson Jeffers, T.S. Eliot, Sylvia Plath, to more recent Beats like Gary Snyder and Diane dePrima.

Now there are those who might suggest that we get our myth today through science fiction. First, there is a miscomprehension by those who make these suggestions, as if science fiction is myth in the sense of true Mythos. We can ask, Who lives in accordance to science fiction books? Or even science fiction movies, for that matter, except perhaps for those fans that might obsess about them like a cult (e.g. Star Wars)? There is no doubt that mythemes come into play in a work of fiction or science fiction, but fiction by its very nature is a work "made up" for a literary audience and is not something in which we live and move and have our being. True, *living,* myth—Mythos—, we must realize, is not simply worked out like sitting down to write a novel. Mythos is our being called by the Word which addresses us and would guide us. Of course, this is why *The Bible* or *The Koran* continue their hold upon billions.

As we noted early in our Story, the inauguration of the Space Age failed to birth a new global Mythos for us too. Our landing on the Moon on six missions was a technological spectacle that enthralled millions at the time, but the culture lost its enthusiasm for space exploits shortly after. Certainly a potential for Mythos was offered by this whole new perspective of Earth from space, but mainstream culture was simply too Postmodern for it to happen. Daniel Noel's extended attempt at *A Search for the Mythic Significance of the Space Age* in *Approaching Earth* (1986) is really only a scholar's search in previous and contemporary culture for indicators of that significance than any originating Mythos. It does appear that no one at that time was fully aware of how a genuine Mythos could have emerged out of our early space ventures.

Science itself is informed by mythic structure, from the 17th Century's development of our modern relationship to Nature, to its tie in with Modernism's Progress, to those scientists and technocrats who still today believe only in science, who have made of it a sort of cult (scientism). Freud himself had said, "Logos is our god," referring, of course, to scientific endeavor. Or consider this quote by contemporary astrophysicist Neil deGrasse Tyson: "After the laws of physics, everything else is opinion." In my youth, especially during the years of the birth of our space program, it was common to hear that science would someday save us from all of our social ills. That was, in essence, a mythic projection.

\*

*Once you connect with Mythos, you are in the process of Mythos-making your way into psychospiritual Reality.*

Hopefully why I've had to go back to the original, ancient Greek word 'Mythos' has become clear by now. So let us finally get to this question that's been hanging in the background all this time, How have I reinterpreted Mythos for our contemporary world? Mythos originally meant 'something spoken—words,' particularly words that tell of events—a story. 'Mythos' is twin to the Greek 'Logos,' which also meant 'word,' on an everyday level, but in a different sense—that of discourse, conversational exchange between persons.[4] We should keep in mind, though, that both, when we consider rather their profound senses, had reference to a divine source. The Word as Mythos and the Word as Logos each revealed something regarding Divine Reality. First, however, Mythos had an original connection with the mouth, therefore with utterance itself—it was *the spoken word* of the oral traditions, which especially meant poetry. Bards told long narratives of Mythos. Whereas Logos acquired a philosophical connotation signifying the interior, intellectually reflective word that then gives an accounting; it referred to our ability to reason, and with the philosophers, it was human reason attempting to reflect Divine Reason, the Divine Order of the cosmos. Mythos, because of its implication of spoken words out of an oral tradition of telling, came to strictly apply then to the narrative word, that is, to a story that is orally told about and passed on. Mythos, therefore, became a story (today's myth), and since a story is never a rigorously rational, investigative endeavor, but is a telling as a sharing with others (oftentimes in the midst of ritual), Mythos over time became the "mere" story that was told by poets, with certain individual embellishments perhaps. In contrast, the Word that is Logos that philosophers preferred revealed Divine Reality as Divine Reason (the pursuit of philosophy), which then included the results of investigative intellect (science), resulting in the "truth" about things. (A few of the earliest Greek philosophers were still poets, such as Parmenides, when he wrote poetic Mythos to convey new revelations about Logos.) But what Divine Reality, then, did the Word of Mythos refer to? Mythos—*a story of what or who?* In its original, primordial sense, it was a Story of *the Gods*—and yet, even more original than that, it was the Story first spoken by the Gods themselves. As Julian Jaynes said, *The first poets were gods.*[5] In other words, the first poets—and for that matter, the first prophets—heard directly and channeled the voices of the Gods: When they uttered their perfectly metered verses or proclaimed their Visions and prophecies, they spoke exactly what the Gods were speaking through them. They were the mouthpiece of the Gods.

The most profound understanding of myth in its original sense as *Mythos* meant precisely then *the Word* coming-to-us from the Gods, the Word given by, and of, the Gods, becoming then the Word told (an utterance of the mouth) about the Gods. In the ancient Greek world, Mythos implied stories told about the Gods, not make-believe, imaginary Gods, but real Gods, what the Greeks took to be real Gods.

We can consider 'Mythos,' then, in its broadest sense, as *the Word spoken by Divinity* that initially some select individuals then speak, share with the community. That Word was also transmitted as Revelation, Vision, or Oracle, and was passed on originally through an oral tradition; those select individuals were the poet, prophet, avatar, or sibyl (today's channel). What happened in the ancient world, however, was that the words about the Gods, as the Gods themselves retired from open involvement with humanity, became over time merely old stories about them, told and retold by poets down through the years, the years slowly turning into centuries. When no one currently living has any direct experience of the Gods, then the words told about them (Mythos) begin to suggest from the new rational perspective of Logos an uncertainty about them in some of their listeners (which were the early Greek thinkers of Logos). The more time went by, the more there was doubt about the source of those words: Who can say then whether these stories actually took place, whether the Gods actually said or did these things? So the stories became simply, *What is told*. The new Greek thinkers of the 6th and 5th Centuries B.C. seriously started to question the reality of the Gods. Xenophanes, for one, famous for his skepticism, in fact held in disdain the old Gods of Homer.

When contact, therefore, with the Living Word—*true Mythos*—is lost, the culture producers are no longer actively Mythos-making in the profound, primordial sense, but work in a secondary literary phase of mythmaking that, though it can still be intellectually creative, stimulating, and nourishing for the culture, is existentially inferior in comparison. The dictionary meaning of 'mythos' has now historically expanded to include the whole interconnected mythological / symbolical / iconographic system in which a people live. But its original meaning as the *Divine Word* has been lost.

*In the beginning was the Word* (John 1:1), as the Gospel says. The Greek word for "Word" here (as The New Testament was written in common Greek) is Logos, rather than Mythos. So the first verse of John states, *In the beginning was the Logos*—the Divine Reason for all things. The implications here are extremely telling. Logos in the Greek world had already become associated with "Truth," with Reality—that is, a Divine Blueprint that, in Plato's dominating philosophy, remains stable and unchanging. Mythos, with its reference to the Gods, could no longer claim that it spoke truly of things, since its foundation depended upon the Gods, and with the Gods no longer around, it lost what it was supposed to hold in view. Mythos, then, did not possess certainty; its stories could be embellished, twisted, changed, since it had nothing immediately in view to lock onto. Therefore, the Apostle John wanted to make certain that it was *truth*—better yet, Truth with a capital 'T'—that he was referring to, a Truth that does not change, that remains dependable, because Reason (it was believed) locked onto it and secured it. The Christian obsession with possessing the Truth can literally go back to this passage. But then we realize that Logos was also the way that science would talk about the world. Science, too, wanted to be certain and so pursued its adventure with Truth. We see once again how Christianity and Western science have been running along on the same track of wanting to secure "Truth" through the Piscean Age.

*In the beginning was the Mythos* is how I believe it more accurately should have been worded. For Mythos *is* the Word spoken by Divinity. Christ was the Word—the Mythos—for Christianity: Beginning with Jesus as the Christ, the divine God-man, the Word then became the Gospel (the Good News told about and shared), unfolding a whole new world that we have known as the Piscean Age of Western civilization. It was destined, however, that the apostle chose to use the Greek 'Logos,' aligning the Christ message with the whole new direction of Greek philosophy and science to seek Truth, so that the Word as Logos of early Christianity came to supplant the dying Word as Mythos of the old, departed Gods of previous Ages.

Mythos-making, then, is our supremely creative act of putting into Form our encounter with that which lies beyond the Veil, which is That-which-is-greater-than-us, that is, greater than the ego-self, whether it is called generically the Greater Reality, or Spirit, Divinity, the Gods, "God," Higher Self, Divine Self, or, beginning with the most primordial of all—*Being* (as Heidegger reintroduced). Interestingly, Logos-making in philosophy no longer claims to connect with any metaphysical Greater Reality, especially as Logos has long become primarily the language and province of science. This is why I had to return to the original meaning of *Mythos*. To genuinely speak Mythos, we must be directly in the flow of, directly engaged with, that Greater Power coming through, and not simply telling stories at secondhand.

A quote from Ananda Coomeraswamy: "Myth embodies the nearest approach to absolute truth that can be stated in words." Note that, though he probably didn't have in mind the distinction between Mythos and Logos at all, he does say "Myth" [that is, Mythos] rather than "Logos." I would expand this statement, however, and say, that can be embodied in *Form*, whatever that Form might be. Today, we, the creative individuals hearing the Call of a new Word, are being called to be Mythos-makers of the New Age. Through our encounter with the returning Gods—ETs, the Visitors, Other-dimensionals, Other Intelligence—, through our encounter with Spirit coming-to-us anew as the Living Image of our Higher Self, as I experience as Psyche, we are called to bring that encounter into new Form, at the same time transforming the established forms of culture that are current. Modernism was a drive to demythologize culture; the New Age is the Vision to remythologize culture, to remythologize, re-enchant, a world that is wallowing in spiritual abandonment. One might suggest that in more preferably contemporary, conceptual terms, the emerging new Mythos that I speak about is another way of referencing the New Paradigm that just about everyone is on the trail of today.

The ancient Greeks, as we saw above, had originated the contrast between Logos and Mythos. Logos became above all the language of science, which in our day is deified as Technos. Let us consider for a moment then that we can view our relationship to Nature as a type of attunement; that is to say, we can attune to Nature in a certain way. Our attunement throughout the Modern period was based on domination and certainty. The scientist wanted to be certain with regard to statements about Nature (the Church had shown that it had failed here), and the only way to be certain, said modern science, is through clear and distinct ideas (Descartes), and these ideas are only to be found in mathematics and physics—specifically, mathematical physics—, which eventually gave birth to Technos. Since science did in fact produce results (which Kant provided the philosophical foundation for in *The Critique of Pure Reason*), Technos, in turn, produced marvellous material riches through this particular dominating attunement to Nature. But let us compare for a moment Technos and the emerging Mythos of Psyche. Technos, originating in this narrow obsession with certainty, and this will to domination, is therefore a limited listening—not everything in Nature is allowed to speak—that within this pre-established limit knows no limits. Technos does not realize Its own limit, thereby does not respect limits. (Technos will ravage and end up destroying Earth to get what It wants.) Whereas our new awareness of Mythos implies an unlimited listening—everything in Nature is given a chance to speak—that is always recognizing and respecting the limit. In other words, there is always a limit as to how far we can go before balance is broken, before the Fabric of Nature is torn. The Greeks had a word for this recognition of limits: *moira*. The new Mythos will show what our limits are, for the emerging new Mythos allows all of Nature/Gaia to speak. Psyche, as Mythos of the New Age, therefore defines a new attunement to Nature (implying thereby to Being): Let us call it *openness*.

Today more than ever we live in a sort of playing field of numerous, competing myths-in-the-making. The challenge for today's Mythos-maker is tremendous and exhilarating. The questions we pose are: How conscious are the new Mythos-makers of their making of Mythos? How existentially satisfying is the potential new Mythos? Does it speak to our soul and provide a foundation for living? How comprehensive of what we know today—of all the various fields of knowledge—is the new Mythos? Does the new Mythos leave out or distort certain areas of knowledge or evidence that would appear to be pertinent? Is the new Mythos but partial, inadequate to the total situation in which we find ourselves? Is it a packaged "myth" that simply asks that we believe it? A truly adequate Mythos is one that assimilates and transforms and launches anew all that it comes into contact with; it is constantly growing and spreading in unexpected ways because it is the new Tree that feeds on all that has come before.

Now we come to some succinct statements about Mythos. Mythos is about relationship—developing a relationship with Divinity—and this relationship is a process, a supremely co-creative process. Mythos, developing such a relationship, is then about bringing that relationship—co-creating it with Divinity—into Form, the new Great Story. Mythos is this process of Spirit-coming-to-us-driving-us-to-manifest-forms-of-our-Divinity-as-we-co-create-these-forms-into-manifestation. These are forms within the Form of the Great Story to be told. Mythos-making is therefore the Supreme Art, the Art of all arts. Mythos-making is our creative encounter with That-which-is-coming-to-us; the form which we choose, or are gifted, to work in doesn't matter, be it poetry, prose, storytelling, painting, sculpture, dance, music, new ritual, philosophical or theological thought, works of scholarship, in developing new forms of relationship to others, new forms of community, a new attunement to Gaia, or new forms of spiritual practice or life-style. It should not go unstated that the *process* of Mythos-making itself is at the center, is of the very essence, of the new Mythos. New Mythos—what I will call The Mythos—and Mythos-making are one and the same.

One thing should be made clear regarding this call to remythologize our culture, as I am aware that certain intellectual types might immediately raise their eyebrows and protest. None of what I am advocating here should be misread as a call to revert back to the mythic stage (as understood by anthropologists) of our cultural evolution. Any kind of unconscious—or even contemporary media-conditioned, and thereby numbing of critical thought—membership defining myths are a way of being of our past, and should be left behind us. It would be a gross mistake to think that what I am promoting here is any new membership myth that would only result in a mass totalitarian New World Order. Mythos-making, in a *contemporary* sense, on the contrary, is a fully conscious, ongoing, co-creative process that engages the highest image we have of ourselves. Its vector is toward superconsciousness, and creatively—super-creatively—bringing that state of being into Form.

We should address an issue that is bound to come up, and that is regarding the notion of creating our own personal mythology, which is considered to be a sort of therapeutic, creative expression, an idea that is advocated today by any number of psychotherapists. We might point out, however: Isn't a personal mythology an oxymoron? How can a mythology, which is always a cultural Form collectively shared, be strictly personal? A living myth—Mythos—speaks to others; it is a Form in which all (potentially) can find the existential significance they need, a Form through which all can live. "Personal myths" can be helpful in therapeutic work, but they can just as easily be called personal *fantasy*—or a delusion. Christianity, Islam, Buddhism are certainly not anyone's personal mythology, or, let us say, anyone's personal religion. For the level from which we have been speaking all along is that of religion, and the call for a new, universal religion. To suggest a compromise here, let us say that contemporary mythmaking cannot be so neatly defined between personal and collective, and that a personal mythology—after all, one is practicing a kind of Mythos-making of one's own psyche—is a contemporary way of preparing the ground—engaging in one's own *soul work*—for the new Mythos. For ultimately, by definition, those who are genuinely Mythos-making from Higher Self inspiration will be spoken to in a way that equally, in turn, *will* speak to others.

My Vision is that Psyche is the Mythos of the New Age. As we develop a relationship to Psyche and bring that firsthand experience into both cultural Form and our own, personal embodiment of it, we are Mythos-making, that is, we are conscious co-creators of our psychospiritual evolution. Psyche as a teacher is our own Higher Self teaching us that we might embody more of our Higher Self, thereby realizing a New Self. The most exhilarating insight we can have today about Mythos-making—and I believe it is what Nietzsche saw at the far end of the tunnel of nihilism—is that we are no longer destined to be the prisoners of previous myth, but that we stand at The Edge, as if before an abyss (that of Being), of a tremendous, new creativity as of yet unimagined—that we can be the Mythos-makers, the transformers, of every aspect of our life. Mythos-making, we will someday collectively come to realize, is our fundamental creative birthright, an existential *human right*. That, I contend, has not yet been fully accepted by our society—that we have an absolute human right to creativity on such a scale. The fundamental reality of our own creativity, a creativity of unlimited potential, is the New Age answer to a Postmodern nihilism that would deconstruct us and leave us dismantled in our tracks.

Realistically, the great majority is nowhere near the point of really understanding this or being ready for it; in fact, when it comes down to it, if there is any gut-level feeling about any of this at all, it utterly baffles or frightens people. Most people we know cling to their conditioned roles and icons—and so many to their Fundamentalism—as if to life jackets in the swirling currents of the Postmodern sea. The Establishment is definitely not advocating anything as liberating as Mythos-making. Which goes to explain again why there is the necessity for a shake-up to civilization by the return of the Gods. The thing is, there will be a shake-up in one way or another when we add into the scenario the unfolding of an abrupt climate change MELE that we are still in the early days of. Perhaps then will the new Mythos be taken seriously.

The image of the Water Bearer of Aquarius is now transformed into the image of Psyche hovering in the Living Fountain. Deep in the interior of the Fountain is found the Sun. Now the Sun is the ruler of the astrological sign of Leo. As we discussed in an earlier chapter, an Age is defined by a zodiacal polarity—the two signs that lie opposite one another on the wheel of the zodiac. Leo is the sign opposite Aquarius; it is the undercurrent theme to the new Aquarian Age, as Virgo was undercurrent to the Piscean Age. Leo is the astrological sign of projecting the personality, which is why it rules acting and theatre; it therefore rules self-expression, creativity, that is, the self projecting itself, expressing itself, in all forms of its inherent creativity out into the world. In the most profound sense, Leo is the sign of the Self and the unlimited creative potential of the Self realizing itself. If we would enter the Fountain with Psyche, we would come to know the potential of Unlimited Creativity—a creativity as superabundant as the Sun in the depths of the Fountain. I introduce here—and those able to dwell in the Living Fountain will know what I am talking about—the notion of a creative state on a whole, new level—*supercreativity*.

Indeed, so central is this notion of creativity to the New Age potential before us (and remembering that soul is our potential-to-become), that I will even suggest that the New Age will be the most profound Art project humanity has ever known, if it unfolds with the conscious intention of Mythos. To those who would wave their authority over us and say that Mythos as religion has nothing to do with art, I would say that creativity on the level that we are speaking about, which throws open the door of the control system cage we are all born into, is attuned to a higher authority. It is to see beyond our fish bowl world. It is creativity engaging Being in the Opening offered by Being. This is also where the New Age Vision birthing The Mythos to come breaks away from the Postmodern.

The astrologer Dane Rudhyar has said that the undercurrent theme of an Age doesn't fully come to collective expression until the halfway point of the Age has been reached, and that appears to have been true. That, at least, is how it has manifested in the past. That would mean that 1,000 years from now humanity would begin to fully manifest its Leo creative potential of Self. Given that change is happening so fast today, it is quite presumptuous to even talk about anything that far in the future. (For that matter, even 30–50 years into the future.) Such acceleration of change, if it is indeed translating into an evolutionary acceleration, could very well mean that the timetables of the past may no longer be valid. Certainly, there are those of us discovering such supercreative potential now. The whole understanding of World Ages may itself change as what we understand by Reality itself changes.

The Self—the New Self, not the narcissistic ego-self we currently know—is destined to become the supreme creative project of the New Age. The New Self—the Marriage of Spirit and soul, of mind and heart—will be the supreme New Age work of art, the Great Work: soul married to the Mythos that is its liberation. Mythos-making, the art of soul liberation—of *soul transformation*—, is today's most spiritually revolutionary act. What we briefly touched on earlier regarding the process of manifestation is only a hint at what the New Self will be capable of. Mythos-making that wields equally the power of spiritual manifestation will be the dream of the alchemists come true.

It is obvious then that we do need to think of Mythos in terms of our encounter with Other Intelligence, with the return of the new-old Gods. We need to bring forth new words about the Gods, as they reveal themselves anew to us. The contactees, experiencers, channels, Walk-ins, ET souls in human form, and yes, even the UFO cultists, are indeed answering that Call; any criticism we may have of them is directed more at how well, how appropriately, they are conducting their Mythos-making, as we have just previously explored. So let me be clear and state that turning one's UFO/ET experience and the resulting Mythos-making into a narrowly defined cult that by its very nature excludes the rest of the world is first of all going down a wrong path. The New Age, as we have said at the very beginning, is not about forming new cults. The New Age is a global shift in consciousness that will potentially, eventually, happen for all. The UFO cultists are right in their attempt to Mythos-make, but the social form in which they generally embody it is too often outdated—that is, unless they see it as only a stage to go through in this co-creative process of bringing UFO reality into the world.

Aquarius is the sign of coming to realize one's true individuality within the collective. This is individuality determined by our ongoing relationship with Higher Self, and as a result of that relationship knowing where we belong, what our work is, within the collective. The myth of individuality is also going to undergo a shift in meaning as we enter the New Age. We will no longer be referring to the rugged individualism of old pioneer America or Type-A entrepreneurial America; or the egocentric personality doing whatever it wants; or the isolated Kierkegaardian individual standing existentially alone; or the narcissistic personality absorbed only with Me Me Me (meaning totally absorbed with one's personal soap opera, with personal likes, dislikes, needs, wants, comforts, quirks, habits, ambitions, neuroses, etc.); nor is this shift implying the Fifties nonconformist beatnik or Sixties rebellious hippy striking out against the Establishment, but without a clue as to where to go next. The true individuality of Aquarius is that of being aligned with our Higher Self and allowing that Higher Self to manifest in the world. It is a return to Mythos—now meaning the Word of the Higher Self, of our own Divinity, addressing us. The Higher Self outside our four dimensions of a space-time continuum has an interconnectedness with the invisible Whole, the Greater Reality. What this means for us living in everyday society is that by coming to know our Higher Self in the collective Mind Field, in the macrocosm, we come to know our place, then, in the microcosm, in our society, in our community. Aquarius implies individuality working within the Whole as the natural development of individuality first defined by the relationship to my Higher Self connecting me with the Whole. Coming to know my Higher Self, I therefore know what my Calling is in the everyday world, what I am meant to be doing in the community. This, then, is my Path. This is not an easy notion to grasp in our contemporary world where the ego-self is so utterly conditioned by the values of mass culture, and so intoxicated with its own ambitions of success defined by that culture. Let us therefore not think that this new understanding of individuality will be realized overnight.

Hopefully it has been apparent that a how-to approach to Mythos-making has not been my intent here. The creative process of engaging and transforming soul through new Mythos Forms would be a whole book of its own. At issue, however, is the old quandary of trying to teach creativity to others: To think that technique alone (shades of Technos) can do it is a misunderstanding, though hints, clues, suggestions, guidance, and the sharing of work, can definitely help others in their process. But to be spoonfed what should be our own vital encounter with Higher Self? We should realize that the emerging Mythos will provide new Forms for engaging Gaia, Technos, the returning ET Gods and all the Intelligences contacting us today, for transforming soul and being able to navigate our way in this whole confusing world of the astral-psychic and the complexities of a multidimensional Self-hood; new Forms also for living in a New Age community, and for embodying New Age ideals. Once we are in the flow of Higher Self inspiration, we will be shown.

When we have reached this point in our understanding of what is opening to us, then we realize how liberating the Aquarian dispensation is. In our youth, the question always thrown in our face was, *What gives you the authority to speak of spiritual things?* This was meant to intimidate us, and to silence us. The right to speak of spiritual matters could only come from Authority, whether that Authority was *The Bible, The Koran*, the pope, the priesthood, a rabbi, some academic theologian, some Buddhist Roshi, or some flashy Eastern guru. The voice of Authority had been built into the old Piscean Age hierarchical social system (astrologically, the Jupiter co-rulership of Pisces). The New Age announces the liberating news—announced long ago, in fact, by the ancient Gnostics—that, if we have seen for ourselves, we are then entitled to speak from our own, firsthand, Higher Self authority.

The New Self learns of all the corridors of the Labyrinth of soul; learns of its body and etheric body; learns of all the subtle energy fields that surround us; it respects and gives voice to Gaia; it allows Psyche to work with Technos, integrating technology and spirituality; it develops its intuition to instantly see through the confusion around us, and learns to move through the Veil to the astral-psychic and how to manifest; it has prepared itself to meet Other Intelligence from this Next Level; it is not fearful of the close encounter with ET in physical form; and it will eventually join telepathic hands with others who have also ascended to the Next Level. The New Self in all its creative projections is the New Age Mythos in-progress.

We will now define *The Mythos* as:

*The Story of our Divinity coming-into Human Reality.*

## ( 13 )

## THE EMERGING NEW STORY OF US

*Nietzsche: God is dead. End of Story.*
*Postmodernists: We agree. There is no Story.*
*Lampi: The Gods return. Beginning of a new Story.*

After all that we have explored up to this point, it is time to provide a preliminary sketch of the new perspective on history that the New Age Vision entails. This sketch is meant only to indicate how another history might be written in the future. For history will undoubtedly be rewritten from a New Age perspective. It might not be an exaggeration to say that the most important influence on humankind has never received mention in any history book, has never even been mainstream acknowledged, to begin with—that is, unless we invoke it from within the religious Traditions. But, then, after all, that has been the very nature of the UFO phenomenon itself, ever since the Gods retired from open involvement with humanity millennia ago, yet remaining covertly active behind the scenes, purposely keeping us in the dark about their presence. How, then, could we have known to write them into our history except as old myths or alleged miraculous encounters out of sacred books? The UFO influence will of necessity be written into our history as we come to finally accept it and learn more about it.

The rewriting of history has been underway, however, in other quarters. I am thinking particularly here of feminism and the women's movement and how women have been reclaiming their importance in the human Story. *Our hidden heritage,* as Riane Eisler[1] called it. Here, again, we see the work of the Water Bearer pouring forth what was hidden. Eisler's work, as but one example, has provided a new understanding of the role of women and the feminine in our history that had been suppressed, a new understanding that the New Age Vision can only welcome. In fact, her advocacy of a partnership society rather than a dominator one is the ideal of the New Age community; it is supremely Aquarian. Here is another Thread to be woven into a complete Story of our history. This aspect of the revisioning of history—after all, women are obviously integral to the human Story—is still only the beginning, however.

For the astrological understanding of World Ages and other major planetary cycles has also been left out of our history.[2] A more thorough telling of history would have to weave in the metaphysical depth that astrology offers. And even more than that, the whole, integrated metaphysical background to the Story of our psychospiritual evolution will have to be woven into our history. A complete history, therefore, would weave the Threads of not only social, cultural, intellectual, political, and material developments, but the Threads as well of the metaphysical/astrological and of our relationship to Other Intelligence. There is a new Story of us emerging. I am not aware of any author who has yet been able, or who has even attempted, to tell this Story in all its complexity. For this, too, is Mythos-making of the highest order. But let us begin here an early attempt at a brief sketch...

*So Threads of The Mythos continue weaving...we are in process...*

Despite the continued perpetration of the Big Lie that we have been alone on planet Earth, more and more evidence is coming forward that a non-human presence has been on this Earth for millennia. When the pre-human hominid species was still roaming the Earth, the alien Other was here. The alien Other, who I have referred to as the Gods, were aware of the slow, plodding pace of biological evolution; at some point in their dealings with Earth, they decided to actively intervene in the genetic upgrade of the pre-human hominids. Zecharia Sitchin believes he has found the original reason why this happened in his interpretation of the ancient Sumerian texts. His interpretation, in a nutshell, goes like this: Those from the planet

Niburu, primarily referred to as the Annunaki, over 400,000 years ago decided to genetically engineer a new species of intelligent creature, homo sapiens; their purpose was that this new species would work for them in their mining operations on Earth, specifically for gold. Now, whether Sitchin is correct in all the details of this (he extensively lays all this out in *The 12th Planet*) is not the issue here. It is the drift of his argument that is important. Genetically integrating their own genes, those of an advanced, intelligent race, with a hominid Earth species, they created a race of workers, or, to put it more bluntly, a race of slaves. A certain class, however, eventually emerged who became the intermediaries between the Gods and worker humanity. They were the priest-rulers and kingship elite.

Two, contrary, competing theories that attempt to explain our origins nicely dovetail with this new perspective. The theories of evolution and creationism can now both be viewed as having validity. There has indeed been biological evolution on Earth, but it is well known by biologists that it proceeds at an enormously slow snail's pace. Some biologists have theorized that if the selection of biological mutations were the only factor in our evolution, we should, by such figuring, still be living in caves. It is quite possible, too, that Earth was originally seeded with life and that genetic alterations were always being made by Others at certain timed intervals. Whatever had previously occurred, the pre-human hominids had evolved to a point where the alien Other decided to "create" us—*the generic Adam, human beings*. This explains why there has always been a so-called "missing link" in the evolutionary chain that resulted in homo sapiens—it was that the ET Gods gave us an enormous quantum jump on evolution. Since the alien Other was the ancient Gods and Goddesses, it is therefore true that we were created by "God"(s). As *Genesis* tells us, "Let *us* make man in *our* image, after *our* likeness…" (Genesis 1:26) I would like to introduce a new term hinted at throughout this work that synthesizes the contrary views of evolution and creationism, and that is, *interventionism*.

The genetic program of the ET Gods was a fusing, as it were, of an Earth being and their "divine" being, of Earth-based genes and "divine" genes. (This does not have to be interpreted so literally, however; they could have altered/added genes in the original hominid gene base, this bioengineering itself entailing a "divine" upgrade.) This, too, explains the age-old notion that *we are* a mixed being—we are part Earth animal and part divine. We are an Earth-based animal with a spark of Divinity within us (the soul-Spirit dynamic). That spark of their being, biologically grounded in a genetic alteration, raised hominid consciousness so that Spirit, the higher divine spark, opened to us. Since the ET Gods were already active in the higher dimensions of Spirit, their intervention allowed the opening to Spirit to occur for us also. So we are doubly part divine—"divine" on the genetic level, but truly divine through the window that opened for us revealing Spirit. The notion that we were originally created to be the servants/slaves of the Gods is not an interpretation merely spun out by Sitchin, however. The ancient Mesopotamians explicitly say that in their writings (taken, of course, as mythology); it can be found in any standard ancient history book or heard in any university ancient history course. But now we begin to genuinely understand the background to the Mesopotamian view. The ancient peoples were not simply telling imaginative stories; they were not simply projecting the harshness of their existence onto "personified Gods." As Sitchin puts it, they were reporting exactly their direct experience. Their myths were based on the Mythos, the Word, revealed by the Gods and about the Gods, *actual* Gods.

This period of our servitude might have been extremely long in comparison to our current, limited view on history. That whole, earlier phases of human development took place leading up to agrarian civilizations that were the first to record stories about the Gods is to be assumed. In these earlier phases, the Gods had undoubtedly a substantial involvement with us. (We will set aside in this brief Story the likelihood that other high-level civilizations existed before Sumer, such as Atlantis. Some investigators of alternative, "forbidden," archeology, such as Michael Cremo, contend that we have actually been active on planet Earth for millions of years. This certainly raises issues of who in fact we originally were, especially in relation to the Gods.) After the Flood (circa 11,000 B.C.), which the ancient record states had destroyed what was then the known world of civilization, the ET Gods were once again our teachers. As the testimony of all ancient peoples worldwide claim, the Gods, Those-who-came-from-the-Sky—and in what other manner than in their UFO craft—, taught them everything they knew. The Gods continued to upgrade us by teaching us the arts of civilization. Language, writing, agriculture, tool-making, metallurgy, pottery, textile making, education, mathematics, astronomy, social codes and mores, law, government, religious practice, all these acquirements were attributed to the influence of the Gods. (It is quite possible that most of these arts, at least in this new phase of our evolution after the Flood, were largely taught in the Age of Gemini, which would make astrological sense.) But there was more—all the arts of civilization would also include the occult arts, astrology being one. Certainly, astronomy itself was originally none other than astrology. The implication is, is that the Gods, therefore, had to have been masters of astrology too. (The UFO-astrology connection, as far as I know, has not yet been fully explored by anyone.) If this were indeed the case, then the Gods already possessed foreknowledge of all the stages of evolution timed to astrological cycles. And they know to this day what stage we are at, and what new evolutionary lesson we are ready for.

Now the arts of civilization are not only the tools for advancing humanity, but certain ones among them can also be considered a *control system* for humanity, and this does not necessarily imply anything nefarious. (Jacques Vallee is apparently correct: the UFO phenomenon itself, in the broadest sense, is a type of spiritual control system.) If we think about it, isn't that what social codes, morals, ethical precepts, customs, law, government, in essence, is all about? And the control system that had the greatest affect on us was traditionally religion. They are all forms of controlling and educating our otherwise wayward, aimless, misdirected, licentious, and violent behaviors—the naïve, unevolved soul. A control system—and this implies myth, our deepest cultural structural form—serves a double purpose: It existentially orients us, guides us, evolves us, in other words, benefits us, but at the same time can play a restrictive, limiting, even repressive role, in our history. The Gods, through the arts of civilization, have apparently played a parental role for us, in turns teaching us, inspiring us, and then repressing us and disciplining us. Terence McKenna had cleverly once said that periodically the aliens show up in order to give us another needed metaphysical spanking.

Yet, all is not as simple as that. If we had originally learned everything from the Gods, then what about war? The ancient record states how these same Gods who taught us how to become civilized also set one city-state, one tribe, one people, against another in war after war. The Gods allowed for—*encouraged*—warfare, especially when we consider the Age of Aries. What does this say about them? That they do have an uncanny resemblance to us? Or, is it more accurate to say that we have an uncanny resemblance to them? And is this but another form of control? William Bramley in *The Gods of Eden* makes a case for warfare as an important part of the control system established on Earth by what he called the "custodial Gods." Referring to Yahweh, Moses said, "The Lord is a man of war," (Exodus 15:3), and we are appalled at all the blood that was spilled in the name of Yahweh in the Age of Aries.

It is quite apparent that any superhuman beings, or any particular superhuman being, who appeared out of the sky and performed wondrous feats—*miracles* we would consider them—would be imaged as Gods and, with the birth of monotheism, seen as the supreme *God* (I am the one God, thou shalt not have other Gods before me.) Keep in mind, though: When we say that the superhuman ETs sound like Gods, we are placing the cart before the horse, sort of speak—our whole concept of Gods originates with the ancient ETs; they are, in fact, the original template for what we mean by "Gods," and for all human imagination down through the ages. As we saw, one ET ruler among them stood out and declared a covenant with humanity—specifically with a Chosen People at that time—, the one Lord, the dominating ruler, the one *God* above all Gods—Yahweh. A superhuman being such as Yahweh (Christian O'Brien in *The Genius of the Few* interprets Yahweh, in fact, as an Annunaki leader) could save a people (the story of Exodus), perform miraculous wonders for them, and claim he was the one Lord above all others. Such a powerful, superhuman being could, in other words, before the highly impressionable imagination of the still young human psyche of that time, stand-in and masquerade as the Absolute Power of all creation. And Tradition has been under this spell ever since.[3]

It is important to make again the distinction that the UFO phenomenon so clearly forces upon us, and that is, between the personal God of history and God as the Absolute. The God of history who intervened in our affairs, we now see, was none other than the alien, superhuman being who could easily masquerade as "God" the Absolute Power of the cosmos. It is the other "God" then, if one still finds this word meaningful, that is the "true God"—the "God" of mystics, "God" the Absolute, the Source, the "God" of Creation. "God" is not, then, a personal, intervening Supreme Being, but is one with the Mystery of Being itself.

There is a whole underlying dynamic, hardly explored as of yet by scholars, between the real events of real beings, superhuman in power, who periodically appeared in the sky and descended to Earth and how that impacted the human psyche, especially the human imagination. We must realize how the human psyche had hundreds, if not thousands, of years to mull over spectacular numinous events that took place in its past. We must keep in mind that our mythopoetic powers can elaborate, exaggerate, embellish, *but also deepen,* and that Language itself is a self-dynamic medium, a human mode of Being, that shapes our experience. The great mythologies were founded upon miraculous, yet real, events that were then worked upon by human imagination, transforming them into human cultural forms. The incomprehensible paranormal event in one way or another comes to be assimilated by the human psyche. We have only to consider the beauty and wisdom that is packed into the Old Testament *Psalms* and *Proverbs,* and the dedication to their Lord of prophets/contactees such as Isaiah and Ezekiel, to realize that the human psyche was feverishly working with and assimilating numinous events and bursts of intense, Spirit-powered inspiration. Spirit-powered would here mean that the God(s) were literally speaking through our psyches, as we know the

ETs do telepathically communicate through those they contact. Julian Jaynes has argued as much in his theory of the bicameral mind,[4] that in the distant ancient world individuals literally did hear the "hallucinatory" voices of their Gods speaking directly into their psyches. Though Jaynes, as a good academic scholar, makes no reference at all to alien ET Gods, his thesis sheds uncanny insight into what was taking place psychologically in the early history of our relationship to the Gods. If we go back to Sitchin for a moment, he has said, in fact, that the earliest of ancient, historical peoples did not actually refer to the ETs as Gods in the later Greek sense, but more mundanely as superior, advanced people who came from the sky. Now the Mythos-making that resulted was not a process of falsification (as the contemporary misunderstanding of myth might suggest) so much as a cultivation of the development of the human psyche. By the time of the Roman Empire, however, the Gods had long departed—or, let us say, largely departed—and faded from living memory (legend has it that a lament was supposedly heard throughout the countrysides, *Great Pan is dead*—like today's "God is dead"), so that the myths, retold now as works of artistic imagination—still carrying, though, psychological import, still playing a role in culture—, became effete, became, in other words, in the Christian era, "mere myths," and were routinely stamped out (the suppression of paganism). Yet, it is still not as black-and-white as that—just as today UFO encounters come and go unexpectedly, stories of the Gods—new versions of them—periodically appearing, continued to be reported down through the ages. The ETs were still visiting, but taking on a role that was clearly behind the scenes. In the Hellenistic period before the full glory of Rome unfolded, start-up religions, cults, decadence, world-weariness, people searching and crying out for a Messiah, was rampant: The time was ripe for the Piscean dispensation of a Jesus Christ, a new type of "divine" man.

But let us go back for a moment to the earlier Age of the Gods from the sky. At some point, at the promptings of some trigger (a Spiritual Hierarchy who were other than the Gods?), we rebelled against our slave status. We had become not only intelligent, but more than that, we had been given a taste of Spirit (which will sooner or later come to imply *freedom*, a la Hegel). An Earth-based soul, once having tasted of the Living Water of Spirit (Living=Fire), only yearns for more. This rebellion against our slavehood, thereby against the Gods—or, as the commonly interpreted biblical version has it, against the Lord God—was our Fall, our disobedience, the Original Sin against Divinity. We defied Divinity, that is, the ET Gods who were at that time what we knew of Divinity.

The Gods began to retire from view, but not before they installed a system of human intermediaries to convey their commandments to humanity. Instead of direct rulership of humanity by the Gods, kingship and priesthoods were instituted. In Egypt, it was pharaoh, the priest-king who was the God apparent on Earth. In Mesopotamia, it was the priests who met with and catered to the Gods who would descend atop the sky-reaching ziggurat temples. In other words, only a select individual or a select group was allowed court with the Gods. (We encountered this same theme in our earlier discussion of the emergence of the ego.) In the Old Testament, likewise, not everyone could enter the tent of the Lord, but only the priests. Moses, in particular, was chosen by the Lord, and it was Moses who went up to the mountain to encounter the Lord. We now understand too the meaning of such an age-old phrase as *The divine right of kings*, for originally kings were undoubtedly given their right to rule and command by the Gods. "Royal blood" could literally have meant a select genetic line that eventually went back to the Gods themselves.

The impact of the Gods on the human psyche was profound, and not only in terms of the development of the arts of civilization. To have been abandoned by them had to have had impact too. I find the theme of abandonment by Divinity to be a major racial memory. Also, ancient peoples were so enthralled by the Gods that we find to this day an archetypal human yearning to be like the Gods. The whole theological concept of a monotheistic God infinitely superior, transcendent, impossible to even think of approaching, let alone even forming an adequate conception of, had not yet been developed. That the Gods were essentially a more superior race, apparently in some ways similar to us—as remember, *Genesis* suggests—implied that early humanity was not utterly deluded to think that somehow we could attain their level. This is most evident with the theme of immortality. We have only to consider the elaborate funerary rites that were conducted for the Egyptian pharaoh in order that he could properly attain immortality, or the Sumerian tale of Gilgamesh who vainly sought to live forever, as did the Gods. The Gods, in comparison to the pitifully short human life span—which may very well have been genetically shortened by the Gods, as again *Genesis* suggests—appeared to be immortal. *Appeared to be*, because their life spans were possibly measured in thousands of years, giving them the ability of visiting succeeding generations of humanity. By Greek times, this became the universal epithet of the Gods: *the Immortal Gods*. So, it was an inevitable spiritual inspiration that we, too, wanted immortality. Thus, we find that the theme of immortality is another racial memory that is still psychologically powerful to this day. We can already anticipate the day—they say it is not all that far in the future—when, through Technos, extended longevity will no longer be simply a vain yearning. This, indeed, is one of the drivers of Transhumanism. Still, to this day, we want so much to be like the Gods.

Our psychospiritual evolution occurs in stages. Again, why is that? I will hint at what I intuit as the beginning of an answer. Let us start with a naïve question or two: If the Gods were so powerful, if they were such advanced bioengineers, why didn't they upgrade us all the way? Why didn't they hand to us evolutionary enlightenment on a silver platter? But then, who are we to assume that we were entitled to instant evolutionary fulfillment? Ignoring their own agendas, would they have advanced us to their level, figuratively speaking, overnight? Perhaps Earth-based biology has inherent limitations, beyond which we are no longer human (as we know human existence to be). There would have been no need then for the Great Story of human evolution; but, as we have eventually come to see, this Story is meant to be our destiny. First, it is perhaps true that there is a "Prime Directive" not to spoon-feed fledgling intelligent beings on their respective planets. That is, there are probably certain assumed guidelines in not blatantly interfering in the evolution of others. As we have seen all along, however, that does not imply total non-intervention. The Gods *have* intervened throughout our history, there is no doubt about that. Another suggestion here that we have already explored (and more below) is that the various agendas of different ET Gods does not imply a singular, uniform involvement with humanity. Last, however, the most important metaphysical insight here is that, given the above, there is something inherent in the dense nature of the material plane of existence—which implies our biological being and the nature of an electro-biochemical body, which in turn defines our soul, our psyche, our psychological being in this life—that does not readily transform or evolve by the sheer force of will power alone, nor simply by mere abstract ideas promoted about enlightenment, at least in any short term. Soul enmeshed in matter apparently requires, for collective humanity at least, millennia to evolve, for it requires so much ego development first just to reach the stage of a fully-fledged responsible, ethical, and rational person. Matter, as the old idealists suggested, is congealed Spirit. How, then, to liberate materialized Spirit? But hasn't that always been the big question? Isn't that The Mythos to come?

We *are* in this sense an experiment in evolution on this particular planet, Earth. Within this Earth context, is it possible that a newly bioengineered intelligent being can evolve? (The reincarnation of soul, as an aside, is of course another complicating factor here.) In other words, can we survive and not destroy ourselves and evolve to the point where our science and our spirituality do merge and are able to work together to transform our biological being into a Godlike state? Yes, *like the Gods themselves*. (But as the abrupt climate change doomers say, it is too late for such pipe dreams.)

To be like the Gods themselves. Yes, the new biology will eventually bring us to the point of mastery of our biological being. We will undoubtedly be able some day soon to genetically alter ourselves, and to acquire superhuman capabilities as cyborgs. (Needless to say, for those wealthy enough to "upgrade" themselves.) Can we deny that this is in our future? Would we want to stop it? Secretly, there are many—and let us not be naïve about this—who, on the contrary, yearn for and find it inspiring that someday in the not too far off distant future we will have this option to become transhuman superhuman. The superhuman ETs are indeed showing us our future. But, like them, this stage in our evolution requires a more enlightened encounter with, and relationship to, Spirit. After all, Psyche, Living Image of our Higher Self, the Divine Androgyne, our Divine Archetype, appearing as the possibility of all Divine Forms, reveals to us the protean possibilities inherent in being human—and, in particular, at this point in our discussion, in our very biological being. But what we would see emerge as the coming Singularity spoken of by the Transhumanists will hopefully be heart (soul, being Earth-based) united to mind (Spirit). Otherwise, Transhumanism will imply an AI dominated future.

If astrology is indeed a roadmap of the evolutionary Ages that we must pass through, then indeed there is a metaphysical underpinning to the human Story. Looked at from another angle, however, astrological cycles might be considered another metaphysical level of the bars of our cage. The astral level has woven the Anima Mundi as a Web throughout all levels of existence on Earth. This is where Psyche, revealing our Divinity from beyond the astral plane, would teach us of the Web, and of how thoroughly we, living an Earth-based existence, are woven. Why the actual physical planets of our solar system have anything to do with this (as the conventional scientist scoffs) is, again, of the essence of the metaphysical interconnectedness of all things. Extrapolating as pure speculation here, this would imply that distinctly different astrological cycles and their meanings are in effect in other planetary systems elsewhere in the cosmos. *Our* astrology is therefore utterly Earth-based.

As we look back in history, we see religions, customs, social mores, economics, government/politics, as one interlocking System of guidance, control, manipulation, of harsh oppression even, and a stifling of full human expression. We have only to think of racism and sexism. The Story, as we see, does not unfold as any one clearly or consistently defined agenda (from our limited perspective) on the part of the Gods. There is, first of all, a rivalry among the Gods themselves (as the ancients knew so well), which played out in a schizoid relationship to humanity. There are enlightening forces as well as repressing forces. (UFO/ET encounters indicate that we are consistently visited by different groups or rival factions of Other Intelligence.) Yet, it is not as if we are utterly passive either. Individuals of our human race are also notorious for wanting and demanding and wielding ruthless power. Megalomaniacal rulers, tyrants, despots, and behind-the-scenes secret societies and shadowy groups, all figure into the vicissitudes of this Story. Personal, ego-motivated, power-hungry agendas have so often twisted and distorted spiritual influences, and have often set us back, exploiting and wasting millions of lives. Consider how the Catholic Church built a huge power establishment on the influence of Jesus. I am not suggesting any outright evil intent here by the Church, but the Church was certainly a major force in this control system with both human and non-human players. (This again is indicated by the Jupiter influence of the Piscean Age.) But behind-the-scenes conspiracies go as far back as history itself. Control and power have long been the name of the game on this planet. However, there is one more crucial factor that drives history forward—something in us, that spark of Spirit (with Divine, ET God, inspiration), that drives us to express our potential, that drives us to evolve, that drives us to expand into the higher levels of Spirit and hopefully, eventually, out into the larger cosmos.

We can begin to see then that the relationship of the ET Gods to us was quite complex, implying, again, that different ET groups were undoubtedly involved. But one constant in our relationship to the Gods remained throughout: It was always a one-way relationship; it was not a dialogue between equals. The Gods, and then "God," imposes a Divine will upon us: The Other has always dictated to us its commandments, its dogmas, its taboos, without us being in any position to directly question the Other in turn. We were not the equal of the Gods—they came and went—entered and departed our Human Reality—at will; it was not the reverse. We had no real capability of responding to them on their level in this relationship. What we did have as a second best was the cultivation of inner dialogue ("talking with God"), prayer, sacrifice, and ritual, which have always had, though, an uncertain outcome with regard to the Gods. But, again, though prayer may not have always reached, had an audience with, the Gods, or "God," it did contact in this oblique way a higher level of consciousness (Higher Self) and so helped us in developing our inner life, an inner culture, an inner art of manifesting. Prayer, too, is another way of talking about contacting the Higher Self and initiating the process of manifestation. (The power of mass prayer for manifesting change in the world is being called upon all the time now in some sectors of the New Age global community.)

Let us look further at the deeper Story of history. In the early tribal phase of the historical period of our psychospiritual evolution, our consciousness had not yet consolidated around a centralized ego. Consciousness was dispersed, as it were, in a multiplicity of directions in response to a multiplicity of Gods or Powers (polytheism). A general psychological tenet—we can also consider it a metaphysical one—is that consciousness is always attracted to power, however that power appears. Whether that power (mana) is an expression of something magnificent and great and good or something evil and violent (and all gradations in between), consciousness makes a beeline to encounter it, or is forced to react to it, as in the case of danger where we must physically fight or flee. Now Judaism during the Age of Aries signaled a change was occurring in consciousness, specifically, that the ego was beginning to consolidate as a unity, by its attraction to the Power of a one Lord "God." A one, unifying ego was falling under the spell of the one Lord "God"; later, Christians would refer to the Father. The ego was realizing the self-conscious stage of having an identity, unconsciously modeled on a one "God." Jesus, who claimed a personal relationship to the Father, then augured the Piscean Age development of full subjectivity—the full-fledged person. What Jesus, a man—an alien-human hybrid most likely—, had (a relationship to the Father), we likewise could have by allowing Jesus to step-in as our link to Father ET (who was in turn to become a stand-in for the Absolute, which, from our New Age perspective implies standing-in for the Higher Self). And so we find that the ego learned how to develop defenses, with its single-minded focus on Christ—actually the Christ archetype emerging into consciousness—, against the inner world of a polytheistic soul (the astral-psychic plane with its multiplicity of beings, including Other-dimensional ETs). The ego was now to follow in the footsteps of Christ, especially the sufferings of Christ. Islam stepped around a need for an intermediary Christ—Allah was apparently sufficient for this single-minded focus. Over the centuries the ego grew in strength and expanded its dominion over our psyche in the Light of a monotheistically-oriented Spirit—that is, Spirit acting through the Jesus Image/Christ archetype, pointing, in turn, as Islam directly did, to the one, abstract "God." It is ironic, however, that the Light of Jesus that had come into the world to bring Light to the world was followed, historically, by the Dark Ages. (The Piscean contrariness once again.)

By the late Middle Ages, especially by Renaissance times, the Virgo undercurrent of the Piscean Age began to tangibly reply to the Piscean dispensation. The sign Virgo is service oriented, like Pisces, but, whereas Pisces denotes universal service to the Otherworldly, to "God," Virgo is personal and Earth-based, and seeks perfection in skills and material matters as service. Once again, we find the thread of scholarly monks and alchemists becoming inspired with a Vision of humankind perfecting itself on the material plane. So the ego began to focus on material concerns, but since it lost the old soul (polytheistic) connection to Earth, these material concerns were ego-centered, an ego already inflating itself with the Vision of an all-powerful "God" who controlled all things. "God" was the Master Clockmaker, and if we could but understand how this clock, which was Nature, worked, we, too, could become all-powerful—and so Technos was born. The rise of modern science—the dissection and analysis of Nature (Wordsworth's poetic line comes to mind, *We murder to dissect*)—, allowing for the birth of Technos, forced Nature into the position of merely being at the service of our human needs. Science, eventually becoming the handmaiden of Technos, became therefore not so much contemplation of cosmos for its own sake (as with the Greeks in the Libran phase of the Arian Age), but had become more of a means: *What can I do with it?* The outer world, for one thing, was to be conquered. The scant record we have from medieval and

Renaissance times of UFOs and visitation by the Other often reveals a scientifically-directed influence from them at work. Reports of luminous beings appearing to the early modern alchemist-scientists often tell of these beings encouraging them in their research. What these visitors often said in so many words was, *You are on the right track. Keep going.*

Our modern Virgoan response to the original Piscean dispensation has turned just about everything into this materialistically-oriented service mode. The universal, God-directed, service of Pisces did a turnabout—now every particular thing on the material plane was taxed into service. How could animals and plants be of service to the human ego? How could the resources of Earth be of service to the human ego? How could others who share this planet with us be of service to the ego—by becoming a labor force. And what must the ego itself do, what training must take place, in order to be of service in the modern world? We thus witness the rise of the modern worker, the great mass of humanity turned into a labor market. Ironically, we still find ourselves in the position that the Annunaki Gods had created for us—socially, the great majority of humanity are here in this life to be workers. But, perhaps, *this* New Age will promise something far more than that.

Which brought us to the 20th Century: Since the old "God" is effectively dead, that is, has no role in our Postmodern world, Technos has become our alter ego God. And Technos has allowed us to create weapons that can now bring about our own collective demise. Technos does not intend on our (premature) demise, however, but Technos is still politically in the hands of the collective, unevolved soul. The dropping of the atomic bomb and the quickly following development afterward of the hydrogen bomb were without a doubt the major events of the mid-20th Century. (The Moon landing some years later, though significant, had not the same major collective impact.) The Mushroom Cloud quickly became a dominant cultural icon that had great impact on many of us as children. And now let us note this time sequence: 1945, the first atomic bombs were detonated; 1947, the "modern" period of UFOs clearly began. Suddenly, they were unbelievably appearing to thousands in our skies. Other Intelligence knew that we had entered a dangerous, critical phase in our civilization. They knew that Postmodern humanity was creating rapid changes on the planet. The Gods had decided to show themselves once again.

Overnight, some years back, an uncanny revelation occurred for me: It was no coincidence that my Vision of Psyche hovering in an enormous Fountain over Monterey Bay had an iconographic similarity to the Mushroom Cloud. That monstrous, terrifying image of death and annihilation that had gone so deep inside of my psyche as a child was now transformed, so many years later, into my Vision of Psyche rising out of the dark depths of Monterey Bay...the saving power that was the new Divinity of Psyche rising into the open Air for all. Remember the lines of the poet Hölderlin: *Where danger is / grows the saving power also.*

What we can always question, though, is the will and wisdom of the Gods. Why have the ET Gods allowed for so much suffering on this planet? It is the old theological, Sunday homily about the mysterious ways of God (e.g. Why does God allow the little child to die?), but with a new twist: Now that we are addressing not some infinitely remote, transcendent, abstract Deity, but superhuman ET beings who can appear as physical as you and me, we can pose this question in a more poignant way. Why did the ETs allow World War II (or any war for that matter) to take place? We have heard it said that this is a free will planet, that we are fundamentally on our own (again, the so-called Prime Directive). That, as we saw, is not as simple as it sounds—they *have* intervened at various times. However, it has been suggested that by and large the ETs are not especially concerned with the fate of individuals per se or the human drama vicissitudes of traditional war and suffering, so much as with the Big Picture of humankind itself, where we as a species—Earthlings—are headed. They appear to be supremely concerned with the long-term agenda of human survival. Which is why they have appeared in our skies so regularly since the mid-20th Century, because the Bomb inaugurated a whole new dangerous phase of our Story. As for occasionally aiding individuals, it appears that only if it serves a larger purpose do the

ETs step in, as we sometimes hear of an alien abductee who is singled out for special treatment regarding his or her well-being (health). Of course, we must keep in mind the long-term genetic program of human-alien hybrids and what this might imply.

This is a free will planet—and yes, according to our everyday ego-self, it seems to be. (The whole notion of free will is a philosophically slippery one, though, which would have to be more fully explored.) Honestly, though, I do not put much stock in appeals to "free will" to genuinely solve our problems, our contemporary crisis; it certainly has not worked yet. The context of free will decision-making is primarily the individual and small groups of individuals, such as we find in communes; in the collective sense, in mass society, it is almost impossible to pin down what exactly is meant by the "free will" of a people. Who decides the "free will" of a people? The President (with an alleged mandate, but then a puppet of powerful elites / the military-industrial complex)? Is it some other official body? Is it the Federal Reserve? The shadow government? The Establishment mass media owned by big corporations? Masses of television-conditioned individuals trapped in their cars on the congested freeways? Is collective free will expressed in the voting booth? Is this a joke? Will it eventually be Technos—the new AI God—who decides our so-called "free will"? (I hope that these questions are not construed as an excuse for apathy.)

My point is, I do not believe that the Gods are simply sitting idly by and watching us exercise our collective "free will." If that were the case, then I do believe we face real catastrophe. So this raises the theological issue again, that we do have a right to question the ways of the Gods. We do have a right to question why they have tolerated such enormous suffering on this planet. Or worse—as certain evidence appears to indicate, some among them have actually been the instigators of our suffering. (Keep in mind what the ancients recorded. Conspiracy research has had much to go on here.) And might the answer of the Gods be that in the cosmic scale of things, in the Grand Cosmic Plan, where Earth is but a speck within the whole, but one small planet among possibly millions of other intelligent life planets, that what has happened and might happen on this planet has happened and is happening on these millions of other planets before and now? That is to say, can we on Earth claim to be uniquely special, the center of all evolutionary action? But then, would this relativistic position not be unlike saying that the silent "God," the "God" who died, the "God" who abandoned us, perhaps moved on to focus "His" divine attention elsewhere? So, are we fundamentally on our own or not?

Our Earth, as I had suggested earlier, is a cosmic experiment in evolution in which another form that Intelligence takes—aka human intelligence—is challenged to manifest its full, divine potential. But this cosmic experiment in evolution is not simply for individuals existentially alone. Too often the view taken of soul, said to be here to learn lessons on Earth, is thought of in a strictly personal, egocentric way. Aquarius, remember, connotes individuality within *community*. The individual truly has a place and responsibility in the community. Despite the propaganda in recent decades about looking out for Number One, and *You can have it all*, grabbing whatever it is we want (still today consumerism and materialism are as rampant as ever) at the expense of others, *we are* responsible to the human family. For we must realize the interwovenness of us all on this planet. We are equally here to help one another, to improve life for one another, and to alleviate suffering. Our "free will" is not exemplified by our choosing whatever we want in the marketplace, be it goods, property, career, success, investments, even a mate, but by our choosing to fulfill the Calling of what is greater than us. Free will is ultimately the decision to open to Spirit and to align ourselves with what Spirit wants of us.

Aquarius will be taking the original Piscean ideals of peace and love to another level, where the Higher Self comes into play. *For the sake of community. For the sake of the human family.*

Is the ego-self sufficiently strong and self-assured by now to face the ET Gods? Some may think that this is overly optimistic. The great masses of humanity are probably still not ready. (This is one of the reasons given why a cover-up is still in place regarding the ET presence, and perhaps why the ETs themselves have an almost universal policy of secrecy.) Keep in mind that we are speaking here of renewing a relationship to a multiplicity of Powers—many Intelligences. Human consciousness will once again encounter this multiplicity, the return to a polytheistic-like scenario, but at a higher level than that of the ancient world, as the astral-psychic plane breaks through the Veil into a highly ego-conscious awareness. Are we—or at least some of us—, with our fully developed egos, now strong enough to withstand the impact of this encounter? But, remember, there is more: It is not the ego alone any longer, but the Higher Self revealing the Living Image of our Guide who will lead the ego to the realization of multidimensional Selfhood. What is showing itself outwardly—UFOs appearing in our skies, ET encounters, the signature of Other Intelligence, such as in the crop circles—mirrors the shift that is taking place in consciousness. A multiplicity of Intelligences mirroring the multiple, multidimensional New Self. With this consciousness raising, as it were, we are now at the point of asking for a two-way relationship with the Gods. This is the CE-5 initiative we have spoken about earlier. Hopefully we are now ready to face the Gods once again and ask that we be treated equally as an intelligent race that is truly attempting to graduate from our previous lessons. At the very least, that there are those of us on the Path who feel that *we are* ready—individually, we have been preparing ourselves for a destiny that implies an ongoing dialogue with Them.

But lest we lose sight of where we are today, let me present a variation on the possible scenario of what this 21st Century we have now fully entered will entail. And let us be honest, it is not sweetness and light. It is the shadow that has been dogging us all along: Earth, as the evidence gathered by thousands of scientists worldwide is showing us, is in deep trouble. We are heading for catastrophic climate change; in fact, the collapse of civilization may only be a mere few decades away, with the extinction of not only a great portion of the biosphere, but of most of humanity. The panic and the chaos—the mass suffering—that would unfold in society is beyond comprehension today. Others have also said that humanity—now at over 7 billion—has taxed Earth beyond Her ability to sustain us. As we know, a taboo topic in public discourse is this theme of over-population. It is thought that the majority of humanity by the end of the 21st Century (if humanity survives to that time) will be living like the masses of the destitute do today on the streets of India. That is, if ecological collapse does not produce radical population reduction before then. We know by now there is a Secret Government, a global elite, with Secret Controllers behind the scenes that manipulate politics and world trends. Richard Dolan speaks about a secret Breakaway Civilization that is already preparing for End Times on planet Earth, with a plan to migrate into space, perhaps, to Mars.

We are also aware of the ET Greys, with a possible one hive agenda working in unison, and their abduction program that centers on a human-alien hybrid breeding program. We are aware that the ETs, as with any being that can access and master the astral-psychic plane, can see into the future. They are profoundly more aware of where we are headed than we ourselves are, at this time. Those of us who have kept abreast of the UFO picture feel that on many levels the ETs are conditioning us into this radically different future, slowly influencing whole new cultural memes and trends. We are also aware of the conspiracy research that claims that the Secret Government is already in contact with particular ET groups, such as the ET Greys and/or Reptilians. If there is indeed any basis for this, then the Greys have probably conveyed to key players in the Secret Government what they already know of future trends. Now let us also add that there are noisy rumors of Secret Controller plans for a New World Order, to be materially put into place by all the latest technologies of Technos, and in principle inspired by the one hive organization of the Greys. The Greys, in other words, may indeed be showing us our future—*in their image*. With human-alien hybrids being groomed for integration into society, perhaps into a world with a much harsher, climate-changed and radioactive environment, we see then a possible, other picture unfolding. In so many subtle ways, civilization may slowly be undergoing a conditioning program that keeps it on track in the direction of this scenario. (Consider also, as we did earlier, the techno-wizards gearing up society for a brave new AI, cyborg, and android populated world.) On the surface, in the political/international arena, the rationale of those in power will always be, *We are doing this for the sake of National Security. We are doing this for the planet. We are doing this for our survival. Only allow us more power and more control if you wish to see future generations alive on this Earth.* Meaning, from the point of view of the Greys, that *if you want some remnant of the human race to survive, then we are your model, we know what you must do. And we are doing much of the work for you already—we are already preparing a new hybrid race for this planet once catastrophe really does unfold.*

This may be the future that some UFO researchers have expressed fear of. And given the forces behind it, what realistically could be done about it? Is this the New Age evolutionary intention? Certainly, Aquarian themes are found in it. Or is the future still one of another, a greater evolutionary, spiritual potential? Is a Spiritual Hierarchy with our best, highest interests in mind working beyond these more alarming and fearful scenarios? Given the potential catastrophe of radical Earth changes, is there any detectable hint that Earth, that some remnant of life and humanity, will be protected?

Spirit is our saving power. All the more then that we should be open to the new spiritual dispensation of the Higher Self. All the more then that we should claim our right to be co-creatively conversant with Spirit. All the more then that we should allow Psyche to meet the challenge of Technos. Other Intelligence appears in many forms. Evidence shows that the Greys and their possible masters (some say the Reptilians) are not the only visitors to this planet. And it is not definitive what the Greys are ultimately intending, to begin with. The scenario presented above may have it all wrong concerning them (as it was only a possible, hypothetical scenario). And their timeframe is certainly different than ours. We at one time wanted so much to be like the Gods, who the Greys obviously do not appear to be at all. The ancients certainly idolized the Gods as far more (super-)human-like. From all the evidence coming in, the old Gods who are other than the Greys do appear to be making their presence known again. Perhaps it is the Nordic type of ET that may very well represent what the ancients knew as the Gods of old. Perhaps they will remain behind the scenes for a while still, as they have for ages, showing just enough of themselves to inspire us, to let us know that they are near. That is to say, for those of us who are not in denial. For those of us who are open to knowing Them. Perhaps, too, the old Gods and Goddesses were shapeshifters, as they must have known of the Higher Self potential for shape shifting. And, again, it may very well be that even higher dimensional beings, on ever-higher spiritual levels, are ultimately our agents of evolutionary inspiration. It is, to say the least, a very complex picture.

We now come to realize that the Higher Self must indeed become our Guide. The Higher Self now defines for us a new teleology for human evolution. Perhaps we are destined not to become "God" in the monomaniacal sense of contemporary Technos, but perhaps individual Divine Beings in the manner of the Gods. As in the manner of Psyche who, once-upon-a-time in the ancient Eros and Psyche story, became divine. As the once-upon-a-time mortal Earthlings we are, sometime in the far future—the far distant Aquarian future of 2,000 years?—might we be destined to become immortal and divine? As Gaia-born and Gaia-nurtured beings, with all the unique implications that that might come to entail, to become Gods in our own right, we will someday be able to traverse the galaxy, and even more—the entire universe…*like the Gods*. Do we, too, not have a destiny among the stars? And soul will have realized itself at that point as Soul/Spirit in an alchemical Marriage of such magnificence. Hopefully, it is the best in us, the Earthling, that is able to evolve to that point. Are the great masses of humanity today ready for this? Obviously not. This all sounds more like far out science fiction. But those on the Path will come to realize that *they* are ready to take the next baby steps. They are ready for the *Next Act*.[5]

We are now on the threshold of consciously co-creating our own evolution.[6] Are we Gods-to-be in some far-off time, in the making?

—*Only if we fully realize what we are capable of—that soul is our potential-to-be and our potential-to-become all that Spirit eventually reveals to us.*

## We, The Aquarians

*All that is hidden is to be revealed*

We, the Aquarians, Water Bearers of a new Millennium,
    we pour forth all that was hidden, repressed & forgotten
    in the Waters of Pisces.
We pour forth the ancient archaic occult wisdom two thousand years
    hidden & repressed in the self-forgetting Waters of Pisces.
We pour forth two thousand years of suppressed Goddess pagan
    Earth-born wisdom of soul flowing centuries underground
    in the self-denying Christian & Islamic Waters of Pisces.

    Into Air
    we pour
    astrology, Kabbalah, tarot, numerology, alchemy, geomancy,
    divination, dowsing, witchcraft, magic, all the old lore

    What was hidden        What is hidden

        *Into Air*
            *we pour*

We pour forth our heretofore untold academic-obliterated history,
    our come-to-light alien/ET origins, obscured dawn-of-history
    Bible-condensed & distorted stories of super-beings who birthed
    our civilizations & through the Ages watched over us, guided us,
    & surreptitiously controlled us.
We pour forth all divine Revelations of all times & places—
    Lao Tzu, sages Hindu, Krishna, Buddha, Hermes Thrice Greatest,
    Abraham, Moses, Jesus, Mohammed, of Zen, Sufi, Gnostic,
    Ascended Masters—all teachings brought forth & freed

of dogma-adulterated Piscean faith Waters to pour forth anew
into Air transformed through Vision.
We pour forth native tradition wisdom of peoples who mysteriously
disappeared or were genocide slaughtered & wiped out,
but a remnant surviving sharing protectively old tribe riches.

Into Air
we pour
all the old stories/legends/epics/myths/poems/prophecies
of Sumerians, Egyptians, Babylonians, Chinese, Indians,
Tibetans, Hebrews, Greeks, Persians, Romans, of Christians
& Muslims, of Celts & Druids, Incas, Mayans, Aztecs, Hopi,
of Africans & Polynesians & Australian Aborigines…

All that was hidden/is hidden
revealed to us
we reveal
pouring forth

pouring secrets
of Sphinx, Stonehenge, Nazca, of pyramids Egypt & Mexico,
of ziggurats, temples, pueblos, serpent & sacred mounds,
mysterious stone monoliths & petroglyphs of silent testimony.

From the Waters
into Air

We, the Aquarians, we pour forth exposing conspiracies & agendas
& behind-the-scenes controlling powers threading through the Ages,
of priesthoods, dynasties, churches, bankers, of secret societies
& secret orders & secret governments, whomever are secret
Controllers of this Earth.
We pour forth naming names, in Brotherhoods, in Vatican, Masons
& Freemasons, Knights Templar & Rosicrucians, in the so-called

Illuminati, in Round Table, Jesuits & JASONS, Skull & Bones,
in Bilderbergers, Club of Rome, in the Council on Foreign Relations,
Trilateral Commission, the Federal Reserve, in the legendary MJ-12.
We pour forth from the self-destructive Waters of Pisces cover-ups
& lies about Vietnam, Kennedy assassination, radiation given
to guinea pig civilians, about depopulation long-term plans,
about vaccines, AIDS, bio-engineered plague, Gulf War syndrome,
government drug trade, 9/11 inside job war on terror conspiracy,
false flag operations, chemtrails in our skies / geoengineering
to alter the planet, climate change denial, HAARP, GMOs,
government surveillance, SmartGrid ulterior motives, MK-ULTRA
& covert mind control, & the deadly destiny of Fukushima.
We pour forth our investigations into Roswell, UFOs & ETs visiting,
into alien contact/encounters/abductions, animal mutilations,
into crop circles & pictograms, black helicopters, alien technology,
underground bases, Montauk, Area 51, into anomalies of Moon
& Mars, of what was found & not told.

Cover-ups, lies, disinformation, media manipulation & fabrication
perpetrated by every Administration, Air Force, NASA, FEMA,
FDA, Robertson Panel, Condon Report, DOD, CIA, DIA, DNI,
FBI, NSA, NSC, NRO, the BATF.

We dive into the obscuring Waters
    of Pisces,
        the illusion confusing
& dissimulating Neptunian Waters
    of Pisces—
We bring up to share

              into Air

        into Light

    for all to see

We, the Aquarians, we pour forth our cutting edge research
    unrecognized, inventions & devices government suppressed,
    lone heroes of new energy manifesting the hyperdimensional,
    & higher vibrational masters who work outside Establishments
    of medicine, institutions & schools that purposely or unwittingly
    promote the Plan of the secret controller elites.
We pour forth our dreams, our visions & inspirations & breakthroughs
    of insight, our psychic healings & precognitions, our close encounters
    with Other Intelligences, our out-of-body & near-death experiences,
    other-dimensional beings & group minds channeled & remote viewing
    present, past & future.
We pour forth our Shadows, complexes, vulnerabilities, subpersonalities,
    the voices within us, giving them the voice of new wholeness,
    inner to become outer, liberating the too long self-undermining
    & self-contradictory Waters of Pisces.
We pour forth the Living Image of Higher Self Divine, transpersonal,
    trans-temporal, outside world, shapeshifting mystical Form of all
    the forms we are, the Fountain of Unlimited Creativity we step into,
    Fire & Water we pour, the Uranian lightning Idea shattering
    old boundaries & seed planting the New Self.

    We drink of the Fountain
    of Living Waters
    deep in ourselves,
    our boundless creativity
    pouring forth,
    our endless revealing
        of what
            is revealed

            to us

        as new Revelation

We, the Aquarians, we pour forth our friendship, love of humanity,
>   our caring & compassion in a biochip love-lacking world, building
>   our grassroot communities of Spirit, distrusting the centralized,
>   hierarchical, mind-controlling, secret agenda, One World Order,
>   the obsolete of paradigms the elites still hold on to.

>   Into Air

We pour forth *our* communication, *our* truth, *our* interconnectedness,
>   the co-creative supreme Art of new Mythos we pour, pouring,
>   pouring, out of the universal, Spirit-inspired, visionary imaginative,
>   *Yes*, the Waters of Pisces.

>   All that is hidden
>   we reveal

>       we bring to Light

We, the Aquarians of Air, we pour forth
>   the mystical Waters

>           of Pisces


>   *All that is hidden is to be revealed*

>       No more secrets

1997

# ( 14 )

# WE POUR FORTH

Let us take one, last, spiral turn in our Story by returning to the Aquarian Water Bearer and exploring more fully what it entails. The Water Bearer, as we remember, has dipped an urn into the Waters and is now pouring those Waters into the open Air for all. It is the Air of open, free, communication. The Air of dialogue. The Air of mind that sees, and in that seeing, *knows*. The Waters represent all that has been hidden. What has been hidden implies that we, in one way or another, have been living an illusion, and perhaps it has been a grand Delusion spanning centuries. After all, these Piscean Waters were Neptunian, the planet that epitomizes illusion, and delusion. Psyche, the Divine Androgyne, the new Image of the archetype of Self, as the Water Bearer, shows us what we must do. Psyche has taken concrete spiritual forms (the urn) and shows us how the hidden is to be revealed—the new forms of culture (Mythos) that we are to birth. When we are at-one-with Psyche, through our own gnosis, then we are playing the role of Water Bearer—we, representatives of universal humanity. We are then doing the pouring *from* Psyche, that is, Spirit's Form (for this next Age) of all forms (the Urn of all urns), which, again, is *the new Mythos—The Mythos*. And it will undoubtedly be an endless revealing.

We must keep in mind that Psyche is always already there, ahead of us. If we take the ancient myth of Eros and Psyche seriously, then Psyche is an accurate beacon of our future. She was once mortal, like us; through a process of self-discovery, she became Divine. *Humanity is therefore destined in some futurity to become Divine.* If we consider Psyche as being the Living Image of our Higher Self, then, again, Psyche is already there for us. We saw that the Higher Self comes-to-us from outside the limitations of the bubble of our 3rd-dimensional Human

Reality. The Higher Self, higher in the spectrum of consciousness than the astral-psychic, embraces—comprehends—past, present, and future, in a transtemporal Now. Psyche, in other words, in broad outline, knows our future, knows where we are headed. Psyche, therefore, is our Guide, showing us the way through the Labyrinth.

What this also means for us individually is that whatever we suffer, Psyche has suffered it before us. Psyche has been there. Psyche knows what suffering is, but Psyche has already transformed that suffering. In a sense—a sense potentially made concrete rather than abstract, implying an existential realization on our part—, Psyche has already done it for us.

We pour forth. What is to be poured forth? All that is hidden. What is hidden? The wisdom of the ancients is hidden, but today it is being revealed. The secrets of our origins and of peoples buried in prehistory have been hidden, but today they are being rediscovered and revealed. The secrets of the Great Pyramids, the Sphinx, of Stonehenge, of Nazca, of hundreds of temples and sacred sites worldwide, are today all being rediscovered, and their secrets are coming to be revealed.

Soul, hidden in its own Waters, is being revealed. All that had been kept in the Dark is being revealed. It is all coming out today, however we might interpret it: all our complexes, fears, desires, subpersonalities, inner voices, hang-ups, racial memories, cellular memories, all are coming out of hiddenness, and through our creative efforts we will provide the necessary and appropriate spaces for all of them in everyday life. Everything is coming out of the proverbial closet.

Soul has been traditionally associated with the feminine. So we see that women have also been pouring forth what has been hidden about them, their influence in history, their unacknowledged contributions. And all the oppression, injustice, inequality, all the suffering they have had to bear in a dominator society. All that they have had to stuff inside themselves. All that they have wanted to say. All that they have wanted to do. And the same goes for all forms of racism.

All the suffering on this Earth will be poured into the open Air. All the sexism, racism, all the oppression, all the injustice, all the crimes against humanity—all to be poured into the open Air. All the cries of the victims of abuse, violence, of hatred, torture, and war will be revealed. All who have met with tragic misfortune. Those who have suffered will not be forgotten. The Story of all who have suffered for being human will be told in the open Air.

And there is so much more to pour forth and reveal—secrets long hidden away from us by secret societies, the Secret Government, the Secret Controllers. Secrets hidden from us by any number of government agencies. Conspiracies kept in place to ensure that humanity remained enslaved and blind to the truth of our Higher Self. All these secret, Illuminati, New World Order, conspiratorial groups are hereby put on notice: The sign Aquarius is not a keeper of secrets. On the contrary, the Aquarian motto is rather: *No more secrets. Everything is to be revealed.*

And a broad range of researchers today are investigating secrets of all kinds: the cover-up regarding UFOs and the alien presence, of mind control projects and our own civilians used as guinea pigs in any number of projects; and other projects such HAARP, geoengineering aka chemtrails, biological warfare agendas; and then cover-ups regarding the Kennedy assassination, AIDS, the Gulf War Syndrome, and above all 9/11. The 9/11 Truth Movement is exactly an example of Aquarian revealing. And then, what is going on in the massive underground facilities at various locations around the country? What is it that NASA doesn't want us to know about regarding what was found on the Moon and on Mars? What are the Secret Controllers planning for the populations of Earth? What is already known about the future impact of global warming, better yet, abrupt climate disruption? Or how geoengineering our atmosphere is making it worse? Is Earth's biosphere truly dying? Again, I pose these questions not as if all or any of this is going to be revealed overnight, or anytime soon. But the Aquarian intention is clear, and that is, that a greater openness, what is called transparency, about all things previously hidden will become the rallying cry as more and more people wake up. And as more people access the psychic plane, the more potential there is for perceiving what had been hidden. As more individuals in the future, as one example, become adept at remote viewing, potentially nothing can be kept utterly secret.

Naturally not everyone engaged in the above-mentioned endeavors of scholarship, research, and investigation will see it in the context of the Big Picture of the New Age, or would even think of associating it with the New Age movement. Many pursue their work strictly out of what interests them, or because of what they find themselves called to do, or are gifted at. But the Big Picture is there nonetheless, and whether they acknowledge it or not, they all play a role in this process of pouring forth.

But Reality will no longer appear as we knew it. For the world we are increasingly entering, at the same time that we are pouring forth, is not one in which "truth" is "out there" only waiting to be plucked. As the Next Level breaks into our world, Reality will no longer have the stability of simple location anymore. Even in matters that should appear to be straightforward, we may find no "final" truth to get at. Our pouring forth, we must realize, is an ongoing process requiring creative effort—what we will be concerned with is how well we can tell the Story from our own seeing, from our own gnosis. As I said above, it is an endless revealing.

All of us who consider ourselves the Aquarians, we will pour forth our insights, inspirations, visions, realizations, discoveries, our new friendships of like minds, our liberating new inventions, our apprenticeship to higher dimensional energies, our super-creative works. We will pour forth our dialogue with The Other.

The Air of open communication. The Air of Mind liberated to think and manifest in ways never before dreamed of. To push the boundaries of Human Reality. When this Vision of a New Age is fully seen for oneself, one cannot help but realize that we have lived as if behind the bars of a cage by our conditioning, our taboos, our dogmas, by the various social and spiritual control systems that Tradition had set in place. But it is time we throw open the doors to our cages. It is time we begin to learn how to live outside of cages. In the open Air, the more will minds unite behind Aquarian ideals of freedom and independence from conditioning and dogma, and the ideal of true

Higher Self-defined individuality. The revolutionary, breaking out of convention and seeing a larger picture, is the Uranian-inspired Aquarian.

And we will take a new, individualized pride in realizing our unlimited creative Self, for this is our Leo undercurrent, human response to Spirit's Aquarian dispensation. Through guidance, we will find our way through the Labyrinth and we will reach the Fountain. The Living Fountain. The Fountain of Fire and Water. And we will taste of its illumined Waters and realize that this is what we have always yearned for. And the figure hovering in the Fountain is none other than our Guide, inviting us to step into the Fountain, to step into its up-rushing flow, and be who we always already potentially were—there, in the Fountain. But we need to do the work, the co-creative, transformational work, to manifest such multidimensional potential. So, we will step into the Fountain and join Psyche and realize ourselves living daily in its flow of Unlimited Creativity. It is what I call *super-creativity*.

We, the New Age Aquarians, represent a new loyalty. Beyond family, beyond faction or political party, beyond our local membership group, beyond loyalty to country, we are first and foremost loyal to universal humanity, to all the human family. What this means is that if family, if any group, if any Authority, is resistant or counter to the evolutionary intention of the new dispensation, then we must have the courage to break away and forsake that which would hold us back. And that is, because we dedicate our lives to a Vision that benefits all from the perspective of Spirit, even if others cannot yet see it. We dedicate our lives to a Vision that is respectful of Earth, that honors Earth, and all of Her creatures. And this Vision shows us that each must be given the opportunity of realizing what it is that he or she is called to do.

Let us be clear about it: The New Age, at least the near future of this new Aquarian Age, is not a Golden Age stroll through a rose garden. The future may very well be catastrophic in any of the various scenarios we have touched upon. And dates will always be offered for some Big Event, some tipping point, some definitive moment when the New, or when chaos, breaks open. The end of the Mayan calendar year 2012 was believed by some to have been that threshold of unfolding prophecy. And as so many ask today, *What will it take for us to change?* A major disaster? Abrupt climate change? Open ET contact? A technological Singularity? But we should not feel immobilized and live in anxiety or dread because of predictions or prophecies of coming trials, disasters, or doom, even if it looks like the appearance of End Times. Yes, an Age *is* ending. There may indeed be horrendous, inevitable birth pangs coming. However the near future unfolds, the New Age beginning will announce at the same time the birth of a humanity such as we have not yet known. But I, myself, am not idly waiting around for that day. Whatever may come, *a Vision is here, now.* I am living it today.

The danger calls forth the saving power—Spirit. *Spirit is again speaking to us.*

The New Age Vision *is Vision*—the ability to see. The New Age Vision is all-comprehensive, for we realize that nothing can be left out of the Big Picture. *We are* entering a New Age where the game rules of Reality itself will of necessity come to be rewritten. And it will not be the previously popular "New Age" pipedream of some overnight enlightenment for all, but will only be another step toward that far-off place. But another collective lesson. Hopefully, this book itself, the Story I have begun to tell, has done its part in the unfolding of The Mythos. The complete Mythos to be told is a very complex, wondrous, exhilarating-to-behold, Reality-expanding Story. I believe that more will take up the challenge to tell it, and to live it.

Let us realize this: There is more happening on this planet today than most people realize. If one only follows the Establishment media and its portrayal of current events, it might seem that everything significant that takes place on our Earth is out in the public and well known. Tragedies happen, scandals happen, politics happens, wars happen, business happens, new scientific and technological developments are reported every day…life goes on. Yet, with thousands of lone individuals and little groups and behind-the-scenes research teams and networks and alliances worldwide, there is such a transformational ferment; but the casual eye simply doesn't see it. Earth's mind sphere is not mono-dimensional; multi-leveled, multidimensional activities are underway somewhere on our planet all the time. I find myself continuously awed by such splendor that as of yet has not fully realized itself as a New Age consciousness.

For those of us who have already awakened to the dispensation of this New Age, let us be honest about it, and take courage in saying it—*we are on a mission.* And our Guidance for this mission is Spirit revealing to us our own Divine Selfhood. And Others who are present among us have come once again to help us take the next step.

There are those of us who believe that we are living in a time of crossing a Threshold—

I believe we are about to encounter a community of Cosmic Intelligences.

I am open to it. I am prepared for it. I am not afraid of a future shared with Others.

Earth is about to step onto the stage of the galaxy. *Are we ready?* Here it comes—

A step, a shift, a moment transformed,

then another, and another…

You see, we have crossed the Threshold—

## A New Age Prayer

Psyche, Spirit of Higher Self,
allow me to fulfill what I am called to do
    in this life,
help me to see my place in the Whole,
and reveal to those of us prepared
the Vision of our working together
for the good of all
        on this,
our so very precious Earth.

June 2005

# Addendum 1: New Age Music

Shouldn't I say something about New Age music? We realize that it is a music genre that is culturally low profile and that never really gets much play on the airwaves. For many people, it is as if it doesn't exist—that is to say, if they recognize it at all, they consider New Age music simply boring, or, let us say, unexciting. To me, however, it is exactly the opposite—it is music I can listen to continuously for hours. Variations of it will be called by different names: mystic, visionary, electronic space, atmospheric, or ambient music, techno-ambient, or psychedelic; some of it blends into world fusion. Almost every coffeehouse we walk into today is filled with pop music of one kind or another; if I owned a café, it would undoubtedly be filled with all varieties of the New Age genre. The ethereal, hauntingly angelic space so much of it opens up is actual balm and true inspiration for the soul. As the drift of our Story consistently tried to convey, this is not merely metaphor for an abstract "soul"; it is the very real impact upon our very real mode of Being that is soul.

More could be said about all New Age art, but that is for another time.

# Addendum 2: The MYTHOS Project

*The Mythos: The Story of our Divinity coming-into Human Reality.*

Numerous times throughout this work I've made mention of The Mythos, always implying by that The Mythos that is to come. As a matter of fact, I have begun a project by that name—The MYTHOS. *The MYTHOS* is, first of all, a work of writing, a massive text, a new Great Story, that I am inviting others to participate in. It potentially will grow to become an enormous work. But the project, in its broadest sense, goes beyond a written work, which would be but only another book—it potentially opens out into many collaborative directions, involving artists of all genres, scholars and philosophers, cybertechies, organizational leaders, networking angels, New Age practitioners, and Lightworkers in all capacities. My performance *The Vision of Psyche*[1] I consider another expression of The MYTHOS.

The MYTHOS, as I see it, is the Word of the new global archetype of humanity (our Divinity) that is about to break into and manifest as a universal culture; we see evidence of it everywhere today downloading into untold thousands of individuals worldwide as the new dispensation of Spirit—the New Age Vision. It should be realized that the New Age Vision, as a visionary Seed of Spirit, unfolds and embodies itself into cultural Form as the New Age Mythos—the global, universal MYTHOS to come.

# Notes

Orientation: Welcome to the New Age

1. My Vision of Psyche, which I share in Chapter 7. The most complete depiction of my Vision can be found my published work *The Vision of Psyche & other poems* (3rd edition 2020), and is also found in another depiction in *Technos & Psyche, A Prelude & other poems* (2019). Other versions are found in the still unpublished *The Birth of Psyche* (1988) and "Song of the New Age" (2002) in my yet unpublished massive collection *Advent*.

Chapter 1 A Preliminary Discussion: Objections to the New Age

1. *New Age Almanac*, J. Gordon Melton, with Jerome Clark & Aidan A. Kelly, is a dense volume of over 400 pages that is a compendium, including historical background, to all things New Age up to 1991. Also, John L. Lash's *The Seeker's Handbook* provides a good general overview of early New Age influences.
2. Jonathan Zap *Crossing the Event Horizon, Human Metamorphosis & the Singularity Archetype*
3. Alice Bailey and the Lucis Trust.

Chapter 2 An Age of Crisis—*and Transition:* Postmodernism

1. 'Postmodern': I am aware of the scholarly difficulties in trying to nicely define Postmodernism, and all the subtle distinctions between Postmodern, Postmodernity, Postmodernist, and Postmodernism. We find similar issues with the word 'Modern.'
2. Be aware that the Postmodernists are suspicious of any attempt to present a Grand Premise or Great Story…a "meta-narrative."
3. Friedrich Hölderlin. Lines are found in the poem "Patmos."
4. Octavio Paz, *Children of the Mire*.
5. 'Human Reality': I am using this as a philosophical term, not merely a general phrase. It would require a full study to explicate what all is implied by it.

6. It is not my intent here to engage in a full-on philosophical confrontation with Postmodern deconstructive thought. I may save that for another work.

7. Spirit: By the recognition of Spirit in the New Age, we will mean, in its most essential sense, this: That the Invisible has an Intelligence, and one that is far greater than our ego-self intellect. Its corollary is: The invisible realms are populated by various Intelligences. We will further define 'Spirit' in chapter 4. There is nothing sanctimonious or religiously biased or theistic about this basic definition. We might consider it very Aquarian. But even Spirit given so basic a meaning would still not be recognized in the Postmodern context. The Postmodern context only recognizes the ego-self.

## Chapter 3 World Ages: The Astrological Background

1. See C. J. Jung's work by that name, *Aion*, which is volume 9, II in his *Collected Works*. In this work he explores in great detail the psychological makeup behind the Piscean Age, which he acknowledges is passing. The Age of the Fish, the Christian era, he said, was dying. He speaks then of the dawning of a New Age—*Aquarius*.

2. *Proceedings of the Aquarian Age Workshop* Held September 18, 1999 in Redwood City, CA. In his paper "The Mystery of the Ages Solved," George Flory believes he has found the zero point of the traditional zodiac, basing his argument on Zecharia Sitchin's work and using a planetarium simulator. It is where the galactic equator exactly crosses the celestial equator and the ecliptic at the spring equinox of 4492 B.C. marking the beginning of the Age of Taurus. Projecting forward in time, he calculates that the Age of Aquarius began on the spring equinox of March 20, 2000.

3. Other major cycles that have collective impact are:

    The Neptune–Pluto cycle of 493 years

    The Uranus–Pluto cycle that can vary from 110-130 years

    The Uranus–Neptune cycle of 171 years

4. Neptune rules all the various forms of illusion, illusion-making, and otherworldliness: glamour, drugs, alcohol, psychedelics, photography, movies, mysticism, delusional beliefs, mass hysteria, dreams and the dream world, the ethereal Music of the Spheres. Neptune also rules the ideals of Peace and Love and the oceanic experience of interconnectedness. In my work, it is the Melody.

5. Uranus is the principle of breaking out of convention, conformity, conditioning, any structure or form that no longer works for us, so it represents the maverick, the revolutionary, the eccentric, the genius. Its action is sudden, electric, unexpected, brilliant, novel. It is the New. It is the breaking into, and opening up of, the Greater Reality—the higher mind suddenly accessed. It is therefore insight, intuition, illumination. In my work, it is the Vision.

6. The Eastern view on the cycles of the Ages: called Yugas.

A note on language

1. My yet unpublished long poem *ENERGY, The Dance of* (2005).

Chapter 4  The Water Bearer: Spirit and Soul

1. *Souls* From my poem "*Souls*" from *Lamp Light* (3rd edition 2020).

2. Huston Smith, *Why Religion Matters*

3. I have chosen to italicize *The Bible* against standard publishing practice. My logic is that it *is* the title of a book, so should be italicized as any other book is.

Chapter 5  The Higher Self: The Aquarian Dispensation

1. 'Divinity': Since I will be arguing that our traditional "God" is dead, how, then, can I use the word 'Divinity'? What might that refer to? 'Divinity' is a title for a state or condition: any being that attains a certain level of spiritual realization can be considered "Divine" or a "divinity." ETs possessing superhuman, miraculous powers can be considered "divinities," once we free ourselves from a certain sanctimonious reverence toward them.

2. See Karen Armstrong, *A History of God*
3. Herbert J. Muller, *The Uses of the Past.* Chapter VI "The Rise of Christianity."
4. Ken Wilber, *The Atman Project.* Though Ken Wilber has provided much helpful organizing information in his various schemas, I cannot subscribe to his thesis of an Atman project as the underlying drive of human culture. His explanation of it in the introduction to *Up From Eden* is much too simplistic, too neatly laid out, and is to me more of a projection of his own proclivity for the Eastern path that idealizes some enlightened state. His view condemns the rich parade of human culture to being merely substitute formations in lieu of genuinely attaining Atman.
5. Gopi Krishna, *Kundalini—The Evolutionary Energy in Man*, reissued as *Living with Kundalini*.
6. Ken Wilber, *The Spectrum of Consciousness* and *The Atman Project*.
7. See the works of Elaine Pagels, especially *The Gnostic Gospels* and *Beyond Belief: The Secret Gospel of Thomas*. Also see Marvin Meyer, *The Gnostic Gospels of Jesus*.

## Chapter 6  Our Psychospiritual Evolution

1. *Upon a weathered shore...* From my poem "A Word" from *Lamp Light* (3rd edition 2020).
2. The word 'psychospiritual': This word indicates that psyche and Spirit are not utterly separated from each other, but interface and interpenetrate each other in an intermediate plane of consciousness where the Creative Imagination is active.
3. Quote from Jean-Francois Lyotard: "Simplifying to the extreme, I define postmodern as incredulity towards metanarratives." (1984)
4. I came across this phrase reading an essay by John L. Lash on his website www.metahistory.org.

### Chapter 7 Psyche: Mythos of the New Age

1. The phrase 'spirit of place' is a context where 'spirit' and 'soul' are more or less interchangeable. I could have referred to the soul of this place. There still ring subtle differences in each.
2. See note 1 under "Orientation: Welcome to the New Age."
3. See my essay "The Sun Experience, An Opening to Being" (2008) in *Toward The Mythos, philosophical essays* (2010).
4. My collection of poems, *The Lessons of Psyche* (1983-1987). The poetic lines are actually first found in *The Birth of Psyche* (1988). Both are as yet unpublished.
5. Lucius Apuleius, *The Metamorphoses* or also known as *The Golden Ass*.
6. James Hillman, *Re-Visioning Psychology*.
7. The ishtadeva discussed by Lex Hixon in *Coming Home*. Chapter X "Designing an Experiment in Contemplation."
8. Definition from John L. Lash, *The Seeker's Handbook*
9. The Active/Creative Imagination: See the various works by Henry Corbin on the Imaginal world as found in Sufism and Gnosticism.
10. The first poetic lines are from my collection *The Birth of Psyche*. The second lines are from the poem "The Lessons of Psyche 2" from *The Lessons of Psyche*.

### Chapter 8 Technos: The New Global Superpower

1. *Giant Technos walked…* From my narrative poem *Technos & Psyche, A Prelude & other poems* (2019).
2. Martin Heidegger, *The Question Concerning Technology and Other Essays*.
3. John B. Watson, *Behaviorism*.
4. Who first brought this to my attention was the remote viewer, formerly with the military, David Morehouse.
5. Building New Gods website www.buildinggods.com

6. See his web site: www.kevinwarwick.com . Also, his book: *I, Cyborg.*
7. Ray Kurzweil's website: www.kurzweilAI.net
8. Consider the enormous potential of IBM's projected new Blue Gene supercomputer. It will be 40 times faster than the aggregate sum of the world's top supercomputers. Will calculate 1 quadrillion (1 followed by 15 zeros) instructions/second. Its bandwidth will have all the power of all the ISDN modems in the world, capable of downloading the entire Internet in one second.
9. The new zero energy devices

Chapter 9 Gaia: Our Earth Web

1. *My dear Earth…* From my poem *"My Dear Earth"* from *Advent.*
2. 'Deep ecology': The term was coined by the Norwegian philosopher Arne Naess in 1973.
3. James Lovelock, article in *Rollingstone*
4. James Lovelock, *Gaia, A New Look at Life on Earth*
5. Dr. Masaru Emoto, *The Message from Water*, with the photo documentation.
6. My yet unpublished long poem celebrating the life of water, *Water, Water…Precious Water* (2004).
7. William Everson, *Birth of a Poet*, pg. 164.
8. I have told the story of the early years of the crop circles in my yet unpublished long poem *The Crop Circle Mystery, A Poem Chronicle* (1998).
9. Denni Clarke, *Crop Circle Wisdom.*
10. The butterfly movement: One of the principal activists behind it is Alan Moore, director and founder of the Butterfly Gardener's Association and Project Chrysalis; also, director of Authors for a Positive Millennium, and tireless promoter of *The Earth Proclamation.* Also see Norie Huddle, *Butterfly.*

Chapter 10  UFOs and ET Contact: Harbingers of the Next Level

1. Dr. Richard Boylan provides an overview on his site www.drboylan.com
2. Barry H. Downing, *The Bible and Flying Saucers*.
3. Richard L. Thompson, *Alien Identities, Ancient Insights into Modern UFO Phenomena*.
4. Hyperdimensional physics and spiritual reality: I am not implying that the hyperdimensions studied by the new physics are identical to the hyperdimensions of Spirit per se. Hyper-dimensional physics studies a realm that is lower on the evolutionary scale or the Great Chain of Being (Ken Wilber's "spectrum of consciousness") than human consciousness, whereas the higher dimensions of Spirit are superconsciousness, transpersonal to the ego-self. Ken Wilber has made this clear. There is the sense, though, that Spirit permeates everything: other-dimensional reality is a new, contemporary way of talking about spiritual reality. All of this refers to the Invisible.
5. In the context of the Santa Cruz UFO Study Group 1992-1995
6. Richard F. Haines, *CE-5 Close Encounters of the 5th Kind* for 242 cases of them.
7. *The "God" Part of the Brain*, Matthew Alper  http://godpart.com
8. My yet unpublished long poem *The Tail of Hale-Bopp, A Poem Chronicle* (1997/2004).

Chapter 11  The Next Level: The Astral-Psychic

1. H*ave you never had intimations…* From my poem "Where Are You Taking Us?" (1999) from *Advent*.
2. Caryl Dennis, *The Millennium Children*.
3. David Jacobs interview [could not locate this interview at the time of this printing]
4. Lyssa Royal and Keith Priest, *Visitors from Within*.
5. Lex Hixon, *Coming Home*, Chapter X "Designing an Experiment in Contemplation."

6. The word 'therapy': From the Greek 'therapeia': to do service. Thus, to do divine service: to be in service to Psyche.
7. To explore the notion of future lives, see Chet B. Snow, *Mass Dreams of the Future*.
8. 'Polyphrenia': I first used the term in my poetic prose manifesto, *The Golden Thread* in 1978. The only other author I am aware of who has used this word is Jean Houston.
9. Walk-ins: I believe originally discussed in detail by Ruth Montgomery in *Strangers Among Us*. See also Scott Mandelker, *From Elsewhere, Being E.T. in America*. He explores at length the whole phenomenon of ET Walk-ins and Wanderers.
10. The abstruse analysis in Kant's classic of Western philosophy *The Critique of Pure Reason* regarding the transcendental possibilities of experience is another way of approach to what I am presenting here.
11. See the latter part of Yuvah Noah Harrari, *Homo Deus*.

Chapter 12 Mythos-making: Art of the New Age

1. My first printed work *The Golden Thread, A Manifesto on the Art of Contemporary Mythmaking* (1979)
2. Zechaaria Sitchin, *The Earth Chronicles:*

    *The 12$^{th}$ Planet*

    *The Stairway To Heaven*

    *The Wars Of Gods And Men*

    *The Lost Realms*

    *When Time Began*
3. Christian O'Brien, *The Genius of the Few.*
4. See my essay "The Word as Mythos" (2008) in *Toward The Mythos, philosophical essays* (2010).
5. Julian Jaynes, *The Origin of Consciousness in the Breakdown of the Bicameral Mind*

Chapter 13  The Emerging New Story of Us

1. Riane Eisler, *The Chalice and The Blade*.
2. Dane Rudhyar was a pioneer here. The most detailed, recent studies that I'm aware of that correlates the major astrological cycles to history, all of history—both are thorough in their own way—is E. Alan Meece's book, *Horoscope for the New Millennium* and the more recent *Cosmos and Psyche* by Richard Tarnas.
3. Consider the title and theme of Neil Freer's book, *Breaking the Godspell*.
4. Julian Jaynes, *The Origin of Consciousness in the Breakdown of the Bicameral Mind*
5. See my long poem The NEXT ACT in *The New Story* (2$^{nd}$ edition planned for 2021)
6. See, for example, Barbara Marx Hubbard, *Conscious Evolution*. Also, she is the founder of the Foundation of Conscious Evolution, in Santa Barbara, California.

Addendum 2  The MYTHOS Project

1. T*he Vision of Psyche* performance was first presented on October 24, 2006 at the E3 PlayHouse in Santa Cruz, California.

# BIBLIOGRAPHY

Abram, David *The Spell of the Sensuous*

Apuleius, Lucius *The Metamorphosis (The Golden Ass)*

Armstrong, Karen *A History of God*

Bramley, William *The Gods of Eden*

Buhner, Stephen Harrod *Plant Intelligence and the Imaginal Realm*

Dennis, Caryl *The Millennium Children*

Devall, Bill / Sessions, George *Deep Ecology*

Dolan, Richard / Zabel, Bryce *A.D. After Disclosure*

Downing, Barry H. *The Bible & Flying Saucers*

Eisler, Riane *The Chalice & The Blade*

Ellul, Jacques *The Technological Society*

Emoto, Dr. Masaru *The Message of Water*

Everson, William *Birth of a Poet*

Ferguson, Marilyn *The Aquarian Conspiracy, Personal & Social Transformation in the 1980s*

Freer, Neil *Breaking the Godspell*

Furst, Dan *Surfing Aquarius, How to Ace The Wave of Change*

Grasse, Ray *Signs of the Times, Unlocking the Symbolic Language of World Events*

Haines, Richard F. *CE-5, Close Encounters of the 5th Kind*

Harari, Yuval Noah *Homo Deus, A Brief History of Tomorrow*

Heidegger, Martin *The Question Concerning Technology and other essays*

Hillman, James *Re-Visioning Psychology*
   *The Myth of Analysis*

Hixon, Lex *Coming Home*

Hopkins, Budd *Missing Time*

Hubbard, Barbara Marx *Conscious Evolution*

Huxley, Aldous *Brave New World*

Jacobs, David M. *Secret Life*
    *The Threat*

Jaynes, Julian *The Origin of Consciousness in the Breakdown of the Bicameral Mind*

Jung, Carl G. *Aion*
    [Alchemical Works:]

Jungk, Robert *Brighter than a Thousand Suns, A Personal History of the Atomic Scientists*

Krishna, Gopi *Kundalini—The Evolutionary Energy in Man*, reissued as *Living with Kundalini*

Kurzweil, Ray *The Age of Spiritual Machines*
    *The Singularity is Near*

Lash, John L. *The Seeker's Handbook*

Lloyd, Donna H. *The View from Olympus, A New Gnostic Gospel*

Lovelock, J.E. *Gaia: A New Look at Life on Earth*
    *The Vanishing Face of Gaia, A Final Warning* 2009

Mandelker, Scott *From Elsewhere, Being ET in America*

Marrs, Jim *Rule by Secrecy*

McPherson, Guy / Baker, Carolyn *Extinction Dialogs*

Meece, E. Alan *Horoscope for the New Millennium*

Melton, J. Gordon, with Jerome Clark & Aidan A. Kelly *New Age Almanac*

Monroe, Robert A. *Journeys out of the Body*

Montgomery, Ruth *Strangers Among Us*

Morehouse, David *Psychic Warrior*

Muller, Herbert J. *The Uses of the Past*

Noble, David F. *The Religion of Technology*

Noel, Daniel *Approaching Earth, A Search for the Mythic Significance of the Space Age*

O'Brien, Christian *The Genius of the Few*

Orwell, George *1984*

Pagels, Elaine *The Gnostic Gospels*
  *Beyond Belief: The Secret Gospel of Thomas*

Paz, Octavio *Children of the Mire*

Royal, Lyssa / Priest, Keith *Visitors From Within*

Rudhyar, Dane *Astrological Timing, The Transition to the New Age*
  *Occult Preparations for a New Age*

Sheldrake, Rupert *A New Science of Life*

Sitchin, Zecharia *The Earth Chronicles* (5 volumes)
  *Genesis Revisited*

Smith, Huston *Beyond the Postmodern Mind*
  *Why Religion Matters*

Tarnas, Richard *Cosmos & Psyche*

Tart, Charles T. *The End of Materialism*

Thompson, Richard L. *Alien Identities, Ancient Insights into Modern UFO Phenomena*

Vallee, Jacques *Dimensions*

Warwick, Kevin *I, Cyborg*

Watson, John *Behaviorism*

Wilber, Ken *The Atman Project*
  *Up From Eden*
  *Eye to Eye*

Zap, Jonathan *Crossing the Event Horizon, Human Metamorphosis & the Singularity Archetype*

# About the Author

Ron Lampi is a visionary New Age philosopher-poet, writer, and astrologer. Over the years, he has lectured on various subjects, and has been a facilitator of discussion groups. His published works thus far are only the beginning of the many manuscripts he has yet to publish. The massive project *The Mythos* is already composed of a number of books. He has lived in Santa Cruz, California, at The Edge, for over 40 years.

www.ingramcontent.com/pod-product-compliance
Lightning Source LLC
Chambersburg PA
CBHW031131160426
43193CB00008B/109